POPULAR
EVOLUTION

POPULAR EVOLUTION

LIFE-LESSONS FROM ANTHROPOLOGY

Joseph L. Popp

Man and Nature Press

Published by:

Man and Nature Press
P.O. Box 3400
Lake Jackson, Texas
77566-3400

For additional information about ordering this book, see www.popularevolution.com
and www.manandnaturepress.com

Printed in the United States of America

Library of Congress Card Number: 00-105072

ISBN: 0-9701255-7-7

Publisher's Cataloging-in-Publication

Popp, Joseph L.
    Popular evolution : life-lessons from
anthropology / Joseph L. Popp. -- 1st ed.
    p. cm.
    Includes bibliographical references and index.
    LCCN: 00-105072
    ISBN: 0-9701255-7-7

    1. Evolution--Popular works. 2. Culture--
Philosophy. 3. Anthropology--United States.
4. Human reproduction--United States. 5. Social
ecology--United States.   I. Title.

HM108.P67 2000   303.4
                       QBI00-560

This book is dedicated to the people who gave sanctuary and succor.

No one whose testicles have been crushed or whose penis has been cut off, may be admitted into the community of the Lord.

Deuteronomy 23:2, The New American Bible

Contents

Acknowledgments

I wish to thank those people who taught anthropology and evolutionary biology to me, especially Chester B. Wike, Jerry F. Downhower, Frank E. Poirier, Stephen Jay Gould, Edward O. Wilson, Robert L. Trivers, Ernst Mayr and Irven DeVore.

I would also like to thank those people who read the manuscript and offered comments, including Ronald E. Schilb, John G. Augustine, Reidulf K. Molvaer, and Christine A. Ryan.

I offer my deepest gratitude to my family for their unfailing support and love, without which this project could not have been undertaken. I would like to mention my father, Joseph, my mother, Dorothy, and my sisters, Susan, Barbara, Laura and Eileen.

Preface

Everything that we think or do makes sense only in terms of its enhancement of our reproductive success. Although this conclusion may seem novel or strange to some readers, it is a logical extension of Darwinism, which teaches that past reproductive success is reflected in present human traits. With the reproductive imperative always in mind, this book offers an unadorned explanation of the purpose of human life and how we can fulfill that purpose. It also suggests that the forces of evolutionary anthropology have a role to play in shaping our lives as individuals and in framing the broader social policy. In so doing, these forces will often challenge traditional sources of intellectual, social, and moral authority.

I do regret that the spirit of this book is very much in conflict with some current thoughts on environmentalism and on human population growth. I have examined the hypothesis with some care and cannot refute it solely on the grounds that it may be unpopular with environmental activists. But there is the belief that some truths should not be known. If this belief is true then it can be argued that I have erred in my efforts to publish some of the herein thoughts.

This book has three purposes. First of all, I introduce evolutionary thinking for application in the daily lives of Americans. Secondly, I familiarize readers with a model of optimal life history strategies and analyze some of the aspects of American life as an anthropologist. Finally, I attempt to provide examples of how these evolutionary strategies can be employed and how they relate to human cultures.

I apologize to those people who are offended by my interpretation of the meaning of life. No doubt there are many with heartfelt opinions about the important role of environmentalism or religion in their own lives. But they have, and likely will use, the opportunities available to them to challenge my views. It may be particularly irksome to some that I have not disapproved of environmentalism or of religiosity outright, but rather have given them special significance as a means of fulfilling, albeit unwittingly, the goals of a completely different world view.

The power of a synthesis is proportional to its ability to bring new meaning to old facts. It would be presumptuous of me to describe the content of this book as a new paradigm, but it does challenge the conventional wisdom of our times in many places.

Much of the content of this book will challenge the *Weltanschauung*, or world view, of the average American reader, for I have made a sincere attempt to dispute some of our common cultural preconceptions as they relate to human survival and reproduction. As I will explain, much of our behavior is influenced by cultural components that exist for reasons other than our evolutionary success. In 1985, 38 percent of all Americans said they believed that every word of the Bible represented divine revelation and was to be taken literally[69]. That *Weltanschauung* is in stark contrast with the conclusions based on the mode of analysis in this book, which asserts that we must look to the evolutionary process to learn the origin and function of the moral, mental, and physical qualities that humans possess. I agree with the comment of Mayr[134] that the theory of evolution has been confirmed so completely that modern biologists consider evolution simply as fact. Evolution is treated so in the book; no attempt is made to argue its irrefutable case (to date) against the various factions of anti-evolutionists.

I would like to imagine that this view of life is politically neutral. However, given the past reactions to evolutionary interpretations of human life by liberals, conservatives, Marxists and creationists, I expect to receive criticism from those quarters. While these movements may seem to form an unlikely opposing alliance, they all have one thing in common: a core belief in free will. For that reason, the proponents of these philosophies object vehemently to any interpretations of human behavior and human morphology that are inherently deterministic, as this one most certainly is. But given the decline of worldwide Marxism as a force and the increase in skepticism in the West concerning animistic beliefs and religious ritual that has occurred in our lifetimes, now may be a more propitious time than any in this millennium to promote the herein views. I expect that one of two extreme reactions will be the prevalent response to this book: The reader may be incited to burn it, *or* the reader may feel an utmost necessity to share it with his children. Either of these two responses may make a lot of sense if the book contains some essential truths about evolution, humans, and culture. The reader may be incited to burn this book because there is an evolutionary battle between humans and their cultures in progress. A casualty of that battle is often our reproductive success. To that end, there are aspects of our culture that would very much like to suppress the contents of this book, which are progenitive. The reader may feel a necessity to share this book with his children because it contains a message that should be passed between generations for the benefit of the parent and the child. Because of the inevitable controversy that will occur with the publication of this book, I briefly entertained the notion of distributing it only among my relatives and close colleagues. I have grown weary of *ad hominem* attacks. But I agree with Gould[74] that determinism is not an abstract matter to be debated only within academic cloisters. While very much in disagreement with him about the role of evolution in human behavior (e.g., Gould[74]), I have attempted, as he does, to reach a broad readership.

In the 1970s and 1980s academia had the sociobiology wars. Sociobiologists held the view that evolutionary analysis of social behavior, including that among humans, was an interesting and valid endeavor. Opponents from a number of quarters objected and maintained that sociobiology was uninteresting and invalid; some claimed it was dangerous. That controversy is not the subject of this book, because it is accepted herein as true that sociobiology can be sound science. But these sociobiology wars have a historical lesson for us. Sociobiologists maintained that it was their duty as scientists to explore the subject, with the disclaimer that to explain a given social behavior in evolutionary terms was not to justify it or advocate it. Opponents argued that the information would be misused and would lead to abuses in the real world outside of academic circles. The point I wish to make is that sociobiologists drew the line at the wrong place. They failed to recognize that an evolutionary ethic is a source of justification for some human behaviors. Namely, I intend to argue that the evolutionary significance of maximizing reproductive success *does* justify the traits that lead to it -- and more. No doubt this hypothesis will give rise to a new controversy that will divide anthropologists yet again as they were divided over sociobiology.

In some fields of science the people who call themselves scientists work toward the practical application of their scientific endeavor. For the most part, anthropologists have kept themselves removed from this type of applied science. For example, there is no tradition of conceptual rigor in anthropology in discussing what people *should* be doing. This book diverges from that general anthropological trend. It provides theory, examples, data, algorithms, and life-lessons, all with application to practical purpose in human activities in mind. This approach of advocating human behavior (that is conducive to reproductive success) is unusual in the context of a scientific publication. It follows from my discontent with leaving what ''ought to be'' to the nonscientists who usually deal with such matters. I do understand that I am violating cherished customs in two fields. Most anthropologists do not prescribe behavior for the cultures they are studying, and many modern moral philosophers hold firm that there is no authoritative statement of how humans ought to live. Part of the reason that anthropologists have not prescribed behavior is that they have lacked a credible model. The reason that moral philosophers have been unable to tell us how humans ought to live is because they believe in the existence of some higher and external source of validation of the concept of ''oughtness,'' to which by definition they have no access. I argue in this book that both a credible model and a true source of validation of ''oughtness'' exist. On the other hand, I wish to say that I have the greatest respect for fellow anthropologist who practice their discipline in the more traditional form of a pure science. I beg their indulgence in this extraordinary digression. Perhaps if a physician-writer can advocate practices that promote the health of his readership, then an anthropologist-writer can advocate practices that promote the survival and reproduction of his readership. Certainly, advocacy of the antithesis of the premise of this book, namely restraint in reproduction, has long been common among environmentalists (e.g., Ehrlich and Ehrlich[54]). The zeal with which some environmentalists urge others to control their fertility is at times truly remarkable. I do not get quite so emotional about my alternative prescription.

Anthropologists and evolutionary biologists may have both theory and data to challenge some of the specific conclusions that I draw. Like all hypotheses, those offered in this book should be challenged and either supported or refuted by the weight of the scientific evidence. I particularly welcome technical, empirical and theoretical comments from my colleagues. The subject matter of the book covers philosophy and the sciences anthropology, evolutionary biology, and sociobiology. This switching among disciplines can be annoying at times to specialists. However, it is an old tradition in works that discuss evolution in broad perspective, and I believe the reader will conclude after reading the book that it serves a clear purpose.

I have intended this book to be both accessible to the layman and of interest to the scientist. It is difficult to satisfy the needs of two such diverse groups in a single writing project. For example, I have retained the practice of citing scientific references with superscript numerals at the appropriate places in the body of the book; a full listing of these materials appears in the section entitled References. I hope that it is not too obtrusive. In contrast, I have avoided statistical analysis and mathematical modeling, which will be unsatisfactory to the scientist but will be a considerable relief to the layman.

I have avoided the use of footnotes and endnotes other than to references. They are a disservice to all readers in works where space is not extremely limited. I have, instead, attempted to be concise yet thorough in the body of the text itself. On the subject of verb tense, references to non-Western cultures are written in the ethnographic present, while reference to other publications is in past tense. **Technical terms are defined in the Glossary to assist the nonspecialist with unfamiliar words and to provide the specialist with the precise meaning intended for nomenclature of possible ambiguity.** It was necessary to create a few neologisms, and they will also be found in the Glossary.

The life-lessons herein described are intended for an American readership. But as supporting evidence I have often drawn examples and data from animal societies and non-Western human societies. This kind of cross-phyletic and cross-cultural review is sometimes used in anthropological writing -- often one can see one's own society more clearly when it is put in an exotic context.

On the subject of further readings, I can do no better than to commend to you the most important book of the last two centuries, *On the Origin of Species,* by Charles Darwin[38]. You probably have not read it and you should. It is superbly written, enlightening, and stimulating. You may have the impression that you understand life in general (and even biology) without having read it, but you would be mistaken.

Joseph L. Popp

Chapter 1: The Meaning of Life

Great thinkers have contemplated the meaning of life. Shakespeare[188] in a prescient representation of nihilism wrote in *The Tragedy of Macbeth*:

> Life's but a walking shadow, a poor player
> That struts and frets his hour upon the stage
> And then is heard no more. It is a tale
> Told by an idiot, full of sound and fury,
> Signifying nothing. (Act V, Scene V)

The view that I offer in this book is in stark contrast to the words of Macbeth. I argue here that life has a clear purpose, that this purpose can be achieved, and that we should attempt to achieve it. Further, I provide an introduction to the theory explaining this purpose, discuss practical steps for making the theory a rule of life, and consider the implications of achieving this purpose.

Many modern Americans, in their frustration at their inability to find meaning in life, would no doubt empathize with Macbeth. I sincerely hope that they can be rescued from that fate. Instead of facing the stark realities of life with only the guidance of art, e.g., the works of Shakespeare, we may add science and philosophy, with gratifying results. The exercise need not be esoteric. Instead, it should serve most Americans, who are so preoccupied with the details of life that the meaning of life goes unfulfilled for them. That is a mistake based in part on ignorance and also in part on something far more sinister. The ignorance is a lack of knowledge of the evolutionary ethic. The sinister component is the way humans are manipulated by antigenitive cultures, and that is discussed in detail in a following chapter.

When we ask: "What is the meaning of life?" we are usually asking what, if anything, is the goal worth seeking in life. Here, without adornment, is **the precept of this book: Life is merely an artifact of evolution -- maximizing reproductive success is why we are here.** That is to say, maximizing reproductive success is the sole activity of which humans are capable that has intrinsic significance. Here we define maximizing reproductive success as exhibiting a strategy that contributes the maximum number of one's genes to subsequent generations. When I use the term reproductive success, I mean it in the modern sense, acknowledging the role of Darwinian fitness[38] and also the importance of inclusive fitness as described by Hamilton[85]. Reproductive success as used here refers not only to offspring produced by the individual, but also to offspring produced by relatives with assistance and devalued by the regression coefficient of relatedness, a mathematical representation of the number of genes shared in common. The subject is discussed in detail in the section on inclusive fitness. What does this definition mean in practical terms? It means that humans are selected to produce as many children as can possibly be raised to adulthood (who will be able in turn to reproduce themselves) and to assist relatives in raising offspring in proportion to their degree of genetic proximity, your costs and their benefits, where costs and benefits are measured in reproductive success. We have known since Watson and Crick[211] published their paper on the chemical basis of heredity that DNA is the *secret* of life. It is strange and interesting that maximizing reproductive success, using those same DNA molecules to replicate our genotype, is also the *meaning* of life.

Let us state the evolutionary ethic herein endorsed in the form of a **life-lesson: That which increases one's reproductive success is good; that which decreases one's reproductive success is bad; that which has no effect on reproductive success is neutral**.

The readership should have foremost in their minds two questions: 1. Is the precept, in conjunction with the evolutionary ethic, valid? and 2. Are the methods described herein effective ways of fulfilling it? All activities other than the maximization of reproductive success are classified into either of two categories: They have derivative significance by being proximate mechanisms that contribute to maximizing reproductive success, or they have no significance. How does maximizing reproductive success, which can confer derivative significance on proximate mechanisms and provide value to life, have intrinsic value itself? That intrinsic value is conferred on it by evolution. Some may object to this view when it is described in short form. Here is the long form of the argument with which it is more difficult to find fault: Evolution, as defined by the synthetic theory, is the descent of organisms with modification due to changes in gene frequency in a population over time. Evolution is driven by differential reproductive success among members of the population. Natural selection is one process that leads to evolution through differential survival and reproduction, i.e. individuals that maximize their reproductive success contribute more genes to succeeding generations than those who do not. In this way, we are selected to maximize our reproductive success -- it is the purpose for which we are designed.

Among organisms there is one basic evolutionary rule that must be followed if they are to continue their kind over time: They must maximize their reproductive success. All other activities are secondary in the sense that they either serve the process of maximizing reproductive success or they devolve. The point of any living thing's life is nothing but the maximizing of the reproductive success of that life itself. Modern evolutionary theory asserts that there is no goal or pattern toward which life in general is heading. Animals and humans may pursue goals of survival and reproduction with apparent purpose, but that is the consequence of a purposeless evolutionary process. However, to maintain that we cannot read purpose into evolution does not mean that we cannot derive purpose from evolution. That is

2

because even though evolutionary forces are without purpose themselves, they are primary causes for the way we are. In that we are the effect of evolution, it is the only legitimate source of purpose that we shall find. For millennia people have been asking themselves what the purpose of human life is, and the answer to that question was facilitated by Darwin[38]. Evolution as a source of purpose of human life has been debated before, but this book offers new arguments in justification of the belief and practical suggestions for living according to that principle.

From a biological point of view, life may be summarized in six simple steps: to be conceived, to feed, to grow, to maintain, to reproduce, and to die. We are each part of a web of replicating entities that transmit their genes to the next generation. And to do precisely that with the greatest success is the purpose for which we are designed or destined. As the precept implies, corporal existence and mind are merely by-products of the process. Self-awareness, emotions, and all higher functions are results of the refinements of this reproductive process imposed by evolution. Other drives such as self-preservation, hunger, libido, and parental care have evolved to serve that end as well. Pugh[167] explained in his discussion of innate human values that they are inherited decision criteria that were built into humans over evolutionary time. In this sense, all living organisms are unique in possessing a purpose. A mountain or a river does not possess a purpose. But a human, a chimpanzee, or a plant does. Also, the objects that humans make possess a purpose derived from their human makers.

People are skeptical now. The meaning of life lies in question for many. Others believe in long discredited theories. Nearly a century ago Moore[143] debunked hedonism, utilitarianism, and love of God as ultimate ''goods''. While Moore's eloquent logic is now largely unfamiliar, many have a pervasive sense of doubt about these kinds of beliefs nevertheless. This book offers an explanation of the meaning of life and simultaneously the way to ultimate self-improvement. Theoretically, once an individual knows the meaning of life, it is possible to organize his life so that all aspects of it are meaningful, i.e. lead to the maximization of reproductive success.

Let us consider the epigraph, a quotation from Deuteronomy that essentially says that a man who is incapable of reproduction is banned from eternal life. Intact genitals, to the extent that the penis has not been severed and the testes have not been crushed (but ignoring the loss of foreskin due to circumcision), are a man's key to heaven. Strangely, this ancient belief is true in a metaphorical sense and in an evolutionary sense. In the context of the precept of this book, it is surprising that humans have previously failed to understand that they have evolved to maximize reproductive success. While knowing that men and women have sex organs, many are ignorant of the fact that maximizing reproductive success is the function for which these organs evolved. Furthermore, it is remarkable that many are likely to continue to deny that, even in light of the considerable supportive evidence that exists and is herein presented. Evolutionary biology argues that humans have been selected to expend their life in maximizing reproductive success, conscious of the fact or not. Genetic posterity is the *ultimate* function of all adaptive behavior and morphology. The distinction between an *ultimate* cause and a *proximate* cause is one worth knowing. An ultimate cause is an explanation of *why* a trait exists. The ultimate cause put forth here for adaptive traits is evolution selecting for individuals who maximize their reproductive success. The ultimate cause for the existence of maladaptive traits is cultural evolution. A proximate cause is an explanation of *how* a trait came to exist. The explanation most commonly presented in this book for proximate cause is genetics and environment. For example, some or many aspects of an individual's morphology, physiology, development, neurology, environmental conditions, and stimuli comprise a proximate cause for a trait, all without necessary reference to evolutionary biology. Reproductive success is the only success that matters. Other, culturally determined, motives may inspire some of our behaviors, as will be explored under the section concerning cultural evolution, but they are most appropriately considered to be riders on the underlying foundation of biological reproduction.

While the individual elements of the proposed strategies presented herein may seem counterintuitive or even absurd, each is consistent with the stated objective of maximizing reproductive success. It is an important point that adaptive strategies are now often different from what they were a century or a millennium ago. Remarkable environmental changes have greatly altered the reproductive consequences of our behavioral and morphological traits. Even behavioral and morphological traits that have large genetic components may not make adaptive sense when the environment undergoes radical change. As primates, humans are generalists, endowed by evolution with considerable plasticity. In the coming chapters I shall be calling upon the readership to make use of that plasticity in the attempt to maximize their reproductive success. That plasticity is, and will be, sorely needed as our environment continues to change.

It is a common fallacy to draw from Darwin's correct argument, that evolution has no purpose, the incorrect argument that humans have no purpose. While evolution has no goal, individuals are selected by evolution to increase the representation of their genes in future generations. That is their purpose. Does the universe itself have a purpose? No, it was not designed to do something. The essential difference between those things that have a purpose and those things that do not is that the former were designed to do something.

Anthropology is the study of humans. The etymology of the word is "anthropos" from Greek meaning man and "ology" meaning science or branch of knowledge. It encompasses the fields of archaeology, paleontology, cultural (or social) anthropology, physical (or biological) anthropology, nonhuman primate studies, and medical anthropology. At the present, most anthropologists are cloistered in universities or isolated by the remote locations of field sites. But one day you may have one in your community with whom you will be able to make an appointment and visit -- an anthropologist, specializing in human reproductive strategies, who cares to help you maximize your reproductive success. In the meantime, this book is your guide.

Anthropological discussions are often accompanied by the fear that evolutionary interpretations will justify undesirable human behaviors. Of course it is true that evolutionary arguments can be subject to abuse, just as chemical formulae or mathematical equations can be subject to abuse. But because evolutionary arguments explain the adaptive significance of social behavior, they are unique in providing a perspective on who will abuse, and in what way. Understanding the evolutionary foundations of behaviors such as cuckoldry and murder is one endeavor. Suggesting that they are rational behaviors under certain circumstances in evolutionary terms is another endeavor. And arguing that they are desirable in human societies is yet another endeavor. I shall use the evolutionary ethic in the following sections to give the reader specific guidelines on how he or she should judge these matters. But first I cite below the views of five prominent evolutionary biologists. All offered objections to the use of evolution as a source of ethical guidance.

Gould[77] wrote:

> We never should have sought either solace or moral instruction in Nature, who was not made for us, or even with us in mind, and who existed by her own rules for billions of years before we arrived. (p. 8)

Gould went on to state that the proper source of ethics and values is human bodies and human minds (true humanism). In response to his view it can be argued that while it is true that nature was not made for us, *we were made by nature.* The evolution of the human species was subject to the basic principle of natural selection. Furthermore, to the degree that human bodies and human minds evolved, human ethics and values based on them are subject to the influence of evolution.

Huxley[106] said:

> ... the only way to escape from our heritage of evil is ... to refuse any longer to be the instruments of the evolutionary process, and withdraw from the struggle for existence. (p. 63)

My response to him is: Exactly how does one withdraw from the struggle for existence?

Huxley[106] also said:

> Let us understand, once for all, that the ethical progress of society depends, not on imitating the cosmic process, still less in running away from it, but in combating it. (p. 83)

When Huxley used the term "cosmic process" he was referring chiefly to evolution. It appears that Huxley's quotation is the antithesis of the view presented in this book. Again, even if combating either evolution or an evolutionary trend is desirable (and I believe it is not unless it is in the interest of one's reproductive success) a very practical question arises: "*How* does one combat evolution?" At first consideration, the answer appears to be something like "have no children and kill one's relatives". But that does not really "combat" evolution, it just means one has decreased one's gene frequencies in the population and has actually effected evolution. The only imaginable way to combat evolution is to be perfectly average in reproductive success, thereby giving rise to neither an increase nor decrease in one's gene frequencies in the next generation and thereby precluding evolution. But to do exactly what the average member of the population is doing anyway hardly seems to be worthy of the description "combating" evolution, with the connotations of action and force that "combating" has. Indeed, one might be doing the same even if one were unaware of Huxley's call to arms. There is another consideration that does not support Huxley's premise. If we define evolution as a product of the basic principle of natural selection, and if we use the word *combat* to comprise in part what is meant by the word *violate*, then Huxley was wrong by virtue of tautology. Because by the very fact that the basic principle of natural selection is a basic principle, it cannot by definition be violated. The most important lesson from the above quotation of Huxley is not that there is any truth to the notion that we should or could combat evolution, but that for some reason the notion has enduring appeal. And that says something about how confused humans can be in their dealings with aspects of their culture, and how certain cultural traits which are devoid of truth or the ability to promote their bearer's reproductive success are nevertheless perpetuated.

Dawkins[40] wrote:

We, alone on earth, can rebel against the tyranny of the selfish replicators. (p. 215)

and

We should not seek immortality in reproduction. (p. 214)

By "replicators" Dawkins meant genes and memes (memes are his concept similar to culturgens, i.e. cultural traits, as used in this book). In contrast to his view, my view is that reproducing and thereby replicating our genes is the ultimate compliance to that process which is favored by evolution and is desirable. However, refusing to support the perpetuation of self-serving culturgens does make sense. Later Dawkins implied that contributing to culture may be a desirable alternative to contributing one's genes to the gene pool because an idea, a song, a spark plug, or a poem may live on intact for a long time. That implication is in complete disagreement with the views herein presented. Unless this contribution to culture enhances one's reproductive success, or that of one's descendants, it makes no sense at all. The reason is simple: We are selected to perpetuate our *genotypes,* not our *phenotypes* or the environment that contributes to making our phenotypes, or the culturgens which are part of the environment. Dawkins seemed to have confused organic evolution, which selects our genes, and cultural evolution, which selects culturgens. What is good for our genes is good for our reproductive success. But that is often not what spreads a culturgen, which is a part of the environment.

Williams[218] wrote:

> So I conclude that natural selection really is as bad as it seems and that, as Huxley maintained ..., it should be neither run from nor emulated, but rather combated. (p. 196)

and

> There is no justification for any personal concern with the long-term average proliferation of the genes we got in the lottery of meiosis and fertilization. (p. 214)

Alexander[1] wrote:

> The challenge of Darwinism is to find out what our genes have been up to and to make that knowledge widely available as a part of the environment in which each of us develops and lives so that we can decide for ourselves, quite deliberately, to what extent we wish to go along. (pp. 136-137)

Most, or all, of the above five prominent scientists seem to fall victim to a common false dichotomy. In this false dichotomy, genetic influences are viewed as sinister or ''bad,'' and cultural (or other environmental) influences are viewed as righteous or ''good''. It is puzzling that men of such erudition should not reject this false dichotomy outright on the grounds that humans are a product of both genes and environment. Perhaps a self-serving culturgen is at work in their minds, making them believe that the cultural component of human life should be increased and praised, and the genetic component decreased and repudiated. Such an assertion would not have obvious benefits for humans but would perpetuate the culturgen itself. This culturgen, if it exists, must be a potent and versatile one, because the five scientists cited above are of different genetic and environmental backgrounds and have different opinions on other subjects. One part of this culturgen may be an idea shared among them for the need to disavow the now largely discredited eugenics movement. Their unconscious motive in finding fault with genes may be that they are attacking the kind of unfair genetic discrimination against people that eugenicists sought.

Darwinism has meant many things to many people -- some have attempted to use it as a justification for war, others as a justification for peace[31]; some have thought it meant justification for change, others thought it meant justification for preserving the *status quo*. Simpson[192] suggested that what T. H. Huxley called the "gladiatorial theory of existence," based on an overemphasis on struggle between organisms in Darwinism, was an ethical view well suited to Victorian *laissez faire* capitalism as well as to its opposite, Marxist socialism.

The study of anthropology provides a broad description of the way that humans act -- the study of evolutionary biology provides clear guidelines on how we ought to act if we are to maximize our reproductive success. For example, we will see in a following chapter why we should be concerned about which social behaviors are optimal in maximizing our reproductive success.

It has been noted by many social scientists that the Darwinian model is less than perfectly realized in the diversity of human social behaviors that have in the past and do now exist. It has been suggested that perhaps the maximization process is operating on some utility other than reproductive success. Vining[209] suggested that humans are seeking social success at a cost to reproductive success in a way that shows a failure by the natural selection model to predict the observed behavior. But as pointed out by Gaulin[71] in rebuttal, natural selection does not work that way: A failure to show fitness maximizing behavior in a novel nutritional, ecological, epidemiological, and demographic environment is what is expected of a species -- it is not a failure of the evolutionary paradigm. There is an important point to keep in mind regarding the word "fitness": It is simply another way of describing reproductive success, evolutionary success, or survival to reproduce; its usage should not be confused with other connotations. Fitness depends upon other aspects of environment and genetics; if conditions change so may the fitness of a given trait. For the reader who is not an anthropologist or biologist, I point out that the term "natural selection" as used above is a process described by Darwin[38], and refers to the differential survival and reproduction of variants of a species, and its evolutionary effects over generations. Harris[90] suggested that humans are maximizing another utility, namely their own well-being, and that they adjust their investment in children to this end. However, this hypothesis is refuted by the data supporting the theory of life history strategies, which are discussed in a following section. We shall see how natural selection favors the self-sacrifice of a parent's health, and even of the parent's life, in the pursuit of maximizing reproductive success. Another view of life is described by the expression: "He who has the most when he dies, wins". But evolutionary theory argues that accumulation of resources for their own sake is not strategic behavior. Limiting resources must be sequestered and then *utilized* in reproduction.

In a more modern, mathematical sense, fitness is the measure of one's contribution to the gene frequencies in subsequent generations. Is there a simple way to calculate an individual's fitness or evolutionary success? According to Williams[217]:

It is certainly possible, under the proper conditions, to measure the evolutionary success of an individual organism. We need merely count its descendants of two or three generations later and compare this count with the mean of its contemporaries' descendants. (p. 103)

Why advocate the maximizing of fitness? To reiterate, it is the meaning of life in the sense that it is that which we are designed by evolution to do: maximize reproductive success.

How ought humans live?

Modern philosophers have argued convincingly that there is no authoritative answer to the question: "How ought humans live?" This position usually comes as a shock to laypersons, many of whom have followed a religious doctrine or adhered to the law of the land all their lives in the belief that they held a uniquely legitimate canon with which one ought to comply. The position of philosophers is usually less confounding to anthropologists, who have found extremely diverse ethical systems in different societies during more than a century of research, showing a wide range of variation in how humans actually live, e.g., Mead, 1977.

It has also been generally accepted by philosophers since the time of Hume[103] that one cannot derive logically a norm from a fact (an "ought" from an "is"), a tendency in the discourses of his time that Hume himself criticized. It is true that when philosophers and scientists recognize that "ought" cannot be derived from "is," there is a fortunate consequence: Philosophers and scientists then refrain to a large degree from sharing moral convictions about how we should live. Free from the task of moralizing, scientists have been all the more productive in furthering science.

But it would seem that if it is not logically possible to derive "ought" from "is," then all ethical systems break down. Under these circumstances, there is no genuine morality. In the absence of ethics, how do we decide what to do? Why is moral subjectivism not the rule rather than the exception? And why do people develop and hold strong convictions about how they ought to live? The answer is that we decide what to do by adopting ethics anyway, even though they are not founded in logic. Moral subjectivism is avoided by adopting these illogical ethics. And the reasons why people develop and hold strong convictions about how they ought to live are threefold: 1. It may be adaptive to do so, e.g., we have moral feelings and moral thoughts because they enhanced reproductive success in previous generations. 2. It may be the work of self-perpetuating culturgens, e.g., people around the world believe that morals, often given to humans by gods, are the proper ones for humans. 3. It may be a consequence of the environment interacting with genes in a way that benefits neither the believer in the ethic nor the ethical system itself, i.e. neither a gene nor a culturgen increases in frequency.

Thus, we reach the unexpected conclusion that people hold values that cannot be proven to be true, but those values are held because they are adaptive, are self-perpetuating culturgens, or are environmentally/genetically imposed. Moral subjectivism is not the rule because of the pressure of the assault by these sources of morality on our intellects. And in answer to how we decide which moral system to adopt, it is simply the result of our environment and genetics. With the three above explanations for why people hold values, we see the beginning of a scientific synthesis. The right question is not whether we shall merge ethics with anthropology, but in what way. From the viewpoint of the evolutionary ethic, only morals that exist for reason number 1 above, i.e. adaptiveness, are legitimate. Reasons 2 and 3 above, self-perpetuating culturgens and environment/genes, are not legitimate sources of ethics because they serve their own interests or the interests of nobody, rather than promote the evolutionary interests of their human holders.

As a philosophy and system of morals, the evolutionary ethic is not like any other; i.e. it has real justification. Other philosophies are unable to explain in logical terms how the normative is derived from the factual. In other words it is usually difficult to justify the use of the word "ought," even with reference to the will of God, by intuition, or by reference to facts from the physical world. But in the case of the evolutionary ethic, it is possible to go from design to function. For example, natural selection favors the maximization of an individual's reproductive success. This fact is assuredly so. But can we conclude that we ought to maximize our reproductive success? Yes, we can draw that conclusion. The evolutionary ethic has one advantage over other philosophies; *namely, that it makes sense to do what we were designed to do*, and evolution was the designer. The evolutionary ethic proposes just that. It proposes that we maximize our reproductive success in order to fulfill the *purpose* for which we were designed. No other system of ethics can truthfully make this claim, to my knowledge. Some philosophies advocate "doing what comes naturally". But doing what comes naturally is not the same as maximizing reproductive success, for the very reason that under some circumstances, for instance in a changed environment, doing what comes naturally may not maximize reproductive success. One may question, isn't maximizing reproductive success "doing what comes naturally"? No, because although adaptations to past environments may lead to the natural expression of adaptive behavior in the present environment, that is not necessarily so. Where environments have changed radically, new, "unnatural" behavior is what is required to maximize reproductive success. There is a final point in logic for those who maintain that the normative can never be derived from the factual. The conclusion that we *ought not* to maximize our reproductive success is equally indefensible to them, in terms of logic, as the conclusion that we *ought* to do so. Ironically, then, and in contrast to that line of thought, it is particularly helpful that the evolutionary ethic derives its principles from an evolutionary fact, whereas some other systems of ethics derive their principles from sources such as revelation.

The evolutionary ethic derives its legitimacy from the fact that it is an effect of natural selection. It is firmly rooted in the process of differential rates of replication of genes. This observation gives rise to speculative comparison with other systems of ethics which lack this genetic basis and are purely cultural -- can they be stable? Will they endure? Many aspects of modern Western morality and philosophy are just a few centuries or a few millennia old. Many of these systems of culturally based ethics which lack biological foundations will not survive to perpetuity. I shall discuss the example of the Shaker religion in a following chapter as one that has recently failed the endurance test. Part of the problem with the culturally based ethics that have existed in human history is that they are not based on science. In my world view, knowledge is found through science. And in this way the source of validation of ''oughtness'' has been found, through science, to be evolution.

Does a law of nature really determine human reproductive behavior? For example, is it a law of nature that one should maximize one's reproductive success? If it were a true basic law of nature, then all people would obey it all the time, and proclaiming it would serve no purpose in promoting adherence to it. On the other hand, if all do not obey it, then proclaiming it would perhaps serve the purpose of promoting adherence to it, but of course it could not then be a true law of nature, since all did not obey it. The answers to the questions at the beginning of the paragraph are: Yes, a law of nature does determine human reproductive behavior. No, it is not a law of nature that one should maximize one's reproductive success. Confused? The next paragraph may clarify matters.

The law, or more appropriately, the basic principle, with which we are dealing in this book is the basic principle of natural selection: differential survival and reproduction produces evolutionary change in succeeding generations. Although evolutionary ethicists endorse the basic principle of natural selection, they do not proclaim that humans should strive to ensure its application. They know it will be applied whether humans strive for its application or not. Rather, they proclaim that individuals should act in their own evolutionary interests and maximize their reproductive success. Maximizing reproductive success is not a law, it is a strategy making use of the basic principle of natural selection.

Since it is the basic principle of natural selection that there will be evolutionary consequences of behavior, with differential effects on survival and reproduction, one has a choice whether or not to maximize one's reproductive success, to devise a stratagem accordingly, and to put the basic principle to use (or not to use) to achieve one's purpose.

Ayer[4] wrote:

> But how can life in general be said to have any meaning? A simple answer is that all events are tending towards a certain specifiable end: so that to understand the meaning of life it is necessary only to discover this end. (p. 7)

I accept this definition of "meaning," and I reject idealistic notions that explanations of the meaning of life require compliance with or sanction of some higher source of the legitimization of values. Ayer failed to discover this end which gives life meaning, doubted that the assumption included in the above quotation was true, and claimed it was a justification for the meaning of life that was being sought, not an explanation. However, for the purposes of this book, I shall accept the above quotation as one that contains a useful definition. We have at hand an explanation of *and* justification for the certain specifiable end towards which all events in life tend to be directed, namely, the process and the consequence of the natural selection for the maximization of reproductive success. For the reader interested in technical detail, I add that non-Darwinian evolution, such as genetic drift and founder principle, may have consequences different from those of natural selection and may not lead to an explanation and justification of an end to which all events in life tend to be directed. There are arguments on both sides of the question and it is worthy of some future debate.

Ruse[177] made some interesting comments:

> It is true that most putative bridging attempts [to go from "is" to "ought"] flop; but I can imagine an evolutionary ethicist agreeing that normally you cannot go from "is" to "ought", yet insisting that in one case you can. Evolution uniquely bridges the gap. At this point, and at this point alone, you can go from the way things are, to the way things ought to be. (p. 87)

As extraordinary as the above proposition first appears to be, it is likely true. Evolution is the unique guiding force of life. Not only is it the source of the legitimization of values, it is the only *possible* source of the legitimization of values. That is because the principles of evolution explain what has been, what is, and what will be in the entire organic world. If evolution is responsible for all that, then it is obviously responsible for moral values, too, which are just a subset of mental states for members of the organic world. All that I know and all that I ever can know, including values, is a product of my genetics and environment. Since genetics are a product of evolution and since environment becomes an evolutionary force whenever it has consequences for differential rates of reproduction, it is clear that all that I know or ever can know is based on a cognitive capability that is a product of evolution.

Since we are created by evolution, it is the cause of what we are and what we ought to be. Since doing is part of being, evolution is thus the cause of what we ought to do. In short, evolution creates its own moral universe.

I contend that we are justified in describing the meaning and purpose of life and that evolutionary theory is unique in providing a valid perspective on these questions. It is equally clear that one is justified in proclaiming what humans ought to do, when a meaning and purpose of life are clear and offer themselves as points of reference. But for the purpose of simplifying the language in this book, I shall use the word ''should'' in the sense employed by a physician when he tells his patient: ''You should take one tablet three times a day''. Of course, the physician is assuming, when he says ''should,'' that the patient wants to improve his health. In the same way I, an anthropologist, use the word ''should'' and assume that the reader wants to maximize his reproductive success. Of course, it is up to the discretion of the reader to decide if he will act in ways consistent with the meaning and purpose of life.

It is my belief that life has its guiding principle, which to some degree we have lost with the advent of advanced culture. This guiding principle is derived from evolution. While I am a devout determinist, I do believe that people's perception of what they ought to do can be one of the determinants of their actual behavior. To be consistent with determinism I would simply maintain that the idea of what they ought to do has deterministic causes itself. But regardless of people's perception of what they ought to do, projections based on differential reproduction in the past suggest that some of us will maximize our reproductive success and that this type of individual will be represented in increasing proportions in future generations.

What use is life if we do not know the purpose of our existence? A great deal! Organisms have been maximizing their reproductive success for billions of years, fulfilling their purpose, without knowing it. It is perhaps true that consciously knowing the purpose of life, an opportunity that only humans have recently acquired, could further our ability to achieve that purpose through maximizing reproductive success.

Anthropologists and evolutionary biologists have previously offered explanations for human variation. My intent here is to help the reader filter through the existing variation and to choose those patterns that are adaptive in the new and greatly changed modern environment. Just as there is an authoritative rule for how one ought to live, there are also evolutionary consequences for individuals, depending upon which lives they choose to live. An important part of the consequences is whether the genotype and the culturgen that gave rise to the ''oughtness'' will be perpetuated. As we shall learn from the example of the Shakers, some ''rules'' for how humans ought to live are self-eliminating, and in the example of the Hutterites, self-perpetuating.

We have no trouble when we ask the question: ''What is the meaning of a word?'' Of course, we are asking for its definition. We may also ask without difficulty: ''What is the meaning of an action?'' We are asking for its intention. So why is there a traditional difficulty when we ask: ''What is the meaning of life?''

The answer is in part because we believe that people have a meaning higher than a definition or intention. Natural selection has conferred on us a nervous system that in combination with our environment leads us to reflect on the meaning of life. Is this search for the meaning of life an adaptation? It is a preadaptation for the coming of the evolutionary ethic. Would a genetic basis for the meaning of life or for a rule on how humans ought to live validate that definition or rule? Yes, if it was also, for example, a useful proximate mechanism to ensure adaptive behavior. Such a genetic basis for a definition of the meaning of life could serve as an adaptive proximate mechanism until the environment changed, when a new philosophy and genotype would make adaptive sense. And why has evolution not conferred upon us an intrinsic knowledge of the ultimate meaning of life, maximizing reproductive success? The only answer is that until the recent accumulation of a large number of maladaptive, culturally determined traits, the system of drives and appetites which guide our behaviors was more or equally adaptive than ultimate knowledge. Of course, with the present and future availability of artificial ways of expressing behaviors that are motivated by drives, and of artificial ways of satisfying appetites, those primitive systems are no longer reliable guides to adaptive behavior -- hence the need for the evolutionary ethic.

If we were to accept the extreme interpretation of Hume's[103] observation and maintain that one can never derive "ought" from "is," then no "oughts" exist. If no "oughts" exist, what rules would we use to choose our actions in life? Ultimately, all actions would occur without justifiable moral bases. Since we cannot live without actions, life itself would continue without final justification. At the endpoint of this inquiry, we reach the level of self-nullification. If we decide that self-nullification is not appealing, we have no choice but to adopt ethics that cannot be proven to be logically correct by Hume's standard in order to merely survive. Indeed, the human brain seems to be designed to either need or to be easily parasitized by ethics. For in order to live, humans accept *some* system of ethics -- typically those ethics that as culturgens have been successful in the past at self-perpetuation. But we should not be misled; those presently accepted systems of ethics may not be good. A few revolutionaries among us pursue a different approach and formulate their own system of ethics. Some dedicate themselves to more or less random and purposeless behavior; we label them insane. But none of these options, or any known option, can be labeled justifiable by Hume's criterion. The conclusion that I draw is that we must be willing to accept a standard for an ethic other than Hume's standard of logical defensibility since it precludes all "oughts," because we need an ethic in order to survive. One such alternative standard is that one may want to live a life that is consistent with the purpose for which one evolved. If so, then the evolutionary ethic is the way. By comparison, all other systems of ethics seem contrived. For example, in America the most common form of ethics, Judeo-Christian, is based on a God whose will is believed to be the source of all morality.

While such beliefs are understandable in the cultural and historical context of Western civilization, it is hard to believe with confidence that Judeo-Christian ethics are really applicable to the modern world where science has provided a powerful alternative to faith in the pursuit of knowledge. Furthermore, the morality of the Judeo-Christian tradition seems increasingly out of touch with modern life. We are living at a time that is between the past inception of Judeo-Christianity as a religion and its future recognition as a mythology in the way that Greek mythology is understood to be by us today. At that future time, Judeo-Christian teaching will suit our biology and ethos even less well than it does now, and it will not be taken as a serious reason to elicit behavior.

Now, after reading the above paragraphs concerning the lack of logical justification for any system of ethics by Hume's standard, we come to a critical juncture in this book where an assumption is made, and I intend to be forthright by making an important aspect of it clear. I assume that you *do* wish to fulfill your purpose in life and to act in accordance with the meaning of life by maximizing your reproductive success. That maximization is what we are designed by evolution to do. Accordingly, I use the words "should" and "good" to describe behavioral strategies that will help you to achieve that goal. The choice is yours, and what choice you make will be determined entirely by past and present aspects of your environment and your genetics.

Naturally, if I believe in the evolutionary ethic, I should be concerned with maximizing my *own* reproductive success. But as an author I also accept the responsibility of sharing information that will benefit my readership. The two operations may be compatible or they may be in conflict at times. What is good for the reproductive success of my readership may not be good for my reproductive success, particularly if my readership is large. I would also like to note that there is no need for you as an individual to preach this philosophy, unless there is some positive feedback for your reproductive success. It is enough that you and your relatives follow it. The reason that I openly advocate it is that by the fact that this book is sold, I am an advisor paid to do so. In effect, I have an unspoken contract with my readership: I will help to enhance their reproductive success, and they will compensate me with something that I hope to convert, perhaps with difficulty, to reproductive success.

The concept of the naturalistic fallacy relates to evolutionistic ethics, as described by Moore[143]:

> Evolutionistic Ethics .... is the view that we ought to move in the direction of evolution simply *because* it is the direction of evolution. That the forces of Nature are working on that side is taken as a presumption that it is the right side. (p. 56)

Moore considered the above view to be fallacious. Moore[143] also defined his often quoted naturalistic fallacy:

> That fallacy ... consists in the contention that good *means* nothing but some simple or complex notion, that can be defined in terms of natural qualities. (p. 73)

Moore[143] also made a point that evolution is a temporary historical process. And it is true that evolution on Earth had a beginning and will have an end. But that fact does not negate the moral imperative of evolution to maximize one's reproductive success as long as the living products of evolution continue to exist.

In a clear departure from Moore's original definition, many modern writers interpret the naturalistic fallacy to state that it is incorrect to use statements about what "is" to derive statements about what "ought" to be. In fact, Hume[103], not Moore, was the correct source of the lesson about the subtle, and by his implication, invalid, tendency to progress from "is" to "ought" in discourses. I discussed his standard in previous paragraphs. The naturalistic fallacy is often taken as a major obstacle in justifying the use of the word "good" to describe any behavior or trait promoted by philosophy. No doubt some may employ it in an attempt to invalidate my evolutionary ethic. But there is an interesting aspect of the naturalistic fallacy that is rarely acknowledged by those who wield it. Richards[172] described it well when he wrote:

> ... the justification of first moral principles and inference rules must ultimately lead to an appeal to the beliefs and practices of men, which of course is an empirical appeal. So moral principles ultimately can be justified only by facts. The rebuttal, then, to the charge that at some level evolutionary ethics must attempt to derive its norms from facts is simply that every ethical system must. Consequently, either the naturalistic fallacy is no fallacy, or no ethical system can be justified. (pp. 619-620)

Richards[172] made an important point: *All* ethical systems fail the test of logic at this level. But I would maintain that there is another level at which ethical systems need to be analyzed, and I would maintain that they are not all of equal validity at this level -- namely, their consistency with the maximization of reproductive success.

The evolutionary ethic

In questioning whether a certain value, like the maximization of one's reproductive success, is right for guiding human behavior, it is appropriate to ask: "Right, relative to what criterion?" Pugh[167] posed a similar question and challenged the logical validity of the naturalistic fallacy, because it depends upon one's accepting the philosophical concept of an absolute definition of "right". If one does not believe in an absolute or authoritative definition of right, then it is meaningless to ask whether a certain value is valid -- except within the context of some specified criterion[167]. In the case of the evolutionary ethic that criterion is evolution itself; no higher authority capable of conferring the status of ''right'' is recognized to exist. Although this concept may sound strange to some at the present, I expect that in the future a smaller proportion of people will defend the concept of the existence of any source of moral authority higher than evolution.

Moral axioms may be considered as a mere special class of culturgens, thoughts and behaviors transmitted among humans, in part because they are self-perpetuating, and in part because they may confer reproductive success on their bearers. Morals are a special class of culturgen because they assert that they *ought* to exist. ''Honor your father and your mother, that you may have a long life in the land which the Lord, your God, is giving you'' is asserted as something that should be done because it is a commandment from God. This type of ought associated with the moral culturgen is absent from interactions with other culturgens. Because of this attribute, moral culturgens have special powers in structuring the form of our lives. And any culturgen that asserts an ''oughtness'' to its existence can help to ensure its own perpetuation. Further investigation along these lines will lead to findings on the evolution of ethics, not to be confused with the related subject of the evolutionary ethic. Perhaps they are most productively but obscurely considered together as the ''evolution of the evolutionary ethic''. Such a subject would be based on the axiom that ethics did evolve *and* that evolution can point to an ethical principle, namely, that the maximization of one's reproductive success is right. Based on this ethical principle of maximizing reproductive success, an entire social order would be justifiable.

Importantly, the evolutionary ethic, with one primary ethic, is a system that is free of the ethical dilemmas common to ethical systems with more than one primary principle. Furthermore, it is an ethical system that is subject to scientific investigation, as secondary and tertiary principles on how best to maximize reproductive success are determined empirically. This susceptibility to scientific investigation is different from most other ethical systems; e.g., how would one determine empirically the optimal method of increasing the glory of God? We need not limit the maximization of reproductive success to a narrow sense. For example, altruism among relatives would of course be natural, but cooperation in remarkably complex ways between unrelated individuals would also exist. The society created by the evolutionary ethic might indeed be a society with some similarity to our own. The difference is that reproductive success would be the ultimate currency by which all actions, social and nonsocial, would be judged.

Earlier scientists who promoted the concept of evolutionary ethics were correct in seeking guidance from evolution for moral human behavior, but they were incorrect in their interpretation of what the guiding message was. Rather than being correctly formulated as an evolutionary mandate to maximize reproductive success, these former models were based on misconceptions of the evolutionary process. For example, views held by Spencer[197] suggested that more evolved is better, that it was desirable for humans to further advance former trends in evolution, and that (borrowing from hedonism) pleasure is the supreme end. Simpson[192] described another of Spencer's views: the life ethic. In this view all life is "good," and ethical conduct is that which promotes life. Another set of views maintains that certain phenotypic characteristics, such as human intellectual faculties, are characteristic of human evolution and should be further advanced. But, in fact, evolution does not have an absolute commitment to the advancement of any particular trait; rather, evolution favors *any* trait that happens to promote reproductive success. Another mistaken view is that we should make an effort to continue evolution itself. Simpson[192] wrote:

> The search for an absolute ethic, either intuitive or naturalistic, has been a failure. Survival, harmony, increase of life, integration of organic or social aggregations, or other such suggested ethical standards are characteristics which may be present in varying degrees, or absent, in organic evolution but they are not really ethical principles independent and absolute. They become ethical principles only if man chooses to make them such. (p. 310)

This quotation from Simpson raises three questions: 1. Is there a standard that is characteristic of evolution? 2. Is it an independent ethical principle? and 3. Can only humans turn a standard into an ethical principle? In answer to the first question, yes, there is a standard that is characteristic of evolution; it is selection for the maximization of reproductive success. In answer to the second question, yes, it is an independent ethical principle in that it is independent of idealistic notions that an ethical principle requires compliance with or sanction of some higher source of legitimization, and it is the fact of evolution that is the foundation of an ethical principle. In answer to the third question, no, humans need not be considered unique in their dealings with standards and ethical principles. Any organism with sufficient encephalization for conscious choice may have to deal with ethics. Some nonhuman primates are likely candidates.

In contrast to these views from the past, by choosing reproductive success as the foundation of my evolutionary ethic, I am not choosing a trend in evolution, but rather a basis of evolution. This foundation for the evolutionary ethic has implications for the central question of ethics, the nature and justification of fundamental ethical values. Fundamental ethical values by this definition have a nature that is founded in individualist costs and benefits measured in reproductive success, vary from environment to environment, and change over the life history. Their justification is evolution. This point is the rational component that defends the fundamental principle in the evolutionary ethic. A final mistake in the recent history of evolutionary ethics is the one made by some sociobiologists, who believe that in describing and explaining all aspects of human behavior that a foundation for ethics is realized. Some sociobiologists believe that knowledge of what we ought to do is based on what we are. While there is no doubt that the fact we are hominids is very much relevant to our behaviors, moral and otherwise, it is a mistake to look at the details of these evolved characteristics for the source of ethics. Rather, the source of those natural behavioral tendencies themselves, evolution, is the correct source of ethics. With that view we arrive at a somewhat surprising conclusion: The evolutionary ethic does not apply to humans alone but instead to all living things which owe their origins to evolution -- which to our knowledge is all living things now on Earth.

Another interesting point about the above quotation is that it conflicts with a view that may be equally popular. Simpson[192] maintained that an ethical principle can only be made one by the act of humans. But a conflicting viewpoint suggests that although morality and ethics may coincide with the customs or laws of the land, morality transcends human-created permissions, obligations, and prohibitions[177]. Clearly, we need to make up our minds on this central issue if we are to claim to know the truth about morality and ethics. It is my view that all ethics are culturgens, and that one of them, the evolutionary ethic, contains a special truth based on evolution. Other secondary ethics have legitimacy to the extent that they derive it from the evolutionary ethic. No ethical principle has been handed down to humans from any source which legitimizes values that is higher than evolution.

Of course, some people think that there is more to life than there really is (namely, to maximize reproductive success), and that is a common fundamental mistake that can lead to the erroneous rejection of the evolutionary ethic. There is also a philosophical inquiry: Do the ends justify the means? The evolutionary ethic has a decisive answer: Yes, they do if the ends are the maximization of one's reproductive success. The words good and bad, n.b., are used throughout this book as defined in the previous elucidation of the evolutionary ethic: That which increases one's reproductive success is good; that which decreases one's reproductive success is bad; that which has no effect on reproductive success is neutral. For the occasional exceptions to that pattern of usage, the words good or bad are placed in quotation marks. To say that the meaning of life is to maximize reproductive success does not involve the naturalistic fallacy. But to say that reproductive success is the same as good, as I have done here, is to commit the naturalistic fallacy *par excellence* as defined by Moore[143]. However, as I explained above, it is appropriate to challenge the logical validity of the naturalistic fallacy on the grounds that there is no ultimate source of authority higher than evolution in establishing values.

It is high time that we analyzed the naturalistic fallacy using evolutionary theory, since for so long evolutionary theory has been critiqued by the standard of the naturalistic fallacy. Could the naturalistic fallacy be an insidious cultural plot to put all value systems on the same loose footing, making the meaning of life (the maximization of reproductive success) obscure, thereby perpetuating culturgens including the naturalistic fallacy itself, at the cost of perpetuating our genes? And could it be that culturgens, in a battle against our true evolutionary interests, have launched a pre-emptive strike against the evolutionary ethic, by attempting to deny us access to "ought" from "is," i.e. to attempt to deny us the normative statement "*ought* to maximize reproductive success" from the factual statement "maximizing reproductive success *is* favored by natural selection"? Culture, not wanting us to have access to the evolutionary ethic, tries to deny us the path to the evolutionary ethic via "ought" from "is". The reason is simple: In ways described in detail in a following chapter, culture is in the business of diverting our reproductive effort from the process of maximizing reproductive success and using it instead for its own perpetuation.

What increases the reproductive success of an individual is dependent on populational, individual, genetical and environmental constraints. Therefore, what is good for an individual may not be good for the same individual at another time or for another individual at any time, although by the very nature of the similarity of the life historical requirements of individuals of the same species, there is much overlap. We find that the evolutionary ethic leads to a consequence of moral pluralism. Thus, in agreement with principles first stated by Wilson[222], I maintain that no single set of moral standards can be applied to all human populations, or sex-age classes. To carry the principles further, moral standards would be based on the life history status of each individual. While this idea initially sounds revolutionary, after examination the concept is not entirely unfamiliar. For example, Muslim countries practicing Sharia law behead a murderer and amputate the hand and foot of a thief. While we would find this bizarre form of punishment cruel and unusual in America, we accept that they are of a different population and culture, and we do not intervene in international courts to stop the practice. Women in American society who are breastfeeding may bare their breasts in public because they are of a special reproductive status; women who are not breastfeeding may not do so. Infants may appear in public in a state of undress because they are of a special age class; adults may not. A starving man might be pardoned by the courts for the stealing of a loaf of bread because of his critical life history status with respect to food, but a well-fed man would likely be sentenced as a shoplifter. There are countless such examples. Wilson[222] was correct when he wrote that imposing a uniform ethical code creates complex, intractable moral dilemmas -- just as are seen in the world today. One outcome of a widespread application of the evolutionary ethic would be a reduction in the hypocrisy in the way our laws are written in contrast to the way they are applied. The starving man who steals bread would not have to rely on the mercy of the courts (or lack of mercy, as in the case of Jean Valjean in the novel *Les Misérables*[102]), but instead he would, in fact, be morally entitled to food. Is it moral to break the law? Yes, if the law is an immoral one in terms of the evolutionary ethic and if one's reproductive success is enhanced by so doing.

The above kind of moral pluralism is different from the type of pluralistic morals that are caused by the merging of two or more different moral systems. When moral systems merge, attributes of each are retained in the new moral system, with the result that there are deep inconsistencies. For example, there are conspicuous inconsistencies between biblical teachings on ethical behavior and the current legal status of those behaviors in America today. There are many systems of ethics practiced around the world. The evolutionary ethic is not identical to any of them, but it does not have to be. There is overlap with some of these systems of ethics, but certainly the evolutionary ethic does not make a perfect fit with present ethics in America. If the popularity of the evolutionary ethic increases, then a stage of pluralistic belief with mainstream ethics will occur. For example, people may attempt to maximize their reproductive success, strive without restraint for wealth, and serve their God all at once. While such a pluralistic ethic is bound to fail in practice, this kind of cultural synthesis is the usual outcome when two or more value systems meet. That, in turn, may lead to natural selection and cultural selection for the expression of the evolutionary ethic in a purer form over time. Eventually, the evolutionary ethic will possibly subvert other beliefs in a pluralistic system.

Symons[200] made a prescient comment:

> Probably no one has seriously maintained that whatever an individual does to further its reproductive interests is right, although DeVore (1977) comes close when he remarks that sociobiology "ultimately lends a certain dignity to behaviors that one might otherwise consider aberrant or animalistic" p. 87. (p. 61)

The state of affairs has changed from the time of Symons' writing -- the evolutionary ethic is now submitted with serious intent for the consideration of this book's readership.

I am a staunch believer in the power of the field of sociobiology as established by Wilson[222] to make important and interesting findings about behavior. However, there is a common misperception among sociobiologists that modern humans are regularly maximizing their reproductive success. It is my view that modern humans are not very effectively doing that, but that they *should* be doing that. The explanation is a simple one: There is no doubt that the majority of human behaviors *were* adaptive, but the environment has changed radically and strategies that once resulted in maximizing reproductive success no longer do so. I ask my fellow sociobiologists to question with me whether reproduction is the imperative driving much modern human behavior. Does it not seem that the conscious goals of average Americans and the actual products of their lives are something quite different from the maximization of their reproductive success? Does is not seem that some ideas and pieces of our material culture are self-perpetuating, even though they do not lead to higher reproductive success of their bearers? Modern contraceptive techniques are among the most vivid examples, which I shall discuss in detail in another

Chapter 2: Evolution

Evolution and phylogeny

The current trend is to think of evolution as a change of gene frequency in a population. An older and still popular view, held at the time of synthesis of knowledge about natural selection and genetics, the synthetic theory of evolution, is that evolution is the twin processes of adaptive change and the origin of diversity. Regardless of whether one thinks of evolution as best being described by the activities of genes or of organisms, it is clear that 141 years of applying the scientific method to questions about Darwin's theories has resulted in irrefutable support of them to date.

Life is what it is because of natural selection. And natural selection is an evolutionary process by which differential survival and reproduction leads to a change in gene frequencies in a population over generations. Darwin[38] pointed out that natural selection is similar in some ways to artificial selection, in which humans choose desirable characteristics for domestic plants and animals and through selective breeding change a variety or breed over time, sometimes with conscious intent and sometimes unconsciously. Sexual selection is the evolution of traits that are not for the survival of the individual but which instead give the individual a competitive advantage in obtaining a mate. Evolution is a process dominated by natural selection and sexual selection as described by Darwin[38, 39], but it also incorporates random components of genetic change based on the founder principle, genetic drift, and mutation pressure. The founder principle is when the smallness of the number of founders of a population gives rise to a genetic drift effect. Genetic drift is the random fluctuation of gene frequencies in a finite population between generations. Genetic drift is due to a difference between the gene frequencies of the random sample of gametes forming the next generation and that of the parental generation[22]. It has a particularly powerful influence on the frequencies of neutral genes, i.e. genes without positive or negative selection value. Mutation pressure is the change in gene frequencies due to mutation alone. A mutation is a random, heritable change in the DNA. Mutation pressure changes gene frequencies very slowly, so it is rarely considered to be a major force in evolution.

A study of phylogeny teaches us that beautiful adaptations have evolved in the human species. We need to briefly examine our heritage to understand the sources of those adaptations. At an early stage of evolution we received from our mammalian heritage hair, dependent young, and lactation for nourishment of young offspring. Later the primates evolved. Primates are an order of mammals including humans that appeared about 65 million years ago. There are about 200 living species. They include platyrrhines, (meaning flat or broad nosed) having a broad nasal septum with flat and widely spaced nostrils. They usually have 36 teeth and are monkeys that occur in the New World. They are all arboreal and some have prehensile tails. The other major group of primates is the catarrhines (meaning hanging or downward nose) having nostrils that are narrow and close together and pointing downwards. They occur in the Old World, and include monkeys, apes, and man. The final group of primates is the prosimians. Prosimians are the oldest group and occur in the Old World. The lemurs of Madagascar are among them.

From our primate heritage we receive a number of traits that people often assume are human characteristics when, in fact, they are older. These traits include less specialization than other mammals, singleton birth of a dependent offspring, being highly social, having a large brain, visual acuteness with stereoscopic vision, grasping, pentadactyl hands, opposable thumbs (and big toes in nonhuman primates), and nails instead of claws. There is considerable genetic similarity among higher primates: Humans share 93 percent of their DNA structure with Catarrhine monkeys. And as Diamond[43] pointed out with panache: Humans share a remarkably high 98.4 percent of DNA structure in common with chimpanzees and with pygmy chimpanzees. I say ''panache'' in reference to Diamond's assertion because he concluded that humans are best described as a third species of chimpanzee!

From our hominid heritage we inherit the remainder of phylogenetic traits. Examination by anthropologists of fossil evidence from the last three or four million years indicates that the earliest species of man-apes (*Australopithecus afarensis*) had an erect stature and bipedal locomotion before later species attained the advanced brain development that we associate with modern humans. This early bipedal adaptation is further correlated with changes in dentition (such as reduced size of canine teeth), changes in the pelvis, and changes in the hands, feet, arms, and legs. So human-like brains and bodies have been evolving for perhaps 250,000 generations, 99.8 percent of which lived as hunter-gatherers -- before agriculture, cities, industry or the other common characteristics of modern life. Older fossil finds of *Australopithecus ramidus* dating to 4.4 million years ago have yet to be fully evaluated; more material from this hominid is needed. As we shall see, this heritage has implications for American life today. The specific traits that we owe to our hominid heritage are: bipedalism, tool use, culture, and language.

Life history strategies

What form should the life history of a human organism take? For example, when should we grow? How should we act? When should we die? Modern evolutionary biology can tell us about which strategies are optimal in terms of their life historical consequences. The first point regarding life history strategies is that organisms are selected to convert resources into offspring. Life history strategies were discussed eloquently by Gadgil and Bossert[68]. They described how growing, maintaining, and reproducing are competing variables in the life history equation. Furthermore, the advantage of expending effort in feeding, growing, and maintaining is only in that future reproduction is enhanced.

Energy budgets, or the calories available to the organism to carry out its life historical activities, relate to the process of maximizing reproductive success. In the natural environment, organisms tend to utilize all the energy they can accrue, and that amount is near the optimum. For example, there is little energy wasted and none surplus in the life of a wild baboon. But when organisms move into a new niche, as humans did during the neolithic period and again in the industrial age, a great and evolutionarily unanticipated increase in the energy available can occur. The average American has two or three more orders of magnitude of energy available to him than he was adapted to process. This fact produces two consequences. The first is that the incredibly efficient operation for which the human body was designed is not as relevant to daily survival and reproduction as it once was. For example, we do not need to be as efficient as we are in locomotion and thermoregulation. Second, we have more energy available than we can possibly utilize in reproduction. Remember, the primary task in the life history is to convert resources into offspring. So a great deal of energy goes unutilized or is wasted when it is overly abundant. If this energy abundance continues long enough, humans will evolve strategies to utilize it for reproduction. In the meantime, this bounty is a liability as well as a potential asset. I will discuss the problem of morbid obesity in Americans as a consequence of bountiful energy sources in a following section. The human brain has a mass of approximately 2 percent of the total body and uses about 20 percent of the total energy budget. That level of metabolism for brain activity was the result of a subtle balance in the adaptive benefits of brain function, e.g., thinking, weighed against the costs of thinking, in terms of calorie consumption, in the millions of years of hominid evolution. That relationship is now totally out of balance. We could afford in caloric terms to have brains that were a hundred times more costly than the ones we have, and if the same rules of efficiency applied, we might be a hundred times more intelligent.

An individual's reproductive success at a given time is determined by his reproductive effort at that time and his net return of reproductive success per calorie (or degree of satisfaction, i.e. an index of the extent to which a resource like energy is limiting) at that time. Kinship effects may be considered in this equation -- reproductive effort may include calories expended in the assistance of relatives while the net increase in reproductive success of those relatives is devalued by the regression coefficient of relatedness. Interestingly, while the energy available for reproductive effort has increased for modern humans, the summation of actual reproductive effort expended over the lifetime and/or the net reproductive success per calorie has decreased. I shall explore the reasons for that trend when I discuss the concept of cultural load in a following chapter.

While the energy budgets of Americans are almost unlimited, the time budgets of Americans are not. Since it is often instructive to look at limiting variables, it makes sense to consider time budgets when energy is abundant. The average American spends the majority of his time in three activities: working, sleeping, and television viewing. Other activities of less importance in the time budget include child care, eating, and driving. Thoreau[202] said that it was a little uncertain whether we should live like baboons or men. Having studied wild baboons in Africa for many years, I am personally in favor of living like a man. But that does not suggest we are unable to learn a great deal from studying these fellow primates. They are a useful model of early hominid behavior because, like humans, they are primarily terrestrial, omnivorous and African grassland-living. For example, consider time budgets of baboons and humans, specifically the time budgets of Masai Mara baboons in Kenya and of Americans. Compared to baboons, Americans do not spend enough time sleeping or eating. The result is that their sleep and the calories in their food need to be more concentrated to compensate. While it may be possible to concentrate some aspects of sleep as well as some aspects of nutrition in the food, other important components may be lost. For example, Americans tend to eat high calorie diets, but are they well balanced in terms of other essential nutrients? Do we all not sometimes accept a quick meal that we know to be less nutritionally complete rather than take the time to prepare and consume one that is more nutritious? From my observation of wild baboons, they never make, or need to make, that choice. Rather, unlike humans they seem to follow the theoretical model for optimal feeding strategies proposed by Schoener[185]. In that model, an individual is considered to be a keen strategist, choosing food items carefully in terms of how well they will enhance his reproductive success. For Americans, spending more time eating and eating fewer calorie dense food items would be a possibly desirable tradeoff.

In the previous discussion of life history strategies, we learned that an optimal life is an exercise in extracting resources and harnessing them as reproductive effort. But infinite resources are not of use. For example, take energy. A biological system like an individual human is designed by natural selection to maximize reproductive success within a narrow range of energy throughputs, those encountered in the environment during previous generations. (This reason is the primary one that modern, adult humans occur in the limited range of body mass that they do). The individual human will be inefficient at higher or lower levels of throughput. This point clearly applies to Americans today. One might think that morbidly obese people might be able to convert their stored energy in fat reserves into reproductive success. But in accordance with the above discussion they cannot. The causes are many. For example, among morbidly obese women ovulation commonly ceases. So rather than the wholesale conversion of the energy in every extra twenty-five pounds of fat into an infant (the production of which requires approximately that amount of energy), reproduction ceases altogether.

Americans often think that what they do is the normal expression of human nature. Often they do not realize that people in other cultures manifest very different ways of living. We shall explore some of those ways as well as others that are novel in a search for life history strategies that maximize fitness. For example, Americans are accustomed to viewing kinship relations bilaterally, i.e. we consider ourselves to be equally related to our paternal and maternal families, discounting the slight linguistic bias toward the patriline given through patronymy. But it is incorrect to assume that this type of kinship pattern is universal; on the contrary, the people in about two-thirds of human cultures have a different view of their kinship network.

Some people try to maximize wealth or longevity, and in popular culture the maxim ''you can't be too rich or too thin'' is often heard -- these are misguided efforts in the evolutionary perspective. Irons[107] provided a cross-cultural perspective on goal-directed behavior. He pointed out that the men in some societies strive to increase the number of their cattle, or the number of their wives. He felt that middle class Americans seek the combined goals of interesting work, moderate economic prosperity, and financial security. However, he offered the example of the Turkmen of Persia to argue that human beings tend at times to behave in a way that maximizes their genetic representation in future generations. I question the correctness of the last view, because as I explain in subsequent sections of this book, I see a great deal of maladaptive behavior in contemporary societies. However, I do hold the opinion that fitness maximization *should* be our goal. The question arises whether we make a conscious or unconscious pursuit of evolutionary goals. We may wish to keep them in our habits if not always in our conscious minds. For example, making a rule of never having contraceptives in the home is a simple algorithm that leads to adaptive behavior without the requirement of constant thinking. Also, not taking the time or trouble to provide traditional sex education to one's children is a counterintuitive way of increasing one's inclusive fitness and need not require a great conscious effort.

Many contemporary social scientists argue or assume that the human mind is a *tabula rasa* which is totally dependent on socialization in the process of forming human nature. Similarly, the school of behaviorism, now on the decline, teaches that behavior is purely the product of operant conditioning. While human culture in some respects takes on a life of its own, so to speak, it is my opinion that the *tabula rasa* hypothesis should be rejected. All human behavior is most fruitfully analyzed in the context of its evolutionary significance, past and present.

Chapter 3: Feeding

It is time for a popular science of living and reproducing -- a new, fitness-friendly ethos. Many of the culturgens we encounter in modern American life are pre-Darwinian. If they further our reproductive success it is by accident or by a cultural selection process. But due to the fact that they predate Darwinism, they could not have been consciously designed to increase our fitness. Now the conditions are different. We have the opportunity to deliberately create a new model that elucidates methods of maximizing one's reproductive success. Culturgens that are post-Darwinian in origin have had the hypothetical possibility of being designed with the maximization of reproductive success in mind, but only rarely, if ever, would that seem to have occurred. Finally, we must recognize that many culturgens are not consciously designed at all, but instead arise and continue according to rules all their own, as we will see. We begin this discussion of a new, fitness-friendly ethos with a discussion of human feeding behavior.

Optimal feeding behavior

Food item selection according to the theory of feeding strategies by Schoener[185] is a process of choosing that food item which provides the greatest net benefit to the consumer. In the natural environment, many animals are selective about what they eat. Humans, too, especially in accordance with cultural patterns, are discerning about what they consume. But among modern humans there is a great deal of confusion and irrational behavior in feeding. It is not clear that modern humans do in any meaningful way exercise optimal feeding strategies, with exclusion of the fact that they do not ordinarily eat large quantities of substances which are impossible to consider as food (ignoring the growing market in non-nutritive diet beverages). The reason for the gap between the theory of feeding strategies and actual modern human feeding behavior is that the food environment has changed radically and rapidly in comparison to the rate of human evolution. We shall learn more about that point in this section. But first let us cover some basics. Here is an anthropological view of the essential diet which describes in the simplest way the basic needs in human nutrition. Harris[90] wrote:

> In addition to air and water, we have to ingest forty-one substances: one carbohydrate that can be broken down into the sugar glucose; one fat that contains linoleic acid; ten amino acids, the building blocks of proteins; fifteen minerals; thirteen vitamins; and a source of indigestible roughage to help clean the lower end of the gut. (p. 154)

Nutrition really does not have to be more complex than that. So in itemizing the balanced diet, what is involved in practical terms? The National Research Council[151] cited in Willett[215] made recommendations for a healthful diet. These recommendations included:

> 1. Reduce total fat intake to 30% or less of calories. Reduce saturated fatty acid intake to less than 10% of calories and the intake of cholesterol to less than 300 mg daily. 2. Every day eat five or more servings of a combination of vegetables and fruits, especially green and yellow vegetables and citrus fruits. Also, increase starches and other complex carbohydrates by eating six or more daily servings of a combination of breads, cereals, and legumes. 3. Maintain protein intake at moderate levels. 4. Balance food intake and physical activity to maintain appropriate body weight. 5. Alcohol consumption is not recommended. For those who drink alcoholic beverages, limit consumption to the equivalent of 1 ounce of pure alcohol in a single day. 6. Limit total daily intake of salt to 6 g or less. 7. Maintain adequate calcium intake. 8. Avoid taking dietary supplements in excess of the RDA in any one day. 9. Maintain an optimal intake of fluoride, particularly during the years of primary and secondary tooth formation and growth. (p. 532)

Another source of information for Americans about diet is the U.S. Department of Agriculture, which has prepared a dietary pyramid of the food groups. It is being used as a teaching tool for improving eating patterns in America. Willett[215] said the following about the pyramid:

> Inevitably, such a document represents a mix of well-supported findings, educated guesses, and political compromises with powerful economic interests such as the dairy and meat industries. (p. 535)

After interpretation of available information, Willett[215] concluded that consumption of partially hydrogenated vegetable fats and saturated fats, particularly those from dairy sources, should be minimized. He also felt that sugar displaces other nutrient-bearing foods in the diet and leads to tooth decay. Finally, he said that most epidemiological data suggest that an optimal diet emphasizes generous consumption of vegetables and fruits. The above review of Willett[215] sums up the informed, conventional view of nutrition. But human feeding behavior looks different when viewed from the perspective of its primate origins.

Early humans

Perhaps it is appropriate to start with an examination of the original state of human feeding activity, i.e. hunting and gathering, and then to consider the changes imposed by agriculture. The anubis baboons of Masai Mara may be a useful model of early human feeding behavior. They feed on a chiefly vegetable diet with some hunting of small game and a very small amount of scavenging. This actual documented field observation is in contrast with what is a popular view among anthropologists today concerning how our primate ancestors fed. For example, Harris[90] wrote:

> Our ancestors must have remained primarily scavengers, at least until the appearance of the first [*Homo*] erectus, 1.6 million years ago. (p. 45)

I cannot support the statement in the above quotation with my own field observations of wild primates. In fact, all evidence that I have is to the contrary. I would add, I hope not unfairly, that most anthropologists who believe the scavenger hypothesis have neither lived on the African grasslands nor encountered the relentless efficiency of the indigenous predators and scavengers. Baboon encounters (and my personal encounters!) with hyenas, cheetahs, leopards, and lions in the Masai Mara portray a picture different from the scavenger hypothesis. Baboon and human scavenging from cheetah kills is occasionally possible, but subsisting primarily on kills scavenged from large predators is totally out of the question. Most meat consumed by baboons is from their own hunting of small game. Only once have I observed baboons driving a cheetah away from a young topi that it had freshly killed, which the baboons then scavenged. Leopards are too rare, dispersed, and secretive to be the source of kills for scavenging. Lions are too formidable; hyenas are too nocturnal and too efficient in disposing of all prey parts; wild hunting dogs are too rare and range over great areas. In many years of life on the wild eastern African grasslands, I had only a single opportunity to take part of a kill from another predator -- the hind leg of a young impala freshly killed and abandoned by a cheetah. Not only are kills already well consumed by other predators and scavengers when found by baboons and humans, they are difficult to find in the first place. How would early human scavengers solve this problem? One way, according to Blumenschine and Cavallo[11] was:

> At night, the loud "laughing" of hyenas at a fresh kill, the panicked braying of a zebra being attacked, the grunting of a frightened wildebeest -- all serve notice of where to find an abandoned carcass when morning comes. (p. 95)

This proposed mechanism for finding kills is simply preposterous; in areas where wildlife is abundant the African night is a veritable cacophony of sounds which are poor indicators of what will be found at that site hours later during daylight. In conclusion, while game meat is an ideal, low fat source of protein, scavenging is not the way to get it.

Perhaps one of the freshest and most rational views of human nutrition comes under the heading of paleolithic nutrition. Paleolithic means "old stone" age, a period lasting millions of years in distant hominid prehistory. On the subject of a paleolithic diet in modern perspective, Eaton and Konner[52] stated:

> The foods we eat are usually divided into four basic groups: meat and fish, vegetables and fruit, milk and milk products, and breads and cereals. Two or more daily servings from each are now considered necessary for a balanced diet, but adults living before the development of agriculture and animal husbandry derived all their nutrients from the first two food groups; they apparently consumed cereal grains rarely, if at all, and they had no dairy foods whatsoever. (p. 287)

The point about cereals (defined here as barley, corn, millet, oat, rice, rye, sorghum, and wheat -- not in the narrow sense of "breakfast cereal" common in popular American usage) being largely absent from the paleolithic diet is well taken. However, their point regarding the absence of dairy foods requires some modification. Considering the mammalian heritage of humans discussed in a previous section, it comes as no surprise to us that milk serves as an important (and sole) food for part of every human's life history. In this sense we had a preadaptation to make use of dairy food -- first as a substitute for lactation in order to feed infants, then later as juveniles, subadults, and adults as natural selection favored the ability to produce lactase (the enzyme that digests lactose, milk sugar) past the time of infancy in those populations with dairy products in their culture. Some human populations which have not been historically exposed to milk products show a high frequency of lactase-deficient adults. These populations include American Indians, some Asian populations, and some African populations.

In my study of anubis baboons[162], which are omnivorous primates living in the same habitat in which our human ancestors evolved, I found that baboons do rarely eat grass heads (the seeds of mature grass plants and the precursors of modern cereals) while foraging, but feeding on them comprises only about 5 percent of their feeding time budget. I would not object in theory to that low level of cereals appearing in the modern human diet, because it is probably close to the paleolithic level. However, that amount is much less than what appears in the American diet; the average American eats an incredible 85 pounds of bread alone per year, and when cereals other than wheat are included in the analysis, the reliance on them is dramatic. There is, in fact, considerable overlap in the diets recommended by nutritionists and anthropologists. But one point of significant departure in my opinion is on this subject of cereals. I suggest that people eat them at their own peril. Do the morbidly obese among us really obtain a positive benefit in reproductive success from that 85 pounds of bread? On this point of cereal grain consumption, Eaton et al.[53] did not remain true to their premise for a paleolithic prescription diet. First, they pointed out that cereal grains are not part of the paleolithic diet; later they proclaimed them healthful and seemed to recommend their consumption in large quantities. It would appear that they were putting adherence to conventionality before adherence to their hypothesis. So while their hypothesis is an interesting and novel one, the actual menus that they suggested for daily consumption seem to be the product of habit.

There are indications that olive oil is a particularly healthful fat source; in technical terms it contains monounsaturated fatty acids, which are effective in lowering serum cholesterol. Is it mere coincidence that wild African olives (*Olea africana*) were an important food source in our primate heritage? Modern African primates like anubis baboons feed nearly exclusively on them for weeks in the riparian forests when the wild olives come into season. Another food that baboons have in common with humans is figs. Concerning food allergies, a legitimate question is: Are they associated more often than randomly with new foods introduced during the neolithic period and during modern times? The question deserves some serious future research, but it is worth briefly noting that foods derived from cereals like wheat gluten and corn are frequently allergenic in America. This observation is no doubt in part because these foods are popular, and thus many people are exposed to them, but it could also be an indicator of the evolutionary inappropriateness of these neolithic foods.

Life-lesson: Eat plenty of fruit, vegetables, and lean animal protein. Eat few cereal grains.

People educated in the benefits of the paleolithic diet make a beeline for fresh fruits and vegetables, fish and lean meats, and milk products, and they avoid cakes, donuts, cookies, breads, pastas, and all cereal grain based foods. In the eighties and early nineties Americans had a love affair with pasta, which was thought to be a nutritious, healthful food -- precisely the opposite of what we now know to be true. So avoid the cereal grain products like pasta and bread, which contain complex carbohydrates that are quickly converted to body fat, and substitute them for more healthful paleolithic foods like fruit and fresh vegetables. A point to remember: All complex carbohydrates are not created equal. The complex carbohydrates in carrots or broccoli are a much better complement to the average American diet than are the complex carbohydrates in a bowl of pasta.

Data on national consumption of alcohol indicate that alcohol contributes 4.5 percent of the total calories in the energy budget of the average American[183]. Rates of alcohol consumption are age dependent, with younger adults consuming more than the elderly. The lower rate of alcohol consumption among the elderly is at least in part a consequence of differential mortality: Heavy drinkers are eliminated from the population by accidents and alcohol-related diseases. In fact, in 1991 there were 19,233 people who died of alcohol-induced causes in America, and that figure excludes causes indirectly related to alcohol use like accidents and homicides[148]. Males are more likely to drink alcoholic beverages and to drink more heavily than females[149]. The lungs (through loss in breathing), the kidneys (through excretion in urine) and the liver (through metabolism) are the only ways of disposing of significant amounts of alcohol. It is in the liver through the enzyme alcohol dehydrogenase that most alcohol is disposed. This explains why only time will restore sobriety. Walking will not -- muscles cannot metabolize alcohol[82]. Alcohol, when consumed excessively, will displace essential nutrients from the diet; it is a form of "empty" calories. It also adversely affects the metabolism of existing nutrients. Heavy drinking is linked directly to pathology: Fatty liver is the first stage of liver deterioration; fibrosis is the second stage; cirrhosis is the third stage. The guidelines for consuming alcohol are clear: never more than three drinks a day for the average-sized, healthy man; never more than two drinks a day for the average-sized, healthy woman[82]. Here a "drink" is defined as the equivalent of $1/_2$ ounce of pure ethanol, or 3-4 ounces of wine, or 12 ounces of beer, or 1 ounce of hard liquor.

Food and its relation to behavior is a topic of some interest to the average American. For example, in the popular culture, sucrose (table sugar) and aspartame (Nutrasweet) are often believed to be the cause of hyperactivity and other behavioral problems in children. But scientific evidence refutes those opinions. In a double-blind controlled trial, Wolraich et al.[225] demonstrated convincingly that neither sucrose nor aspartame affects children's behavior or cognitive function. That does not mean that there are no valid behavioral correlates of nutrition. One clear, established relationship is that excellent nutrition, especially during childhood, increases IQ. Another clear relationship is that excellent nutrition increases rates of aggressive behavior, while severe food deprivation results in docility. That relationship is discussed further in a following section on aggression. Another behavioral response to food, or rather to the rejection of food, is the vomiting-salivation reflex. People often notice that immediately before vomiting they salivate profusely. That salivation is a reflex action in order to protect the teeth from the corrosive stomach acids that are contained in the vomitus. Saliva contains chemical buffers for exactly that purpose. Another relationship between food and behavior is the reflex response that we have to foods of distinctive taste that we have consumed before becoming nauseous and vomiting. As a child I once became nauseous and vomited shortly after eating a bar of black licorice, which I loved. My illness was not caused by the licorice, rather by influenza. To my utter amazement when I tried to eat black licorice again weeks later, I gagged; the taste was so revolting that I could not swallow. That response is a subconscious mechanism to avoid repeat poisoning and would have adaptive significance under the conditions in which hominids evolved, particularly experimenting with new plant foods that could contain toxic substances. Many plants do indeed contain toxins. It is their own adaptation to avoid being eaten by herbivores. Since my childhood experience this phenomenon has been described in print. Seligman[187] referred to it as the *sauce béarnaise* phenomenon.

Food fads are part of the American heritage. Generally, they do little to improve nutrition and may actually be harmful. One of the biggest food fads in America today is vegetarianism. The truth is that no culture is strictly vegetarian.

Animal protein may be scarce as a source of food in some human populations, but it is valued. Even the Eastern cultures, the dietary patterns of which some Americans seek to emulate, include animal protein in their diets. After extensive field studies in the wild, it is clear to anthropologists that most nonhuman primates are omnivores as are human primates. We also can be certain from archaeological evidence that our hominid ancestors ate meat. No better example of silly food fads exits than the change in preference for egg color among Americans. A few decades ago white eggs were preferred over and sold at a premium above brown eggs. White eggs were then associated with ''clean,'' and brown eggs were associated with ''dirty''. Now brown eggs are preferred over and sell at a premium above white eggs. Brown eggs are now associated with ''organic'' and white eggs are associated with ''processed''. But nutritionally they do not differ. Some chickens just produce brown pigment and deposit it in their feathers and in the shells of their eggs. Many food fads are promoted through the mass media by self-appointed nutrition and physical fitness advisers. Their real objective is to sell a ''package'' to as many of the millions of people interested in improving their diet as possible. In the process they provide an incredible disservice through spreading gimmicks, half-truths, and outright falsehoods about nutrition. For example, a few nutritional plans promoted through the mass media advocate ''no fat diets''. They make promises of spectacular weight loss in return for forsaking the indulgence of fat. Often they perpetuate the myth that a fat calorie is always an empty calorie, when in truth some fat is needed. What they fail to point out is that some fats are indeed an essential component of every balanced diet, and while not desirable in excess, they should be consumed in modest amounts by adults and liberally by children.

Do you remember the breakfasts of the fifties? They commonly included bacon, eggs, sausage, white bread toast, cereal, butter, whole milk, and were prepared with plenty of saturated cooking fat. Today that kind of meal will seem quite out of date and unhealthful to the average reader. But food trends are not now fixed in time. Fifty years from now what you ate for breakfast this morning will appear just as outdated and unhealthful as the breakfasts of the fifties appear to us today. In the year 2050 we shall look back with little amusement at how we were duped by the advertisements of giant corporations to pay inflated prices for and to eat breakfast cereals full of ''empty'' calories and indigestible fiber based on neolithic grains. Most breakfast cereals made of oats, wheat, corn, or rice are so low in nutrients that I am reluctant to call them foods but will do so because they are, in fact, eaten. For example, the health benefits of oat bran have been grossly exaggerated. And the problem is *not* the processing of the food as is most commonly assumed. The actual problem is the intrinsic deficiencies in the raw cereal grain products. For example, they lack a proper balance of amino acids for use as food by humans. Processing, if well designed and executed, can actually improve the nutritional value of the final product on your table. This point is so opposed to the popular view in America today that I recognize it is unlikely to gain general acceptance quickly. For those who doubt my point and who are willing to take a challenge, try going a week without eating any food that has been cleaned, refined, enriched, pasteurized or cooked and still manage to get the recommended RDA's of vitamins and minerals.

Because of the junk food that people consume at breakfast, such as commercially packaged cereals containing wheat and oats, it is all right to skip breakfast -- it is the least important meal of the day, contrary to what you have probably been told your entire life. Millions of years of the hunter-gatherer lifestyle, during which food was not available until the day's work had begun, adapted us to begin eating later in the day. Indeed, eating breakfast may be implicated in modern American obesity.

While it is true that no known culture in human history is strictly vegetarian, some individuals, particularly in postindustrial age Western countries, may forgo all animal foods. Often they do that out of a misguided sense of morality. Fortunately, high technology food supplements are available to enhance the diets of these people. Because it is so difficult to obtain a balanced diet that is derived entirely from plants, we do not see much strict vegetarianism in non-Western peoples. Ironically, many vegetarians in the West think that they are emulating the practice of the Hindus of India, but in fact Hindus consume milk products and eggs, and some even eat meat. Recently, Ornish[156] advocated a mostly vegetarian, very low fat diet along with philosophical insights, points for meditation, and exercise, with the intent of reversing cardiac disease, specifically as a treatment for coronary artery blockage. Whether this program/diet actually clears clogged arteries in the heart is one question, and whether it actually achieves the gold standard in medical science by prolonging life is another question. He addressed the first question but not the second in his publication[156]. In the context of this book, we would also want to question: "Does his program increase reproductive success?" Macrobiotics describes a group of cults among which the most zealous believe it is proper to eat only brown rice. Sadly, contrary to their firmly held belief that they were getting the best possible nutrition, whole families of children have been dreadfully stunted in their development by malnutrition on this diet. In the less extreme form, macrobiotics allows other vegetable foods in addition to brown rice, particularly other grains. But in view of the arguments presented above about paleolithic nutrition, it is not clear that even this form of macrobiotics provides any special benefits or that it has the right to be considered natural. Rather than being based on old wisdom about food, it is a modern digression from healthful paleolithic nutrition, and this digression took place primarily to oblige neolithic farming practices, not to meet the nutritional needs of humans.

Undernutrition and overnutrition

Severe undernutrition, to the point of being life threatening, is rare in America and is usually associated with behavioral pathology rather than with food shortages. Moderate undernutrition, often associated with dieting, is a greater overall risk to maximizing reproductive success in America through the phenomenon of fertility suppression. Both in human females and males, reproductive functions are interrupted by undernutrition because both the cost and the chance of success in reproductive efforts at such a time are unfavorable. One point about undernutrition is the lack of a generally agreed upon definition. For example, fertility experts and cardiologists disagree over optimal body mass, because they are treating different things. It is not surprising that the optimal weight for fertility in a woman might be higher than the optimal weight for cardiovascular fitness. In the view of this book, if you are a woman in your reproductive years, the fertility experts should have the final say about your weight. The definition that I propose for undernutrition is a state of body mass that is below the optimum for maximizing reproductive success. In the Third World, where undernutrition is common, it is associated with increased risk of disease. Mortality from starvation is usually a combination of the nutritional deficiencies and the diseases that opportunistically infect the undernourished. In America, pathology in the form of anorexia nervosa and bulimia nervosa is the most common cause of severe undernutrition. These conditions afflict a disproportionately higher ratio of women to men. Frankly, their evolutionary implications are obscure, other than the fact that they have a highly disruptive effect on reproduction. Anorexia and bulimia may be best considered to be manifestations of mental illness that have no past or present adaptive advantage.

Unlike undernutrition, overnutrition is a common problem in America. One out of three American adults is overweight, defined as weighing 20 percent or more above their ideal weight. In 1993, Americans spent approximately thirty billion dollars on goods and services related to dieting; three hundred diet books were in print in 1984[108]. At present there is a lively debate on whether obesity is always the product of hyperphagia or if it may be the result of low metabolic rates or other problems. We need not have the answer to that question to explore the adaptive significance of overnutrition, because obesity can be a product of overnutrition, and it has an evolutionary explanation. In prehistory, the ability to accumulate fat during times of plenty evolved because the fat was an essential store of energy during times of food scarcity, helping to ensure its carrier's survival and reproduction. In this way obesity was impermanent and actually desirable. Some archaeological evidence supports this view. The Venus of Willendorf, a paleolithic fertility symbol, is an example. It portrays in limestone a woman from about 30,000-25,000 B.C. with exaggerated obesity. It seems that optimal fat storage is lower in environments where food resources are predictable and evenly distributed over time than in environments where they are unpredictable and unevenly distributed. Americans live in the former environment but eat too much because their feeding behavior is adapted to the latter environment.

In the current environment, obesity is primarily a cosmetic issue, but it does have some important correlates. Brown and Konner[16] pointed out that obesity is positively correlated with females, modernization, and fertility and inversely correlated with social class. It was their view that in the course of human evolution fatness arose as an adaptation for the successful completion of pregnancy under some conditions. Many women in America today want to be slim because they feel it is becoming. But perceptions of desirable weight vary over time. The body shape now considered most attractive may have been considered too slim by previous generations. There also may be a sex difference in the perception of the ideal female figure. In a study by Fallon and Rozin[58] of preferences for silhouettes of women, the silhouettes that men labeled most attractive were heavier than those preferred by women. It is true that obese women are less likely to marry, but unless they are morbidly obese, they have more children than women who are normal or under-weight. Naturally, it is the number of children, not the number of husbands a woman has, that determines her reproductive success. This important point remains generally unknown in America today, where people are keenly aware of marital status and appearance, but are generally oblivious to reproductive success. Obesity is a risk factor for heart disease, diabetes, and high blood pressure. But it has not been scientifically demonstrated that losing weight and achieving one's ideal weight increases longevity. However, it would appear that losing and regaining weight repeatedly is an unhealthful practice.

Culture specific values in overnutrition are apparent in America, as they are around the world. There will always be a role for feasting in populations where there are famines. Feasting is a way of storing energy for times of food deprivation. In some cultures obesity in women is considered to be a sign of beauty. Among the Bahima of Uganda a woman who is too fat to walk is thought to be beautiful[173]. There is little doubt that this kind of love for obesity would make sense if it were correlated with environmental cycles of plenty followed by famine. In America, obesity is correlated with minority subcultures; half of African American woman and Mexican American woman are overweight. In America, poverty and obesity are positively correlated. Poverty is primarily the cause but also may be to some degree the effect of obesity, to the extent that it can be a physical and social handicap. People receiving food stamps, arguably the sector of society nearest to the threshold of poor nutrition, often make surprisingly poor nutritional choices, using their food stamps to buy candy, potato chips, and soft drinks.

Eighty million Americans go on a diet every year, and 9 out of 10 of them gain all the weight back within five years. Seligman[187] stated:

> Maybe someone will have that new insight into maintenance [of weight loss] that has thus far eluded everyone. But in the meantime, the clearest fact about dieting is that after years of research, after tens of millions of dieters, after tens of billions of dollars, *no one has found a diet that keeps the weight off in any but a small fraction of dieters.* (p. 181)

I would like to venture to offer one more diet in addition to the plethora of existing diets. It is called the modified Masai diet. My approach to the problem is to go to the study of people who are traditionally thin for their entire lives, but who also are healthy, well nourished and most importantly, highly fertile. These people are the Masai. I lived among them for many years in eastern Africa. The Masai are among the leanest, slimmest people in the world. They derive protein primarily from cow's milk and to a lesser extent from the meat of cattle, goats, and sheep and from the blood of cattle. They have low body fat and a low serum cholesterol level when living the traditional lifestyle, even though they consume a large amount of cholesterol in their diet each day. These seemingly disparate facts are explained by some unexpected interactions among the things we eat. Drinking milk, especially skim milk, and consuming a diet with low saturated fat, lowers serum cholesterol levels, and the Masai do both. They have no traditional source of carbohydrates other than lactose (milk sugar) and, rarely, wild honey, which is usually brewed into a traditional drink. When Masai leave their traditional village, referred to as an *ang*, and live a more Western lifestyle, their serum cholesterol levels increase and their weight often increases markedly. Those facts indicate something that is not the least surprising, namely, that physiological variables like serum cholesterol levels and body weight have a large environmental component and are not highly heritable.

For most of human history and prehistory and in the majority of non-Western cultures today, it is not appetite but a shortage of food that keeps body mass under control. Most people in America will overeat if food is constantly available. One approach to healthful eating patterns is to control the amount of food that one brings into the home. With the modified Masai diet that is easy. It includes simply four cups of milk and plenty of fruit and vegetables daily, and occasional lean meat. Like any diet, if you go off this one you will probably regain the weight lost, and more. It is better to think of this diet as a permanent change in the way that you eat rather than as a temporary weight loss measure. Think of it as a permanent cross-cultural experience. One final note: It is true that the traditional slimness of the Masai people is partly genetic; they are examples of Allen's rule in biology -- protruding body parts such as arms and legs are relatively longer in the warmer parts of the range of a species than in the cooler parts. The Masai are best described as Nilo-Hamites with historical origins near the equator and hence show this adaptive complex.

Morbid obesity (200 percent or more of ideal body mass) is likely to lead to premature death. To solve that problem, it is advisable to curtail caloric intake. The human body is incredibly efficient in its use of calories, so exercise alone is unlikely to succeed. It takes only a hundred calories to walk a mile. One can run a marathon on a typical Thanksgiving dinner. There are only two ways in which to lose a pound of fat: One can eat 3,500 fewer calories than one usually does, or one can burn 3,500 more calories than one usually does. The most practical method may be a combination of both ways. Morbidly obese people eat so much that they often handicap themselves. Indeed, morbid obesity can be a disability in terms of locomotion, sleeping, and sitting in chairs designed for people of normal proportions. As the morbidly obese person's mobility is decreased, activity is reduced, thus promoting further weight gain in an unfortunate cycle. Among the worst disabilities associated with morbid obesity is fertility suppression in women who suffer from it. This condition is a clear indication of pathological obesity. Studies of morbidly obese women show that excessive fatness is associated with amenorrhea and infertility[66]. If asked why some humans have appetites that lead to morbid obesity, we can answer that natural selection has rarely had the opportunity in human prehistory and history to promote a physiological or behavioral mechanism to reduce caloric intake, since it has been a scarcity of food that has been the prevailing condition. Some overweight women have the option of becoming pregnant and nursing -- if they keep their caloric intake constant they will stabilize their weight or lose weight. Brewer et al.[15] have shown that lactating women tend to lose weight gained during pregnancy more easily than nonlactating women.

Life-lesson: If you are cosmetically obese (less than 100 percent over your ideal body weight), do not worry about it. Instead, use the stored calories to raise additional children. If you are morbidly obese, consider a diet and an exercise program. Your weight goal is that which maximizes your reproductive success, not necessarily that which makes you look nice or be healthy.

What should we eat? The modified Masai diet, the paleolithic diet[52, 53] or the guidelines listed above from the National Research Council[151] cited in Willett[215] might help you to achieve better nutrition, depending upon your current nutritional state. The guidelines cited by Willett[215] are especially attractive if cereals are deleted and increased quantities of legumes are substituted for them. Lean game meat and fish, wherever possible, should be substituted for the fatty meat of domestic stock.

Social feeding and courtship feeding both have implications for human eating patterns as well as those of other species. There is a phenomenon known as social facilitation of feeding. Individuals feeding in the presence of other feeding individuals eat faster and eat more than they would if they were feeding alone. In humans, dining at social occasions where food is served, or simply eating at a table with family members, may promote overindulgence. I expect that dining alone might help a dieter to lose weight. Courtship feeding is usually ritualized but often meaningful in terms of calories. Most commonly, males courting females present suitable food items to the females. It may be a symbolic representation of ability and willingness to invest in the female, or it may be an actual contribution to the costs that the female incurs in the period of reproduction following courtship, or both. There are numerous examples of courtship feeding in animals. The male Mormon cricket provides a large, nutritious spermatophore to the female at the time of mating. Among some species of birds, the male typically feeds the female during courtship as though she were a dependent offspring. The males of some species of insects, e.g., the hangingfly and the scorpionfly, present a nuptial gift to the female and copulate with her while she consumes it. And, of course, the food habits of Americans while courting are too numerous and too well known to mention. Suffice it to say that both special and ordinary foods are presented by the male or female on occasion as an integral part of forming or maintaining a sexual relationship.

Chapter 4: Growing

Physical growth

The purpose of physical growth is to achieve the optimal body mass for reproduction and to develop ancillary structures to the extent that they also maximize reproductive success. Generally, the larger an organism, the greater its metabolic costs for maintenance. At the same time, the larger the organism, the greater the possible gross throughput of energy, sometimes disproportionately small or large for the size increment. The object is to gain a selective advantage by processing a greater net amount of energy that can be diverted into reproductive effort. Knowing how long and how large to grow is simply an exercise in following those two functions: overall energy throughput and metabolic costs over the range of possible body sizes, and choosing that size with the net maximum energy that can be diverted to reproductive effort.

Americans go through a period of approximately thirteen years of growth after conception to the time of sexual maturity, then continue to grow in stature for another six years for males and thirteen years for females. In part because of the abundance of food resources, Americans grow faster and larger than the people of many other populations. Throughout the prepubescent growth period, ancillary structures like dentition, the respiratory system, the circulatory system, the skeleton, muscles, skin, and the central nervous system all grow while the reproductive organs are mostly dormant. But at the time of the adolescent growth spurt, the reproductive organs mature, providing a start to the reproductive life of the individual. Human females reach sexual maturity earlier and at a smaller body mass than human males because, in the past, males who have had a large body mass at the time of sexual maturity have produced more offspring than males with a smaller body mass, largely due to the advantages of a large body mass in male-male competition. At the same age, females, not requiring the large body mass for intrasexual competition, divert energy to attaining earlier sexual maturity and producing additional offspring with that reproductive effort. In previous research I have plotted growth curves for anubis baboons. They, too, go through the same amazing growth spurt in adolescent years as do Americans in junior high school.

Mental growth

Through most of human history and all of prehistory, mental growth or learning was a product of informal education and brain growth. Certainly the most important aspect of informal education in relation to fitness is attitude toward sexual intercourse. Nearly any proximate mechanism that leads teenagers to have sexual intercourse early, such as "seeking experience," "satisfying curiosity," "experimentation," "peer pressure," "proving manhood or womanhood," "looking for a conquest," "scoring," "seeking physical pleasure," "affection for partner," "wanting to have a baby" or "putting a notch in one's belt," is a highly acceptable way of initiating reproduction and focusing their lives on reproductive success. Although this frank appraisal of the usefulness of these mechanisms in the adolescent rite of passage is sure to offend most Americans who have a prudish attitude about adolescent sexuality, the adaptive significance of the sexual behavior and the proximate mechanisms that prompt it are not diminished. Many of these proximate mechanisms are learned through informal education. But they are easily subject to being supplanted by culturgens provided in formal education or deliberate inculcation, with behavior modification as its goal. Not all teenage girls report that they want to get pregnant. That fact is no doubt a consequence of informal and formal education of the teenagers that implants antigenitive messages. Fortunately, consciously wanting to get pregnant is not the only way or even the best way of getting pregnant in terms of adaptive significance. Getting pregnant when one does not want to may be highly adaptive. Instead of focusing on becoming pregnant, other behavioral variables like mate selection, pair bonding, or unimpeded expression of sexuality might be the proximate goal. These proximate goals could then in turn lead to higher reproductive success.

Another aspect of mental growth among Americans is formal education. Formal, compulsory, public education is a recent First World experiment. Regardless of what its goals might have been when first established and what its goals are now, it has had some surprising effects on our lives, particularly in the area of fertility. When all variables relating to reproductive success are accounted for, it may be that formal, compulsory, public education is inferior to family based, informal, observational learning.

It is apparent that even early in life, education and fertility have an adverse relationship, because the major cause for teenage girls' dropping out of school is pregnancy or motherhood. Also, high school dropouts begin having intercourse earlier and marry earlier than college-educated women. That adverse relationship continues into adulthood long after the education has been completed. The more education, the less fertile, is a well established pattern, not just in America but around the world as well. In America the total fertility rate among women who did not complete high school is 2.5; for college graduates the total fertility rate decreases to 1.4. But in Kenya there has been a positive correlation between the number of years of formal education a woman has had and total fertility rate. Unlike most other populations, Kenyan women with more education had higher fertility than those women with less education. This pattern in Kenya is a rare exception to the general trend. In a *naïve* model, education prepares us for the challenges that we meet in life.

No doubt to some degree it does. But after a point increased education also leads to a critical threshold in increased burden of culturgens and subsequently lower fitness. In other words, formal education in America comprises the transmitting of some essential facts combined with fitness inhibiting misinformation. I do not use the word "misinformation" here to refer entirely to lies, but more in the sense of the word "disinformation," which may include some truths but which has an overall effect of diverting people from their true purpose. Modest exposure to formal schooling can lead to increased reproductive success. To see the effects of no formal education and little formal education on fertility we must look at non-Western societies. Gille[73] reported that in some countries, e.g., Bangladesh, Benin, Kenya, Philippines and Senegal, women with a few years' schooling have a slightly higher fertility than uneducated women. But it is also clear that higher education consistently depresses fertility. Considering the example of the Amish, who are an American subpopulation with very high fertility, an eighth grade education may be near the optimum for maximizing reproductive success in the present American environment.

A rigorous evolutionary analysis turns much conventional wisdom on its head. For example, just as schools teach mathematics and health, they should also be in the business of teaching how to succeed in reproduction. And this teaching is certainly not what passes for sex education in many school curricula. Sex education as now commonly taught is the antithesis of preparing students to maximize their reproductive success. It is quite possible that it actually *reduces* the reproductive success of the students with its emphasis on contraception, delaying pregnancy, and scare tactics couched in terms of health messages. Instead, sex education courses should: 1. Teach students that sexual intercourse at an early age is good, 2. urge students to have sexual intercourse, 3. urge students not to use contraception when having sexual intercourse, 4. tell students that abortion is not an option when pregnancy occurs, and 5. provide a practical sex laboratory at school. Today, many messages from formal education and from the mass media are heavily permeated with industrial values. Children get a heavy dose of the glory of industry from such seemingly innocuous sources as the Public Broadcasting System. Do we question why the children who view PBS television shows see the making of brooms in a broom factory instead of the birth of babies in an obstetrics ward? The fact that we do not ask that question tells us much about our greater orientation toward industrial productivity than toward the ultimate human productivity, i.e. reproductive success. When parents talk about raising an achievement-oriented child, almost invariably they are talking about scholastic achievement and economic achievement. It could be different. Almost everyone takes some pride in becoming a grandparent. A natural extension of that emotion could be supportive parental behaviors that urge our children to achieve reproductive success. Americans commonly express the view that "there is nothing more important than family". We should include the children of our children in our families with enthusiasm.

University education is a depressant of reproductive success in three ways: 1. The financial cost of a university education could be directed toward reproductive effort, 2. the time allocated to university education usually occurs during peak reproductive years, thereby reducing the time available for reproduction, and 3. new, antigenitive values are learned at university, further reducing fertility. The result is a 44 percent decrease in the total fertility rate among women who have a university degree in comparison with women who never completed high school.

Fundamentalist Christians and political conservatives object in particular to one aspect of formal education, i.e. sex education. They want to deny teenagers access to information about contraception. Instead of teaching them about the normal expression of sexuality, they prefer to urge them to abstain from sexual intercourse altogether. Ironically, I share in this opposition to traditional sex education classes in school, but for a reason contrary to the purposes of the fundamentalists and the conservatives. I know that denying children this information is a sure way to increase the fertility of teenagers, contrary to the expectations of the fundamentalists and the conservatives. In other words, the result of a ban on traditional sex education would be an increase in teenage pregnancy, which is fully in accordance with the philosophy discussed herein.

Certain aspects of growth, such as some infant development, are under direct control of the mother. Fetal alcohol syndrome is the deleterious effects on the fetus as a result of maternal consumption of alcohol. It comprises a set of behavioral and morphological abnormalities in the infant with stunted growth both mentally and physically. It can be entirely avoided by modifying maternal behavior during pregnancy to avoid all alcohol. It is the commonest cause of retardation in America today.

One topic on growth that is surrounded by confusion is the claim by the promoters of self-help and motivational courses that these courses enhance it. There is a major industry in self-esteem and motivational courses, through publishing, through organized public lectures, and through mass media. Often they are touted as a cure-all for subclinical personality disorders. But that claim is nonsense. This judgment is true for one simple reason: A person can have too much as well as too little self-esteem or motivation. Education is most effective when it teaches knowledge or skills, not emotions. Sadly, the people who are most in need of new knowledge and skills for survival and reproduction fall victim to these quick and easy, and often expensive, "personal development" courses. The result is that people may feel better for a short while, having false expectations and overconfidence. That short-term "feeling of elation" effect is part of the reason the courses are popular, along with the slick promotion by the course providers. But they promise, then fail, to provide long-term solutions to life's problems. Broadly, the popularity of these courses demonstrates that many people are dissatisfied with their economic and social success. These courses reinforce this dissatisfaction and teach variations on why we should want more money and more peer approval, two common but mistaken goals in life, in the view of this evolutionary discussion. The possibility exists that people are actually harmed by these courses, in that they are given erroneous reasons for and bogus solutions to problems rather than focusing on the real issues, resulting in wasted time and energy that could otherwise be allocated to maximizing reproductive success. Real social success comes not from amassing wealth, status, or fame, but rather from using the social environment to maximize reproductive success.

We need to keep in mind that intelligence is not the variable in our life history equation that we are selected to maximize. And according to the evolutionary ethic, pursuit of intelligence should always be subordinate to the pursuit of reproductive success. ''What price knowledge?'' is a pertinent question, where price is measured in the consequences for one's reproductive success. The simple answer is that reproductive success should *never* be lowered in exchange for a gain in knowledge. While it is a common belief in American society that intellectual achievement, say publishing a learned volume, is superior to physical pleasures, such as sexual intercourse or perhaps even having a large family, the evolutionary ethic stands in stark opposition to this view. Consider this fact: The people who have chosen intellectualism as a way of life are usually both more eloquent and more convincing in the defense of their philosophy than those people who pursue a nonintellectual lifestyle are in defending their philosophy. Which point of view do you think will be most successful in spreading through the culture? Obviously, the point of view of the intelligentsia will dominate. And the spreading of that view does not make it right, it just means that it spreads. Although the pleasure of coitus and fulfillment in parenthood are two nonintellectual experiences, they are as close as any person can get to knowing the meaning of life as a personal experience. It is not a coincidence that these two remarkable experiences are associated with the process of maximizing reproductive success. By comparison, intellectual achievements can rarely offer the passion or the reproductive success of progenitive behaviors, i.e. behaviors that perpetuate one's genes.

Life-lesson: See that your children get a good eighth grade education.

Do not be dissuaded by the claim that people with an eighth grade education are ill-equipped to serve an advanced technological society. That is not an effective rebuttal to the life-lesson which teaches us that an eighth grade education is optimal for maximizing reproductive success. Advanced technologies are superculturgens, and we do not necessarily benefit from blindly serving them or perpetuating them. Instead, they should exist to serve us and to aid our attempts to maximize our reproductive success. In future generations Americans will become increasingly aware of the fact that they do not truly want to be slaves to an advanced technological society, but at the present we are all too enamored of the comforts of technology and largely unaware of the real costs. Instead of encouraging our children to get "good" grades in school, we should be encouraging them to get good grades in reproductive success. Some may worry that this philosophy is self-defeating. For example, if everyone has an eighth grade education, from where will the obstetricians come to deliver the subsequent generation? The answer to this question is found in statistics. No matter how pervasive this philosophy becomes, there will always be variation around the mean years of formal education in the real world. Some will receive less than eight years and some will receive more. The reasons for this variation are numerous and need not concern us here. The point is that professions like obstetrics requiring higher education will continue to exist in a progenitive society even though far less formal education is optimal for reproductive success for the average American.

Chapter 5: Maintenance

Risk

Here I shall define risk as the probability of permanent debilitating injury or death. There is risk in everything we do: eating, drinking, sleeping, exercising, working, traveling, reproducing. High risk-taking in American society is often "involuntary" and associated with poverty, e.g., poor nutrition. But some risk-taking is voluntary and associated with wealth, e.g., high Himalayan mountaineering, which is very dangerous, indeed. When we reduce a risk, we are actually reducing a risk from a particular cause, which in turn increases risks from other causes in the future. So when we reduce risk and save a life, it is more accurate to say that we are prolonging a life[112]. This perspective makes it clear how risk is omnipresent. The theory of optimal risk-taking is based on the fact that the value of an individual's life at any point in time is assessable in terms of expected future genetic contribution to succeeding generations. In an argument based on the principles of natural selection, changes in tendencies toward self-preservation or self-destruction over the life history should be molded by this parameter. The rate of survivorship and the rate of reproduction are competing variables in life history strategies[68]. It follows that increasing longevity is not necessarily the same operation as maximizing reproductive success[216, 84]. Selection can favor a decrease in the rate of survivorship in a tradeoff for an increase in the rate of reproduction if, on the average, it results in a greater number of offspring.

When people think about the subject of longevity, they usually feel that they would like to have as long a life as possible. Life is considered precious and its preservation is often thought to be a goal in itself. But according to the theory of life histories, the belief that we should try to maximize this variable is merely a common misconception.

Mean life expectancy at birth has roughly doubled during the past two centuries and has increased approximately 50 percent since 1900. In the United States, the mean life expectancy at birth is about 72 years for men and 79 years for women. Many people live beyond these ages, but the maximum lifespan for humans, which appears to be about 120 years, is rarely approached. However, an increasing percentage (about 1.5 percent) of people born now are expected to live to 100 years and beyond[195]. Mean life expectancies at birth vary by a decade for men and by nearly seven years for women according to states of residence -- Hawaii having the most longevous population for both sexes and the District of Columbia having the shortest life expectancy for both sexes[195].

The theory of optimal longevity maintains that individuals are selected to live to the age that maximizes their reproductive success. As mentioned above, there is a tradeoff with other variables in the life history equation. Longevity is a variable that is readily exchanged in the life history equation for higher overall reproductive success. There is no behavior or physiological process that is free from risk. And simply by living we, and all organisms, are exposed to risk of death by accident, disease and, in natural environments, by predation. The best we can do is to allocate our behaviors to distribute risk over the life history in a way that is adaptive. For example, Popp[162] demonstrated that old male anubis baboons living in a wild population in eastern Africa take exceptionally high risks in male-male aggression over access to estrous females because they are of low reproductive value and are unlikely to survive or reproduce much longer even if they do not make a terminal reproductive effort. They can afford to become severely injured in aggression, and they do often receive debilitating and even lethal injuries, while younger male competitors cannot afford to take these risks because of the potential greater loss of future offspring. In this sense, old individuals of low reproductive value have a competitive advantage over young individuals of high reproductive value when the competition is risky.

Given that life must be finite, the theory of life history strategies asks what additional risks are acceptable in the process of maximizing reproduction over the lifetime. This life history strategy of trading off longevity for gains in other variables in the life history equation is the ultimate refutation of the philosophy of egoism. We have not evolved to preserve ourselves as individuals at all costs. Rather, our bodies and minds are built as though they are designed to be expendable in the pursuit of reproductive success. Only entities that reproduce can beat the long-term odds against becoming extinct through accidents. Another implication for philosophy follows from the study of life history strategies: Life's problems are real, they are not an illusion. The life history equation consists of *competing* variables. Increase one desirable variable, say, growth, and you may correspondingly decrease another desirable variable, say, longevity. Finally, there will always be a limiting variable or resource to the ultimate function of reproduction, for which humans as organisms are selected to strain to obtain. Utopian dreams, which envisage a perfect society, are equally unrealistic. Life history strategies demand the pursuit of essential resources. Limits on these resources often have a social component, e.g., availability of mates. To the extent that this relationship is true, genuine harmony (total overlap of reproductive goals) cannot exist in a society of individuals that are not genetically identical.

The various causes of mortality due to senescence have coevolved as the deleterious pleiotropic effects of genes that confer high reproductive success early in the life history have had their expression delayed until late in the life history, when their impact on reducing reproductive success is lessened[216]. Because all physiological systems have been selected to senesce at the same rate, a "cure" for senescence will be a futile pursuit for modern medicine because of the plethora of deleterious pleiotropic effects with which we must deal. A single panacea, such as intensive supplemental vitamin therapy, is not likely to extend maximum longevity. For example, antioxidant vitamin supplements, although in popular belief considered to be beneficial in preventing cancer, have, in fact, been shown in clinical trial to have no effect in reducing the risk of colorectal adenoma. In that study[79] supplements of beta carotene, vitamin C, and vitamin E had no efficacy in preventing the precursor of invasive cancer of the large bowel. The risk of hypervitaminosis is just as real as any potential benefits from overdoses of vitamins. Neither a single panacea nor a combined approach of polypharmacy, surgical intervention, and lifestyle modification offers any meaningful reduction in senescence. In spite of the inevitability of senescence, claims concerning a fountain of youth are ever-popular. It is simply something that many people want to believe. Chopra[25] is among the popular writers now promoting life without aging through a variety of alternative medicine remedies and procedures. The phrase *ad captandum vulgus* comes to mind when reading his book. Its contents are wholly in conflict with what is known about aging from evolutionary biology. Chopra[25] stated:

The evolutionary purpose of aging is itself a puzzle to biologists .... (p. 64)

It is certainly not a puzzle to the evolutionary biologists whom I know! It is only by disregarding the sound, existing evolutionary explanation of aging by Williams[216] and by Hamilton[84] that these erroneous beliefs put forward by Chopra[25] can persist at all. Why do Americans gravitate so readily to New Age mumbo jumbo when simple but elegant scientific explanations exist revealing the real truth about life?

The real methods for increasing our longevity as individuals may not be as appealing as are the herbal placebos. Taking holy orders is one very successful way to stretch out a human life. Individuals who forgo reproductive effort, such as celibate monks in monasteries and nuns in convents, have a considerably longer lifespan than do ordinary members of the population from which they are drawn. Near starvation, especially during early development, is a very successful way of lengthening the lifespan. For example, it has been known for decades that food deprivation of rats and mice in the laboratory results in the prolongation of mean survival and maximum lifespan by up to 50 percent[195]. Harrison and Archer[91] showed that food restriction in mice reduces aging, depending upon genetic differences in the mice. This trend also appears to hold true in wild populations of primates when comparing poorly nourished desert dwelling hamadryas baboons with well nourished grassland dwelling anubis baboons[162]. The trend most likely holds true for humans as well. Another means of prolonging life is castration -- it leads to increased male longevity. Eunuchs are spared several androgen-dependent and male-selecting pathological conditions[83]. Clearly, as a review of the actual means to increase longevity above indicates, the goal is not to increase longevity but, instead, to increase reproductive success through increasing longevity where possible. The above methods of taking holy orders, starvation, and castration achieve the opposite effect and cannot be generally recommended.

Limitations to longevity are ultimately determined by the life history equation, but average lifespan has been slowly increasing in America. For example, declines in the frequency of diseases of the heart, cerebrovascular diseases, and atherosclerosis have been the general trend since 1950[148]. However, continuing this trend of increased longevity is not likely for the long-term. Dawkins[40] suggested that the way to delay senescence would be a breeding program that he recognized as impractical, involving a gradual increase in the minimum age permissible for reproduction. Older and older people would be selected to breed, eliminating those genotypes that contributed to early senescence. I agree that such a breeding program is impracticable, but it would increase maximum life span meaningfully.

Remember this important **life-lesson: Age is not the life history variable that you should be maximizing. Life is a tradeoff between longevity and reproductive effort. And because, other things given being equal, higher reproductive effort leads to higher reproductive success, one should accrue and expend reproductive effort at the expense of longevity.**

Here is a vivid example. One of the least fertile countries, Japan, has the greatest longevity. And the most fertile nation, Ethiopia, is among the lowest in longevity. Minor increases in individual longevity can be accomplished through what are primarily lifestyle choices. A study of elderly residents of Alameda County, California, found predictors of high survival and high levels of functioning 20 years later. These predictors were: race (other than black), higher family income, absence of hypertension, absence of arthritis, absence of back pain, being a nonsmoker, being of normal weight, and the consuming of moderate amounts of alcohol[80]. Schoenborn and Cohen[184] identified unhealthful habits and they include smoking, alcohol consumption, sleeping less than six hours per day, never eating breakfast, daily snacking, a sedentary level of physical activity, and being overweight. Married people (at every age over 20 years) live longer than unmarried, divorced, separated, and widowed people according to the National Center for Health Statistics[147], with mortality rates up to 50 percent higher for the unmarried groups.

In a cross-species comparison, large animals generally have a longer lifespan than smaller animals, e.g., an elephant lives longer than a horse, which lives longer than a dog, which lives longer than a mouse. But in a comparison of subspecies within a species, large animals generally have a shorter lifespan than small animals, e.g., the lifespan of a wolfhound is shorter than the lifespan of a miniature pinscher. The fact that large breeds of domestic dogs have a shorter lifespan than small breeds is common knowledge. The same relationship is true for baboons and perhaps for many other mammals. The explanation for this pattern comes from life history strategies. The cross-species comparison holds true because a large body mass is positively correlated with a long period of growth, and a long period of growth is correlated with a long lifespan. The comparison within a species shows a negative correlation between body mass and longevity. That is because well-fed populations are growing quickly (to a large body mass) and pursuing a life history strategy of early and intense reproduction, which shortens the lifespan. On the other hand, poorly-fed populations are growing slowly (to a small body mass) and pursuing a strategy of late and less intense reproduction, which lengthens the lifespan.

Exercise

America is on a physical fitness craze. What does that mean in an anthropological context? The first striking observation that an anthropologist might make is the apparent reverse cause and effect relationship between exercise and health. In other words, there is no doubt that what exercise enthusiasts tell you is true, i.e. exercise and healthiness are correlated. But here is the surprise: In an important sense healthiness is the *cause*, not *effect*, of exercise. This view is contrary to the current popular belief that exercise makes you healthy. Compare two hypothetical populations (A) exercisers and (B) couch-potatoes. Group A includes only those people who are healthy enough to take rigorous exercise. They live long because they are a healthy group of people. Group B includes some people who are too ill to take exercise. On the average they die younger than group A. Sampling bias in this way explains most of the observed trend in the correlation of exercise and health. In fact, when one considers the increased risk of sudden cardiac arrest that is associated with strenuous exercise, no exercise more demanding than a brisk walk is likely to be justifiable in the pursuit of increased longevity. This example of how physical fitness conscious Americans confuse cause and effect is not unusual. Belief in the philosophy of determinism is helpful in getting the lines of causation in a hypothesis correct. However, much of the American ethos, even on important matters like finance, politics, crime, and punishment, is confused on matters of cause and effect. In following chapters we shall explore related topics.

Humans have evolved behavioral mechanisms to minimize exercise and to achieve an economy in required motion. That is why Americans tend to lay around the house and why they take the car when they could just as well walk. But the behavioral mechanisms that lead us to minimize exertion evolved under circumstances where it was impossible to survive without some minimal exercise, thereby providing a useful amount of exercise for maintenance. We have left that stage of prehistory and history where some exercise was required daily in order to feed, drink, and reach a sleeping place. Now essentials are self-contained in our homes and resources required from the outside are obtained with the help of labor saving devices, e.g., automobiles and elevators. Our behavioral mechanisms to minimize exercise may lead us to a minimum that is below what could be achieved in the past or what is healthy. Another consideration is what I call exercise opportunity cost. The average white American woman lives approximately 79 years. If she spends on the average an hour a day in exercise and sleeps eight hours a day, then she would have to live an extra five years just to recover the waking time spent in exercise over her lifetime. In fact, it is not clear that exercise offers this required compensatory increase in longevity.

If you do choose to exercise, walking is the best exercise. It is also part of our hominid and primate heritage. From sunrise to sunset baboons spend 29 percent of their time walking. One germane aspect of walking is that it is not an exclusive activity, so exercise opportunity costs are reduced. For baboons, they feed, provide infant care, and consort while walking. For humans, while it is possible to walk and think constructively or talk at the same time, more vigorous exercise like running is usually the sole preoccupation when it occurs. Walking can also be a mode of travel, as strange as that might seem to modern Americans. Walking to work or walking to school may be a viable option for some. Walking also contributes to a low rate of injury in comparison to other sports. I used to run marathons but never had any illusions about that improving my health or increasing my longevity. The average long-distance runner has slightly more than one running related injury at any one time. If simply changing your appearance is your goal, and it should not be, running ten kilometers a day and eating as much of anything you want will get you thin, and keep you thin, due to a combination of the powerful appetite suppression associated with long distance running and the actual caloric expenditure in running. Warning: Some strenuous activities are inversely correlated with female fertility. These include marathon running, excessive jogging, frequent high-energy aerobics and triathlon training[120]. These exercises may reduce a woman's chances of conceiving by suppressing ovulation. Further, there is some evidence that regular, strenuous exercise during a girl's developing years postpones the age of menarche. In closing this section on exercise, I conclude that it is absurd that Americans are more concerned with their physical fitness than with their evolutionary fitness. This situation is a historical accident and cannot persist.

Death

Let us begin our discussion of death in an evolutionary context by considering some of the age/sex-specific causes. In the United States trauma is the leading cause of death for people below the age of 44. The leading cause of trauma is motor vehicle accidents. Forty-two percent of all major injuries are to motor vehicle passengers. The average amount of loss of life over a lifetime for various causes, activities, and events in America (adapted from Stossel[198]) is: flying = 1 day of life lost; hazardous wastes = 4 days; house fires = 18 days; pesticides = 27 days; air pollution = 61 days; crime = 113 days; driving = 182 days; smoking (for smokers only) = $5^1/_2$ years; poverty = 7-10 years. Diseases of the elderly are disproportionately emphasized in our society because of the political and financial power of the elderly and the fact than our national leaders, including the congressmen who make funding decisions for health programs, are elderly themselves. One striking trend in American health statistics is the higher male than female mortality in all age classes. In 1991 the age-adjusted death rate for American males of all races was 1.7 times the female death rate[148]. Evolutionists have an explanation for this pattern of male biased mortality. In discussing this explanation we must first discount two other proposed explanations, the societal stress and the unguarded X chromosome hypotheses. Although our close relatives among the nonhuman primates do not have social organizations like the modern Western society that is hypothesized to cause stress on working American men, the males in those species suffer the same kind of differential male mortality. Concerning the unguarded X chromosome hypothesis, higher male mortality is still true in species where the female is the heterogametic sex and bears hemizygous loci. (Among mammals the male is hemizygous for the genes of its single X chromosome, i.e. it has only one allele for each X-linked gene.) Trivers[206] pointed out that differential mortality by sex in animals is not predicted by sex-determining mechanisms. Birds and fish, in particular, fail to support the hypothesis because in those taxa the males are not heterogametic and still tend to suffer higher differential mortality. Trivers[206] provided data and theory that discount convincingly the societal stress argument and the unguarded X chromosome argument in higher male mortality. Trivers[206] concluded:

> It is easy to show that differential male mortality in humans does not result from a difference in the way in which the two sexes are treated by the larger society. It is likewise clear that the difference in sex chromosomes between the two sexes cannot account for the pattern of differential male mortality. Instead it seems likely that males suffer higher mortality than do females because in the past they have enjoyed higher potential reproductive success, and this has selected for traits that are positively associated with high reproductive success but at a cost of decreased survival. (p. 314)

The real cause for differential male mortality is a long evolutionary history of greater male-male competition for access to females. For example, males may be above the optimum size for longevity, display rates of aggression higher than optimum for longevity, expose themselves to risky behaviors, and be susceptible to more disease in the pursuit of reproductive success.

Mortality levels for each of the 14 leading causes of death are higher for males than for females. Nine of the leading causes of death show differentials in which death rates for males are at least 1.5 times those for females[148]. In rank order the 14 leading causes of death and their ratio of male to female age-adjusted death rates are: all causes = 1.73; diseases of the heart = 1.89; malignant neoplasms = 1.47; cerebrovascular diseases = 1.19; chronic obstructive pulmonary diseases = 1.74; accidents and adverse effects = 2.63; pneumonia and influenza = 1.65; diabetes mellitus = 1.14; suicide = 4.37; homicide and legal intervention = 3.84; chronic liver disease and cirrhosis = 2.25; nephritis, nephrotic syndrome and nephrosis = 1.54; septicemia = 1.31; atherosclerosis = 1.36; certain conditions originating in the perinatal period = 1.27 (adapted from National Center for Health Statistics[148]).

Euthanasia and suicide

The drive for self-preservation is usually a strong one, but sometimes self-destructive behavior emerges in humans as well as in other animals. Suicide is almost always a bad choice in the evolutionary context, especially under the circumstances in which it tends to occur in America. However, considering the life history approach to analyzing strategic timing of life history events, it is not desirable to survive at any cost. For example, one should be willing to trade some longevity for increased reproductive success. The suicidal behavior of worker honeybees is an appropriate place to begin our considerations. Honeybee workers are particularly adapted to sting mammalian and avian predators in ways that are maximally effective deterrents to the predator but are also lethal to the worker herself. When a worker uses her sting against such an enemy, the sting becomes firmly fixed in the elastic integument of that enemy by the sharp barbs at the tip of the lancet[181]. Consequently, the sting is torn from the worker's body, together with associated organs. Stings that remain in the enemy's wound in this way are thought to be more effective -- perhaps through a greater or more prolonged injection of venom. The adaptive significance of such suicidal behavior is clear when one considers inclusive fitness. Worker honeybees are sterile females. Ultimately, this altruistic and suicidal behavior benefits the future offspring produced in the defended hive, i.e. the future sisters (related by $3/4$) and brothers (related by $1/4$) of the stinging worker. Indeed, the very basis for eusocial life in the honeybee appears to be the fact that a female honeybee is more closely related to her sisters than she would be to her own offspring, so she has evolved sterility and assists her mother in producing more siblings instead of starting a nest of her own. From my personal and rather painful experience, I have noted that queenless hives of African honeybees are defended more fiercely than queen-right hives because they lack a reproductive alternative. When a queen-right hive is disturbed, the bees can leave the site of the hive and begin a new one elsewhere. But when a queenless hive is disturbed, the bees have no such alternative. The workers must stay and defend the hive, where they are raising brood to become a replacement queen and, sometimes, to become additional drones. Their future reproductive success is totally tied to the site of the hive. For lack of an alternative, they defend their hive more ferociously than do bees in hives with an alternative.

Another observation in honeybees is that it is young bees that serve as guards. Guarding behavior is risky, but it is less risky than foraging behavior outside the hive. Because a younger bee has more additional time to be of service to the reproductive success of its mother, sisters, and brothers, it is adaptive for it to be allocated the least risky task in the hive. However, I hypothesize that when the requirement for suicidal defense of the hive arises, that older bees should do a disproportionately large amount of the suicidal stinging of potential vertebrate predators. This hypothesis follows from the fact that the older worker bees have a lower *extended reproductive value* than the younger worker bees. Extended reproductive value is a concept introduced by Popp and DeVore[164]. It is an individual's reproductive value plus the expected future contribution made to the production of offspring by relatives devalued by the regression coefficient of relatedness. Reproductive value is the expected future number of offspring. Because a worker honeybee is sterile, she has no reproductive value. But because she can contribute to the reproductive success of her relatives, she does, during at least part of her life, have an extended reproductive value above zero. In this way, something as small as the difference of the extended reproductive value of a young bee and an old bee, even when they appear superficially to be just two out of tens of thousands of identical workers, can shape the difference between self-preservation and self-destruction. There is evidence from ants that supports this extended reproductive value hypothesis for risky defense. Hölldobler and Wilson[98] reported that among the green tree ant of Australia the aging workers play a special role in colony defense, leading the authors to conclude that a principal difference between humans and ants is that humans send their young men to war and ants send their old ladies.

In a previous section I discussed how old male anubis baboons of lower reproductive value take greater risks of permanent debilitating injury or death than young males do. In order to achieve an optimal competitive strategy, the reproductive value of the individual, along with the probability of being killed or receiving a permanent debilitating injury, must be weighed against the potential increase in reproductive success conferred by winning and other variables listed in Popp and DeVore[164]. Other variables remaining equal, an individual with a low reproductive value can afford to take greater risk in competition than an individual of high reproductive value, when the resource that is the object of competition is of equal absolute importance to both, since the former has less to lose if killed than the latter. The application of this principle to animal behavior is relatively straightforward. Most birds and mammals in stationary populations have a reproductive value that increases from 2 at the first day of life up until about the time of sexual maturity. This trend of increasing reproductive value from the time of birth to the time of sexual maturity is due primarily to the fact that not all newborns survive to reproduce. Shortly after the onset of reproduction, an animal's reproductive value begins to decrease, slowly at first, and then at an increasing rate so that at the time of old age it is nearing zero, since the probability of producing more offspring before death is very small. In a population of wild anubis baboons in Masai Mara, Kenya, I was able to collect data on the age of the subjects through dental casting, and on the risk-taking by the subjects through examination of injuries and behavioral observation. Age information was gathered through the taking of complete upper and lower dental casts using standard techniques with alginate impression material and dental stone. Information on injury was taken by measuring the scars and open wounds caused by the slashes of the canine teeth of opponents on the individual's skin. Total length of all injuries and scars appearing on an individual was then calculated based on the measurements. Since even small risks taken over time will eventually result in injuries, the best way to calculate an individual's tendency toward risky competition is to look carefully at the rate at which that individual accumulates injuries. I concluded in this study that the old adults sampled had a significantly higher rate of injury than both young adults and middle-aged adults. Old individuals not only had more injuries and scars than members of the younger age classes, but the significant difference in the number of injuries per year indicated that old animals incur injuries at a higher rate as well. These observations in the field laboratory were consistent with the behavioral observations in which old male baboons fought for access to estrous females with the result of great injury to themselves and sometimes their death.

Generalizations from age-specific risk-taking in male anubis baboons demonstrated in Popp[162] must be drawn with caution. For example, an amendment to the basic line of argument is required in species where kin effects are a major portion of an individual's genetic contribution to succeeding generations. Human females after the fifth decade of life and members of worker castes in social insects like the honeybee have a reproductive value of zero according to the definition by Fisher[60]. In a *naïve* application of the male anubis baboon model, it would seem that unlimited risk in competition would be appropriate in these two examples. However, through potential aid-giving behavior to relatives, including partially dependent offspring in the former and through kin effects and service to related reproductives in the latter, it is evident that the future genetic contribution made to succeeding generations in these two cases can be large. For example, helping a mother, sister, or daughter to raise more offspring is a common strategy. Accordingly, Fisher's reproductive value is insufficient to calculate optimal risk-taking strategies under these circumstances. Unconfined risk-taking in these two cases is not, in fact, expected. In the place of Fisher's reproductive value, the concept of extended reproductive value introduced by Popp and DeVore[164] should be used in determining optimal patterns of risky behavior when kin effects exist.

Older human mothers of low extended reproductive value should be willing to take greater risks in defense of their children than younger mothers of high extended reproductive value, but investment not involving large amounts of risk should not vary. Extended reproductive value is at its peak near the beginning of a woman's reproductive life, perhaps around age eighteen in America. Younger girls have a lower extended reproductive value because of the higher risk of mortality during the time until reproduction and care giving to relatives begins. Older women have a lower extended reproductive value because the remaining time in which to reproduce and to provide care has been shortened. But unlike Fisher's reproductive value, it may never drop to zero during life. A fixed risk of permanently debilitating injury or death to an individual of low extended reproductive value imposes less real fitness cost than it does to an individual of high extended reproductive value, but behaviors not involving risk impose equal cost on the two individuals.

The male praying mantis "dies" during copulation when he is eaten, head first, by his mate. The reason why I put "dies" in quotation marks will be apparent in the next section. The consequence of the decapitation is that the male proceeds with the copulation with even greater facility. The adaptive significance of the greater facility is clear: He has no reason to save sperm for a future copulation, because without his head he cannot find another mate. Decapitation by the female may be the ultimate in sperm extraction strategies -- more effective but considerably more brutal than the sperm extraction strategies used by human females discussed in a following section. Of course, the female praying mantis also gets a meal at the time when she can put it to direct use in egg production.

Spawning salmon end their lives in reproductive effort. Those individuals who expend all their reserves in a final act of reproduction maximize their reproductive success. It is common for a dying plant to use its last energy to bloom and fruit. Is there an analogous phenomenon in humans? Are "dirty old men" pursuing a similar strategy of terminal reproductive effort?

The ephemeroptera merit special examination because of their interesting approach to adult life. This order of insects includes the well-known mayflies. The aquatic nymphs in this order are chiefly herbivorous. The eggs are laid in the water after a mating flight; soon afterwards the adults die. During the entire adult life, which lasts only a few hours or a few days, no food is consumed -- the mouth parts are degenerate and incapable of feeding. This example is a striking one of reducing adult life to its essential and bare minimum: reproduction. The adult mayfly does nothing else. The essential function of all adult organisms is also reproduction, but in viewing more complex life histories, e.g., human life histories, it is easy to become confused with the details of the ancillary strategies of feeding, growing, and maintaining, which are not elements of the life of adult ephemeroptera. The purpose of an adult mayfly's life is unmistakable because it is so simplified, but that purpose is no less so in other organisms, including humans, simply because additional ancillary strategies support that purpose.

Suicide is the third most frequent cause of death among the young in America. From the viewpoint of the evolutionary ethic, among the worst crimes imaginable is to kill oneself (or to have oneself sterilized or to kill one's identical twin at the age of peak extended reproductive value). For reasons that are not entirely clear, of the thirty thousand Americans who kill themselves yearly, most of them *are* young adults near peak extended reproductive value. I speculate that this pattern is often due to some defect in ordinarily adaptive parent-offspring conflict over access to resources. The suggestion is based on the fact that scholarship students in college have a lower rate of suicide than do non-scholarship students. Could it be that non-scholarship students, more dependent upon parental investment, feel morbidly guilty at times at the fact that they continue to draw upon parental resources, whereas scholarship students, being more independent, do not? As important a source of lost fitness that suicide is in America, it cannot compare with the higher frequency of elective abortions as the most common evolutionarily unethical act in America today. Simply put, elective abortion is devastating to fitness. Granted, it would be worse to kill one's eighteen-year-old child than to kill one's fetus, but it is not much worse considering the small difference in extended reproductive value of the two, due to the fact that an undisturbed fetus becomes a teenager with considerable reliability in the current environment.

Euthanasia may be justifiable under carefully controlled circumstances for those in the final stages of a terminal disease and who are unable to reproduce or to be of assistance to others with whom their inclusive fitness is linked. Invalidicide and senilicide, long reported by anthropologists in traditional societies, continue in the Third World. For example, people with severe congenital defects are rare in eastern Africa, because they are killed as infants. In America they tend to be physically abused, institutionalized, and abandoned by their parents[33]. Among the Eskimo, senilicide was often accompanied by cannibalism. "Having grandma for dinner, and we mean it" is a phrase with special substance in some cultures. Senilicide occurs in modern America, but it is concealed and gradual. The physical abuse, sometimes lethal, of the elderly in our society parallels the senilicide observed in some other cultures. The U.S. population is aging, and increasing numbers of the elderly are under the care of their relatives. Giving long-term care to the disabled can be frustrating, and sometimes this proximate mechanism of frustration leads to abuse. Most of the abuse of the elderly in America is by care-givers who are relatives.

A study of the opinions of physicians in the state of Washington indicated that the attitudes toward physician-assisted suicide and euthanasia are polarized, but that a small majority favor legalizing it[29]. Miller et al.[140] stated that voluntary, physician-assisted death serves the moral goals of self-determination by the patient and of relief of suffering. When the palliative and supportive treatment used in hospice programs, elsewhere known as comfort care, ceases to be effective for the termi-nally or incurably ill, euthanasia becomes permissible. They emphasized that euthanasia would be used ideally in relatively infrequent but troubling cases. It will come as no surprise to the reader that the evolutionary ethic does not condone euthanasia on the grounds of pain and suffering. Instead the criterion for euthanasia should be the maximizing of inclusive fitness.

Invalidicide in termites is like that in humans. It occurs between close relatives. The killing of an invalid termite by its sisters and brothers occurs, presumably, because an invalid is less efficient than the termite that will replace it, from the viewpoint of the killer's inclusive fitness. The logic of the argument in favor of invalidicide in termites is based on ergonomics and energetics. A termite that is an invalid costs the colony the same to maintain as a healthy termite, with the invalid termite being less able to do useful work for the colony but consuming energy resources nevertheless. Thus, even though the invalid is likely to be a sister or brother sharing at least $\frac{1}{2}$ of its genes in common with the other termites in the colony, the invalid is, for practical purposes, easily replaceable with a healthy termite which is more useful and more efficient, and also related by $\frac{1}{2}$, from the nearly limitless supply of eggs carried by the queen. This replacement of the healthy termite for the invalid termite is no doubt facilitated by the cannibalism of the invalid that usually occurs. In this way, scarce nutrients like protein are recycled. In fact, Wilson[221] interpreted cannibalism in termites, which is far more intense than in other social insects, as a protein-conserving device.

Extended reproductive value may be something that the average person judges intuitively and unconsciously. Do we grieve equally for the death of a very old person, or of a premature infant, as we do for the death of a person in the prime of life? There are countless allegories in anthropology of the elderly in non-Western societies sacrificing their lives for the preservation of the lives of related children. Is the traditional view in Western law that all human lives are equal a valid view? The question is more than an academic exercise. Funds for medical research are limited. There has been much debate about which diseases should been given funding priorities. The answer is simple and sound when the concept of extended re-productive value is utilized in conjunction with the evolutionary ethic. That medical research which offers the greatest recovery of the sum total of extended reproductive value from the sum total of patients per unit cost (where cost is measured in reproductive success) is that which should receive funding priority. Such a policy might involve saving a few people of very high extended reproductive value, or many of low extended reproductive value. This guideline is a useful one in determining whether a specific disease with specific effects on the reproduction of the afflicted, and affecting perhaps a specific age-class disproportionately, should be a main focus of research. This guideline solves a current problem in medicine, in which it is conceptually difficult to make judgments about the value of different people's lives. On a related subject, physicians sometimes face the choice of saving the life of the mother or of the baby. Consider these examples: The mother is fifty and has no other dependent children, or the mother is twenty and has three other dependent children. In the first example, the life of the child would be saved preferentially, because the child has a higher extended reproductive value than the mother. In the second example, the life of the mother would be saved preferentially, because the mother has a higher extended reproductive value. There is also the subject of the hypothetical choice to save the life of one's spouse or the life of one's child. This choice is obviously an unlikely one to be encountered, is unpleasant in the extreme, and would be made under duress. Yet, many Americans have given some consideration to just such a circumstance. Perhaps because it is a cruel choice negatively affecting fitness with either of the two options, the mind lingers on it. In an evolutionary analysis, once again extended reproductive value is a key consideration. The optimal choice of life for spouse or for child would depend on their relative extended reproductive value, the probability that you and your spouse will stay together to reproduce again and other aspects of the fitness linkage with your spouse. These variables would be weighed against the extended reproductive value of the child, devalued by the regression coefficient of relatedness.

Why do groups of people in the form of cults often have apocalyptic visions, some self-fulfilling? We know that when the end of life is near that it can provoke exceptional adaptive behavioral and morphological strategies, e.g., as among old male anubis baboons discussed above. Likewise, self-deception about an imminent end to life or an end to the entire world could imbue a special significance in the cult members and also impart a fervor in them regarding the perpetuation of the cult's creed. Such a cult, embracing an apocalyptic vision, may proselytize at higher rates and achieve higher rates of continued participation than cults that do not embrace such a vision.

Strategic behavior given the inevitability of death

There are, for humans, some practical implications for strategic behavior in anticipation of death. One of them concerns life insurance. Cost-benefit analysis is particularly applicable to choosing life insurance coverage. In all types of life insurance, one is establishing a financial safety net at a known cost to cover the occurrence of an unlikely and disastrous event: premature death. Life insurance should name dependent relatives as beneficiaries. Its only purpose should be to save one's relatives from a financial catastrophe that could turn into a fitness catastrophe, by ensuring that they have adequate financial resources, and no more. It should be designed to maximize one's reproductive success. The analysis of the optimal amount of insurance to buy becomes more complicated when the family income is less than or equal to the optimal income for maximizing reproductive success. Under such circumstances the cost of the insurance must be weighed against its benefits, in terms of reproductive success, to determine the optimal expenditure on insurance. To this end, "term life insurance" is a better buy than "whole-life" policies because it does not dilute the basic purpose: All the money is allocated for protection. Term life insurance also provides the maximum coverage that can be obtained per unit cost. That is important early in the life of a family when dependent children mean that there is a real need for good coverage and when, at the same time, the budget is usually tight. Life insurance is best considered as a tactic for reducing variance in reproductive success.

Another strategic behavior in anticipation of death is the preparation of a will. The correct purpose of a will is, in traditional language, the protection of one's bloodline. In modern terminology, one's will serves one best if it maximizes one's inclusive fitness. And there is evidence that conferring benefits on kin is, indeed, the conscious or unconscious intent of most people who prepare a will. For example, distribution of inheritance is nonrandom. There are strong kinship effects on the distribution of property. Nobody picks up a telephone directory to find inheritors at random. I say that conferring benefits on kin is the intent of most people who write a will, but is it the actual consequence? Perhaps it is not. The problem is that fertility depression by wealth may thwart strategies that bequeath considerable assets. The solution to this problem is to establish a trust fund to cover the costs of child raising of relatives. In this way, one's inclusive fitness is maximized because the will defers the costs encountered by one's relatives in raising additional offspring, thereby encouraging them to have additional children. The more common alternative of simply bequeathing considerable assets to relatives in a lump sum may have the reverse effect and lead to the birth of fewer related children. Explore estate planning with your attorney. Distribution of one's assets can be done through a will, gift giving, trusts, and joint ownership.

Trusts seem to offer the greatest promise of maximizing inclusive fitness. Since you have no personal use for your financial assets after you are dead, it behooves you to plan your estate with the maximization of your inclusive fitness in mind. Use the following guidelines. In the near future, I expect that all attorneys handling matters of estates will have a standard will for the maximization of one's inclusive fitness on file, and it will be adapted to the needs of individual clients.

In the meantime, you need to be well-informed yourself about genetic relationships within the family. The correct approach is to distribute inheritance by the regression coefficient of relatedness and by the reproductive benefit the inheritance confers. While this procedure may sound strange at first, I pointed out above that many people already write a will with the intention of providing for or protecting their family after their death. This new concept of a will designed to maximize its maker's inclusive fitness is an extension of that existing pattern of conferring benefits on relatives. It is simply more rigorous to do so according to your regression coefficients of relatedness to the recipients and the reproductive benefit they will enjoy as a function of the inheritance. Murdock[146] pointed out the surprising number of types of relatives that we have. There are thousands of categories of relatives theoretically distinguishable, but which are reduced in all cultures to a number around 25. Below are some of those most important in America in preparing a will for protection of your bloodline. Some regression coefficients of relatedness for various relatives are: child, parent, full sibling = $\frac{1}{2}$; half sibling, grandchild, grandparent, nephew, niece, uncle, aunt, double first cousin = $\frac{1}{4}$; first cousin, great-grandchild, great-grandparent = $\frac{1}{8}$; half first cousin, first cousin once removed = $\frac{1}{16}$; second cousin, great-great-great-grandchild = $\frac{1}{32}$.

Allot your estate by means of trust funds to the unborn children of relatives to increase rates of reproduction among relatives and avoid an inverse correlation between wealth and reproductive success. Consider not only genetic proximity to a relative but also the benefit conferred, e.g., the births of two nephews are worth more than one grandchild in terms of shared genes. If a more distant relative can utilize an inheritance to produce more offspring than a closer relative, then there is a threshold in terms of the regression coefficient of relatedness times the number of children to be born to the individual, where investment in the more distant relative makes evolutionary sense. Leaving an entire inheritance to a reprobate son who shows no intention of producing a family is the kind of error to which some people are already sensitive. Also, from a grandparent's point of view and from a grandchild's point of view, they are equally related to each other, but that does not suggest that inheritance should flow equally in both directions. Under most circumstances the grandparent would gain more by contributing to the reproductive ability of the grandchild than the grandchild would gain by contributing to the reproductive ability of the grandparent. This asymmetry in the relationship is a consequence of the usual stage of the life history in which grandparents and grandchildren find themselves. Grandparents are often near the end of their reproductive years and grandchildren are often near the beginning of their reproductive years. This fact leads to asymmetry in the costs and benefits of social behavior between them. Remember, your goal is to distribute your assets in a way that maximizes your inclusive fitness. It is often helpful to prepare a genealogy and use it as a guide in distributing inheritance, as well as a guide in distributing social acts during life. In this sense research into one's genealogy could have benefits, if it led to adaptive social behavior with one's relatives. Perhaps the natural curiosity we seem to have about our lineages evolved to serve just that purpose.

One problem in bequeathing one's estate is that it may go unwittingly to unrelated inheritors. The classic fear of the false inheritor is the stuff of legends. Until recent advances in genetics were made, it was not possible to distinguish a relative from an unrelated individual except by monitoring reproductive events themselves. Now the situation is very different. When in doubt about your genetic relation to a potential inheritor, utilize genetic profiling to assure that genetic relationship. How commonly is an unrelated individual mistaken for a related one? Some anecdotal evidence suggests that perhaps 10 percent of assumed fathers in America are not the genetical fathers[43]. This assessment was made by way of paternity exclusions using genetic markers from blood samples. While used today primarily as evidence in court in cases involving disputed paternity, there are no technical reasons why a man cannot institute such an investigation seeking assurances of paternity certainty for his own peace of mind. The current cost of paternity determination is about six hundred dollars. Knowledge that one did or did not engender a person assumed to be one's child can have important consequences. If you object to genetic testing but exist in an environment where paternity uncertainty is high, we need only borrow from the ethnographic literature and use the approach of non-Western cultures in a similar situation: The strategy is to bias inheritance toward one's consanguines of one's matriline instead of bequeathing to affines or to the patriline. There is an old tendency in Western society to deny illegitimate offspring an inheritance. That is a cultural trait neither supported by a genetic basis nor advisable in trying to maximize inclusive fitness. In other words, illegitimate children should not be disinherited simply because they are illegitimate. One's illegitimate child is just as closely related to one genetically as a legitimate child. Primogeniture, the custom of leaving the bulk of one's assets to one's first born son, is more common in Europe than in modern America. It is a way of preserving fine estates and keeping them intact over generations, not necessarily a way to maximize inclusive fitness. Such a custom should be replaced with an evolutionary approach as described herein.

Life-lesson: Use an inclusive fitness maximizing approach to estate planning.

One final point about bequeathing is on the subject of organ donation. Organ donation makes sense if you are donating an organ to a relative. But there is little incentive to offer to donate your organs to members of the population at random, with the possible exception of primary sex organs, i.e. testes or ovaries. This conclusion follows from the fact that a transplant of one's testes or ovaries will perpetuate one's genes, while one's heart or kidney will not do likewise. But, primary sex organs do not seem to be much in demand by transplant recipients. In spite of the demand for transsexual operations among people with gender identity problems, and the frequency in which primary sex organs are surgically removed in other people due to pathology, it does not appear that these people desire to receive transplants. Could it be that they are unconsciously aware of the fact that if they did so they would be reproducing for someone other than themselves? Another point about donating organs in general is that there may be some increased risk of receiving less than the best medical care if the medical bureaucracy anticipates a profitable use of your organs when you are pronounced "dead". It is highly disconcerting that it is standard medical practice to pronounce a person "dead" prematurely by evolutionary standards.

Brain death and persistent vegetative state, two medical conditions, have given rise to a medical and legal standard of accepting brain function as the criterion for death. In a previous section I mentioned the fact that the male praying mantis is often decapitated by the female during copulation, but he continues to function very well in maximizing his reproductive success. If Western concepts about brain death were really true, i.e. that it is the valid criterion for death, the various species of praying mantis either would not show that behavior pattern or would be extinct! I consider that to be a *reductio ad absurdum*. That observation leads us to the obvious consideration that humans with severe impairment of the central nervous system might also be capable of maximizing their reproductive success. And that brings us to question the concept of "brain death" as a criterion for actual death. While it may seem preposterous to consider an infertile person to be dead, it is equally preposterous to consider a fertile but neurologically impaired person to be dead. Full protection of the reproductive rights of the severely disabled is likely to require revisions in the present legal codes. This example is just one demonstration of how evolutionary arguments give new meaning to what is rational and irrational. What is the meaning of declaring a pregnant woman who could go on to have a child legally dead by virtue of brain death? If one ignores reproductive potential and refers to the absence of certain brain waves as death, what term is then appropriate to the later state of ceased circulation, halted respiration, termination of metabolism, and the abatement of reproductive capacity? In relying on the output of an electroencephalogram to determine the state of death, physicians are making one of the classic errors in science: failing to assure both reliability and validity in their work. Reliability is the extent to which an experiment can be repeated with the same result. Validity is the extent to which one is measuring what one thinks one is measuring. Electroencephalograms are reasonably reliable. A finding of the absence of certain brain waves today will likely be repeated by a similar test tomorrow. But the flaw is that an absence of certain brain waves is *not a valid* measure of the state of death when viewed in an evolutionary perspective. Therefore, the reliability of electroencephalograms is irrelevant. Technology can be dazzling, but even if reliable, it is not an acceptable substitute for clear thinking on this matter. A similar problem arises with the legal decisions to terminate the lives of people in persistent vegetative states. Often their brains are active, at least in the brain stem; their eyes are often open; they go through sleep-wake cycles, and they move. Contrary to the common legal practice at present, there are good reasons not to terminate the lives of these people as long as spermatogenesis or oogenisis, i.e. the production of gametes, is occurring within them. All that is required for the lives of these victims to take on renewed purpose is that someone comes along who wishes to have a baby with them!

Death is often accompanied by a rite of passage in humans. The social significance of a funeral goes beyond organized mourning and the paying of homage to the deceased. It can also serve to reunite an extended family that may have lost a genetic ''link''. While many cultures provide for elaborate funeral rituals, no ritual at all may serve the purpose under some circumstances. The custom among the Masai tribe of eastern Africa is that a baby is not recognized as a person until it reaches one year of age, at which time it has its head shaved and is given a name. This delay in cultural recognition of a baby as a person is an obvious social mechanism to minimize the emotional loss in a population with high infant mortality. In the event of the death of the infant in its first year, a common occurrence, life of the parents quickly returns to normal. The dead, unnamed infant is not buried; it is left under a bush for the scavengers. The avoidance of undue grieving over a tragic but commonplace event may make adaptive sense if it allows additional resources to be allocated to the parents' reproductive effort.

To conclude this section on death, let us examine a question that is sometimes asked: How can there be any meaning of a human life if it ends inevitably in death? This question has long perplexed some philosophers and laypersons alike. Not only are we as individuals mortal, but the entire human species will eventually perish. The question about our individual lives ending in death is easily addressed from the evolutionary perspective: The occasion of mortality is not a negation of meaning, rather it is ''planned'' as a life history strategy to maximize reproductive success. The meaning of our lives, i.e. maximizing reproductive success, is not dependent on eternal life. If we succeed in maximizing our reproductive success, we leave a living legacy in the form of a genetic heritage in descendants and in relatives whom we helped to reproduce. The point regarding the fact that the entire human species will perish eventually is a more difficult philosophical question. I can only suggest that when human life ceases to exist that there is not, indeed, any meaning of human life any longer. A universe, some time in the distant future devoid not only of human life but also devoid of the meaning of human life, is not a pleasing prospect. But there is no law of nature that says the truth has to be pleasing.

Economic considerations

The interaction between economics and maintenance is fairly straightforward. Higher economic status is associated with longer lifespan. Graham et al.[78] suggested that a higher income leads to lower long-term individual risk. This trend has implications for public policy concerning debt. Keeney[111] suggested for illustrative purposes that 7.25 million dollars of debt born collectively by a group of people may induce one death because those people are consequently less wealthy and are therefore unable to make life-sustaining choices. The choices that cannot be made by this less wealthy group include better health care services, eating more healthful foods, living in safer communities, and others[112]. It is not entirely clear if this relationship between debt and death also applies to the 4.9 trillion dollar national debt. If so, it explains approximately 680 thousand deaths. Richer, in simple terms, is safer. But we shall learn in a following section that compensatory mechanisms exist that provide a surprising conclusion regarding the overall adaptive significance of wealth.

Health issues in maintenance

Medical care

It is perhaps appropriate to consider medical care as a new ''limiting resource'' in the life history equations of modern humans. First, it has considerable direct impact on our survival and reproduction. Second, it influences other variables which in turn affect survival and reproduction, e.g., economics. One dollar in seven in the U.S. economy is spent on health care. In keeping with the antigenitivism prevalent in our culture, Americans debate the increasing costs of modern medicine rather than the fitness increasing potential of modern medicine. For example, there is much talk about medical costs being inflationary. I consider the truth about the matter to be rather unremarkable and feel that it is unworthy of extensive consideration. For while it is correct that health costs are rising yearly, some of that increase is not inflation *per se* but is rather the price of new technology and improved methods. Benefits are thus going up as well as costs through these improvements in medical science. Some politicians, ever eager to inspire and lead a populist movement, have sadly misled Americans on the topic of health care reform.

Fortunately, the only commodity really wasted in that effort was the time of the politicians, and that is perhaps desirable in that it prevented them from doing real harm elsewhere. A progenitivist politician would instead emphasize issues like the importance of good nutrition and medical care during pregnancy and birth. For example, the birth weight of an infant is positively correlated with survival, and the birth weight is positively correlated with the pre-pregnancy weight of the mother and with her weight gain during pregnancy[50]. The practical conclusions based on these data are that prenatal care along with proper nutrition for the mother before and during pregnancy are useful in increasing women's reproductive success.

Preventive medicine

Much of the increase in the lifespan of the average American has been gained in past decades by a reduction in mortality early in the life history from communicable disease by means of improved sanitation. Future increases in lifespan will be in relatively smaller increments gained from a reduction in mortality late in the life history. Long-term prevention will be the key. I shall mention a few related subjects in this section. To begin, the use of aspirin as a prophylactic drug has long been overlooked. It reduces the risk of heart disease and colon cancer. But it does increase risk of hemorrhagic strokes and of duodenal and gastric ulcers. Consult with your physician about whether aspirin as a prophylactic is right for you. Mammograms for women make sense as a diagnostic tool that may uncover disease which, if found and treated early, has a high cure rate. We know now that the risk of breast cancer is associated with diet, genetics, and behavior during early reproductive years. In contrast to the belief of great health risks of pregnancy at a young age, a younger age at first lactation is significantly associated with a reduction in the risk of premenopausal breast cancer[153]. A regular physical examination also makes sense. Immunizations are largely used for infants and people who intend to travel abroad. Their role in infant health can hardly be overemphasized. Yet, I find the public health messages about immunizations often misleading. For example, it is said that Houston, Texas, has a lower rate of infant immunizations than some countries in the Third World. This fact is used as part of a plea to motivate parents into compliance with standard immunization schedules for their infants. What is not pointed out is that America benefits from what epidemiologists call "herd immunity". That means there are so many immunized people in America that by their high percentage, along with good conditions for health and sanitation, they prevent the outbreak of epidemics and protect the whole "herd," including those who are not immunized. So while immunization is crucial to the survival of an Ethiopian infant, it is less important to an American infant. Because of the risk of side effects from immunization, the ideal situation would be if everyone in the world were immunized except for you and your close relatives.

Another point on preventive medicine is the use of sunscreen among light skinned Americans. There are thirty-two thousand cases of the most dangerous form of skin cancer, malignant melanoma, diagnosed yearly in America. Most of those cases are associated with excessive exposure of the skin to the sun. Sunscreen, if used properly, can reduce the skin damage done by ultraviolet radiation and reduce the risk of skin cancer. Some dermatologists, who are well aware of the damaging effects of sun on skin, apply sunscreen to themselves even on days when they do not expect to spend much time outdoors. Tanned skin was once a sign of working class or peasant status; pale, untanned skin was then desired as a sign of higher social status. Later a tan was associated with the outdoor leisure activities that connoted wealth, and a tan was then seen as desirable. Now a tan is rightly considered to be a sign of ultraviolet radiation damage to the skin, and it is for health reasons not considered desirable, even though there is still an association with the leisure class, winter vacations to the tropics, and so forth.

One form of preventive medicine that is greatly underutilized in America is donating blood. The concept is that one donates blood in order to establish a supply of one's own blood, especially before surgery but also in case of unexpected trauma, in what is called a preoperative autologous blood donation. The Prince of Wales has a supply of his own blood carried with him wherever he travels around the world. Although he is healthy, the concept is that his own blood is safest in the event of emergency surgery. This practice has given rise to indignation among the foreign people that he visits. During a visit to Kenya, some of the local people were insulted -- they felt that this precaution meant that Kenyan blood was too low for the veins of members of the royal family of the United Kingdom. (It is not a coincidence that the United Kingdom is the colonial power with former rule over Kenya -- animosity lingers.) Specialists in this field of transfusion medicine report that preoperative autologous blood donations are not cost effective. However, it is certain that they can save lives at a price as low as $235,000 per year of life saved[56]. Another point about donating blood regularly in America is that it might be a means of losing some weight for people who wish to do so. This topic is one that merits further study.

For a healthful diet, follow the recommendations in the chapter on feeding. In this section I shall focus on the complex role of alcohol consumption. In the U.S. alcohol is a factor in approximately 50 percent of motor vehicle deaths. Alcohol causes more than 19,000 auto fatalities each year. About two-thirds of those who die in these auto fatalities are victims of their own drinking. The explanation is straightforward. A single drink, the equivalent of $1/2$ ounce of pure ethanol, improves motor skills. Additional drinks reduce driving performance. The following is a list of brain responses to different alcohol blood levels (adapted from Hamilton et al.[82]): euphoria, relaxation, impaired judgment -- 0.05; impaired emotional control -- 0.10; impaired muscle coordination and reflexes -- 0.15; impaired vision -- 0.20; drunk and totally out of control -- 0.30; stupor -- 0.35; total loss of consciousness and finally death -- 0.50-0.60.

The adverse effects of maternal consumption of alcohol on the developing fetus are well documented. Alcohol consumption should be avoided by pregnant women. Alcoholism is associated with premature death due to various diseases. Long-term consumption of large amounts of alcohol can cause cirrhosis of the liver, pancreatitis, gastritis, hypertension, cardiomyopathy, dysrhythmia, hemorrhagic stroke, degenerative nervous system conditions, and/or cancers of the mouth, pharynx, larynx, esophagus, and liver[64]. Moderate alcohol consumption may result in lower rates of cardiovascular disease. Gaziano et al.[72] showed an inverse association of moderate alcohol consumption with the risk of myocardial infarction, and supported the view that the effect is mediated by increases in high-density lipoprotein cholesterol. Friedman and Klatsky[64] suggested that the health benefits or costs of moderate alcohol intake may be a function of other variables in the consumer's life history. For example, a 50-year-old man who is a moderate drinker would gain more benefits from the reduced risk of heart disease than costs from the increased risk of large-bowel cancer. In contrast, a 30-year-old woman would lose more due to increased risk of cancer than gain from reduced risk of heart disease. Friedman and Klatsky[64] concluded the following:

> Currently, indiscriminate advice to nondrinkers to take up alcohol for health reasons is inappropriate, but some people (e.g., those at high risk for coronary heart disease but low risk for problem drinking) may benefit. (p. 1883)

Recent evidence from Fuchs et al.[67] did indeed support the belief that light to moderate drinking reduces mortality among women older than 50 years and among women at greater risk than the average for coronary heart disease.

Anthropologists have a perspective about moderate alcohol consumption that classifies it as normal behavior[93]. Although alcohol consumption occurs in most cultures, most cultures do not have what Americans would describe as drinking problems or alcoholism. This cross-cultural perspective makes anthropologists unique. Many other disciplines suggest alcohol consumption is a deviant behavior. But given the cross-cultural presence of alcohol consumption and the possible health benefits mentioned above, prohibition seems both out of touch with the worldwide use of alcohol in the anthropological context and perhaps unwarranted on grounds of medical science.

Protecting your fertility is one of the most important aspects of maintenance. One key step is the avoidance of sexually transmitted diseases. Of course, it is important that this avoidance of sexually transmitted diseases does not lead to a large reduction in fertility. One is not selected to minimize sexually transmitted disease but to maximize reproductive success, and the two operations are not identical. A basic rule is that it makes sense to know the medical history and sexual history of one's sexual partners. The probability that any given act of sexual intercourse will lead to a pregnancy is small but cannot be dismissed in pursuit of absolutely safe sex. This topic is discussed in the section on contraception, where behavioral strategies to stay healthy *and* be fertile are discussed. For example, it is suggested that under rare circumstances a woman could employ a condom in order to conceive and to simultaneously protect the health of her sexual partner. Another basic is to get tested for sexually transmitted diseases when one has had sexual intercourse with a person for whom one does not have adequate health information. One of the best ways for a woman to protect her fertility is to be on the lookout for pelvic inflammatory disease, including vaginal discharge and pelvic pain, and to seek early treatment. Also, the best way to protect one's fertility against endometriosis and fibroid tumors is early diagnosis and treatment.

Adults who have not had the mumps should discuss a vaccination with their doctor. Adult-onset mumps can lead to permanent sterility in men. Men who participate in vigorous sports should wear genital protection including cups and athletic supporters. A man who is trying to impregnate his partner should avoid exposing his genitals to the abnormally high temperatures sometimes encountered in hot tubs, spas, saunas, and steam baths. Many pharmaceutical agents can affect libido and sexual function. For example, oral contraceptives, tranquilizers, sedatives, and ulcer drugs can reduce libido. Blood-pressure medications can cause impotence. The Food and Drug Administration should more closely scrutinize prescription and over-the-counter medications for sex-impairing effects, and require appropriate warning labels. Men who smoke have a 50 percent higher rate of impotence than men who do not smoke. Smoking is the most important lifestyle factor in causing spontaneous abortions. Spontaneous abortion may be 20 percent higher in women who smoke. Rubella (German measles) is an example of how maternal disease can have profound effects on the fetus. In the last major epidemic in America (1963-1965), about fifty thousand fetuses were affected. Most of them died and the remainder were born with serious birth defects. As a general practice, women should be vaccinated for rubella prior to pregnancy. It should neither be given to pregnant women nor to women within sixty days of conception. Other maternal diseases with highly adverse effects on the fetus are hepatitis B and syphilis. Lead is the best documented source of danger to fetal development in the workplace and in the home. See Blank[10] for a discussion of issues concerning fetal protection. The connection between regular computer use and infertility is certain, but only a small part, if any, can be attributed to histological effects on the reproductive organs and on the fetus. Rather, regular computer use places the user into the middle class or upper class, two groups with depressed fertility. Avoiding computers, then, would have a meaningful impact on increasing fertility only if accompanied by other extensive lifestyle changes. The people of some cultures are very concerned about protecting their fertility. Kenyan women have the highest documented total fertility rate of any country in the world. Aware that their high fertility is of concern to population control minded Americans, Kenyans are suspicious of the yellow maize meal sent by the U.S.A. as food aid -- they think it might surreptitiously contain contraceptive drugs. To the Kenyans, this conjecture explains why the maize is not white like their own maize meal and why the Americans bother to send it at all. While Kenyan women worry about yellow maize meal, Kenyan men worry that their fertility might be damaged by witchcraft employed by their wives for the purpose of reducing their extramarital liaisons.

Firearm ownership and maintenance is an issue worthy of brief note. A firearm in the average American home is 43 times more likely to kill a family member than an intruder. These odds are grim. Self-infliction of gunshot wounds, rather than self-defense, is the chief use to which families put their firearms. Firearms make a great deal of sense if one is living a frontier existence and if they are used to procure a substantial portion of one's food through hunting. Only a small minority of Americans, perhaps mostly living in Alaska, fit this description. Keeping firearms for sport or self-defense does not make sense. If you feel that you need a firearm because you are bored or frightened, change your lifestyle instead of getting a gun. This argument is not the same as saying that there are too many firearms in America. Compared with countries like Switzerland that have virtually no firearm related crime, and where every adult male keeps an assault rifle under his bed as part of a national military preparedness program, America has too *few* firearms to prevent their abuse. Given the fact that the right to bear arms is guaranteed by the Second Amendment of the Constitution of the United States, it is unlikely that there will be no firearms in America. That being the case, it does not seem that there could ever be too many, since a hundred million of them appear to be more dangerous than if they were *really* numerous. But be rational in your assessment of risk and reproductive success -- let others bear the cost of bearing arms.

Heroic medical intervention for the elderly can be a mixture of costs and benefits. Such intervention is a mixed blessing if heavy costs are incurred on relatives. However, it is not clear how often that is the case. Prolonged home care after the medical intervention may be a greater cost to the relatives than the intervention itself. While financial considerations may also enter into the analysis, they do anything but clarify it. First of all, someone else often pays the medical bills. Even if that is not the case, we have an inverse relationship between wealth and reproductive success in America that will be discussed in detail in another chapter. Although the last few months of life incur disproportionately high health care costs, studies on how to humanely reduce these costs have turned up surprisingly few solutions[55]. It may be that we do not need ways to reduce these financial costs from an evolutionary perspective.

Hereditary disease relates to maintenance. While one cannot choose one's own genes, one can be selective about half the genes that one's children receive. One approach is to be discretely selective in mate choice. There is no doubt that a meaningful proportion of the behavior and morphology demonstrated by humans and other animals during courtship is a process of display and assessment of the pair's genetically predisposed traits with fitness implications. Picking good genes in a mate may have important effects on one's reproductive success, depending upon the type of mating system and the genetic variability in the population. Among humans, there are diseases that limit reproductive success of a mate or of potential offspring. There are modern solutions to some of these problems, and recommendations vary for different human populations. Difficulties and misunderstandings can be minimized by pointing out that screening should be entirely voluntary. Here are some suggestions. Consider screening for Tay-Sachs disease among Ashkenazi (eastern European) Jews, thalassemia among Mediterranean and southeastern Asian populations, sickle-cell disease among African Americans, and cystic fibrosis in families with histories of the disease. Tay-Sachs disease is a fatal condition resulting from the lack of an enzyme that breaks down fatty substances in the neurons; thalassemia is a genetic blood disorder; sickle-cell disease involves deformed red cells and is caused by a gene that makes an abnormal form of hemoglobin; cystic fibrosis is a condition involving thick secretions in the respiratory tract[171].

In vitro fertilization and selection of a healthy zygote by genetic testing will become increasingly available for couples with hereditary diseases. There are over five hundred genetic diseases that are currently known. Amniocentesis is advisable for older mothers to reduce the chance of having a baby with Down's syndrome, and for anyone who might be passing on genes for fragile X syndrome, Huntington's disease, cystic fibrosis, or other conditions. The Human Genome Project will provide considerable enhancement of opportunities for the genetic screening of the unborn. It will not be without controversy. Some genetic diseases with variation in penetrance and expressivity will be borderline cases. Does one terminate a pregnancy if the fetus carries genes that might lead to obesity or to cancer late in life? The cost of genetic testing is perhaps as little as one percent of the cost of raising a child, so the break-even point is well within the range that many people can afford. And because the cost of raising a handicapped child is usually greater than the cost of raising a healthy child, the threshold for genetic testing is lowered further. Of course, we must also consider that the benefit in reproductive success may be higher if one produces a healthy child rather than a child with certain handicaps. In conclusion, genetic testing makes a great deal of sense for high risk pregnancies.

Among the stranger and more interesting proposals I have read is the one by Pirsig[160], who suggested that the insane be sent to anthropologists instead of to psychiatrists for a cure. There has long been overlap between anthropology and psychiatry. Mead[e.g., 137] was enthusiastic in her application of psychoanalytical models in her studies and writings on anthropology. And in recent years there have been attempts to reinterpret psychiatry through sociobiological analysis. Anthropologists might be particularly appropriate people to treat the causes of mental illness. Sadly, treating the symptoms of mental illness instead of the causes (unhealthful environment and genetic propensities) is a cheaper short-term remedy, and will likely remain in the firm control of psychiatrists for some time.

Darwinian medicine is more than a century overdue but its time may have come. It promises to offer a powerful synthesis of evolutionary biology with modern medical science. Williams and Nesse[220] argued that the theory of evolution by natural selection has recently gained new power in explaining many aspects of human disease. In particular, it brings new understanding to infection, injuries and toxins, genetic factors, and abnormal environments. After offering some vivid examples in support of their argument, they suggested that the study of evolutionary biology be made a formal part of medical curricula. In their publication they discussed a range of topics such as a host-parasite arms race, the adaptive significance of fever, diseases caused by modern environments, and diseases of senescence. One example of the relevance of Darwinian medicine to our everyday health is the new understanding of the adaptive significance of fever. Once thought to be something that required a cure, fever is now believed to be an adaptive response which helps rid the body of pathogens. By reducing a fever with antipyretics (drugs that reduce high body temperatures, e.g., aspirin), one may actually be prolonging the time required to recover from the infectious disease. There is a related point not covered by Williams and Nesse[220]: Should physicians reassess their purpose? Should they be attempting to maximize their patients' reproductive success rather than maximize their longevity or whatever it is that physicians are maximizing?

An advantage of Darwinian medicine is that it offers possible explanations for the origins and original adaptive significance of conditions that we now think of strictly as pathology. Seasonal affective disorder is an example. The people subject to this disorder of seasonal depression, particularly in winter at high latitudes, could be displaying behavior that was formerly adaptive. People with this disorder sleep a great deal in the winter and put on weight through excessive consumption of carbohydrates. The cause of seasonal affective disorder is not yet known, but it may be linked to mechanisms to control temperature and hormone production. Light therapy usually makes the symptoms subside within a few days. The result of this disorder is reduced mobility and reduced energy expenditure at a time when food resources would have been scarce historically. It would have been most adaptive among people inhabiting high latitudes, where immobility during winters may have conserved energy and increased the survival rate. Adaptive benefits associated with some symptoms of the disorder, such as irritability and crying, are not clear. But consistent with the hypothesis, this disorder is most frequent among people of northern ancestry.

There are a few other unrelated, interesting points that I would like to mention on the subject of maintenance. Educational enrichment provides a safety net against the ravages of senile dementia and Alzheimer's disease. Intellectual pursuits can be considered a maintenance strategy for the brain. For example, university professors may have lower rates of senility than the general population. Premenopausal women who have lactated have a reduced risk of breast cancer[153]. There is an inverse correlation between frequency of sexual intercourse and the occurrence of prostate cancer. It is interesting that the preventive behavior for this disease is precisely the behavior for which the prolonged capability is enhanced when the disease is prevented. About four hundred thousand deaths a year in the United States can be attributed to smoking. There are 45 million American cigarette addicts. In terms of maintenance, not smoking is among the most important variables in promoting the proper functioning of one's organs. But because of the strong correlation among teenagers between smoking and having sexual intercourse, that is the one age group where smoking may provide a reproductive benefit. Sometimes behavioral phenotypes occur in clusters. For example, most teenage smokers drink alcohol and have sexual intercourse, while far fewer teenage nonsmokers drink alcohol and have sexual intercourse. The correlation of smoking and drinking with sexual intercourse greatly increases the adaptive advantages of those two behaviors among teenagers.

Life-lesson: Avoid smoking tobacco, unless you are a teenager who would otherwise not be having sexual intercourse.

Illicit drug abuse is a common social issue in America and has been since the sixties. The panacea of our time touted by a subculture for American youth is ''sex, drugs, and rock-'n'-roll''. There is no doubt that many teenagers do want these things. What is there to this slogan in evolutionary perspective? First, teenage sex, i.e. sexual intercourse: It is natural, they cannot get enough of it, and it leads to higher reproductive success. It should be commended. Drugs, i.e. illicit drugs, can be a serious health risk and therefore should be avoided, with the exception of circumstances where usage leads to an adaptive pregnancy that would have not otherwise occurred, e.g., through intoxication leading to sexual intercourse that would not have occurred or by deflecting contraception that would have occurred. A similar relationship may hold for the use of illicit drugs and having sexual intercourse among teenagers as holds for the relationship of smoking among teenagers and having sexual intercourse described above. Of course, it is necessary that the health effects and other effects, e.g., legal and financial, not be so high that they negate, through a loss in reproductive success, the gain in reproductive success from the pregnancy. Rock-'n'-roll is inexplicably fascinating. It may or may not be a culturgen that competes with reproduction. Love of music may be a side effect of unconscious language acquisition processes. We are most compelled to listen repeatedly to a song when it is still relatively novel. Once we know it well, the impulse to listen to it declines. What better way is there to learn sounds with possible communication content? At another level, music has all the signs of being a self-promoting culturgen. A survey of world music suggests that the only required attribute for the perpetuation of a work of music is that it attract listeners, i.e. have appeal. In very real ways music competes with other music; consider the music industry and the role of music in mass media for examples of competition. It also competes for time and space allocation in our brains. It is grounds for speculation whether music takes more time and space in our brains than what we would prefer to allot it based on the principle of maximizing reproductive success. Is any style of music superior? Yes, that which is correlated with high fertility; in America that would be the style of music preferred by youth.

Personal hygiene is often assumed to be linked to personal health. But the truth is that it is the health of someone else you are protecting through personal hygiene, not for the most part your own. For this reason, we can classify most personal hygiene behaviors as altruistic. Personal hygiene is taught to Americans with an emphasis on personal health, when it would be more correct to emphasize the community health aspects. When you wash your hands after using the toilet, you cannot be protecting yourself, or even your close family, from disease. Rather you are protecting other members of your community. Could this personal health message associated with personal hygiene be a deliberate piece of misinformation that is designed to help perpetuate what is an altruistic behavior by representing it as a matter of personal health? Along with this line of thinking comes the recognition that much hygienic behavior is based on fashion rather than health fact. Bathing, which is something that most Americans do many times a week, does not seem to have a sound purpose relating to health. Americans may be making themselves less soiled and less odorous by bathing regularly but are probably not assisting in the maintenance of their body in a meaningful way, unless they have a high rate of exposure to ectoparasites like fleas and ticks which may be discovered and removed during the act of bathing. The one part of your body that does benefit from regular washing is the teeth. The need to brush teeth is a product of our neolithic diet, which is high in carbohydrates. Nonhuman primates like baboons in the wild have excellent teeth, without dental caries or gum disease and, of course, they never brush them. Finally, they wear down to the gums in old age due to abrasives in the food.

There are a few aspects of shelter that relate to maintenance. With the trend toward residences with little outside ventilation, residential radon exposure has become a concern. Pershagen et al.[158] showed that residential exposure to radon is an important cause of lung cancer in the general population. The risk may be greater for inhabitants of well insulated, northern homes. Because of the multiplicative effect of radon and smoking in causing lung cancer, Reimer[170] offered a simple algorithm for the practical application of the findings of Pershagen et al.[158]: Stop smoking, and if you do not stop, then conduct a long-term test for radon in your residence.

In recent years it has become common in America for parents to share their bedroom and bed with their babies. In many cultures, children share a bed with their mother. Much less commonly, they do so with their mother and father. With this cross-cultural reference in mind, it would seem perfectly acceptable for mothers in America to share a bed with their babies. But this conclusion ignores one important factor. Parents in Third World cultures are often accustomed to having sexual intercourse while their children sleep in the same small room or small hut. In contrast, Americans are strongly inhibited about expressing sexuality in the proximity of their children. So, although sharing a bed with baby may promote closeness between parent and child, it may also reduce the parent's reproductive success by reducing the frequency of sexual intercourse. It is clear that one could commonly lose more reproductive success than one gains in this tradeoff.

A final note on maintenance concerns our intuitive perceptions of risk, and the biases in risk perception that it involves. While accurate risk perception is a trait that one would expect to be under selection, it seems that once again the environment has changed much faster than natural selection for genes can track. Slovic et al.[194] reported strong judgmental biases in the layperson's assessment of the frequency of lethal events. Lethal events whose frequencies are most poorly judged include overestimated items that are dramatic and sensational, such as accidents, pregnancy and childbirth, tornadoes, flood, fire, venomous bites or stings, and homicide. Underestimated risks involve those that are unspectacular and include diabetes, stomach cancer, stroke, tuberculosis, asthma, and emphysema. They also found that there was a strong similarity between the amount of newspaper coverage given to a particular cause of death and the observed judgmental biases. For example, disease takes about a hundred times as many lives as does homicide, but there are three times as many articles published in newspapers about homicide as about disease[194]. While crime is not rare enough in America, homicide is only the tenth most frequent cause of death and it is getting rarer each year; as the age distribution of the U.S. population shifts toward higher age classes, most types of serious crimes are on the decrease. Reijnders[169] argued that humans appear to be poor intuitive statisticians when it comes to judging matters of life and death. If so, this condition is a consequence of recent environmental change in the risks that humans encounter. An example of that change is in the modes of transportation used by humans, which have undergone a revolution in the last century, and humans do a poor job of assessing their relative risks. The chance of being killed on any commercial airline flight in America is approximately one in a million. But the chance of being killed on a transcontinental automobile trip is one in eight thousand, 125 times greater than the risk by airline[135]. Humans have not yet evolved the ability to discriminate between these new forms of transportation. And the general impression that most people have, i.e. that flying is more dangerous than driving, is wrong. The correct conclusion is that when you have to travel, fly by commercial airline.

Chapter 6: Reproduction

We have already defined the meaning of life as the maximization of one's reproductive success. But what is the meaning of reproduction itself? Its meaning is to perpetuate genes from one generation to succeeding generations. And this task has been selected to be accomplished with remarkable efficiency and high accuracy in the replication process. Reproduction is not only our future, it is our past. The sole enduring legacy of our distant ancestors is that they reproduced and contributed their genes to subsequent generations. Can you specify anything that you inherited other than your genes from the generation of progenitors as recent as your eight great-grandparents? Can you even name your eight great-grandparents? Yet you share a full $1/_8$ of your genes in common with each of them. And what do you intend to give to your great-grandchildren? The only thing you can be sure about is that you will give them $1/_8$ of your genes.

Genes, discovered by Mendel[138], are remarkable self-replicating entities. Long known to be units of heredity serving the organism, a new interpretation of their role has emerged in recent decades. Dawkins[40] argued that living organisms exist for the benefit of the DNA in their genes rather than the other way around. In this view, an organism is a gene's way of making another gene, in the kind of reversed sense that Butler[19] remarked:

... a hen is only an egg's way of making another egg. (p. 109)

There is much to be said in favor of this view of life. See Dawkins[40] for a very readable explanation of evolution from that perspective.

But regardless of whether our genes are serving us, or we are serving our genes (the two operations need not be mutually exclusive), we should be in the business of reproducing our genes. This viewpoint gives rise to an honest question. Should we reproduce all our genes, even deleterious alleles in our genotypes? First, we need to be sure what the fitness outcome of the allele in question is. Some genes assumed to be deleterious, like the ones that produce sickle-cell anemia and colorblindness, actually provide benefits to the carrier in some environments. People with the sickle cell trait (they are heterozygotic for the gene) are resistant to malaria, and that is the reason the gene has evolved to high frequencies in Africa and surrounding areas, even though people with sickle cell disease (they are homozygotic for the gene) have a debilitating and eventually lethal condition. Colorblindness, though of no obvious benefit, is a trait that is increasing in modern human populations. It is reasonable to speculate that the gene for colorblindness has unknown beneficial, pleiotropic effects, i.e. other effects on the survival or reproduction of the carrier that are unrecognized at present. Another possibility is that the gene for colorblindness causes meiotic drive (also known as segregation distortion). In other words, the gene creates a condition for its own spread by increasing the frequency that it appears in gametes above the random frequency normally associated with meiosis. If it were such a rogue gene, serving its own evolutionary interest while decreasing its carrier's reproductive success, it would be reasonable to take a firm stand against perpetuating it. Our technology is at the beginning of an ability to determine the genetic make-up of zygotes and to implant those of desirable qualities selectively. Another example of a condition with two related physical manifestations is the level of serum testosterone in women. High levels of serum testosterone in women probably lead to high rates of sexual intercourse for those women, due to increased libido. That condition is probably adaptive in the context of the depressed rates of coitus among Americans today. At the same time, high levels of serum testosterone in women may lead to increased hairiness. The benefits of increased hairiness for reproductive success are questionable. Will the Earth be inherited by hairy, horny women?

Should we reproduce deleterious alleles in our genotype? Yes, if it increases one's reproductive success measured in grandchildren. But since the very word deleterious can imply reduced reproductive success, we must confront the possibility that certain genes are best not transmitted to our offspring. Since meiosis usually provides a random assortment of alleles in our gametes, such deliberate discrimination against an unwanted gene was not formerly a possibility. But now, through the genetic screening of zygotes, it is possible to select the genotype of one's offspring. Further advances in this area are no doubt forthcoming. Genes that have high penetrance and that are invariably lethal when expressed are of the type that we would want to remove by artificial selection.

Sexual and asexual reproduction

When considering types of reproduction, one may ask: Why bother with sexual reproduction? For it is apparent that one disadvantage of sexual reproduction is that it produces offspring which are related to a parent by as little as $1/2$ of their genes in common, while asexual reproduction produces offspring which are genetically identical to the parent. By forgoing sex and reproducing by cloning, a race of females might be able to double the number of genes that they contribute to succeeding generations. Indeed, asexual reproduction does happen consistently among lower organisms and occasionally among higher organisms including vertebrates such as some lizards, even though the rule is sexual reproduction among higher organisms. Why is asexual reproduction not more common among higher organisms? The traditional answer is that it provides only a short-term advantage. Sexual reproduction, while having the disadvantage of decreasing relatedness to offspring, also has the advantage of increasing variability in offspring which in turn is suited to providing adaptations to environmental change over the long-term. Mutations are the ultimate source of all genetic variability, and they are also a source of unrelated genes between parents and offspring. Most importantly, and commonly not recognized, is that the variability offered by sexual reproduction is not the low quality available from raw mutations, but rather variability that has been tried, tested, and filtered by the generations that gave rise to one's mate. Since some variability is required for long-term evolutionary success and since mutations cannot be eliminated entirely anyway, sexual reproduction can be viewed as trading relatedness to one's offspring for good variability among the unrelated genes. This pattern accounts for some of the negative effects of inbreeding, because inbreeding reduces the number of generations over which new mutations are filtered before they are expressed in one's own offspring. At the same time, sexual reproduction is a way of introducing needed variability to one's offspring while keeping the mutation rate to a minimum.

Sexual reproduction at the level of the individual

Reproductive effort can be divided into two categories: mating effort and parental effort. Males and females may be selected to pursue different strategies. Females among the primates tend to be biased in using reproductive effort as parental effort. Males among the primates tend to be biased in using reproductive effort as mating effort, with some parental effort in those species where mechanisms exist for males to invest in their offspring. In this section we shall consider reproduction as it relates to individuals. Later we shall examine it as it relates to the kinship group, the population, the species, and to interspecific questions.

Individual reproduction

Reproduction in humans occurs at age-specific rates and its onset begins with sexual maturity, which occurs at an age strategically selected in the life history. Genes that cause humans to reproduce when too young and too small will not propagate themselves as efficiently as genes tending to produce an optimal time of sexual maturation. Likewise, genes that cause humans to start reproduction too late will be partially eliminated from the gene pool by mortality of the carriers. It is true that as nutrition improves, the age of sexual maturity for boys and girls declines. Recently improved diets in Western societies have led to just such a decline over the last few generations. This fact gives rise to an old view that is still widely held. It was expressed by Short[190] in the following quotation:

> One might imagine that in times past, sexual maturity coincided with the intellectual maturity needed to handle it. Unfortunately, today's accelerated onset of puberty does not seem to have been accompanied by a comparable advance in our intellectual development, so we now acquire our sexuality before we have the intellectual maturity to bring it under control. (p. 418)

I would like to raise two objections to the above view. First of all, recent declines in the age of sexual maturity are not new at all, but rather recapture the peak reproductive years of earlier human populations when viewed over evolutionary time. In other words, unduly late sexual maturity is not normal. Rather, it is evidence of the loss of the previously discussed nutritious paleolithic diet by recent human populations. It is only now with great advances in modern agriculture that we are attaining sexual maturity at the younger age that our distant ancestors did. Secondly, why must sexuality be brought under mature intellectual control? The theory of life history strategies tells us that both brain development and the development of sexual behavior will occur at a rate that maximizes reproductive success. That means that for part of a lifetime reproduction may be occurring at a time when the brain is too young or too old to be optimal, but still within an age range that makes attempting reproduction adaptive. The facts speak well on this point: A half million teenagers in America give birth each year (about one in seven of all births). An insight can be derived from a study of life history strategy: Sexual intercourse and reproduction beginning at puberty is the adaptive strategy. Thus, the opposite of what was implied by Short is correct: The average American in fact begins reproduction too *late*, not too early. The intellectual development that occurs after puberty often decreases rather than increases an individual's reproductive success, because it is accompanied by an increase in the cultural load, a concept that will be discussed later, in which parasitic aspects of our culture seek to perpetuate themselves at a cost to their human hosts. In this sense, Short's lamenting about sexual maturity preceding intellectual maturity is preposterous in evolutionary terms. It is our human destiny to recapture in the future those years of high teenage fertility that were lost. The time chosen by evolution for humans to begin reproduction is indeed at puberty. And while there may be some additional risks and health effects of reproducing while young or old, the same argument that was applied above to brain development holds true for all other organs: Reproductive ability is physiologically allocated to a time frame in human development that is adaptive, and artificially truncating it reduces reproductive success. The small decrement in future reproductive success from the negative effects of reproducing while young or old is trivial in comparison to the large increment in reproductive success gained through the increase in the number of offspring actually produced. Considering the complex picture of overall behavior and morphology on reproduction and *vice versa*, attempts to second-guess the optimal time and rate of reproduction are likely to return reduced reproductive success.

Menopause, the cessation of female fertility around the fifth decade of life, would seem at first inspection to be a trait that could not evolve, since it decreases rather than increases fertility. But, in fact, it would seem likely that menopause evolved in human females to allow an older woman to help existing relatives to survive and to reproduce instead of risking additional births herself. The evolution of menopause in humans may, in part, be related to the long period of dependency by their offspring. Mayer[132] in a study of New England families found that women who went through menopause had a higher lifetime inclusive fitness than those who did not.

In previous chapters we referred to the concept of reproductive value and extended reproductive value. Fisher[60] introduced the concept of reproductive value and defined it as an average individual's age-specific expectation of future offspring. It is a summation of intervals from age x to age t, carried to infinity, of the probability of surviving from age x to age t, times the reproductive success of an average individual at age t measured in terms of Darwinian fitness. The reproductive success of any age class can increase with decreasing magnitudes of the probability of surviving that interval, as long as there is a corresponding increase in reproductive success of sufficient size during that age class interval, a past interval, or future interval. It is logical to argue from this mathematical relationship that there could be times when it is adaptive for an individual to reduce his probability of survival in attempting some immediate or distant reproductive goal, as long as, on the average, an increased rate of reproduction more than compensated for the shortened reproductive life. When the summation of probabilities of survival in future age intervals is large and the reproductive success in those intervals is large, then a trait decreasing the probability of survival through the current interval can only be justified by a correspondingly great increase in the rate of reproduction achieved in the current or future intervals. However, it is important to note that with small probabilities of survival and low reproductive success in future age intervals, it requires only small corresponding increases in immediate reproductive success to justify further decreases in the probability of future survival. These mathematics are the theoretical explanation for the risk-taking behavior actually observed in old male anubis baboons as discussed previously. Extended reproductive value, not particularly applicable to the behavior of old male anubis baboons because of their limited ability to interact differentially with close relatives, does apply to other social species like bees and humans. Extended reproductive value is similar to reproductive value, the key exception being that instead of measuring the reproductive success of an average individual at a given age in terms of Darwinian fitness, reproductive success is measured in inclusive fitness. In this way, workers in sterile castes of eusocial insects, and humans past the age at which they can engender or bear children, may have an extended reproductive value when their reproductive value is zero. Extended reproductive value should be a more powerful tool of predicting behavior than reproductive value in these circumstances. In a previous section I offered the example of a hypothesized differential rate of stinging behavior according to age in worker honeybees. Age should also be a predictor of risk-taking behavior in humans.

Mate selection falls between a cooperative endeavor between males and females to have offspring, and an evolutionarily promoted battle of the sexes. In humans, this potential for discord may be reduced in a fashion common to the animal world called bonding. The variable added to bonding in all cultures is the institutionalization of marriage. Pair bonding and marriage are by no means a way of eliminating all biological conflict of interests. Infidelity, under-investment in mate or offspring, abandonment, and feeding conflict of interests are examples of problems that can still arise. The method by which the pair bond is maintained can itself be a source of conflict. Male hamadryas baboons maintain harems of females by herding those females with a ritualistic but obviously painful bite on the nape of the neck. Whenever the female strays more than a few meters from the male, he chases and bites her. As a result she follows him more closely during the subsequent progression. But rather than being well trained to always follow attentively after years of conditioning, female hamadryas baboons appear to adopt a strategy of straying deliberately to test their male harem leader's ability to herd. The result is that the females, in most cases, are returned to the harem with a neck bite. But in rare cases the females will steal copulations with other males, or leave their harems entirely. Thus, by deliberately straying, the females are ensuring that their offspring will be fathered by males who have the essential ability to maintain harems or to steal copulations. The reproductive success of sons and other male descendants produced by this strategy will be higher than those produced by unchallenged submission to the male's attempts to herd females. When males and females have totally opposed methods of enhancing their reproductive success, it is perhaps fair to say that an evolutionarily promoted battle of the sexes exists.

Weak psychological models of familial conflict purport that communication is the main problem in strife-ridden families, and that better communication will solve marital problems. If communication were the only problem, why did it not improve long ago? Humans are nothing if not verbose. This case is one well described by the *cliché*: "confusing the medium for the message". Communication is merely the method by which we convey information and misinformation about physical and mental states. It has no inherent value *per se*. In contrast, the model favored in this book is one that suggests that there can be, and often is, a real biological conflict of interests between husband and wife and between parent and child.

Sexual selection is the process by which traits that favor reproduction, not survival, evolve. Darwin[39] thought of it primarily as a form of competition, in which the loser did not suffer death, but rather, fewer offspring. A common expression of sexual selection of this form is intrasexual competition for mates. Among primates, intrasexual competition for mates is primarily male-male competition for access to females. And there, Darwin's view that sexual selection was not a struggle for existence, but a struggle for mates, comes into question. In practice, sexual selection often merges into natural selection. Take the example of two male anubis baboons competing for access to an estrous female through escalated aggressive competition. Though it is clearly sexual selection in progress, the outcome of the competition can often be death.

Another form of sexual selection recognized by Darwin[39] is the evolution of attractiveness to the opposite sex. In particular, males are adorned in ways that enhance their courtship abilities. Because of the disparity in parental investment by males and females, with females generally investing more, females become the limiting sex[204] and males are selected to compete for them through the evolution of this kind of attractiveness and through male-male competition. Female-female competition occurs in some primate societies. Among humans it occurs primarily due to female-female competition for access to optimal males where great variance in male access to resources exists. Women, even those who are friends or relatives, will often show intense competition to get access to a desirable man and his resources. This pattern of female-female competition is also prevalent among gibbons, in which the females of the species sing at each other in territorial disputes.

Runaway selection[60] is an extreme form of sexual selection. Fisher proposed that the females of a population might arbitrarily find a certain male trait attractive. The result is that those males with the trait have increased reproductive success. But by the fact that the male offspring of these males have this trait and also benefit from increased female preference, the females themselves who have the preference have increased reproductive success via their male descendants. The result is an intense and accelerating selection for males with the trait and for females who prefer the trait. Eventually, stabilizing selection will be encountered, but perhaps not before the evolution of an extravagant male trait that has no broader function than having at one time been arbitrarily attractive to females, such as a peacock's tail plumage.

Sexual selection can take the form of social selection, as it does among the San Blas Islands Indians of the N.E. coast of Panama. A high rate of albinism has evolved in that population and it seems to be associated with a cultural preference for albinos. Among the San Blas Indians, albino men are thought to be lucky with women and corn. Because of their sensitivity to the sun, they may be spared some of the heavy labor in the fields. As a result of these factors they appear to have higher reproductive success than albinos in other populations.

Historically, assortative mating, or the pairing of individuals of similar phenotype and similar genotype, has been the overwhelming trend in America. We tend to marry people who look like us, act like us, and live near us. While such a trend may be rooted in demographics, probability theory, and genetically predisposed behaviors, it is also a cause of many of the problems in American marriages.

For example, let us take the topic of interracial marriages. They are the antithesis of the observed assortative mating trend in America today, and they are relatively rare. Yet, interracial marriages are far more stable (less likely to end in divorce) than marriages within the same race. They also lead to a generally desirable state in the children produced from them: heterosis. Heterosis, a phenomenon well-known in genetics, is an expression of hybrid vigor and is the opposite of the phenomenon of inbreeding depression.

One exception to assortative mating that holds true in America, in other cultures, and in nonhuman primate societies, is that males tend to mate with females who are younger than themselves. This trend is a function of male-male competition for access to females, who, according to the theory of parental investment[204], are the limiting sex by virtue of the fact that they invest in offspring more than males do. Therefore, males require more time and energy, often expressed in terms of growth to a large body mass (sexual dimorphism in body size), in order to be able to compete successfully for access to females. In human and nonhuman primate societies, competition for status (social dominance) and accumulation of resources are two processes also facilitating mating but requiring time beyond that needed by females for their own onset of reproduction. In part, as a function of the adaptiveness of this pattern of older males mating with younger females, we find in America that marriages that have a sizable age differential, in the range of the husband being twenty years senior to the wife, are the most stable. Contrary to the rule of assortative mating, rates of divorce are high in America because people tend to marry others of the same race and of similar age.

Mating systems and related topics

While Americans accept monogamy as the mating system that is right and normal, in fact there is considerable diversity in mating systems among animals, including humans. For a thorough discussion of mating systems see Daly and Wilson[34]. In this section I shall cover promiscuity, monogamy, polygyny, polyandry, and also mixed strategies. A large portion of the history of the social sciences has been spent speculating on which mating system is the primordial one among humans from which all others arose. Another question regarding the first system of inheritance, patrilineal or matrilineal, has also often been asked. Studies of modern nonhuman primates and of fossil hominid evidence provide insights that, for practical purposes, end the speculation. There are two key groups of evidence. First, hominid fossils, as far back as they currently go, indicate that our most distant hominid relatives (*Australopithecus afarensis*) had high degrees of sexual dimorphism in body mass. High degrees of sexual dimorphism in body mass in the primates are always associated with polygyny/promiscuity, usually with a group structure based on a dominance hierarchy or on an age-graded system. Monogamy is out of the question as the early hominid mating system. The second group of evidence comes from our living nonhuman primate relatives. Once again, monogamy is rare in Old World monkeys and apes. Because of a high rate of breeding male turnover in dominance hierarchy and age-graded systems, and because of uncertainty of paternity that can occur in dominance hierarchy systems, the only plausible form of inheritance for early hominids was matrilineal. The West, including America, seems to be out of step with our hominid heritage in this respect, as it explores some new aspects of evolution with its system of imposed monogamy. The results are not entirely satisfactory for those people within this imposed breeding system. In the following paragraphs I shall discuss the problems and some potential solutions.

Promiscuity

Promiscuity is defined as reproductive behavior in the absence of a lasting bond between the male and female. Promiscuous mating systems occur where the distribution of mates in time and space is not conducive to bonding, or where resources occur in such a pattern that reproductive effort is best spent on repeated mating efforts rather than combined parental effort. Because there is little opportunity for investment in a mate or by a male in his offspring in promiscuous mating systems, there is selection for preference for maximum fertility in a mate instead. Since the age of highest fertility is greater than the age of peak reproductive value for women and less than the age of peak reproductive value for men, two predictions follow. Women in promiscuous mating systems should prefer younger men than do pair bonding women. Men in promiscuous mating systems should prefer older women than do pair bonding men.

Evolution of the avunculate

Many of the people of the tribes of the Pacific were promiscuous, did not understand that sexual intercourse was the cause of pregnancy, and traced descent only through the matriline. Men had closer ties, e.g., economic relations, to their sisters' children than to their wives' children. This kinship system, the avunculate, which provides special relations between men and their sisters' children, makes perfect genetic sense where certainty of paternity is low. One's sisters' children are related to one by at least $1/_8$, but one's wife's children may be unrelated to one! Kurland[117] established a paternity threshold of 0.268, the probability of paternity below which it makes biological sense to invest in one's sister's children instead of one's wife's children. This figure allows for the probability that one's sister is a half sibling or full sibling according to the prevailing rate of fidelity in the population.

Malinowski[129] reported that the Trobriand Islanders believed that there was no genetical relationship between a man and his wife's children even though he assumed the role of sociological father. Instead of a male playing a role in conception, they believe that a spirit of a dead clan ancestor (called *baloma*) enters the womb when a woman is wading in the sea. Although failing to understand the role of males in reproduction appears strange, it may be in this culture an accurate description of the real genetic unrelatedness of the sociological father to his wife's children. Another social phenomenon associated with the avunculate is cross-cousin marriage. Cross-cousin marriage is another way of reconciling genetic and cultural, e.g., economic, interests in a society with low paternity certainty. When a man marries his sociological father's sister's daughter, he is assuring his sociological father that the sociological father will be related to the grandchildren. This pattern provides a genetic interest by a man in his grandchildren which would not be so otherwise. This trend follows from the fact that a man does not know he is genetically related to his putative son, but he does know that he is related to his son's wife, who is his sister's daughter.

Sowing wild oats

The expression "sowing wild oats" has hidden meaning. To the wheat farmer, wild oats (*Avena fatua*) are weeds that get into his wheat field. They are accidentally harvested with the wheat and are further perpetuated in the next generation when the crop is sown from a contaminated seed source. Ultimately, as wild oats spread, there is risk that they will ruin the wheat harvest. Sowing wild oats in a farmer's wheat field would be figuratively much like promiscuous sexual intercourse with his wife. The first undermines the faithfulness with which he can perpetuate his wheat crop; the second undermines the faithfulness with which he can perpetuate his lineage. The phrase "sowing wild oats" has come to mean to philander and its interesting literal meaning goes widely unknown.

A true promiscuous mating system is not common in human societies. Murdock[146], in a survey of 250 societies, reported that only the Todas of southern India and the Kaingang of Brazil lack sex restrictions sufficiently closely to justify speaking of them as promiscuous. However, even in these extreme cases mating is not random. For example, the Todas, while indifferent toward adultery, observe incest taboos, sib exogamy, and moiety endogamy. Murdock[146] found only 12 instances of societies that have generalized obligatory sexual relations such as wife lending and sexual hospitality. In the culture of the Masai of eastern Africa, wife lending is a practice extended to all members of a man's age set, specifically, the members of his circumcision class (where circumcision occurs after puberty). If a man refuses to lend his wife he is subject to the fine of a bull.

Bonding

Bonding includes the mating systems of monogamy, serial monogamy, polygyny, and polyandry. The only mating system characteristic of humans that is excluded is promiscuity. It is difficult to imagine a strategy other than bonding that could maximize reproductive success for the average American in modern times. If humans were really trying to reach a target family size that maximized reproductive success, males and females would both encounter difficulties with other strategies such as promiscuity. Males would likely find an inadequate number of female mates outside of a pair bond, and females would perhaps require the resources that could be provided by a pair bonded mate.

Monogamy

Monogamy is defined as long-term pair bonding. Approximately 16 percent of human societies are monogamous. That is a fairly low percentage, but it is high by the standards of other primates in a survey of mating systems across the order. It is a mating system that is more common in birds. So why is it relatively more prevalent among humans? Alexander[2] suggested that monogamy, along with monotheism, and related traits, has spread around the world by conquest in war. In monogamous mating systems there is selection for preference for maximum extended reproductive value in a mate. That is why in America teenage girls appear on the pages of *Playboy*. Human males find 19-year-old women most attractive because humans are for the most part a bonding species. A male's reproductive success is linked to his mate's long-term reproductive success, and 19-year-old women have peak extended reproductive value. There is no evidence for a similar phenomenon in chimpanzees of male preference for young females, nor should there be. They are promiscuous and male chimpanzees should prefer to mate with females of high fecundity, not necessarily of high reproductive value. As a result they might prefer older females. Male hamadryas baboons form harems and are bonded to their females in a way that has consequences similar to human bonding. Male hamadryas baboons adopt and care for young females who are approaching peak reproductive value to form their harems in a way that is consistent with this model. This model suggests the existence of a biological basis for "youth worship" in many human populations. Youth worship is not a temporary cultural phenomenon but is rather founded in selection pressures generated by our bonding mating system. It is here to stay as long as bonding is prevalent. There is also a sex difference in youth worship. Men, as a function of male-male competition for females, reach a peak reproductive value later than women. Therefore, women prefer to bond with men older than the age men most prefer women to be when they bond. Extended reproductive value is the explanation of why men grow old more "gracefully" than women do. It is also the explanation for why men marry younger women and women marry older men in a wide diversity of cultures. It is a simple case of sexual selection. Men who marry women of high extended reproductive value leave behind more offspring than men who marry women of low extended reproductive value. Women who marry men of high extended reproductive value leave behind more offspring than women who marry men of low extended reproductive value. The type of individual who makes the wrong mate choice becomes less frequent in succeeding generations. More than 50 percent of American marriages end in divorce, but following divorce about 80 percent remarry. Thus, monogamy is the marriage form of preference in the ideal American culture, but in the real culture the marriage form is *serial* monogamy.

Within the mating system of monogamy there are questions regarding fidelity and cuckoldry. Males are generally believed to cheat on their mates to increase the number of offspring they produce. If a male can be bonded to one female and then produce additional offspring by copulating with other females, he may have an increase in reproductive success. The reverse question regarding female fidelity is somewhat more complex. First, we may ask, why do males have such concern over the fidelity of their mates? The answer is that a female always knows when an offspring is hers, but a male does not. When a male provides investment in his mate's offspring, he is under "double" selective pressure to protect himself against cuckoldry: He loses once if the offspring he supports are not his; he loses twice if they are the offspring of an unrelated male competitor and he invests reproductive effort into them. Women have observed, astutely, I think, that "men are all about control". But to some extent that tendency is due to biology, not choice. As discussed above, men have an evolutionarily promoted drive to avoid being cuckolded and then raising, often unwittingly, an unrelated offspring. To avoid that outcome they attempt to control the behavior and movements of their mate. In turn, that might predispose males to dominate females economically, politically and socially as well. Females cheat for reasons that are not entirely clear at present. Here are some hypotheses. Females might be selected to accept investment from one male while seeking better genes from another. Females might be seeking insurance against infertility in the mate. Females might form a relationship with another male as insurance against desertion by her mate (see Wagner[210] for a related discussion in birds). Another possible adaptive explanation for female infidelity is that it is used as an attempt by the female to increase her frequency of copulation to nearer the optimum. Ironically, at the same time her mate, who is unwilling or unable to provide sufficient copulations for her to achieve optimal fertility, may be practicing infidelity himself. For example, he could maximize his reproductive success by seeking copulations with another female whose fertility is enhanced more per copulation that he provides than his mate's fertility is enhanced. Female infidelity may be high even among human populations considered to be monogamous; for example, between 5 and 30 percent of American and British babies may be the product of adultery[43]. Deception often goes with infidelity in nature. In the liberal environment, it is sometimes asserted that the deception that accompanies an extramarital affair is worse than the affair itself. While that view does not hold up under evolutionary analysis, the role of deception is important. Even among the Trobriand Islanders, where the role of males in procreation was not recognized, infidelity was a secretive matter. There is reason to believe that there is evolution-arily promoted deception during infidelity. Unfaithfulness in the pair bond can lead to a biological conflict of interests. That fact is more important than, but is reinforced by, the discrepancy between the ideal culture and the real culture. The ideal culture is represented by faithfulness and happiness in the pair bond. The real culture is represented by infidelity and conflict in many pair bonds. One of the ways to reduce the costs of infidelity is to deceive one's mate. If one's mate does not know about the infidelity, then retaliation by that mate in the form of withdrawal of investment, aggression, or desertion is precluded. So mates are selected to be discrete or deceptive when unfaithful. Paternity certainty can be given by a wife to a husband -- if you are a married man, stipulate it.

Circumcision

There are some correlations between male circumcision and the health of the circumcised man and the health of his long-term female sexual partner. In particu-lar, cancers of the reproductive organs are reduced. The assumption is that it is easier for a circumcised man to keep his penis clean than it is for an uncircumcised man to do so. But it is also clear that circumcision was not originally performed for this reason. Rather, it is one aspect of what anthropologists call penile rituals, which seem to be culturgens fulfilling obscure cultural purposes. Subincision is another penile ritual which consists of the cutting of an opening into the urethra on the underside of the penis.

Female circumcision, a ritual of surgically altering the female genitalia, may have a relationship to paternity certainty. What is often referred to as female circumcision has a variety of meanings: Commonly it is a clitoridectomy and sometimes a complete excision of the clitoris and all or part of the labia. Anecdotal evidence suggests that some women who are circumcised still enjoy sexual intercourse and experience orgasm, but it is not unreasonable to assume that the enjoyment might be considerably or somewhat diminished by the operation. The consequence may be as it is intended by its practitioners: to reduce female lasciviousness. Among the Masai of eastern Africa, female circumcision occurs after puberty and makes a girl marriageable. In that tribe, a circumcision candidate chooses to participate in the ritual and actively desires it. It is now a fashionable cause in the West to condemn the practice of female circumcision and to refer to it with deprecation as ''female genital mutilation''. However, it is a ritual in which the teenage participants willingly join or which is passed from mother to daughters when they are young children. Perhaps the right to condemn the practice may properly belong to the women who are circumcised. Certainly, in many societies, a girl would not likely choose to forgo this rite of passage -- uncircumcised adult women in some cultures would be subject to their own sense of humiliation and would feel subject to ridicule. Without first-hand experience of the full cultural context and its reproductive consequences, how can outside observers from the West really know if the custom is good or bad? My words on the subject will no doubt lead to reproach from self-appointed crusaders in America. They couch their intrusive opposition to female circumcision in legalistic or medical terminology to hide their ethnocentric motives. But I am adamant that the choice to circumcise or not should be made by the women who choose the ritual for themselves or for their daughters. In the current social environment in many societies, where it is difficult for uncircumcised women to marry or to have children, they are making and will continue to make this adaptive choice in favor of circumcision. People of European descent have a long history of criticizing the habits of people in non-Western cultures. Much of the Western opposition to female circumcision is a combination of ethnocentrism and prudish aversion to discussing an embarrassing sexual subject. In another example, it is also common to condemn the practice of scarification, which is the cutting of an ornate pattern of scars on the face, chest, belly and back, practiced by some central African tribes. It is an alternative to tattooing, which does not show on the black skin of people in heavily pigmented populations. In fact, with a little exposure to it, one can find scarification to be quite beautiful. Of the great variety of body alterations, only ear piercing, male circumcision and tattooing are common in the West. Nose piercing, lip piercing, incisor tooth filing (so that the front teeth have sharp points), incisor tooth extraction (to create a conspicuous gap in the front teeth), footbinding, and subincision are generally thought to be bizarre or unattractive in the West. But, strangely, we sanction a great deal of cosmetic surgery (approximately 1.5 million operations per year) including breast implants, buttock implants, face-lifts, tummy tucks, eyelid tucks, chin implants, reshaped noses, and liposuction[59]. A number of these procedures lead to a state that mimics the attributes of an age class with higher reproductive value than the real age class of the patient. For example, women seek breast implants and face-lifts; both are sought in an attempt to regain the appearance of a nubile, young woman. There is one final point that contains some irony: Many Westerners criticize female circumcision but at the same time condone or encourage the West's own form of female genital mutilation -- tubal ligation. Unlike female circumcision, tubal ligation deserves to be censured because of its devastating effect on fertility.

Polygyny

Approximately 83 percent of human societies are polygynous. The curve of male and female reproductive success as a function of number of wives is not well known for a large number of cultures. It is an example of critical data irrevocably lost by early anthropologists in their studies of non-Western societies, before they were changed forever by contact with the West. But the original fitness implications of polygyny may be reflected in traditions in many non-Western cultures that often come as a surprise to Americans: Women often do not object to their husbands' taking on additional wives. Indeed, they sometimes look forward to the addition of wives to the family. Sometimes new wives are considered to be coworkers who will share the family's burden of labor. Sororal polygyny in some cultures effectively reduces the conflict of interests between co-wives. Sororal polygyny is the mating system in which a man marries two or more sisters. The sisters have a low conflict of interests in such marriages, in comparison to those in which the co-wives are unrelated, because they share many of their genes in common. Helping a full sister to survive and reproduce means that nieces and nephews, each related by $^1/_4$ to the actor, are produced.

Polygyny is often assumed to be of benefit to the male and to occur at a cost to the females. Downhower and Armitage[47] demonstrated that monogamy is the best mating system for female yellow-bellied marmots, large squirrel-like animals that live on the ground, burrow, and sometimes live in concentrations in subalpine meadows in western North America. Yet polygyny exists in this species and is correlated with higher male reproductive success. Thus, male reproductive success increases with increases in harem size, while the number of young per female decreases with increases in harem size. The little data that exist on mating system and reproductive success for humans follow the same model: Polygyny benefits males and costs females. Dorjahn[46] found that, among the Temne people of Sierra Leone, infant mortality increases and the frequency of live births declines with increasing degrees of polygyny. But models and data exist which indicate that this assumption of a reduction of female fitness with polygyny may not always be true. For example, a female may prefer to be the second mate of a male if that male is able to provide better for her and her offspring than other unmated males. For example, a polygynous male might provide for his mates and offspring better by having a territory with superior resource availability or through greater male parental investment. This model, described as a "polygyny threshold," at which females choose to be one of the multiple mates of a male because of circumstances of advantage to the female, was advanced by Verner and Willson[208] and Orians[155]. Also, there may be, under some circumstances, interactions between co-wives that are mutually beneficial, such as division of labor, so that a few co-wives cooperating among themselves do better than single wives and, perhaps, better than many co-wives. In my experience in Africa and in the experience of other anthropologists around the world, it is repeatedly observed that the women in polygynous societies often do not object to and sometimes enthusiastically promote their husbands' marrying additional wives, even when they are unrelated to those new wives, a situation that would provoke greater conflict of interests than if the new wives were genetically related. Thus, based on the preferences of the women themselves, we would want to be cautious in dismissing the female fitness enhancing model for polygyny in these cases.

Polyandry

Approximately 0.5 percent of human societies are polyandrous. Polyandry is not to be confused with promiscuity. Rather, it is a group of brothers or other male relatives who share a wife in common. It tends to occur is societies which express patrilineal ideals[121]. Among the Bahima of Uganda, Roscoe[173] described the following:

> Sometimes a man finds he is too poor to marry, his cows are insufficient to supply milk for the daily need of even one wife, or it may be he cannot afford the number of cows for the marriage dowry [brideprice]: in such a case he asks one or more of his brothers to join him, and together they raise the necessary number of animals; a woman will readily agree to this arrangement and become the wife of two or three brothers. (p. 105)

Polyandry is also common in Tibet. Durham[49], in a complicated analysis, concluded that part of the explanation of the presence of polyandry there is that:

> [It has enhanced] ... survival and reproduction in the special social and natural environment of the Tibetan plateau. (p. 82)

Sperm competition, a strategy to be discussed in detail in a following section, is usually lower in polyandry than in promiscuous mating systems because the males are relatives.

Serial monogamy

Americans have only two forms of marriage: monogamy and serial monogamy. In monogamy a man and a woman are married for an average period of 4.9 years and occasionally for life. In serial monogamy a man and a woman have a marriage that is one in a series of such marriages. There are elements of both polygyny and polyandry in serial monogamy. Mainstream modern American society has one of the unusual cultures that does not permit polygyny. While no doubt based on democratic and religious principles, true and lasting monogamy cannot be established by law. The result of married people wanting another mate, whether for reasons of reproduction, economics or psychology, is serial monogamy. In the majority of other cultures the result is polygyny. In that way, the family continuity is preserved -- the family does not dissolve, it expands, with the possibility of considerable psychological and evolutionary benefits. With serial monogamy comes the possibility of conflict of interests between children from a previous marriage and their new step-parent. The sororate in some cultures effectively reduces the conflict of interests between a man's previous children and his new wife. In this system the new wife is the sister of the former wife. Because of the close genetic relationship between her and her sister's children, biological conflict of interests between them is reduced.

One-parent families, often including a never married mother and children, are becoming more common in American society. In the 1990 U.S. Census, 22.6 percent of white households, 33.3 percent of Hispanic households, and 60.5 percent of black households were one-parent families. About one in three women who gave birth was not married. Two out of three teenagers who gave birth were not married; one-third of daughters of teenage mothers become teenage mothers themselves. This subject is one of hot political debate and much moralizing. Conservatives complain about the high rate of birth out of wedlock because they feel it is a sign of the breakdown of the traditional American family. They point out with a censurious tone that children of one-parent families have more children themselves, many also outside of marriage, than children of two-parent families. They seem to be unaware of the evolutionary implications. First of all, familial behavior evolved to increase the fitness of the family members -- individuals do not exist for the sake of the family. So holding preservation of the family as the ultimate goal is misguided. Secondly, if one-parent families produce more children, who in turn produce more children than two-parent families, then it is the one-parent family strategy that has an adaptive advantage. As a result, the one-parent family will continue to increase in frequency and to prevail, conservative sentiments notwithstanding. Furthermore, given the high fertility of members of one-parent families, I would conclude that they are actually desirable. This view follows from the fact that the children raised in impoverished, one-parent homes and with poor educations have the best prospects for reproductive success, in part because of a novel environment created over the last few generations. Why are attacks on unwed teenage mothers a perennial favorite among politicians? I shall discuss in detail the theoretical implications of the roots of the causes later. These roots are: 1. an overextended expression of an intergenerational familial conflict of interests over reproductive opportunity, 2. evolutionarily inappropriate spiteful behavior in order to deny another individual the opportunity to reproduce, which could only be adaptive in a much smaller population, and 3. culturgens carried by the opponents, which attempt to perpetuate themselves at the expense of the reproductive success of others. In this third cause, only the culturgens benefit by their increase in frequency. The reproductive success of the teenagers is decreased and the reproductive success of the opponents is decreased or remains constant.

Teenage pregnancies are a topic of some considerable importance. Some Americans object to the high rate of pregnancies among teenagers. About 1 in 10 unmarried teenage girls gets pregnant each year in the U.S. Among the objections often raised are that it ruins the girl's life because: 1. It makes continuing her education difficult, 2. it leads to financial insecurity, 3. it has adverse effects on her health, and 4. she is assuming an adult role as a parent too early. I am in sympathy with the "quality" of life issues raised. Namely, education, financial security, and health are valuable, but only to the extent that they serve the maximization of reproductive success. Few people would argue that either education or financial security should be maximized for their own sake. Rather, the common view is that these should, in turn, serve a function, e.g., as tools useful in raising a family. Thus, we see that in these two points of objection that there is, in fact, some overlap with the argument for the process of maximizing reproductive success. We learned earlier that any expenditure of reproductive effort is likely to reduce longevity, sometimes quite abruptly, as for spawning salmon. Forgoing reproduction among humans at any stage in the life history, not just during the teenage years, reduces health risks and increases longevity, so the logic of applying this argument to teenagers alone is dubious. The final point that a teenage mother is assuming a parenting role too early is the product of thinking associated with a weak psychological model of human life histories. In contrast, I maintain that humans are beautifully adapted through the process of natural selection to begin reproduction in their early teenage years. Consider the argument presented earlier about intellectual maturity and reproduction. Viewing teenage pregnancy in a positive way in the current environment is one of the cornerstones of this philosophy and is based on the evolutionary ethic.

Rape

There is a remarkable difference between the estimated frequency of rape in America, perhaps one woman in five, and the estimated frequency of rape worldwide, perhaps one woman in two thousand. The discrepancy is perhaps due to a problem of definition and reporting as much as real differences in the frequency of rape. The biological definition of rape and legal definitions differ. The woman who claims to be raped by her husband rarely has solid legal grounds for prosecution because sexual privileges are considered concomitant with marriage in most legal systems. But it is not difficult to imagine circumstances under which a woman was raped according to the biological definition of rape, which merely states that the woman was forced to have sexual intercourse with the threat of, or realization of, bodily injury from aggressive behavior by her husband. No doubt the high figures often mentioned regarding rape in America as compared to the rest of the world are due to more overreporting in America, more underreporting elsewhere in the world, and a greater frequency of nonaggressive compliance by non-Western women in cases where sexual intercourse is demanded by a male from their society. This last point raises an issue: Rape is less frequent in the natural world under circumstances where the females of the species under consideration have no practical means of resistance. No means of resistance undermines motivation to resist, because inevitably futile resistance is not adaptive. During estrus, a female anubis baboon is in the business of attracting any high ranking male baboon that can gain access to her through male-male competition. The female advertises her state of sexual receptivity and proximity to ovulation with a conspicuous red sexual swelling of the perineal region. Also, the males are much larger and stronger than the females, and unlike the females they are equipped with lethal canine teeth. In such a breeding system, females have neither the reason nor the ability to prevent copulation with the dominant males. Therefore, rape is not observed among anubis baboons by the anthropological fieldworkers who study them. Likewise, rape is uncommon in species in which females have highly effective deterrents to rape. Among such species, males are selected to pursue species-specific courtship rituals rather than waste time and energy in attempts at rape that are certain to fail. Since rape is often a single act of coitus, the percentage of acts of sexual intercourse that are associated with rape is small in humans. When all the variables are considered, e.g., risk of injury or death, contraction of disease, impregnation, future sexual dysfunction due to psychological damage, damage to the existing pair bond, and legal implications, it is difficult to assess the actual fitness consequences of this behavior for either the woman victim or the male rapist. It would be useful in future assessments of this behavior to have access to data about the frequency of conceptions and births that are the product of rape and to have information about the reproductive history of the rapists and the victims. Although one commonly hears the claim today that rape is a crime of violence, not a crime of sex, the sexual component of rape is real. Rape victims are not random members of the population, rather they tend to be females of reproductive age. Rapists are not random members of the population, rather they tend to be males of reproductive age. Victims of rape sometimes get pregnant, thereby rendering arguments denying a sexual component to rape illogical. Rape appears as a reproductive strategy in other species. For example, among primates, rape occurs in orangutans.

Prostitution

Prostitution is often referred to as the oldest profession. It is not. A medium of exchange is necessary for prostitution, by definition. So hunting and gathering must have come first. Prostitution followed, as in chimpanzees. Popp and DeVore[164] reported that prostitution behavior occurs among chimpanzees. Female chimpanzees in estrus exchange the opportunity to copulate with males possessing a highly prized prey item for a share in the meat. It is instructive to consider prostitution as a human economic and reproductive strategy. In its simplest form, prostitution is an exchange of an opportunity to reproduce for something of monetary value. In turn, the monetary value of the payment received may itself be convertible into reproductive success, the ultimate currency. But the observed situation in the U.S.A. today is more complicated than that. As practiced in modern American society, prostitution is risky reproduction for the prostitute and risky reproduction for the patron. It is also relatively costly, considering that the increment of reproductive success is usually low for the patron. The increment of reproductive success is lowered to near zero if the patron minimizes the risk of contracting sexually transmitted diseases by using a condom. Legalized and controlled prostitution might be a rational step, after admitting its role in our primate heritage and its role in many cultures and in the history of Western society. Opposition, especially from married women who would naturally object to the possible diversion of their husbands' resources, is likely. Some European countries and the state of Nevada, which have cultural similarities to mainstream American culture, do have legalized prostitution. But perhaps the most important point is that the intrusion of government into our lives by denying us the right to pursue this alternative reproductive strategy is unacceptable.

American attitudes toward sexual intercourse

Cross-cultural comparison tells us something about how unusual the attitude of Americans is toward sexual intercourse. In striking contrast to the Western ideal of sexual intercourse only within marriage (an ideal formerly held more widely than it is now), it seems unlikely that a general prohibition of sex relations outside of marriage occurs in as many as five percent of societies[146]. Murdock[146] went on and stated:

> The bias of our own highly aberrant traditional sex mores has not only distorted the analysis of sexual restrictions but has led generations of writers to postulate for early man or for primitive peoples the antithesis of our own type of regulation, namely, a generalized sexual permissiveness variously called "hetairism," "primitive promiscuity," or "sexual communism". (p. 264)

Indeed, in the decades since Murdock's publication, it is clear that promiscuity is just one of many mating systems not only for humans but for other animals as well. Similarly, it would be realistic to view our own Western monogamy as just one alternative in mating systems and to recognize that it lacks intrinsic superiority or moral advantage in a broad sense. It is just a strategy by which organisms reproduce under given genetic and environmental constraints.

Regardless of the mating system in which you find yourself, the following is a useful **life-lesson: If you are a man, find a fertile woman; if you are a woman, find a virile man.**

Reproduction and wealth

Poor people in America are actually rich in terms of reproductive success. Should extraordinary provisions be made to care for the children of economically disadvantaged parents, whose numbers will likely increase if the policies advocated in this book are implemented? No, because their fertility is enhanced by the relative degree of deprivation they experience, and from their viewpoint, in accordance with the evolutionary ethic, that increase in reproductive success is the ultimate good. I have compassion for the highly educated and wealthy people in America, because those traits are both the causes and symptoms of depressed reproductive success. Looking after money can be extraordinarily time consuming. This demand on the time budget, along with the principle of allocation, may be one of the reasons that wealth reduces reproductive success. Social status in America is highly correlated with wealth. Striving to achieve it does not make evolutionary sense at the present. According to the evolutionary ethic, anything occurring in excess that depresses reproductive success is bad.

While this statement could be considered a tautology, it contains a **life-lesson: The truth of the fact that we should not maximize the amount of food we eat has slowly become apparent to the average American. By the same slow process Americans will realize that we should not maximize our wealth, education, longevity, physical fitness or any variable other than reproductive success. Too much of anything can lower reproductive success.**

Nowhere is this trend more apparent than in the twin negative correlates of fertility: too much wealth and too much education. In some societies, like Ethiopia, no money and no formal education is the optimum for reproductive success; in other societies, including America, very little of both is the optimum. Very basic food, crude shelter, utilitarian clothing, and primary health care appear to be variables with properties that lead to the maximization of reproductive success. But luxuries such as higher education, leisure, a varied and interesting diet, suburban housing, fashionable clothing, and advanced health care appear to be variables with properties that lead to the lowering of reproductive success. Luxuries, for the most part, are not only dispensable, but are actual hindrances to maximizing reproductive success.

Sexual intercourse

The reason that individuals will undergo severe deprivation including hunger, sleeplessness, and risk of death for sexual intercourse is that it is a prerequisite for reproduction in ''higher'' organisms. Those individuals that make a determined effort to mate reproduce their kind; those that do not, fail to reproduce their kind. This selection occurs generation after generation, instilling in the inheritors a powerful drive. According to the evolutionary ethic, that which maximizes reproductive success is good. Thus, having sexual intercourse and getting pregnant or impregnating is among the best things one can do, if alternatives to maximizing reproductive success are lacking, which would be commonly so. Sexual abstinence among fertile individuals is very difficult to justify. Such an evolutionary justification of sexual abstinence would require the unusual circumstance that inclusive fitness be enhanced by so abstaining. While this condition is regularly met in the neuter castes of social insects, it is rarely met in humans. Purported justifications such as fear of contracting sexually transmitted diseases, waiting until a time of greater maturity, or being of an age past the peak reproductive years are, for the most part, inadequate. Rather, one should choose a healthy sexual partner, start reproducing as soon as is physiologically possible, and continue reproducing as long as it is physiologically possible.

Cross-cultural comparisons of patterns of sexual intercourse show some interesting variation. Murdock[146] summarized below restrictions on sexual intercourse in relation to the life history of the woman:

> Events in the reproductive cycle are widely associated with sex restrictions. Most societies impose a taboo against sexual intercourse during a woman's menstrual periods, during at least the later months of pregnancy, and for a period immediately following childbirth. Many extend the latter taboo throughout most or all of the period of lactation .... Sexual intercourse is occasionally made obligatory in the belief that it is beneficial to reproduction. Thus the Azande and the Kiwai enjoin copulation during pregnancy in order to promote the development of the fetus. (pp. 266-267)

The right age for first sexual intercourse is a question best left to the application of life history strategies. The delay in reproduction among humans in Western cultures past the age of puberty is to a large degree caused by culture perpetuating itself rather than perpetuating our genes. This pattern amounts to the co-option of a number of years' worth of each individual's reproductive effort by culturgens furthering their own interests at the expense of our reproductive success. In contrast to the Western cultural tradition, the Muslim custom is that a girl is old enough to marry when she reaches menarche. This custom is highly admirable from the viewpoint of maximizing reproductive success. The average American abounds with reproductive effort. And an equally large amount of potential reproductive effort is available, through progenitive strategies. In almost all cases, only a fraction of this reproductive effort is expended and that at a low efficiency of conversion into reproductive success. Starting sexual intercourse early is just one of many steps to utilizing reproductive effort well. Nature's social signal indicating the beginning of the awakening of sexuality is the appearance of pubic hair. From data presented in Wu[229] it is clear that spermarche and menarche fall in the middle of the time range for the development of pubic hair.

The timing of sexual intercourse can, of course, effect fertility. On the average it takes about 108 random acts of sexual intercourse to produce a pregnancy, based on data from the well nourished, healthy population of Hutterites, who use no artificial contraception, studied by Eaton and Mayer[51]. This number is high in comparison to other primates, and supports the idea presented in a following section that cryptic ovulation is a strategy by which human females reduce male-male aggression. By concealing the time of ovulation and by being sexually receptive throughout the menstrual cycle, a female devalues the probability that an act of sexual intercourse will produce a child to less than 1 percent of what it could be in theory. This strategy reduces the rate of male-male competition by reducing the value of the object of competition. There is no reason that the human system of fertilization should be so inefficient unless it is designed to be so by evolution. This pregnancy success ratio can be greatly improved by using a simple method. The menstrual cycle is the time counted from the first day of one menstruation to the first day of the next menstruation. If a woman has average length menstrual cycles of 28 days then ovulation will occur around the 14th day. A woman can also know the time of ovulation and peak fertility because as the egg matures her cervix makes mucus which lubricates the vagina. A woman can learn to recognize this mucus just like she recognizes and knows when she is bleeding during her menstrual period. The mucus can be seen and felt. Ordinarily, after a menstrual period there are some dry days without any mucus discharge. Then the mucus begins to form. At first it may be thick and sticky, white or yellow. As the egg matures the mucus becomes thinner and watery. Then it becomes clear, stretchy and slippery. It is like the white of a raw chicken egg. The last day in the menstrual cycle that this mucus appears is the most fertile time. Sexual intercourse around this time is most likely to result in conception. Perhaps 12 acts of intercourse out of 100 will result in a pregnancy during this most fertile time. Wilcox et al.[214] reported that the probability of conception is 0.10

when intercourse occurs five days before ovulation and is 0.33 when it occurs on the day of ovulation. Another technique for use in increasing the pregnancy success ratio is the basal body temperature guide to ovulation. In this method a woman takes her temperature every morning for a few months, thereby allowing her to pinpoint the days on which her temperature drops slightly and then increases, thus indicating the time of ovulation and the most fertile days in her menstrual cycle during which sexual intercourse is most likely to result in pregnancy. Some suggest that a woman's interest in sexual intercourse increases in the 3 days around ovulation and that, consequently, rates of sexual intercourse increase about 25 percent at that time. If true, it is a natural way of achieving what the mucus method and basal body temperature method do artificially. The average American has in the range of four thousands acts of coitus in a lifetime. The total fertility rate in America is approximately two. These two numbers provide a rather shocking statistic of only one birth for every two thousand acts of coitus. I doubt that there is another organism on Earth with rates of birth per act of coitus that are lower than that figure. This fact is just another indicator that we are doing something seriously wrong in our reproductive behavior.

Frequency of sexual intercourse and the Coolidge effect

Based on a survey by Michael et al.[139] the average American male in the age range of 18-59 years has sex 6 times a month. (Unfortunately, they do not define "sex" as sexual intercourse, but we will have to ignore that for the sake of this discussion.) That is a latency period of about 5 days. If the Coolidge effect applies to humans, that latency period would be reduced if males were not having sexual intercourse with the same females every time. The Coolidge effect is defined as a reduced male latency period with novel females. Not surprisingly, reproductive success is, in this sense, the ultimate aphrodisiac. It may be especially true in species with a polygynous social structure. Bermant[8] described the legendary origins of the term Coolidge effect:

> One day President and Mrs. Coolidge were visiting a government farm. Soon after their arrival they were taken off on separate tours. When Mrs. Coolidge passed the chicken pens she paused to ask the man in charge if the rooster copulates more than once each day. "Dozens of times" was the reply. "Please tell that to the President," Mrs. Coolidge requested. When the President passed the pens and was told about the rooster, he asked "Same hen everytime?" "Oh no, Mr. President, a different one each time." The President nodded slowly, then said "Tell that to Mrs. Coolidge." (pp. 76-77)

If sexual intercourse is withheld in a long-term relationship, it is usually by the male. This fact is contrary to the general greater eagerness for sexual intercourse in the male and requires some explanation. Why do some husbands withhold sexual intercourse? Could it be that, due to the longer reproductive life of a man, he values each unit of reproductive time less than his female mate and thus has a means of expressing his discontent? Females sometimes withhold sexual intercourse. Females outside a pair bond may do so to exercise female choice. Females inside a pair bond may also do so. "I have a headache." Why is this stereotyped female response to a male invitation to sexual intercourse so familiar? One speculative idea is that a female might withhold sexual intercourse under some circumstances in order to get her mate to desert in frustration, because of extra-pair copulations and a desire to form a pair bond with another male. There is something of a reverse Coolidge effect as well: Sexual interest is at its highest during courtship, declines when cohabitation occurs, declines further after marriage, and declines further still after the birth of a child. A final note about the Coolidge effect is that it should not be taken to mean that we should copulate to the exclusion of all else. Other behaviors have fitness implications, too. For example, among lions, where meals are rare and copulations are common, a single meal may contribute more to fitness than a single copulation does.

Duration of coitus

What is the optimal duration for coitus? In polls most Americans report that their last episode of sex lasted between fifteen minutes and an hour[139]. But, in fact, we know neither the duration of the average act of coitus nor the optimal duration. Since the most important consequence of coitus is that insemination occurs, there could be two or more optima for duration. One would be a prolonged act of coitus providing maximum psychological satisfaction (perhaps enhancing the pair bond), another would be a brief act minimizing time and energy expenditure. This theoretical speculation supports something that sexually active couples already know: Long, luxurious sexual intercourse is nice, but a "quickie" is also a satisfactory experience.

Contraception and sterilization

Contraception is a new and very powerful selection pressure. The pleasurable sensations associated with sexual intercourse have evolved for the very reason that they are conducive to reproduction. However, through cultural evolution Americans have adopted behaviors that subvert the natural connection between sexual pleasure and reproduction. The necessity of male orgasm to ensure ejaculation under the right circumstances, and subsequent fertilization, has served as a successful proximate mechanism throughout the phylogenetic history of our primate ancestors and beyond. Variability in female orgasmic response is a result of its not being essential to impregnation. Since the beginning of the 19th century, the mean number of children produced by a European woman who survives to menopause has fallen from approximately seven to fewer than two[196]. The United States has a total fertility rate of 1.7-1.8, which is below the replacement rate of 2.1[227]. More recent data from the 1990 U.S. Census suggested that the United States was at the replacement rate. Modern contraception is the product of a technological environment that is very different from the one in which human genes were naturally selected. There is no reason to assume that such behavior is ''adaptive''; indeed, it appears maladaptive in most forms. It is a thwarting of a proximate mechanism that helped ensure reproductive success from a time long before hominids arose. The use of contraception could rightly be called an epidemic in America from the viewpoint of reproductive success. Approximately sixty percent of American women of reproductive age use contraception. Of the remaining forty percent not using contraception, most are not going to become pregnant anyway, for a variety of reasons including: not having sexual intercourse, sterility, or being already pregnant or postpartum. Family planning promoters assert that most forms of artificial contraception are safer than pregnancy. For example, Lee et al.[122] stated:

> The various contraceptive methods have health risks, but pregnancy itself has attendant risks of morbidity and mortality. (p. 49)

They fail to point out that there is an evolutionary return from the risk taken in a pregnancy (a child) -- but what is the return from artificial contraception? Furthermore, as pointed out by Sachs et al.[180], by 1975 mortality patterns had changed so that pregnancy prevention was responsible for nearly as many deaths as pregnancy itself. Because fertility control causes nearly as many maternal deaths as does pregnancy, it is unrealistic to ignore the costs of contraception in the strategic planning of the optimum life history. Indeed, for older women the risk of death from oral contraceptive usage is greater than the risk of death from pregnancy. Jain[109] reported that oral contraceptive use carries a greater risk of mortality than pregnancy and childbirth for women who are both over 40 and smokers. This risk pattern may also be true for women aged 30-49 who are heavy smokers. Even allowing for changes in the pharmacology of oral contraceptives over the years, it is a tragedy of dramatic proportions that pregnancy prevention in America is (or was) responsible for nearly as many deaths as pregnancy itself. It is not only a tragedy, but also a clear indicator of how terribly misinformed Americans are about their reproductive behavior. Intrauterine birth control devices (IUDs) are still promoted in the Third World, while most Western women have become wary of them because of the adverse effects on reproductive health. There is evidence that they should be avoided by all. Levonorgestrel implants (Norplant) have been demonstrated to be a particularly effective form of contraception for adolescent mothers[161], and their contribution to the prevention of teenage pregnancy is thought to be great[92]. But it is my view that teenage girls are too young to be able to make an informed decision about whether they actually want implants placed in them for long-term contraception; they might, if fully aware of the consequences of implants, choose instead to remain fertile and have additional children. Of all married American women of childbearing age in 1982, approximately 23 percent had been surgically sterilized, and about 12 percent of married American men had undergone vasectomies[145]. At present it is reasonable to estimate that over 30 percent of all American married couples have at least one person who has been surgically sterilized. This high percentage of sterilized people reflects a gradual build-up of a permanent form of contraception. Sterilization represents only a small percentage of each year's new contraception adoptions, but because the dropout rates for other types of contraception are much higher, the overall percentage of contraception by sterilization grows. In spite of the highly visible movement protesting abortion in America, abortion, in most cases, actually has a smaller impact on reproductive success than sterilization, a procedure which attracts surprisingly little attention considering its ruinous effects on fertility.

There is evolutionary conflict in the family planning message of ''health for mother and child,'' especially when it is used to promote suppression of female fertility with artificial contraception. There is additional risk for infants born to very young and very old mothers, for first births and for infants at very high birth orders, and for infants born after a very short birth interval[81]. But deliberately spacing births at greater intervals than would occur naturally is likely to be an evolutionary mistake. In an evolutionary context, a woman is not trying to maximize the chance of survival of any one infant (or even maximize the chance of her own survival), rather she is trying to maximize the number of offspring (raised to the age of reproduction) produced over her lifetime. Natural processes such as hormonal feedback systems working in the woman's body are among the best determinants of optimal fertility. Use of artificial birth control, in comparison, involves the possibility of delaying reproduction too long and consequently under-reproducing. Starting reproduction young seems to be an important factor in producing a large family. Delaying reproduction reduces risk slightly at the cost of reducing total number of offspring produced. While there is increased risk to infants born to very old mothers, there is a natural process to terminate female reproduction when a woman is too old on biological grounds to bear a child; it is menopause. Menopause has evolved to terminate female reproduction when it is adaptive. It should be trusted over the opinions of artificial contraception purveyors who have their own social agenda. An example will serve to clarify the optimal birth spacing question.

Compare the reproductive success of a woman (A) who has a birth interval of one year and gives birth to children yearly over a five year period with woman (B) who has a longer birth interval of four years and gives birth only twice during the five year period. Woman (A) gives birth to five children and woman (B) gives birth to two children. If none of the infants of woman (B) die, mortality of the infants of woman (A) would have to be 60 percent for woman (A) to be less successful in net reproduction than woman (B). In practice, such high rates of infant mortality are not observed in the West for even closely spaced infants. Instead of the 600 infant deaths per 1000 births required of woman (A) to negate her reproductive advantage, it is difficult to identify even 1 infant death per 1000 births from this cause in the West. And this example is a simple demonstration of why long birth intervals do not represent an optimal reproductive strategy. For practical purposes, an American woman is not likely to be able to produce too many offspring in her lifetime, considering the abundance of resources and the brevity of her fertile years.

Maternal mortality varies from culture to culture, being much higher in non-Western societies. The World Bank[226] reported that an African woman has one chance in 22 of dying from causes related to childbearing; a South Asian woman one chance in 34; a South American woman one chance in 115; a northern European woman one chance in 10,000; an American woman one chance in 6,500. This differential mortality is a consequence of a number of causes, including the greater risk associated with pregnancy and delivery in the Third World due to lack of adequate medical care; the greater prevalence of infectious diseases, which are cofactors in some deaths; and the higher incidence of pregnancy and the greater number of pregnancies per woman[230]. In America, not only is giving birth desirable in accordance with the evolutionary ethic, it is also safe. In 1983 the maternal mortality rate in the U.S.A. was only 8 per 100,000 births[228].

The **life-lesson here is: Individuals should not use any form of contraception.**

It might be said that this prohibition of contraception is the *pièce de résistance* of the life-lessons, considering its impact on fitness. Further, one should curtail one's mate's use of contraception. If one cannot prevail by discussion, one should resort to subterfuge or to sabotage in stopping a mate's use of contraception. These conclusions may come as a surprise, and it is not clear which may shock the average American reader more: starting reproduction at 13 *or* stopping at 50 for a woman and later for a man. We must also keep in mind that in a growing population it is an adaptive strategy to shorten the generation time. In this sense one gets disproportionately high benefits in reproductive success from children born early in life, and this reason is another good one for starting reproduction while young. Because contraceptives are more dangerous to one's reproduction than most illicit drugs, one should support new legislation for contraceptives interdiction. Federal regulations against contraception would be the start of a spectacular increase in reproductive success for Americans.

Since it is clear that I object in general to the use of contraception, it is appropriate to ask if the use of contraception is justified under extreme circumstances, say by a nutritionally deprived family who cannot provide enough food to raise a child. The answer is no, it is not. An act of coitus requires approximately one hundred calories. Rather than use contraception and continue having coitus, it would be better for the energy limited family to abstain from sexual intercourse until such time that the energy budget has increased. Five hundred acts of sexual intercourse are the energy equivalent of producing a newborn baby. So under unusual circumstances there can actually be a tradeoff of reduced rates of sexual intercourse for an increased number of offspring. A brief note on a related issue: Because coitus is so costly in energy, it may not be a coincidence that fasting is accompanied by abstention from coitus in some cultures. Of course, it could be argued that sexual intercourse might, under some circumstances, have a function in addition to fertilization that helps to maximize reproductive success. However, that possibility of an additional function does not necessarily mean that the possibility of fertilization needs to be precluded in order to attain it. But under rare and strange conditions the use of contraception might lead to increased reproductive success. This statement is not a loophole that one should consider exploiting to avoid the no contraception rule given in the life-lesson above, because conditions for the adaptive use of contraception are not prevalent in America today.

Safe sex

Contraception is an issue that is linked to safe sex, especially the use of condoms. There is no substitute for being informed about the state of health of your sexual partner. A healthy partner means that it is almost impossible to imagine a justification for the use of a condom. However, since there are sexually transmitted diseases and other health problems among humans that preclude normal coitus, let us consider them in relation to the condom. The first point that needs to be made is that there is a tradeoff of a decrease in fertility for a possible increase in health when using a condom. Four scenarios can be considered. In the first scenario, both the male and the female are healthy. In this scenario, a condom is not used because both the male and the female benefit when insemination occurs. In the second scenario, the female is healthy and the male is unhealthy. No sexual intercourse should occur. In this scenario a condom is not used because sexual intercourse does not occur. It does not occur because the semen or sex organ of the male is infectious and can transmit disease from the male to the female if an attempt at fertilization is made.

In the third scenario, the female is unhealthy and the male is healthy. In this scenario, a condom is used, but because both the male and the female will benefit if insemination occurs, the semen in the condom is used in the fashion of artificial insemination after sexual intercourse is completed. In the fourth scenario, both the female and the male are unhealthy. If they have different sexually transmitted diseases, then the approach of the second scenario applies. If they have the same sexually transmitted disease, then it is not clear that sexual intercourse without a condom is risky. Both the female and the male benefit if insemination occurs, so no condom is used in this scenario. So of the four scenarios, none of them employ a condom in the style ordinarily advocated by condom advocates. This analysis is another example of how evolutionary thinking can bring clarity to controversial topics and even challenge the logic of a *cause célèbre* like condom promotion. This argument does not imply that the medical aspects of sexually transmitted diseases can be ignored. Even if the tactics described above are used, it would almost always make sense to have a sexually transmitted disease treated by a physician. Some sexually transmitted diseases can permanently threaten one's fertility, adversely affect one's health and also can have highly adverse effects on the development of the fetus.

Proception

The term proception, as used by Miller[141], is behavior that is intended to increase the likelihood of successful conception, and in this sense is the opposite of contraception. As Americans grow aware of the importance of maximizing reproductive success, the use of proception is likely to increase. Miller[141] wrote:

> Proception begins after an individual or couple decides to have a baby. Once this decision is in place, a question naturally arises concerning how this goal may be achieved. For most the answer is simply to have regular sexual intercourse while discontinuing the use of any contraception. Many go further in their efforts to achieve conception, increasing the frequency of sexual intercourse and/or timing intercourse to occur during what they perceive as a fertile period in the woman's menstrual cycle. If these efforts are unsuccessful over several months, many will make additional efforts, such as further altering their sexual practices, altering other aspects of their behavior in ways that they believe will facilitate conception (e.g., changing their diet, pattern of exercise, sleep habits, work schedule), or seeking additional information or medical help. It is this entire set of activities that is encompassed by the term proception. (pp. 580-581)

At present, proception is sometimes associated with a woman's earlier choice to delay childbearing, and it is intended to counter the adverse effects of attempting to reproduce at a later reproductive age, such as increased time required to conceive, partial sterility, and high risk of losing a pregnancy. Miller[141] explored the antecedents to conception in a study of 967 women residing in the San Francisco Bay area and using multiple regression analysis. He found that proception is by far the most important factor out of a group of factors including, among others, frequency of sexual intercourse and frequency of contraceptive non-use in determining the occurrence of conception. One day the commonness of proception may be on parity with contraception in America, or perhaps will exceed it, as occurs in some traditional non-Western cultures with their fertility rites and practices.

Life-lesson: Practice proception.

Sperm competition

I would like to begin this section on sperm competition with an observation by Camus[20]:

> You must have noticed that men who really suffer from jealousy have no more urgent desire than to go to bed with the woman they nevertheless think has betrayed them. (p. 105)

It is indeed true that some men have noted that their sexual appetite has become voracious when they suspected their mate of infidelity. This trend is counter to the behavior that might be expected at such a time in a weak psychological model of infidelity, which would predict a resulting aloofness toward and rejection of the unfaithful woman by the cuckolded man. But that weak psychological model results in a failed prediction. In contrast, an evolutionary analysis offers a subtle and comprehensive explanation. It would appear that Camus anticipated my co-discovery with Irven DeVore in 1974 of the application of sperm competition to primates (see Popp and DeVore[164]). Here is a brief outline of the argument. Male-male competition for reproductive success does not necessarily terminate after a copulation with an estrous female. Competition between males is extended to the gametic level in those cases where more than one male copulates with a single female during a single estrous period. Competition between gametes from different males for access to a mature ovum is called sperm competition. Although humans do not have estrus, the same effect is achieved when more than one man copulates with a woman near the time of ovulation in a single ovulatory cycle. Sperm competition is now a popular concept, especially in discussion of nonhuman primates which show it as a response to some common social organizations. The result of sperm competition is the evolution of large testes relative to body mass and copulatory rates that are high in populations where it occurs. Sexual selection for size of testes occurs as a tradeoff for the benefit of increased sperm production with increased testes size *versus* increased metabolic cost for increased testes size. The combined weight of mature male testes is known to be highly correlated with daily sperm production, in both continuous breeding and seasonal breeding mammals[3]. In some species, like chimpanzees, it is common for more than one male to copulate with an estrous female during a single ovulatory cycle. Popp and DeVore[164] stated:

> Under such conditions, one expects that sexual selection will favor those males that deposit the largest quantity of sperm in the female reproductive tract -- hence, the extremely high relative testicular weight among male chimpanzees as compared to the other great apes and man. Thus, ... male chimpanzees employ sperm competition as a reproductive strategy. Schultz (1938) and Wislocki (1942) report the following body and testes weight for the great apes: chimpanzees weighing an average of 44.34 kg had an average combined testicular weight of 118.8 gm, or 0.268% of their body weight; gibbons weighing 5.54 kg had 4.6 gm or 0.083%; orangutans weighing 74.64 kg had 35.3 gm or 0.047%; gorillas weighing approximately 200 kg had 36 gm or 0.018%; men weighing 63.54 kg had 50.2 gms or 0.079%. Chimpanzees clearly have testes that are significantly heavier, both relative to body weight and absolutely, than the testes of all other Hominidea [Hominoidea]. Such divergence cannot be attributed to allometric growth, but relates directly to differences in the breeding strategies of chimpanzees from the other species mentioned. (pp. 334-335)

The interpretation of the above data is straightforward. The gorilla breeding strategy is to exclude other reproducing males from the harem of females -- one adult male has exclusive sexual access. Therefore, there is little sperm competition. Gibbons are monogamous and adult males defend a territory that contains their mates from intruding males. Again, this condition is not one that favors a large amount of sperm competition. Adult male orangutans range over a large area that contains one to many adult females, and they exclude other adult males from this area. There is little opportunity for sperm competition with such a social organization. But among chimpanzees, many males often mate sequentially over a period of a few hours or days with a single estrous female. The conditions are precisely those that favor maximum sperm competition. Humans vary greatly in their mating strategies. The figures reported above for relative testes size indicate that humans are in the middle of the range observed in the Hominoidea for the degree of sperm competition: less sperm competition among humans than among chimpanzees and gibbons, more sperm competition than among gorillas and orangutans. I propose the hypothesis that testes size varies in human populations according to their mating system. The men in populations that historically were promiscuous should have larger testes (relative to body mass) than men in populations with high fidelity to long-term mates. And because of the increased autonomy of women in matrilocal and matrilineal societies, and the possibility of subsequently increased sexual freedom among the women, one might expect to find the effects of sperm competition there. Although this hypothesis may seen peculiar, it follows logically from the obvious biological fact that in humans, just as in our nonhuman primate relatives, a sperm is just an organism's way of making another organism. When substantial quantities of sperm are required, the evolution of increased testes size is one of the simplest ways to do the job. So there is some reason to believe the folklore that some races of men are capable of more frequent copulation and make more virile lovers. Preliminary evidence cited in Silber[191] suggested that there is indeed interpopulational variation in testes size among humans. In a study of testes size based on autopsy data from Hong Kong, Chinese males had testes one half the size of testes of Caucasian males. Silber correctly invoked the Popp and DeVore[164] argument based on breeding system, but in my opinion further data on the relative rates of promiscuity in historical context for the Hong Kong Chinese population and for the Hong Kong Caucasian population are needed to support the hypothesis in this case. Since the relationship between breeding system and relative testes size is well established, and because we lack data on the historical rates of promiscuity among the Hong Kong Chinese population and among the Hong Kong Caucasian population, the Silber[191] inference is actually in the wrong direction. We may hypothesize that the historical rates of promiscuity were lower among the Hong Kong Chinese population than among the population of Caucasians that settled in Hong Kong because the testes size of members of the Chinese population is small, not that the testes size of members of the Chinese population is small because promiscuity rates were low. It is possible that if one is looking for a faithful wife, the best place to look would be among the women in a population in which the males had small indices of relative testes to body mass.

I predict that among the largest testes found in humans relative to body mass occur in the Trobriand Island population. Historically in that culture sexual intercourse was not recognized as the cause for pregnancy. In the social environment there shaped by the avunculate and promiscuity, women had high rates of sexual contact with men other than their husbands.

Sperm competition occurs only where more than one male copulates with a female during a single estrous period -- thus, its appearance among baboons and their close relatives is dependent upon mating patterns and the social organization of each species. Conditions for sperm competition are not met in baboon populations with a one-male unit type social organization, nor in an age-graded social organization, because in such systems one male has a near monopoly on estrous females in his group. In contrast, baboon species with multi-male troop social organization do meet the conditions required to promote sperm competition as a strategy, since commonly many males may mate sequentially with a female during a single estrous period. Popp[162] demonstrated a highly significant correlation between type of social organization and relative size of testes to body mass among species of baboons and their close relatives. Gelada baboons and hamadryas baboons, both with one-male units, had the smallest relative testes. The mandrill, with age-graded social organization, was intermediate. And anubis baboons, with a multi-male social organization, had the largest relative testes size.

Age-specific strategies in spermatogenesis

Another variable in sperm competition is its variation over the life history of the individual. Although the differences in sperm competition and resulting selection for testes size are most striking in interspecific and interpopulational comparisons, subtler differences are expected among the males of a single population as a function of life history strategies. In the anubis baboon population of Masai Mara, there are clear age effects in male mating success and male dominance in mating contexts. Although mating success is highest among middle-aged prime males, testes are largest in very old males. Data presented by Popp[162] showed a highly significant correlation between age and testes size among subadult and adult males in that population. Testes seem to increase in size among the oldest males just before their deaths. For example, one old male baboon's testes increased in size by 148 percent over a 14 month period while undergoing only a 4 percent increase in body mass during the same period. This increase in the size of testes among very old males is relevant to the last minute reproductive spurt observed in the same males. Increases in testes size and sperm production among very old males represents an increased commitment on their part toward diverting what remains in the energy budget toward reproductive effort. It is a morphological strategy that is compatible with behavioral strategies of intense and risky competition observed in the old males, in which very old males compete at the highest levels of escalated aggression, exposing themselves to extreme risk with resultant severe injuries[162]. Younger males, because of options that exist for them in the future use of reproductive effort, are unwilling to make as large an immediate investment in sperm as is a very old male with no long-term reproductive future. Thus, it appears at three levels: the interspecific, the interpopulational, and the life historical, that something as seemingly trivial as the caloric expenditure in ejaculation is a selected parameter in reproductive effort. The relative size of testes has evolved in primates to accommodate the social and physical environment in which they function.

The penis and penis-like structures have evolved independently many times among arthropods, chordates (e.g., fish, birds, mammals), and other phyla. One view of the function of the penis is to place sperm closer to the site of ovulation, thereby giving the possessor an advantage in fertilization and in sperm competition. Although the relative size of the human penis is a less interesting scientific subject than the relative size of human testes, it is often mentioned in the popular literature. Morris[144] and Diamond[43] pointed out with a semblance of sensationalism that the human penis is the largest among our primate relatives. However, it is not entirely clear that this large size is of the social significance they imply. Rather than being a social signal, it may be a simple adaptation in the male to the diameter and length of the human vagina, which is also the largest birth canal among the primates for the purpose of delivering the human infant, also the largest among the primates. Thus, the evolution of the large size of the human penis may be a secondary consequence of the adaptive value of having large infants. A final thought related to sperm competition involves the relative complexity of life roles played by the diploid stage of humans (men and women) and by the haploid stage of humans (sperm and eggs). While we take for granted that men and women have long and complex lives and that gametes have short and simple lives, such a scenario is not the only possible one. For example, among ferns the haploid stage forms into a plant that has a life of its own. Among insects like the hymenoptera (ants, bees and wasps), with haplodiploid sex determination, the males are haploid and by that fact contain precisely the same genes that each of their identical sperm cells contain, with the exception of new mutations. In effect they are flying gametes. Imagine, if you will, a human sperm that had a life and a ''mind'' of its own. Perhaps it would have instincts that could guide itself unassisted to the reproductive tract of a fertile woman. That could be quite adaptive -- a kind of sperm competition *par excellence*. It would also change the human world. So why has such an adaptation not evolved? See the chapter on ecological considerations for a discussion of organisms as polyhedrons and the limits of natural selection.

Artificial insemination and sperm donation

At the beginning of this discussion about artificial insemination, we need to make an important distinction between artificial insemination by husband and artificial insemination by donor. In the former, a man provides sperm for the fertilization of his wife's egg. In the latter, a donor, often anonymous, provides sperm for the fertilization of an unknown woman. Artificial insemination by husband is useful in treating some forms of infertility. Artificial insemination by donor uses the sperm of a man other than the husband to achieve fertilization when the husband is unable to provide the quality or quantity of sperm required. In an evolutionary analysis, wives should want artificial insemination by donor if the husband is infertile. Husbands, in turn, should choose one of their relatives as a sperm donor in a high technology equivalent of the pattern of polyandry seen in some populations. Artificial insemination by donor is, for practical purposes, adultery from the husband's viewpoint. It is better, and an outright good according to the evolutionary ethic, that he perpetuate some of his genes from a close male relative rather than accept insemination of his wife by an unrelated male. When the opportunity for artificial insemination by husband or artificial insemination by donor occurs, men should be willing donors. Men should also consider the establishment of a bank containing their own sperm for use in case of future infertility or for use after death. Let us consider for a moment the concept of an evolutionarily perfect market and its implications for artificial insemination by donor. An evolutionarily perfect market is very unlike our current economy, for in an evolutionarily perfect market reproductive success is openly bought and sold on the willing seller/willing buyer principle. Participants in the market are rational, i.e. they want to maximize their reproductive success, and they buy and sell accordingly. In such an evolutionarily perfect market, men would actually pay to donate their sperm, rather than be paid, as they are in the current economic system. Some employers now provide exercise facilities to promote the physical fitness of their employees. However, if those employers had the evolutionary fitness of their employees in mind, they would provide masturbatoriums, facilities for the cryogenic storage of sperm samples, and artificial insemination services instead. And in addition to lunch breaks, sexual intercourse breaks in suitably furnished facilities could be a standard part of the workday.

One medical procedure that has more than a little controversy and theoretical significance attached to it is the extraction of viable sperm from men who have been "dead" for up to twenty-four hours. I place "dead" in quotation marks because it is questionable that an individual who is capable of reproducing is actually dead in some important respects. In this procedure, an incision is made in the scrotum, a needle is inserted into the vas deferens (the tube that carries sperm out of the testes), and sperm are retrieved. This operation is ordinarily done only at the special request of the wife or relatives of the patient, who presumably want to use the sperm in an attempt to continue the patient's lineage after his "death". This example of reproducing very late in the life history leads to another practical point about sperm: Male readers should consider cryogenic storage of their sperm while they are still healthy. Most men who store sperm cryogenically are cancer victims who intend to undergo chemotherapy (and in the process lose their ability to make sperm), but there is no reason why healthy men cannot bank their own sperm. Doing so can serve as reproductive insurance in the event of a sexually debilitating injury, disease or premature death. This process is analogous to sperm donation to an infertile couple, with the interesting qualification that your future self is a member of that infertile couple. It is now possible for women to bank their eggs or freeze part of their ovaries in the event of illness or as insurance against delaying reproduction until it would otherwise have been too late.

Orgasm and faked orgasm

Some women, and even some men, fake orgasms during sexual intercourse. Women, beware, if you catch a man faking orgasm during coitus with you, he may be trying to hide his inability to provide sufficient quantities of sperm to bring you to optimal fertility. Analogously, a faked female orgasm may occur in order to extract greater quantities of sperm from the male (who is stimulated by the signs of female orgasm and who ejaculates in greater quantity with greater levels of arousal). Faked female orgasms may also exaggerate the probability of conception occurring subsequent to a given act of coitus, if the assumption is correct that the female orgasm provides an aid to fertilization by increasing the mobility of the gametes in the female reproductive tract by means of contractions. Some might object to this explanation for faked orgasms and assert that they occur because they are intended to please one's sexual partner or to hide embarrassment. But such feelings are merely proximate mechanisms which elicit the behavior, which occurs for the ultimate mechanism of increasing the actor's reproductive success.

This discussion leads to questions regarding exactly what the adaptive significance of the orgasm is. Among males, the interpretation is easy because the male orgasm is closely linked with ejaculation, and ejaculation is a requirement in achieving male reproductive success. Among females the interpretation is not so easy because there is no absolute requirement for a female to have an orgasm in achieving reproductive success. The possibilities for the evolutionary significance of the female orgasm are: 1. it is adaptive, i.e. it serves a useful purpose in increasing the reproductive success of women who have them, as stated in the sperm mobility and sperm extraction hypotheses above, 2. it is maladaptive, i.e. it is harmful to reproductive success, by increasing the metabolic cost of coitus and increasing female autoeroticism that interferes with reproductive behavior, 3. it is a pleiotropic effect, i.e. it is the chance by-product of selection for something else, as put forth in the hypothesis that female orgasms are just a side effect of the anatomy of female genitalia having structures homologous to the anatomy of male genitalia, (e.g., the clitoris is homologous to the penis,) which were selected to function in a certain way in the males, but do so in females without selective purpose. 4. It is vestigial, i.e. it once served a useful evolutionary purpose, but no longer does so. 5. It is a preadaptation, i.e. it existed in the past for reasons other than the current or future adaptive significance that it has or will have.

Egg donation and surrogate mothers

Sperm donation is perhaps more easily accepted than egg donation at the emotional level. A wife giving birth to children who are not the genetic offspring of her husband is common as adultery. But a woman giving birth to children who are not *her* genetic offspring is quite novel. Egg donation accompanied by fertilization by the husband's sperm may be desirable to some women who want to experience the birth process. The egg donor, or more often egg "seller," undergoes treatment with fertility drugs and surgery; in return her genotype is perpetuated and she receives at present about three thousand dollars. Some concern has been expressed regarding the rights of economically disadvantaged women who may be induced to act as egg donors for the financial compensation offered. However, it appears that the risk to the donors is small, and quite obviously the reward of having a child without the need for additional investment beyond producing an egg is an unusual and good opportunity from the evolutionary view. Therefore, even if the financial compensation offered is the immediate reason for the decision to serve as a donor, it is not a bad decision. Few people raise the question about the outcome for the women who are the recipients of the donor eggs. It would seem that their position is far more tenuous from the evolutionary viewpoint. After all, the recipients of the donor eggs are serving as surrogate mothers, who would ordinarily be financially compensated *themselves*. In an evolutionarily perfect market, egg recipients would be paid for their gestational and socializing services by the egg donor. A related topic is that of embryo freezing. This procedure might be a viable strategy to extend the reproductive life of a woman and a man, particularly in reference to extending childbearing years into the less fertile later years in a woman's life and actually beyond menopause. Frozen embryos will retain their viability almost indefinitely, ready for implantation into the female donor's uterus or into the uterus of a surrogate mother.

To become a surrogate mother can involve either of two very different procedures: surrogacy with zygote donation and surrogacy with sperm donation. The viewpoints of sociological mother and genetical mother should differ if they are not one in the same. In an evolutionarily perfect market, surrogates who carried an unrelated zygote would charge more for their services than surrogates who provided the egg. At present, there is a standard surrogacy fee of approximately twelve thousand dollars. And a surrogate who is a relative of the woman providing the egg (an increasingly common situation) should perhaps charge less for her services than unrelated surrogates. Today we must make a clear distinction between the term birth mother and the term genetical mother. Once the term birth mother meant that the same woman was the genetical mother. But with the advent of egg donation and *in vitro* fertilization, it is no longer necessarily so. Egg donation and sperm donation give rise to some questions about our traditional view of parenthood. For we now have genetic parenthood, uterine parenthood, and social parenthood. When it comes to the question about who has the rights to form a family with the child, we must conclude unequivocally that it is those who are the genetic parents, unless they have given informed consent to forgo that right. A child has only one mother and one father, and they are genetic relatives who provide the gametes for the creation of the child. Other roles, such as gestation and socialization, are often associated with parenthood and are sometimes confused for parenthood, but in fact do not constitute true parenthood. From the mid-eighties to early nineties, about one thousand five hundred babies were born by surrogacy in America. That number will increase considerably in this decade and in coming decades. It might be an appropriate time to apply the evolutionary ethic in determining the parental rights of those involved. Another anomaly could be corrected by an evolutionarily perfect market: At present the woman who gets possession of the baby pays for the services of the other woman, regardless of whether the other woman is the egg donor or egg recipient!

Masturbation

The adaptive significance of masturbatory behavior has on occasion been discussed by sociobiologists. For example, in elderly males it may help them to retain sexual function during periods when intercourse is not possible. But a central question is: Why is it prevalent among adolescent males? Does it serve as an adaptive substitute for sexual intercourse by developing or maintaining sexual function? Or might old, perhaps less potent sperm be discharged in the process, thereby increasing the male's fertility[5]? Another hypothesis is that it may be a way to improve the chances of being chosen by a mate. In this tactic, males masturbate in order not to appear desperate for a mate and thereby increase acceptance by a potential mate. This hypothesis also posits a tendency among females to avoid males with low previous mating success, and that they have a means of detecting it which can be duped by males who practice masturbation. Culturgen manipulation is another hypothesis. In other words, masturbatory behavior is elicited by culturgens such as erotica in the mass media. This hypothesis is not well supported because of the fact that masturbation is prevalent in other mammals including primates, where culture is absent. But do humans masturbate more than other animals? My field studies of hamadryas and anubis baboons living in the wild indicate that they are less likely than humans to engage in autoeroticism. This comparison is a useful one because anubis baboons are rather sexually intense as far as primates go. A final hypothesis is that masturbation is a cost of having a responsive reproductive system that would be much more costly to eliminate than to simply allow to exist. A fellow anthropologist, who shall go unnamed, declared about the sexual frustration caused by the isolation of fieldwork in remote places: "One in the bush is worth two in the hand". He intended it to be a mischievous jest, and with equal mischief I shall elevate his declaration to the status of an anthropological truism and thereby conclude this section on masturbation.

Pornography

If pornography replaces normal sexual activities, it is not desirable. But if it enhances the frequency of sexual intercourse, it is desirable. It is almost impossible for the average modern American to have too much sexual intercourse because, historically, lower resource availability required lower frequencies of sexual intercourse to achieve optimal fertility. Now, with high resource availability, more sexual intercourse than we are casually inclined to have is required to reach the optimum. Accordingly, if males, who seem most interested in pornography anyway, are stimulated by it to increase their frequency of copulation with their female partners, it would make sense to describe pornography as good.

Ovulation and menstruation

Today, American girls start to menstruate on the average when they are 12.6 years old; a century ago the age was 15.5 years[66]. This reduction in age is the result of reaching the critical weight and fatness for menarche earlier as a result of improved nutrition. One of the remarkable things about ovulation in human females is that it is cryptic, unlike in other primates where it is advertised. The main selection pressure is not entirely clear at present. There are a number of competing hypotheses that I do not intend to discuss. But the hypothesis which is most plausible is explained here. First, we know that the evolution of exaggerated sexual receptivity in baboons (the opposite of the cryptic ovulation in women) is associated with greatly increased levels of aggression, mostly male-male aggression (but also the occasional fatal injury of an estrous female by males competing over her), and the reverse may also be true. As in many human societies in which males are always present, male baboons stay in the troop and in association with females even when those females are not in estrus. The adaptive significance of cryptic ovulation could be due to selection for reduced mating aggression in humans. Rates of escalated aggression and murder in human society, even with the presence of potentially lethal weapons are, in fact, much lower than in the wild anubis baboons that I studied. Reduced mating competition could result in lower rates of injury to the female herself, or to mates who could invest in her offspring, and could facilitate social group harmony and cooperation with subsequent benefits to kith and kin. Synchronized menstrual cycles, which have been observed in women living together, help to accomplish the same end, because ovulating synchronously would also reduce male-male competition.

Recent speculation about the adaptive significance of menstruation suggests that it may be a method of avoiding infection due to germs carried on sperm. However, medical evidence indicates that rates of female pelvic infections increase rather than decrease after menstruation. But under natural conditions menstruation is rare anyway. Women in non-Western cultures are either pregnant or infertile (due to lactational suppression of ovulation, undernutrition, delayed menarche or menopause). Nutritional stress in lactating mothers leads to prolonged lactational amenorrhea and subfecundity[128]. This relationship holds particularly true for Third World women on marginal diets. Either a better diet or a reduction in the mother's workload during lactation can be expected to reduce the period of lactational infecundity[128]. But it is clear that lactational amenorrhea occurs in well-nourished Americans, too[179]. In Africa, breastfeeding prevents about four births per woman, whereas modern contraceptives only prevent about half a birth there (based on data in the World Fertility Survey[227]). Demographic studies of the hunter-gatherers of the Kalahari (the !Kung) in southern Africa show that even though they had no modern form of contraception, they had a mean interbirth interval of 4.12 years and an average completed family size of 4.7[99]. The !Kung are known to have high suckling rates which are believed to reduce the fertility of the mother. Breastfeeding delays the resumption of normal ovarian cycles by disrupting the pattern of release of gonadotropin releasing hormone from the hypothalamus and hence luteinizing hormone from the pituitary[136].

Infertility

In some cultures, a woman's marriage prospects increase after her first child because she has proven her fertility. In America, a high percentage of brides are pregnant at the time of their wedding. In the antigenitive environment in which Americans find themselves now living, being pregnant at the altar is usually viewed as a condition that forced the marriage. But could there not also be a component of the couple having proven their fertility as well, and accordingly being more willing to make a long-term commitment to each other? Lack of offspring in a pair-bond over an extended period should, theoretically, weaken the pair-bond because it may be a sign of infertility in the other partner. One species of bird, the kittiwake gull, is three times more likely to change mates if it failed to hatch eggs in the previous season than if it had success in breeding; Wilson[222] stated that this correlation suggests that "divorce" may be adaptively advantageous to birds paired with a reproductively incompatible partner. Both consciously and unconsciously, childlessness in human society has been a traditional grounds for divorce. It is somewhat surprising that ethnographers have not documented a broad pattern of divorce associated with infertility in cross-cultural studies. One partial explanation for the failure of this pattern to emerge more conspicuously is that most cultures are polygynous. In that pattern of marriage it may be that the common behavior is to add a wife when an existing wife is infertile, but to allow the infertile wife to retain the status of wife. In such a system divorce would not be associated with infertility, even though new pair bonds are formed.

There is evidence that the reproductive functions of the human body decrease or cease when reproduction is too risky or futile. Women who are very lean experience amenorrhea, and men who are too lean experience a loss in libido, reduction of prostate fluid, and lessened motility and longevity of sperm[66]. Menstrual disorders associated with extreme leanness are associated with the activity of the hypothalamus, the part of the brain that regulates reproduction as well as food intake and other basic functions[66]. Frisch[66] put the argument in terms of adaptive response:

> It is not surprising that the reproductive function of the hypothalamus falters when a woman becomes too lean. Such a response would have given our female ancestors a selective advantage by ensuring that they conceived only when they could complete a pregnancy successfully .... In ancient times, when the food supply was scarce or fluctuated seasonally and when breast milk was a newborn's only food, a woman who became pregnant when she lacked an adequate store of body fat -- the most readily mobilized fuel in the body -- could have endangered both her own life and that of her developing fetus and newborn infant.
>
> Indeed, one can speculate that females who continued to ovulate in spite of being undernourished left no viable offspring or did not survive themselves; they therefore left no descendants. Thus natural selection had its way: today most women have more than [25 percent] of their weight in fat .... Men, in contrast, have roughly from 12 to 14 percent of their weight in fat at maturity. (p. 88)

A basic reason why many American couples today are having trouble in having children is that they have waited too long to start a family. Over the last two decades American women have added three years to the age at which they have their first child. Many are trying to have a baby for the first time in their thirties and forties. Because of the risk of disease and senescence, those decades are past the prime years of fecundity. Endometriosis, the risk of which increases with age, causes about thirty percent of female infertility. Women who smoke have greater than a three times greater chance of not conceiving for a year than nonsmokers. The quality or quantity of the man's sperm is responsible for about 40 percent of infertility cases. Inexplicably, infrequent intercourse may be the cause of infertility in some couples wishing to conceive. This cause may be a holdover from times when the caloric cost of intercourse was consequential in the energy budget. Today, with our expanded energy budgets, the cost of intercourse (about one hundred calories) seems trivial, but this triviality may not always have been so. The fact that sperm production per gram of testicular tissue is low (about one-sixth the amount of sperm) in humans compared to many other animals[191] indicates that there has been selection for a reduced male reproductive effort in terms of the cost of ejaculating. But that is strictly the historical perspective and not very relevant to optimal copulatory strategies among Americans today with their grossly inflated energy budgets. Here are the facts relevant to the new American environment: Since the positive correlation between coital frequency and the probability of conception is clear in measures of fecundability, even at intercoital intervals as small as 24 hours[165,166], the average American would probably be displaying adaptive behavior by having sexual intercourse more frequently than he or she is casually inclined to have.

Fertility clinics offer treatment of infertility, and are based on the fact that many problems causing infertility are treatable, e.g., with fertility drugs or *in vitro* fertilization. Seek the care of a fertility specialist if you are having fertility problems. The cost-benefit ratio in trading wealth for reproductive success is almost always to your advantage in doing so. While fertility drugs help many women to conceive, a recent report by Rossing et al.[175] linked fertility treatment and ovarian tumors. For example, there is a statistically significant increase in ovarian tumors after using the drug clomiphene citrate to help induce ovulation. This book provides a theory for weighing the costs and benefits of just such reproductive decisions: health or reproductive success. It supports the choice that many women are already making intuitively -- to continue to take the fertility drug in order to get pregnant. The logic is simple: If alternative reproductive strategies are lacking, the personal risk involved in the existing strategy of using a fertility drug is acceptable from an evolutionary perspective. The high cost of *in vitro* fertilization is an indicator of the intense desire for some couples to have a child. In 1994, on average the cost incurred per successful delivery (defined as at least one live birth) ranged from $66,667 for the first cycle to $114,286 for the sixth cycle of *in vitro* fertilization[152]. In the year 2000, the costs are much lower, and some parts of the procedure can be covered by health insurance. A cycle is defined as a four step procedure: taking fertility drugs, retrieval of eggs, fertilization of eggs, and finally the implantation of zygotes. Neumann et al.[152] entered the debate on whether health insurance should cover the cost of *in vitro* fertilization when they stated:

> Even those who believe that procreation is a fundamental right would not provide unlimited resources for a couple's pursuit of a child. (p. 242)

Since "unlimited resources" do not exist in reality, I take that expression to mean very large resources. The appropriateness of providing "unlimited resources for a couple's pursuit of a child" depends very much on who is doing the viewing. From the couple's viewpoint (and there were forty thousand of these couples in 1993 employing *in vitro* fertilization), if they lack alternative opportunities to help other relatives reproduce, if someone else is bearing the cost of the medical procedure, and if these benefits are not transferable, they might indeed think that the utilization of very large resources is quite appropriate. For alternative views we need go no further than the insurance company or members of the insurance pool --

they might favor a more guarded expenditure of their funds. It is interesting that proception has made the greatest impact in aiding couples to reproduce who have some form of pathology. Both the desire for children and the willingness to take extreme steps to have them seem to occur in proportion to the difficulty involved in becoming a parent. But advanced techniques in proception may remain the exclusive domain of the fertility clinics not much longer. With the spread of progenitive philosophy, proception may be in wide demand among individuals with normal reproductive capacities.

Treatment is available for most of the two million American men with fertility problems. One of many techniques for men with low sperm counts involves injecting a single sperm into the egg under laboratory conditions in a special kind of *in vitro* fertilization. Though treating male fertility problems is usually more expensive than artificial insemination by another sperm donor, it is highly preferable in terms of the evolutionary ethic. Even if the sperm donor is a close relative, such as a full brother, one would have to raise twice the number of children to equal the inclusive fitness of any number of children engendered by oneself. Since humans have evolved a tendency to produce few offspring, it is important that the few children one does raise be closely related to oneself -- there is little opportunity to compensate low regression coefficients of relatedness by producing increased numbers of offspring.

There are only two alternatives to individual reproduction that are adaptive. The first is to assist relatives to reproduce at levels above what they could achieve without assistance. The second, only applicable under the difficult to achieve conditions of a small population of mostly distantly and unrelated individuals, is spiteful behavior, in which one impedes the reproduction of individuals of less than an average regression coefficient of relatedness to oneself. Among humans, neither alternative has proven to be a major strategic success. While almost all humans do help relatives to survive and reproduce, this kin directed altruism rarely becomes the main mode of reproduction as it does among sterile workers in the eusocial insects. Instead, most humans participate in individual reproduction as well, and that strategy comprises most of the reproductive success that they attain.

It is interesting that infertility is not more often the result of sexual maiming in the animal world. In a small population with long-term competition for mates, one individual might theoretically gain by maiming a same-sex competitor. Or an individual might maim his/her mate to deny him/her the opportunity for reproductive success outside the bond and to further his/her commitment to investing in their joint existing offspring. Sexual maiming of this sort does occur in banana slugs. They are hermaphroditic mollusks that cannibalize each others' penises after copulation. This bizarre strategy reduces the probability that the mate will copulate again, thereby decreasing the chance of sperm competition and increasing the commitment of the victim to the production of eggs, both to the advantage of the cannibal. There is also a group of parasites that castrate their new hosts as a first order of business in their parasitism. Castrated hosts live longer than uncastrated hosts, and divert reproductive effort to somatic use; both of these consequences are to the adaptive advantage of the parasite because more time and energy is provided for its own reproduction. Suppression of sexual reproduction by conspecifics is common in the social insects where, by chemical means, castes are rendered infertile. This suppression of sexuality by pheromones covers the range from outright exploitation to cooperation by the affected individuals. Among humans we have the phenomenon of eunuchs. Male castration is prevalent in history. Ottoman Turks, Persians, Greeks, Romans, and Chinese all had eunuchs. Tannahill[201] wrote:

> In Christian Byzantium eunuchs really came into their own. The violent record of imperial succession led its rulers to choose ministers and even Church patriarchs who were believed to have been freed from family ambition by their inability to father children, and eight of the chief posts of the empire were reserved for them. The result was that parents with several sons began to have one or two of them castrated, on the principle that they would be able to exert influence on behalf of their uncastrated brothers. (p. 248)

Castration has also been used in the West as a deterrent to anti-social behavior. In recent times castration has been a form of punishment/deterrent for sex crimes. Tannahill[201] wrote:

> In San Diego, California, between 1955 and 1975, 397 sex offenders chose to be castrated rather than serve a long jail sentence. In Denmark between 1929 and 1959, 300 prisoners or detainees made the same choice. In Britain, chemical suppressants of the sex urge are preferred. (p. 247)

Pregnancy

The average woman needs about 2,100 calories a day. This requirement rises to between 2,500 and 2,700 calories per day during a pregnancy. It takes about 50,000 to 80,000 calories to produce a baby[66, 114]. Because of the increased caloric requirement with pregnancy, an increase in body weight for women who are at the ideal height to weight ratio makes sense during pregnancy. The optimal body weight increase during pregnancy above the ideal not pregnant weight is 20-30 pounds. Also consult your physician regarding any special nutritional requirements that you may have during pregnancy. For example, a daily dietary supplement of 1 mg of folic acid is highly desirable for pregnant women, because it greatly decreases the infant's risk of neural tube defect. Some species show nutrient specific hungers, i.e. they have a desire to eat certain foods that contain the nutrients of which they are in short supply. It is not clear that humans do. However, pregnant women do often have cravings and if they go uncontrolled can lead to pica, which is defined as a depraved appetite for unwholesome substances like dirt. Some pregnant women in eastern Africa do eat soil, and go to considerable lengths to get certain soils such as the clay from termite mounds.

Patterns of sexual intercourse during pregnancy vary with cross-cultural attitudes. In some cultures it is prohibited. In others it is believed to be important for the development of the fetus *in utero*. It is easy to imagine that sexual intercourse during pregnancy could be a mechanism for ensuring male presence and material support for the pregnant woman, thereby providing indirect assistance to the pregnancy. In the West there is medical evidence relating intercourse during pregnancy to spontaneous abortion. Some physicians believe that sexual intercourse during the first few weeks of pregnancy and during the last few weeks of pregnancy can endanger the pregnancy in some women who are at high risk for spontaneous abortion. Men in Western cultures sometimes find that they lose sexual interest in their partner while she is pregnant. This lack of male interest is often accompanied by regret over the lack of sexual intercourse on the part of the pregnant woman. This conflict of drives may have a biological basis. From the viewpoint of the husband, additional copulations with a pregnant wife will not lead to additional conceptions, but extramarital sexual intercourse might. From the viewpoint of the wife, additional copulations while she is pregnant may be a way of keeping her husband from straying.

Birth

Humans follow the primate pattern of tending to give birth in the early morning hours, to the inconvenience of obstetricians. The example of baboons giving birth in the early morning hours is instructive. The natural environment of baboons contains predators that can quickly eliminate females who fall behind the troop progression to give birth during the day. Instead, females give birth in the early morning hours in the comparative safety of the sleeping trees, where the troop is stationary and safe for a number of hours. Humans, too, were once more mobile and more exposed to predators during the day in their natural environments. Giving birth at night meant benefiting from the comparative safety of a sleeping place.

Considering how few births there are in America, there is an inordinate amount of lively discussion about birth techniques. Natural childbirth is advocated by some, and it may be acceptable in most cases. Only about 1 percent of births in America require the high technology available in a hospital obstetrics ward. When giving birth at home, it is very helpful to have an experienced midwife present. Giving birth while immersed in water, a popular fad, is preposterous. It is entirely out of keeping with our primate heritage. A more enlightened practice in phylogenetic context would be to give birth in a tree! But I am not making a strong argument in favor of an arboreal mode of birth, because many nonhuman primates descend from the sleeping trees to give birth on the ground. Until the newborn nonhuman primate can cling to the mother's ventral surface shortly after birth, it is not equipped to survive in a tree.

Cesarean section is now commonplace and is among the most over-prescribed major surgery in the U.S.A. today. It is strange that the other two most commonly abused major medical procedures, elective abortion and hysterectomy, also deal with aspects of female reproductive function. It would appear that a strong antigenitive bias exists in operating rooms manned by American physicians. While elective abortion and hysterectomy could not be confused with procedures that have neutral or positive reproductive outcomes, cesarean section is sometimes thought to be unoffensive to reproductive potential but, in fact, it has negative effects on the future fertility of the woman. Flamm[61] wrote:

> In 1970, about 205,000 cesarean operations were performed in the United States, representing 5.5 percent of the total 3.7 million babies born. By 1987, 934,000 cesarean operations were performed in American hospitals. This fivefold increase took place despite the fact that the total number of births remained fairly constant at about 3.7 million per year. Thus, by 1987, 25 percent of all American babies were delivered by major surgery. (p. xix)

The obstetrician's preference for it may not be in your best long-term reproductive interests. Sadly, the great increase in the number of cesarean operations being performed is not because of medical necessity, but rather because it reduces the number of lawsuits, increases the fees payable to physicians, and increases the convenience to the attending physician. For example, there is a nonrandom distribution of cesarean section by time of day that increases the ability of attending physicians to get sleep at night. Cesarean operations reduce the maximum number of children who may be born to a woman who receives multiple cesarean operations because there is risk of complications due to scar tissue formation and adhesions. There is also a higher risk of maternal mortality in cesarean operations than in vaginal births. Flamm[61] recommended that 70 percent to 80 percent of woman who have had a cesarean section would be able to have vaginal birth after cesarean, if cesareans were not routinely repeated on them. The benefits associated with this recommendation are obvious: reduced risk of maternal death and increased reproductive life, because there does not seem to be any increased risk of giving birth several times by vagina after having had a cesarean operation.

There has been an increasing trend in recent decades for the husband to be present in his wife's delivery room and to witness the birth. This trend, although motivated by caring intentions, is contrary to the pattern of giving birth in most other cultures, where women give birth in the presence of other women or alone. A husband is out of place in the midst of obstetric procedures, and any suggestion that he should or must participate is bizarre. Some men report a lasting decrease in the drive to have sexual intercourse with their wives after witnessing birth. This consequence is reason enough to excuse husbands from the delivery room.

Birth spacing

Maximizing reproductive success means having the maximum number of offspring survive to reproduce in the next generation. This goal is achieved by a woman starting childbearing as early as possible, i.e. at menarche, and having the maximum number of births as close together as possible for as long as possible. While such behavior is known to increase risks to the mother's and child's health, it is the way to produce the maximum number of offspring over a woman's lifetime. We have already learned that humans should not be trying to maximize longevity. There has been much hyperbole, mostly by population control disciples, claiming that having too many children too close together jeopardizes the survival of the children. But the fact is that while risk increases with many closely spaced children, so, too, reproductive success increases under normal circumstances. Natural selection has ensured that women's bodies begin reproduction and continue reproduction, by controlling ovulation entirely naturally through a number of feedback mechanisms only when the benefit of so doing exceeds the cost. Not surprisingly, in comparison to the beautiful systems that have evolved over millions of years to control women's fecundity, our attempts to second guess this natural process in the late 20th century using poorly conceptualized models of when women should get pregnant almost always reduce reproductive success. If between the years of 13 and 50 a woman gives birth on the average every 22 months, she will deliver 20 children. And that number is probably near the theoretical optimum for Western societies at the present time. The theoretical optimum is lower for non-Western populations lacking proper nutrition and adequate primary health care. Among other factors, unrealistic fears of being unable to provide adequate parental investment for our children has lead most Americans to have a family size that falls below the parents' potential to raise children.

In phylogenetic perspective the choice of a singleton birth or multiple birth is simple. There has been an advantage for singleton birth in terms of reproductive success in humans and among most nonhuman primates. A singleton historically produced more grandchildren than did two twins, three triplets, four quadruplets, and so forth. In this way each twin produced fewer than half the offspring of a singleton, each quadruplet produced fewer than a quarter of a singleton. This trend is often thought to be a surprising one by people when they first encounter it, but it follows from the decreased survivorship and reduced reproductive success of children in multiple births in the past. However, among humans the pattern has slowly changed. We appear to be on a trend toward the evolution of an increased rate of multiple births. Due to a combination of factors including birth control, abortion, and medical advances, multiple births now have a selective advantage over singleton births. Multiple births in a single pregnancy produce more children than the average American woman has in a lifetime. With improved medical technology there is now a much greater chance that the children so born will survive to reproduce than there was during other times of history or prehistory. We know for certain that dizygotic twinning rates have a large genetic component. In fact, high twinning rates have already evolved in some cultures due to benefits conferred on twins. For example, the Yoruba of Nigeria practice twin worship, believe in twin gods, and give gifts to twins. Because of the preferential treatment given to twins in that tribe, they survive and reproduce better than in other cultures that lack these customs. The result is that one of the highest twinning rates in the world has evolved among the Yoruba. This case is another example of what I call social selection: a social custom creating a selection pressure that changes gene frequencies. The environment is more complex in America today. Luke[125] reported that between 1973 and 1990, multiple births increased by 26.6 percent in the United States. The frequency of twin births increased from 1 in 55 to 1 in 43. Triplet and higher order births increased from 1 in 3323 to 1 in 1341. The increase in multiple births is primarily the result of the use of fertility drugs. Luke[125] also stated that more children are being born to older women, who are more prone to multiple births. Is this an evolutionary process? Are these mothers with multiple births genetically different and are gene frequencies in the population changing? In a previous section we discussed the idea of proception, namely, steps taken to increase fertility. While multiple births, perhaps induced by fertility drugs or by *in vitro* fertilization, may seem a simple solution to increasing fertility, we must in turn ask what is the fertility of the children of multiple births in comparison with the fertility of singletons. As in the above discussion, one child has been the optimal number per pregnancy, and while this trend is changing toward multiple births, we lack sufficient data at present to specify the new optimum. For example, until we know the long-term effect of low birth weight among quadruplets on their reproductive success, we cannot endorse with certainty a practice that would deliberately attempt to achieve the birth of quadruplets.

Abortion and infanticide

Infanticide was reported in 45 of 542 non-Western societies (8.3 percent) cataloged by Hobhouse et al.[96]. Infanticide may take a number of forms: as a method of reducing the number of dependents (e.g., the killing of unwanted infants and twins), as a sex ratio selection method, as a reproductive strategy of an unrelated male competing for a woman's reproductive effort, or as part of cannibalism (sometimes to feed starving older siblings). Hrdy and Hausfater[100] provided an exhaustive explanation of the conditions under which infanticide occurs. Of those they list, three have particular relevance to humans: sexual selection (killing the unrelated offspring of a mate), parental manipulation (as in sex ratio selection mentioned above and discussed below), and social pathology (where infanticide is maladaptive but occurs anyway). Even where infanticide occurs in humans it is usually uncommon, but in some Asian cultures it is a prominent cause of death. In contrast to humans, ornithological field data demonstrate that infanticide is often the most common cause of nestling mortality in certain species of birds[142]. Among birds infanticide usually takes the form of fratricide, an older nestling killing a younger sibling. Among fish the common form of infanticide is cannibalism[45]. Among carnivores it takes the form of infanticide by males (discussed below in the unrelated male strategy section), fratricide, female-female competition within a social group, and extragroup infanticide[157].

Among the most common forms of infanticide today is parental manipulation in the form of sex ratio selection. The differential killing of infants according to sex, which usually results in female infanticide, has evolutionary implications beyond simply those which would be associated with the killing of one's offspring. Fisher's sex ratio principle[60] explains that there is selection to produce the sexes in a ratio in accordance with the cost of producing each and comparative to the reproductive success obtained from male and female offspring. Natural selection favors a primary sex ratio (the ratio of males to females at conception) which maximizes the grandchildren the individual produces. Among humans, more males are born than females. This follows from the fact that there is selection in favor of equal investment in each sex class. Because male offspring die at higher rates than female offspring throughout the period of investment, from conception to independent adulthood, more of the males must be conceived and born in order to bring the total investment in males to equality with females. Female infanticide in humans is commonly associated with high costs of raising female children, particularly in parts of Asia such as India, where cultural characteristics involving costly rites of passage and a dowry prevail. Because parents expect their newborn daughters to be an economic burden to them, they kill them and hope for the birth of a son the next time. The irony of this pattern of female infanticide is that if the daughters pose a higher economic cost but not a higher cost in terms of a decrement in their future reproductive success than sons to the parents, then Fisher's sex ratio principle predicts under certain circumstances the evolution of a decrease in the sex ratio, i.e. *more*, not fewer, daughters will be born in the future if this pattern of differential infanticide continues long enough. The honeybee model demonstrates sex ratio bias in the extreme. The queen must produce many sons (drones) to equalize the investment in the male sex class with the female sex class because of the high cost of producing a daughter. Among honeybees, the daughter inherits the hive and a large number of sterile sisters to work in it. Among other human societies, infanticide may be due to a reduced cost of male children. Male children, especially when they approach maturity, may make a contribution to still reproducing parents by hunting, as among the Eskimo, or by male participation in family defense as among the Yanomamö, or by plowing the family farm with oxen as in cultures in India. In such circumstances, the net investment required to raise a son may be reduced, compared to the net investment required to raise a daughter, and selection for an increase in the sex ratio will occur. For example, in tribes where the role of a son in warfare reduces the net cost of raising that son, female infanticide might be used to reduce the number of daughters in order to balance the optimal ratio of investment by sex class. However, it would require truly extreme conditions to counterbalance the loss of the investment already made in the daughter that occurs when she is killed in order to achieve a more favorable sex ratio.

Infanticide also exists as a form of "birth control". Theoretically, a mother, particularly one of high extended reproductive value, might find herself in circumstances where her own reproductive success was threatened by a birth to the degree that she was better off without the infant than with it. For example, the newborn might require resources that were better allocated to older siblings and to the mother herself. But in recent decades such grim conditions have been eliminated from the cultures of the West and eased in most non-Western cultures. Most infanticide today in the name of birth control is actually social pathology. It involves old patterns of behavior that no longer make evolutionary sense in a new, resource-rich environment.

Abortion is the most common surgical procedure in America. The high percentage of pregnancies terminated by elective abortions observed today (about 1.6 million per year in the U.S.A. as compared with about 3.6 million live births) is likely to be a short-term trend. Elective abortion does not just cause the death of a viable offspring *in utero*. Rather, elective abortion almost always comes with a heavy dose of contraceptive counseling to the patient by the abortion providers, thereby further diminishing her reproductive prospects. It is sometimes asserted that elective abortions are merely a cure for a symptom, i.e. unwanted pregnancy, and that sexuality in the absence of desire for children is a disease. That is a freewheeling use of the words "symptom," "disease" and "cure". The evolutionary ethic embraces another view that is starkly contrasting. The lack of wanting the unborn child is the symptom. The abortion is the disease. Sexuality is the cure. Next to the aborted fetus, the mother is the biggest loser in evolutionary terms. It is often (and strangely) misconstrued that the right to an elective abortion is a highly desirable goal in women's rights. The evolutionary view is that a policy ensuring the availability of all possible assistance to help avoid an elective abortion would be the one best serving women's rights. In other words, it is not the right to elective abortion that is worthwhile, but rather the right to be free from the conditions that cause the want or need for an elective abortion. There is strong selection pressure acting against mothers who voluntarily terminate a pregnancy without good life history justification. Of course, if the mother is medically unfit to carry the pregnancy to term and has other dependent relatives, it makes perfect sense to terminate the pregnancy. But that is rarely the case. One of the interesting facts about abortion is that it is a particularly ineffective form of birth control. At the individual level an abortion seems to prevent a birth. But from the viewpoint of the population (different from the viewpoints of a gene or an individual), a thousand abortions may only "prevent" a few hundred births. This result follows from the fact that many women who have an abortion promptly get pregnant again during the period that they would have otherwise been infertile due to pregnancy and lactation. In part this short-term enhancement of fertility explains why approximately forty percent of elective abortions are repeat abortions. So the actual number of births prevented by a thousand abortions depends upon other reproductive factors of the population in question. For those people who are concerned about preserving fetal human life, they might do best to start an educational program to show men and women that they themselves stand to lose the most (next to the unborn child) in an evolutionary sense if they have an elective abortion. Ultimately, this kind of evolutionary cost-benefit analysis will prevail in coming generations.

While maternal mortality is low in America, that is not so in much of the Third World. Tragically, in Third World countries abortion-related deaths account for a large proportion of maternal mortality: more than half in some Latin American cities, more than a quarter in Addis Ababa, Ethiopia, and a fifth in rural Bangladesh[228]. Do not be duped when antigenitivists cite the risks of maternal mortality as a reason to avoid having children, for on a worldwide scale much of that mortality is caused by attempting to terminate the pregnancy with elective abortion. Hardin[88] provided an environmentalist's guidelines for deciding whether to abort or give birth. In these guidelines he compared the costs of an abortion and the costs of having a child. Costs of early abortion: about $250; loss of a day's time; minimal physical pain; negligible psychological pain; very slight risk of death. Costs of child: about $1,000 for prenatal care and birth; loss of at least a week's time; considerable physical pain; variable psychological pain; risk of death 8 times that of abortion; allocation of 16 years of life to caring for child; about $30,000 for rearing child to age 18, with no college. Note the narrow analysis, especially in terms of financial costs. While the figures he provides are obviously out of date, it is the mode of analysis itself that I reject. It is neither the relative pain of childbirth as compared to abortion, nor the relative financial costs of childbirth to abortion that should be the criteria for reproductive choices.

Life-lesson: Never have an elective abortion. You would be killing an individual with whom you share $^1/_2$ of your genes in common.

Infanticide is common among the nonhuman primates as an unrelated male strategy. It is a consequence of male-infant competition for female reproductive effort. By killing an unrelated dependent infant, a male increases his own reproductive success, because the mother of the infant returns to estrus sooner than if the infant were allowed to survive. He thus engenders more offspring than if he did not demonstrate infanticidal behavior. The trait is thus perpetuated in the population even though it does considerable reproductive harm to infants, mothers and to the males that fathered the infants that are killed. This pattern is common among the primates because of the huge investment in each offspring in this order, the long period of infant dependency, and the subsequent potential conflict of interests with unrelated male-infant competitors. However, it is not confined to primates and occurs in many places where there is conflict between unrelated adults and immatures, e.g., in lions. This pattern of infanticide also appears in humans, although it is not the most common type. For example, warfare among the Yanomamö of the Amazon is primarily for the purpose of abducting wives from neighboring tribes in order to enhance the reproductive success of the men who go to war. When a woman is abducted, her dependent children, especially sons, are killed by the men who are abducting her. Taking the little children by the feet, the abductors have been reported to kill them by beating their heads against rocks or trees[9].

Examination of child abuse statistics

I was puzzled in the mid-seventies about the evolutionary basis of child abuse in America. The high prevalence of child abuse did not seem to make sense. What advantage could parents gain by harming their offspring? Then I discovered the statistics from the state of Florida. A shocking trend emerged from the Florida data. The majority of child abuse was by men who are unrelated to the abused child -- they are stepfathers and boyfriends of the child's mother. Re-examination of the data from all over America is warranted. What we observe in child abuse in the U.S.A. today may be analogous to that behavior described by the primate infanticide model mentioned previously. Now the picture is nearly complete with elegant publications like Daly and Wilson[35] in which they demonstrated the clear relationship between the presence of an unrelated stepparent in the home and the occurrence of child abuse and infanticide. In other cultures there are institutionalized ways of reducing the frequency of child abuse that results from the natural biological conflict of interests between a stepchild and a stepparent. For example, marriage of a woman to her deceased husband's brother is known as the levirate, and it is the most common form of affinal marriage in cross-cultural comparison. The levirate in some cultures effectively decreases the conflict of interests between previous offspring of a woman and her new mate. Wife-lending may accomplish the same thing to a lesser degree. Another example of a strategy to reduce conflict between stepparent and stepchild is the marriage of a widower to his deceased wife's sister. That pattern of marriage is called the sororate, and this institution was particularly common among the indigenous tribes of North America. Some psychologists believe that American children do not do well in one-parent households and do even less well when living with a stepfather. These psychologists appear to be incorrect in the evolutionary sense about one-parent households, because children with this background reproduce disproportionately well. But fitness data are lacking for the eventual reproductive success of children living with stepfathers. Certainly a plausible evolutionary mechanism exists for potential fitness reducing conflict between stepfathers and stepchildren, as seen in the model of competition for female reproductive effort mentioned above.

Infanticide among humans often takes the form of social pathology. With environmental changes in recent centuries, in particular the increase in energy available for reproductive effort through improved nutrition, and the legislation of legal sanctions against killing infants (surprisingly only a few centuries old even in Western cultures), it is likely that most of the infanticide occurring among humans today is maladaptive behavior from the viewpoint of the actor and the infant killed. For example, sex ratio selection by infanticide and abortion (after an ultrasound scan for sex determination) in India provides only a small increment of fitness via Fisher's sex ratio principle in comparison to a large decrement in fitness via loss of a daughter who would have otherwise survived to maturity and reproduced. In America, the pattern of murderous abuse of children by a mother's new husband or new boyfriend has deep roots in the primate pattern of infanticide in male-infant competition for a female's reproductive effort. It, too, appears to be maladaptive behavior from the viewpoint of the actor, since the average American family is so much smaller than the optimal family size that the existence of children unrelated to the new husband or new boyfriend is not a hindrance to his reproductive success. Also, legal sanctions in America against infanticide are powerful and potentially fitness-threatening to the perpetrator.

The Bruce effect

The Bruce effect is a female strategy to pre-empt infanticide. It is named after its discoverer, H. M. Bruce[17, 18], who published papers indicating the existence of a pregnancy block in mice caused by the proximity of strange males. The smell of a strange male mouse causes a pregnant female mouse to have a spontaneous abortion to terminate maternal investment in offspring that are likely to be killed by the strange male. Although a spontaneous abortion means the death of the offspring *in utero*, it makes sense to cut losses early rather than incur even greater losses later through the actions of an infanticidal male. Huck[101] pointed out an important event associated with the pregnancy block: The female who experiences it returns to a state of estrus 4-5 days later. Of course, that is what the unrelated male strategy of infanticide is designed to accomplish, but returning quickly to estrus serves the female's purposes, too. It gives her the maximum amount of time for pregnancy and for caring for the litter before another strange male appears and starts the cycle all over again. Cannibalism of offspring by the mother to recover invested nutrients also occurs among rodents. The Bruce effect is similar in some respects to spontaneous abortions when the embryo or fetus is defective. Spontaneous abortion is the source of much sadness in humans, but often it is the best strategy for avoiding further commitment to what would be a child with a severe congenital disorder. Unlike elective abortion, spontaneous abortion is often fitness enhancing. Abandonment of unwanted newborn children among humans is a behavior associated with new mothers under stress. No longer likely to be adaptive because of good alternatives, such behavior once might have protected the reproductive success of the mother and her family if caring for the newborn was impossible with existing resources. In Kenya there is such a propensity for mothers to abandon unwanted newborns by dropping them live into pit latrines that an extraordinary measure was taken: A law was passed making it illegal to conceal the event of a birth. Although data are lacking, we might expect these mothers to be among those least prepared to give birth and the least able to nurture an infant.

Parental care

Breastfeeding

Breastfeeding is healthful for the baby, but it suppresses ovulation in the mother. We might ask: "What is in the baby's and mother's evolutionary interest?" Theoretically, a woman who bottle feeds her baby could produce additional offspring, and if she produces enough additional offspring it outweighs in an evolutionary sense the risk to the baby from being bottle fed. From the mother's viewpoint, the required increase in reproductive success to justify bottle feeding is smaller than from the baby's viewpoint. Does this happen in practice? The European aristocracy of times past exploited the fact that the contraceptive effect of breastfeeding could be circumvented by the use of wet nurses and by artificial feeding, thereby making it possible for women of this social class to produce a child a year. Queen Victoria, the mother of nine children, is an example -- the Prince of Wales was conceived within three months of the birth of her first child, whom she did not breastfeed[190]. For these reasons, mothers should consider bottle feeding their infants if they live under conditions that they can keep feeding equipment clean and can prepare the baby formula properly. While such conditions are taken for granted in Western cultures, it is difficult sometimes for mothers in non-Western cultures to do either. Cost of baby formula may also be a factor to consider in low-income families, but whether it is a factor that would limit reproduction is not clear. Infant mortality in America reached a record low in 1991 with a rate of 8.9 infant deaths per 1,000 live births[148]. This rate is so low, even in the presence of widespread bottle feeding, that it is difficult to imagine how it could be lowered measurably by an increase in breastfeeding. Indeed, the leading causes of infant death in America (congenital anomalies, sudden infant death syndrome, disorders relating to short gestation and low birth weight) have no link to the type of infant nutrition provided whatsoever. The above argument is a powerful one useful in the rebuttal of the militant pro-breastfeeding hyperbole that is directed at mothers of newborns in America. In short, bottle feeding in an evolutionary perspective is often best for mother and baby.

Life-lesson: Bottle feed your baby and support stronger legislation against breastfeeding, e.g., strict prohibitions against breastfeeding in public.

While it may first appear that, in order to increase the relative contribution of one's genes to future generations, one might encourage others to breastfeed rather than pass laws against it, the analysis is more complicated than that. I discuss in a following section the effects of advocacy of progenitivism on the reproductive success of the advocate through feedforward and other mechanisms.

Nutrient requirements per day for infant growth are as follows: 117 calories/ kg body mass from age 0 to 0.5; 108 calories/kg from age 0.5 to 1.0; and 1,300 calories from age 1 to 3 years[150]. A woman uses approximately 900 calories to produce a liter of breast milk[151]. A lactating woman produces about 30 ounces of milk a day. At 20 calories an ounce, the caloric requirement for lactation is 750 calories per day when the total costs of production are calculated[82].

Breasts are secondary sexual characteristics of human females that have powerful stimulatory effects not only on babies but on American men as well. But the sexual stimulatory effects of breasts on men may not be a populational constant. In many non-Western cultures women go bare-breasted in public, and it is not a source of undue attention or moralizing. Nonhuman primates lack breasts enlarged with fat deposits. But unlike human infants, nonhuman primate infants are able to cling unaided to the mother's chest in order to suckle. This observation gives rise to the hypothesis that the enlargement of the human female breasts may be an infant feeding adaptation, but not in the way that one might expect. In Africa, where infants are carried in a cloth sling on the mother's back, it is surprising to the anthropologically uninitiated to see a mother suckle her infant while carrying it on her back by stretching her elongated breast over her shoulder or under her arm. This capability represents an adaptation to being able to breastfeed regularly and conveniently even while walking long distances. However, size of breasts does not appear to be correlated with actual milk production capability; enlarged breasts may simply be a more convenient delivery device. The alternative but not mutually exclusive hypothesis, the hypothesis that enlarged female breasts evolved to attract males, assumes that this stimulatory effect on males is adaptive for the males and that they have, accordingly, evolved an affinity. The males' response must have an effect on the females, since access to females is the only pathway for male reproductive success. What could the effect on the females be? Could it be a releasing mechanism for male-initiated coitus?

On the subject of parental care, it is evident to the astute that some temporary alternatives to actual parental investment exist for humans. Sperm donation, egg donation, and putting your newborns up for adoption all reduce parental investment but probably achieve the same reproductive success as raising a child yourself to adulthood. If such strategies allow one to have more children than traditional parenthood would, they make evolutionary sense. Sperm donation is clearly a good strategy: About thirty thousand babies are conceived yearly by artificial insemination by a donor other than the husband. About fifty thousand children were adopted in 1992; the number has decreased considerably from the approximately eighty-nine thousand that were adopted in 1970 before the easy availability of birth control, legal abortions, and the acceptance of single mothers keeping their babies[189]. Approximately one thousand five hundred births via egg donation occurred between 1986 and 1992. While this number is small, it is important to note that it is doubling every year. How do these figures for sperm donation, adoption, and egg donation compare to the total number of births, 3.7 million per year, in America? Sperm donors other than the husband are the fathers of about 0.8 percent of all babies. Adoptions occur in approximately 1.35 percent of all births. And approximately 0.02 percent of all births are by egg donation. Combined, these figures show that 1 out of 50 births in America today is involved with these methods. Thus, in spite of the increase in popularity of the new reproductive technologies, the great majority of Americans who do reproduce rely on the conventional, fitness enhancing approach of producing and rearing offspring to whom they are genetically related. Indeed, it would be surprising if it were otherwise.

Kenya has the highest documented total fertility rate of any country. While not scientifically documented, Ethiopia probably has the highest total fertility rate of any country, even greater than Kenya's rate. These populations contain individuals with the highest reproductive success in the world, and I admire that. Keeping this high fertility in Kenya and in Ethiopia in mind, it is clear that parents in these populations are doing something right when raising their children, because in turn the children have such high reproductive success. We must remind ourselves, however strange it might sound, that the sole measure of one's success as a parent is the number of children one raises to sexual maturity and the reproductive success of those children. By this standard, the parents of the American baby boomers did something wrong as indicated by the low fertility of their offspring. Attributes that parents traditionally value in their children and which parents often attempt to impart, such as proper manners, academic achievement, and athletic accomplishments are of no importance whatsoever if they do not lead to higher reproductive success. It is a strange coincidence that Ethiopia is likely to become the birthplace of humankind twice: first, three million years ago with the appearance of our distant ancestor *Australopithecus afarensis*, and again at the coming of the second millennium with a population of Hamitic people growing so fast that they may eventually populate the Earth. In 1950 the United States was the fourth most populous nation and Ethiopia was twenty-third; by 2025 projections suggest that the United States will fall to sixth and Ethiopia will rise to eleventh. Demography is destiny.

Life-lesson: Start reproduction early, preferably at puberty, have a long reproductive life, and maximize your reproductive success.

Risk in reproduction

Risk is a component of sexual reproduction. A tradeoff of survivorship for offspring is a natural consequence of optimal life history strategies. So let us take a rational look at risk in human reproduction. Ignoring the actual risk of attaining sexual maturity, which sequesters time and energy that could be otherwise allocated to achieving optimal growth or improved maintenance, it can be itemized in four main categories: 1. risk in finding or keeping a mate, 2. risk of sexually transmitted diseases, 3. risk during pregnancy and birth, and 4. risk in parenting. The risk in finding or keeping a mate can be divided into these subcategories: searching, competition, and courtship. All have a risk component, and they take a familiar form. Teenage boys tend to spend endless hours cruising in automobiles looking for girls. Because they drive with bravado intended to impress, they have the worst auto fatality rates of any age/sex class. Male-male competition for females is also a source of conflict, aggression, and violent death. The risk of courtship may involve all the risk associated with searching and competition. Sexual intercourse involves a tradeoff of fecundity for health. Ordinarily, fecundity is increased and health is decreased through coitus. Sexually transmitted diseases are a group of organisms that increase their own reproductive success by exploiting the fact that humans ordinarily need to have genital contact in order to procreate. Other health problems, such as an allergic response of women to semen, are increasingly common in America. Risk during pregnancy and birth is represented by maternal mortality. The statistic cited in a previous section is 8 maternal deaths per 100,000 births in America. There is risk in parenting because parental investment has its risk components. The probability of permanent debilitating injury or death can be elevated for parents by virtue of the fact that they may intercede in dangerous situations for the purpose of protecting their children. But other variables like additional travel from commuting with the children to school, exposure to disease through poorer nutrition by sharing limited food resources with children (primarily in the Third World), and, rarely, parricide at the hands of deranged children contribute to parental risk.

Kinship effects

Inclusive fitness

Inclusive fitness theory provides an explanation why each of us finds our relatives to be special. Anthropologists once thought that humans were unique in the establishment of kinship relations; indeed, kinship systems are a universal aspect of human societies. But in recent decades abundant evidence for the importance of kinship in the lives of other animals has been published. Not only do other primates and social insects have complex relations among relatives, but so do species in other phyla (see Wilson[222]). Hamilton[85] provided a comprehensive theory explaining how an individual is expected to maximize the transmission of his genes to the next generation, not only through producing offspring but also by assisting other relatives to reproduce. Offspring are just a special class of relatives, with which in diploid, sexually reproducing organisms, parents share $1/2$ of their genes in common in the absence of inbreeding. But a diploid individual also shares $1/2$ of his genes in common with a full sibling and with a parent. Similarly, an individual shares $1/4$ of his genes in common with a grandchild, with a half sibling, with a niece and with a nephew. These regression coefficients of relatedness can be extended to a first cousin and great-grandparent ($1/8$ of their genes in common) and so forth. Whenever the cost to the actor is less than the regression coefficient of relatedness times the benefit to the recipient, an altruistic behavior will be favored by natural selection. Commonly, the costs and benefits of such a social behavior are represented with the following inequality: $C < b_{AR}B$, where C is the cost of the social behavior to the actor, b_{AR} is the regression coefficient of relatedness between the actor and recipient, and B is the benefit to the individual who is the recipient of the act.

A question often asked by people when they first encounter inclusive fitness theory is: Then why not inbreed in order to produce children that are more closely related to you? The answer is that one is selected to maximize one's reproductive success, not to maximize one's regression coefficient of relatedness to one's offspring. Inbreeding depression and the expression of deleterious recessive genes associated with inbreeding, which lower reproductive success, plus the opportunity for one and one's relatives to find unrelated mates, mean that inbreeding is not a viable strategy under most circumstances.

Dismissing the group selection model

Williams[217] eloquently demonstrated that natural selection acts at the level of the individual. In other words, individuals are designed to promote their own reproductive success, not the success of a larger group like a population or the species. Notions to the contrary are generally designated "group selection" arguments. While there is little doubt that under certain special circumstances group selection might occur, its intensity is insignificant in its evolutionary consequences in comparison to natural selection at the level of the individual. Modern anthropologists look to selection at the level of the individual and at the level of the kinship group to explain social behavior. They do not profess to see evidence for social traits that evolved for the benefit of the species. There is no need to look beyond the level of individuals and kinship groups for explanations of observed adaptations.

Familial conflict of interests

One of the great issues of family conflict in America is over teenage sexuality and teenage pregnancy. In general, parents want their children to delay sexual reproduction. Originally, this desire arose out of an adaptive strategy that permitted parents to thereby produce more of their own children. This desire follows from the fact that one's own children are related by $1/2$ -- but one's children's children (one's grandchildren) are related by $1/4$. Children prefer to be sexually active earlier than their parents wish them to be because the children would prefer to produce their own $1/2$ related offspring instead of allowing their parents to produce siblings related by $1/4$ to $1/2$. Parents usually have the advantage of size and various sources of authority in the argument, and are likely to be able to prevail in direct confrontations with their still dependent offspring. So teenagers sneak sexual intercourse rather than confront their parents with overt sexuality. This evolutionary conflict of interests is the source of much of the shyness regarding sexual matters within the family. Every generation of children wants to start sexual intercourse early. Every generation of parents will want their children to start sexual intercourse late, even though they themselves as teenagers had the reverse opinion in the argument. This evolutionary battle is a real one between the generations. It is not the case that each generation of children is only less "moral" than the generation of their parents. This concept of cultural load, it will be seen later, also explains some of the delay in reproduction among teenagers.

Monogamous mating systems and promiscuous mating systems generate different parent-offspring conflict. Children in promiscuous mating systems are selected to start reproducing earlier than in monogamous systems. In this sense, weak nuclear family structure does promote adolescent sexuality. The extent to which this trend explains the cycle of "illegitimacy" in contemporary society is not yet clear. The basis for the trend is that populations in which half siblings are common create a selection pressure for those half siblings to start their own reproduction earlier than populations in which full siblings are common. Trivers[205] proposed the basic model of how a parent, equally related to two offspring, is selected to encourage altruism between the two offspring whenever $B > C$. But the two offspring, depending upon whether they are full siblings (related by $1/2$) or half siblings (related by $1/4$) will have a different view of altruism between themselves. For an actor who is a full sibling of the recipient, altruism must occur at $C < 1/2 B$ to be favored by natural selection from the actor's viewpoint. For an actor who is a half sibling of the recipient, altruism must occur at $C < 1/4 B$ to be favored by natural selection from the actor's viewpoint. So parents wish to support more altruism and less competition among their children than the siblings themselves favor. This fact is particularly true among half siblings, who would be acting adaptively by starting reproduction early, even at the cost of pre-empting further reproduction by the parent, since the half sibling is related to its own offspring by $1/2$ but to its half siblings by only $1/4$. Full siblings are related to their offspring and siblings equally, thereby reducing the parent-offspring conflict over the age of onset of offspring reproduction.

The process of maximizing reproductive success does not mean that a parent provides unlimited and obsessive parental care to the child without discrimination. Trivers[205] provided the theoretical framework of how parent and offspring are expected to disagree regarding parental investment and other issues relating to their overlapping, but not identical, inclusive fitness. It is certainly true that it is the right strategy at times for parents to reduce or withdraw investment in their offspring. This theory has practical implications for Americans, who overall tend to invest too much in too few offspring. In fact, in the majority of American families it would benefit the inclusive fitness of even the children to have additional siblings, because with the abundance of resources available to families, a child's ultimate reproductive success is not usually limited by competition with siblings for those resources. The tendency of an only child to become spoiled may be a manifestation of excessive parental investment in that child, to the point that undesirable characteristics develop in the child. The fact that, on average, an only child has lower fertility in America than a child with one or more siblings is of the utmost relevance to our rejection of reproductive patterns leading to families that are too small to be adaptive.

Weak nuclear families also lead to higher rates of sexuality due to sperm competition. It is an interesting prediction that a cycle of illegitimacy in a population should be both the cause and effect of high rates of promiscuous copulation.

The only family members who have perfectly overlapping interests in an evolutionary sense are identical (monozygotic) twins -- this pattern follows from the fact that they are genetically identical. Some of the familial conflict observed today can be described in a long list of cultural attributes that Americans usually wish to deny to their teenage children: illicit drugs, alcohol, tobacco, firearms, and gangs. These prohibitions probably make evolutionary sense, because things like illicit drugs are self-promoting culturgens with a likely negative fitness consequence for individuals who use them. But it is important not to include adolescent sexual intercourse among the behaviors prohibited, unless you as the parent are still reproducing yourself and your child's child would be dependent upon you, thereby restricting your own ability to have another child. The fact that Americans generally do include adolescent sexual intercourse among the behaviors prohibited is a demonstration of how terribly confused our value system is. Adolescent sexuality is a normal part of life in many human societies and in many nonhuman primate societies. And when the high frequency of adolescent sexual intercourse in America is considered, it is clearly normal *de facto*.

The most effective mediator of a conflict between relatives is a closer relative that they share in common. It is not surprising that parents help to socialize their children into patterns of family reciprocity and altruism because the parents are more closely related to the extended family than the children are. For example, it is expected that an individual would serve as an effective mediator of altruism between his sibling and his child.

Adoption

The commonness of adoption in America is often given by opponents of evolutionary thinking as an example of how evolution does not dictate human behavior. They ask, if the evolutionary model of social behavior is true, why should the adoptive parents want to burden themselves with an unrelated child? What is the adaptive significance to them? Fortunately, the answer is rather straightforward. The urge to adopt children can be easily understood by examining the social organization of early humans, which consisted of small groups of close and distant relatives. Many species of nonhuman primates living under natural conditions have that kind of social organization today. In that social setting, adopted children would almost always be genetically related to the adoptive parent. In that context, adoption was often adaptive for both the adopted child and the adoptive parent. Thus, we are expressing a pattern of behavior that increased inclusive fitness in the past environment, but which now due to changes in population structure and social organization, usually fails to confer a fitness benefit on the adoptive parent. In this sense the behavior is vestigial (a trait that in its present form was a suitable adaptation in previous generations, but no longer leads to increased reproductive success), but it clearly owes its origin to evolution. Adoption by a relative is a rule in nonhuman primates, and it still represents a large portion of the adoptions in the Third World and some of the adoptions in America today. In some societies adoptions occur with the intent of putting the adopted person to work, or to betroth the adopted to a genetic offspring. The general point that we can draw from this phenomenon is that primordial social propensities, like the urge to care for a helpless infant, evolved in primordial and very different environments from those in which we now live. Their origins can only be understood in that perspective.

Two million families want to adopt in America. If you are adopting, consider adopting a relative and giving the child a progenitive education. If you are putting up a child for adoption, choose well-qualified unrelated recipients if possible, but consider allowing relatives to adopt as a last resort. While it is true that related adopters may provide better care than unrelated adopters under some circumstances because they are related, it would appear, superficially at least, that most people who do adopt generally provide fitting homes for the adopted children. One advantage of allowing a relative to adopt your child is that you may be able to influence the direction of the child's education toward progenitivism. But in allowing relatives to adopt your child you may be depressing the number of children they produce themselves, and this loss represents a potential decrease in your inclusive fitness. More data on how well adopted children thrive with related and unrelated adoptive parents and eventually reproduce would be useful. When putting a child up for adoption, choose an adopting family that does not have too much money, that is rural living, and has little or no higher education. These conditions are likely passed from adoptive parent to child and are correlated with reproductive success.

Incest avoidance

The incest taboo, once thought by anthropologists to be uniquely human, is actually a common behavior among "higher" organisms to avoid the costs of inbreeding depression and to gain the benefits of outbreeding. The degree of inbreeding depression is proportional to a mathematical concept called the inbreeding coefficient in the offspring. It is not an absolute but a relative cost, and under some animal mating systems the costs of inbreeding can be outweighed by benefits. However, in no known human society is it conventional for father and daughter, mother and son, or brother and sister to have sexual intercourse or to marry[146]. Brother-sister matings among hymenoptera and human royal families (as once seen in Hawaiian aristocracy, the pharaohs of ancient Egypt, the Inca royal family, and among the elite of other non-Western societies) are examples of exceptions. All of these exceptions can be explained by extenuating circumstances: in insects the inaccessibility of unrelated mates and in humans mostly the rarity of appropriate mates of the same social class and the desire to preserve wealth and status within the elite family.

It is my opinion that incest avoidance in humans has a strong biological base, while many of my fellow anthropologists feel that it is a cultural phenomenon. There are two types of theories in traditional social anthropology that attempt to explain the incest taboo. The first emphasizes principles of social structure and the importance of marital alliances as a means of broadening the scope of social interaction. The second rests on psychological principles and emphasizes the potentially disruptive effects of sexual competition within the kinship group[97]. Combined, these two theories argue that exogamy is a method by which sons, daughters, brothers, and sisters are exchanged to strengthen social, economic, military and political bonds with neighboring groups, and that it is a means by which intragroup sexual conflict is reduced. Harris[90] maintained that view and stated further:

> I should point out that one of the consequences of incest that keeps the emotions boiling may have little to do with incest *per se*. Mother-son and father-daughter incest not only threatens the maintenance of external relationships, but it threatens the basic bonds of family organization. After all, these two forms of incest are also two forms of adultery. Mother-son incest is a special threat to the institution of marriage. Not only is the wife "double-dealing" against her husband, but the son is "double-dealing" against his father. This may explain why the least common and most feared and abhorred form of incest is that between mother and son (as in the Ancient Greek myth of Oedipus). It follows that father-daughter incest will be somewhat more common since husbands enjoy double standards of sexual conduct more often than wives and are less vulnerable to punishment for adultery. Finally, the same consideration suggests an explanation for the relatively high frequency of brother-sister matings and an additional reason for their legitimization in elite classes -- they do not conflict with father-mother adultery rules. (p. 206)

But it appears that Harris[90] is wrong about the rates of different types of incest, and his hypothesis is not supported by the facts. In fact all rates of incest by dyadic interaction in the nuclear family are in accordance with a competing hypothesis. It has been known by sociologists that incest in the nuclear family follows this pattern of frequency: father-daughter > brother-sister > mother-son. Weinberg[212] reported 203 cases of incest in Illinois, of which 78.33 percent were father-daughter incest, 18.23 percent were brother-sister incest, 0.99 percent were mother-son incest, and 2.45 percent were combined father-daughter and brother-sister incest. My alternative explanation, which to my knowledge has not been hypothesized before, is that this pattern of frequency is based upon genetic concerns. Namely, whenever the probability of paternity of a husband being the genitor (genetical father) of his wife's children in a population is less than 1, then the inbreeding coefficient for the children of the same nuclear family pairs is: child of putative father-daughter < child of brother-sister < child of mother-son. The inequalities of rates of incest coincide in perfect inverse with the inequalities for the degree of inbreeding. Thus, the rates of incest within the nuclear family are in accordance with inbreeding avoidance expectations. Dawkins[40] proposed an alternative hypothesis which also fits these data. He suggested that females are less willing than males to engage in incest and that the older member of the pair of relatives is the active initiator of sexual intercourse. It appears to me that this hypothesis can be simplified to state the obvious: Males are usually older than the females with whom they have sexual intercourse. That hypothesis, being the simplest one, would be the strongest one for explaining patterns of incest were it not for the fact that all matings in humans, not just incestuous ones, are biased toward older male-younger female pairs. Freudian theory, which postulates that sons go through a childhood phase of sexual attraction to their mothers is also not supported by the evidence -- mother-son incest being the rarest form of incest.

Economic considerations

Many Americans live too extravagantly and devote too much time to earning the living needed to sustain a high level of consumption. Time and energy that could be allocated to reproduction is instead expended in earning and managing money, in making expenditures and in collecting and managing assets. While it is theoretically true that financial assets could be converted to reproductive success, assets not converted have no intrinsic worth in an evolutionary sense. Rather, in recent times the correlation between wealth and reproductive success seems to be a mostly negative one. I discussed earlier how richer is safer, but richer is also less fertile. Are the two causally related? For example, is less fertile in some meaningful way safer? Probably so, since the cost of reproduction shortens life. And is safer in some meaningful way less fertile? Yes, by the same argument safe behavior for the individual might exclude reproduction entirely.

What seems to be lacking in the modern American ethos is a workable concept of a wealth-to-offspring value tradeoff. In other non-Western cultures there are often implicit assumptions about the economic worth of children. For example, brideprice is in some sense the purchasing of a woman's reproductive capabilities from her relatives. Among pastoral peoples, brideprice is often measured in quantities of livestock, which is a relevant measure of wealth. Likewise, a price may have to be paid by a man to a woman's relatives for engendering a child out of wedlock. In some non-Western cultures the concept of blood money is prevalent, in which a family is paid for the death of a relative by the accused. For example, among the Masai of eastern Africa, if a man kills his wife, he must give a bull to her parents in restitution. This payment is obviously for the lost reproductive success of the daughter, not for economic loss, because among the Masai, who are patrilineal and patrilocal, a married woman does not represent an economic value to her parents after the brideprice has been paid. The closest we come to this kind of wealth-to-fitness assessment in the West is through the courts on the occasion of paternity suits and in cases where child-support from a separated spouse is sought. But few Americans have a clear sense about how much a child is actually worth in dollars. This point arises tragically under the circumstance of kidnapping for ransom -- how much should one be willing to pay for the return of a child unharmed? Ultimately, the correct measure of any action is a question of the offspring gained due to the action versus the offspring lost due to the action. This standard can in turn be converted by approximation into dollar terms for newborns by calculating the going costs for the services of a true surrogate mother, who, by not supplying the ovum, is expending the reproductive effort required to gestate and give birth to an unrelated individual. The current value of a surrogacy contract to a woman providing gestational services for an unrelated fetus is about twelve thousand dollars plus medical expenses. Of course, the first nine months of life are a small fraction of the total parental costs of producing a child to the stage of adulthood. But the actual observed dollar costs of raising a child, perhaps three hundred thousand dollars among the upper-middle class, is not an indicator of what the essential costs are. Many costly contributions by parents to their children actually lower, not increase, the children's reproductive success. So the question is: "What are the basic investments that a parent can make in offspring that increase the number of grandchildren that will be produced, and what is the monetary value of these investments?" I offer a rough estimate of fifty thousand (in year 2000 dollars) for the absolute essentials of life during eighteen years of parental investment. Compared to non-Western cultures, Americans appear to be too strict on emotional issues and at the same time too financially generous with their children. Thirty years ago, the cost of raising an upper-middle class child was approximately thirty thousand dollars -- about one tenth the cost today. It appears that the cost of raising a child has increased to consume the means available. And rather than raise more children with the greater resources available, we actually raise fewer. This pattern represents a fundamental error in our current child raising strategy.

It is a *cliché* that "the business of America is business". There is certainly much truth in it, but it ignores a higher value. It is the goal of evolutionary ethicists to see that expression changed to "the business of America is the business of maximizing reproductive success". Commerce will no longer occur for the sake of commerce *per se*, rather it will be a method of supporting our attempts to maximize reproductive success.

Societal differences

We find little evidence of fitness maximizing behavior in modern Western societies. We find the remnants of it in non-Western societies. And we find full expression of it in nonhuman primate societies living in their natural environments. That is a reason why some anthropologists conduct field studies of non-Western peoples and of nonhuman primates -- to learn about evolutionary principles as applied to social life. It is not a coincidence that fitness maximizing behavior follows the pattern of Western societies < non-Western societies < nonhuman primate societies. Rather, it is a measure of how these societies have recently undergone relative degrees of cultural (and particularly technological) change in ways that are incompatible with older, genetically based reproductive strategies. The nonhuman primate societies, with the greatest amount of fitness maximizing behavior, are the least changed. The non-Western societies are intermediate in their degree of change and in their fitness maximizing behavior. And Western societies are most changed with the least fitness maximizing behavior. Harris[90] wrote this instructive passage on the processes involved in reproducing well or poorly:

> Among nonhuman primates, sexual stimulation usually leads to coitus and coitus virtually guarantees conception. And once sperm and ovum unite, pregnancy usually proceeds relentlessly to the stage of labor and birth. Thereafter, powerful hormones compel the mother to suckle her infant, carry it about, and protect it from danger.
>
> In human beings, this system of genetically controlled guarantees for linking sex with the birth and the rearing of progeny no longer exists. Sex does not guarantee conception; conception does not lead relentlessly to birth; and birth does not compel the mother to nurse and protect the newborn. Cultures have evolved learned techniques and practices that can prevent each step in this process from occurring. (p. 210)

When we imagine the precise interventions involved in breaking the chain between sexual attraction and coitus, e.g., personal choice of mates, cultural constraints in mate choice, and between coitus and pregnancy, e.g., contraception, and between coitus and birth, e.g., elective abortion, we begin to understand the process by which the least fitness maximizing societies mentioned above, Western societies, fail indeed to maximize reproductive success. I shall present further analysis of this topic in the section on cultural evolution.

Religious considerations

Animistic and other religious beliefs are found among some of the members of all cultures ever investigated by anthropologists. These beliefs are always accompanied by a set of rituals that may be used for getting benefits: improved crops, peace, success in warfare, happiness, immortality, and so forth. In some practitioners these beliefs provide immense psychological satisfaction. Pluralistic beliefs are a particularly illustrative example of diverse and internally inconsistent belief structures that exist because of a practitioner's desire to be the recipient of the benefits promised by more than one religion. Today, in the West, religious practices and rites are on the decline. While many religious traditions continue in America, many people cannot trust in the belief of the existence of an all knowing, all powerful God who intervenes in human affairs.

Intellectuals in America have sometimes overemphasized the logical absurdity of religious belief. Some have even concluded that because religion is absurd, it will eventually vanish. They have overlooked two important points: 1. Although absurd, it is comforting, and 2. although absurd, it can enhance reproductive success under certain circumstances. Thus, there are mechanisms in religion's favor: a proximate mechanism, psychological comfort, and an ultimate mechanism, fitness. The question of the inherent truth of a religion is irrelevant to our evolutionary analysis. What does matter is whether a belief system, true or false, helps to promote the survival and reproduction of its adherents. It is with this mode of analysis that I shall examine religion. Anthropologists often think of religion as a universal human need, when in fact it is a universal human symbiont, commensal or parasite depending on a given religion's effect on the fitness of its practitioners. A symbiont has a mutually beneficial association with its host. A commensal coexists with its host and does not increase or decrease the host's fitness. A parasite coexists with its host but reduces the host's fitness. So a belief in God does not necessarily conflict with the maximization of an individual's reproductive success. The fitness effects of religion on humans vary from sect to sect. We shall see that America has achieved ''freedom of religion'' long before it will achieve ''freedom from religion''. This conclusion follows from the fact that by a variety of mechanisms religion enhances fertility and promotes its own transmission.

Because religiosity shows such a strong positive correlation with unplanned teenage pregnancy, I feel it is appropriate for me to offer my endorsement of religion in general. Parents desiring that their teenage daughters become unwed mothers can help accomplish this end, ironically, by ensuring that they are devout in attending church. In support of this argument, Jones et al.[110] found in a study of 37 developed countries, including the United States, that birthrates of both older and younger teenagers were very strongly positively correlated with the importance of God in the lives of the population sampled. Countries with the highest levels of religiosity have the highest teenage birthrates. In that study, America scored higher on an index of religiosity than any other developed country in the sample -- accordingly, it also ranked higher in teenage birthrates than 27 out of 30 other developed countries for which there were data. The explanation for this correlation is not entirely clear. According to folklore, the preacher's son is often responsible.

Below I compare the Hutterites, a population with high resource-high fertility, the Shakers, a population with high resource-low fertility and the !Kung, a population with low resource-low fertility. Eaton and Mayer[51] reported that the Hutterites, people of interconnected anabaptist religious communities in the U.S.A. and Canada, have the highest known fertility of any population. The total fertility rate is 10.2 births per woman. For women married continuously during the years of reproduction (15-49) the average number of births is 12.4. Howell[99] made an interesting point:

> The Hutterites are useful as a standard of comparison for fertility achieved by other populations ... against which we can measure the ways in which other populations fail to achieve maximal levels of fertility. (p. 154)

How are they maximizing reproductive success? Howell[99] pointed out that they are healthy, well-nourished, do not use contraception and desire large families for religious and practical reasons.

The Dobe !Kung of southern Africa were found by Howell[99] to have the lowest natural fertility schedule known, in contrast with the Hutterites, who have the highest. The total fertility rate for !Kung women is 4.7 births. By the term "natural fertility" I mean it in the sense defined by Henry[94], which in brief terms means a population that does not use artificial contraception and has other special characteristics. Howell[99] explained the difference by pointing out a striking feature of the !Kung pattern in parity progression ratios: Among the !Kung there is a sharp decline in ratios after the fifth child; among the Hutterites there is a slower decline at higher parities. Contributing factors to the low fertility of the !Kung are sterility caused by untreated sexually transmitted disease, suppression of ovulation by lactation, and possible suppression of ovulation by a diet with limited calories. Frisch[65] suggested that when the fertility rate of a population like the !Kung is lower than normally found in a well-nourished population with modern contraception, it could be explained wholly or in part by the effects of inadequate nutrition on reproductive physiology: delayed menarche, long adolescent sterility, irregularity or cessation of menstrual function, higher pregnancy wastage, longer lactational amenorrhea, and early menopause. The !Kung also provide a vivid example of how the notion of some environmentalists that natural human populations voluntarily control the number of offspring they produce is in error. !Kung women at nearly five births each have more than twice the total fertility rate of American women!

The Shaker religion began in 1774 and at its peak there were thousands of adherents. But they did not believe that anyone, even married people, should have sexual intercourse. Today only a few adherents survive. Ethel Hudson, last of the Canterbury, New Hampshire, Shakers, died in 1992 at age 96. The only remaining Shaker community is at Sabbath Lake, Maine, and has eight members. This example of a human population approaching extinction because of a culturgen (religiously imposed chastity) contains an important lesson. Natural selection does not force any individual to act in ways that are adaptive, but it is rigid in dispensing the evolutionary consequences when an individual acts contrary to his own reproductive success. This sad example of the Shakers is one of downtrodden people, mostly orphaned and destitute, joining the Shakers only to be parasitized by a virulent, antigenitive religion. Contrary to their heartfelt belief, that is not salvation. In the evolutionary sense it is the antithesis of salvation and gives rise to pathos because the Shakers were so appallingly misguided.

Contrary to popular expectations, the reproductive performance of Roman Catholics is much the same as that for members of other religions when cultural and economic status is controlled. Official prohibitions of artificial contraception by the Roman Catholic church are clearly ignored wholesale by people who consider themselves to be Roman Catholics. Muslims are reproducing faster than any other large religious group, with an average completed family size of six children. The Muslim preference for patrilineage endogamy, e.g., parallel-cousin marriage (a man has the absolute right to marry his father's brother's daughter), resolves the conflict between female rights of inheritance and a patrilineal principle of descent[121]. In other words, wealth is kept within the male lineage in this system even though daughters have rights of inheritance. It might be noted, coincidentally perhaps, that patrilateral parallel-cousins are less closely genetically related than the other types of cousins, i.e. matrilateral parallel-cousins, and cross-cousins, when there is paternity uncertainty.

There is irony in the fundamentalist Christian attitude toward evolution. They oppose beliefs in evolution, but they demonstrate behaviors as though they were guided by the evolutionary ethic, namely by opposing elective abortion and having large families. One positive effect of religion in an evolutionary context is that it may be a convincing counter to Mammon, for as we mentioned previously, wealth for wealth's sake has a negative effect on reproductive success. However, religious beliefs often place life of the soul above life of the body. If those beliefs result in deferential behaviors that reduce resource extraction and decrease reproductive success, then the effect of religion on reproductive success is negative. And based on the principle of allocation, religion must have a depressing effect on fertility when fertility is high. Thus, the battle of faith *versus* reason is most likely to have consequences for reproductive success only in environments where fertility is already high for other reasons. The concept of an afterlife for humans is an expression of the wish for perpetuity. It may be merely a side effect of our biologically based motivation toward self-preservation carried to fanciful extreme. Marx was correct on the point that religion is the opiate of the masses, especially when it offers heavenly rewards for sacrifices on Earth and those sacrifices reduce reproductive success. It is important not to lose sight of evolutionary goals in pursuit of religious ones.

There are two ways that religion is perpetuated: heritability (spread to descendants) and conversion (spread to unrelated members of the population). It is no coincidence that some religious culturgens take the form that is most extreme in promoting retention and transmission. For example, Christianity offers a choice between heaven (eternal bliss) and hell (eternal suffering). Obey (carry the culturgen) and be saved, turn away (reject the culturgen) and be damned for all eternity. Such a culturgen proclaims the ultimate imaginable reward for accepting it and the ultimate imaginable penalty for rejecting it. It is not a coincidence that the projected outcomes for carrying the culturgen or not carrying the culturgen are ecstasy, in the case of the former, and are so dreadful in the case of the later. Similarly, religions reserve their most dire consequences for followers who leave the fold. The principle is: Keep followers once you have them. Another self-perpetuating culturgen, chain letters, often take a form similar to religious messages: They promise a reward (sometimes financial) if they are disseminated and a penalty, often in the form of a curse, if they are ignored. Were the Ten Commandments a chain letter from God?

God blessed them, saying: "Be fertile and multiply; fill the earth and subdue it."

Genesis 1:28, The New American Bible

In the millennia since that quotation was first written, Judeo-Christians have certainly done just that. This culturgen is perhaps an archetypal example of how a religion can incorporate doctrine that contributes to the religion's self-perpetuation through reproduction of its followers. Similarly, some religions proscribe elective abortion and artificial contraception, with the possible and not surprising effect of increasing the numbers of their adherents. In a conflicting fashion, some religions ban artificial methods of proception like artificial insemination and *in vitro* fertilization with the possible, although probably minor, effect of decreasing the numbers of their adherents.

Perhaps in the 21st Century, our conception of humans should not be taken from theology but rather from a scientific examination of humans themselves. There is validity in what Lumsden and Wilson[127] said:

Religion ... is an enchanted hall of mirrors, a powerful device by which people are absorbed into a tribe and psychically strengthened. But in an age of scientific understanding it offers nothing concrete about man's ultimate meaning. (p. 7)

Many religious ideas are conspicuously incompatible with the real nature of humankind. Other religious beliefs, such as God as a "shepherd," are clearly derived from a past ethos, namely the pastoral lifestyle of our Judeo-Christian ancestors[222]. But many modern religions are not greatly incompatible with living or reproducing in an industrial or postindustrial age. Contrary to the publicity currently given to the matter, the real battle is not between creationism and evolutionism; it is between fitness depressing culturgens and the operation of maximizing reproductive success. The battle between creationists and evolutionary biologists is primarily an intellectual pursuit, and it may have surprisingly few fitness implications. But the battle between fitness depressing culturgens and the operation of maximizing reproductive success is the very essence of the evolutionary process itself in that it contributes greatly to the observed variance in fitness. It will be primarily epistemological forces with relatively weak adaptive significance that lead to the continued decline of religiosity in the future. And what does *science* tell us about God? Hutchinson[105] stated:

> There is a story, possibly apocryphal, of the distinguished British biologist, J. B. S. Haldane, who found himself in the company of a group of theologians. On being asked what one could conclude as to the nature of the Creator from a study of his creation, Haldane is said to have answered, "An inordinate fondness for beetles." (p. 146)

Haldane made this memorable statement because there are many species of beetles, more than any other group of animals, representing perhaps 25 percent or more of all higher organisms. This quotation, as attributed here to Haldane, is a famous one in biology, but by virtue of its popularity its authenticity deserves investigation and has been discussed in detail by Gould[76].

How would a modern anthropologist respond to the same question asked of Haldane? Perhaps with a book not unlike this one. In a strange but interesting publication, Galton[70] investigated the efficacy of prayer and found that the laws of nature are not suspended by God to grant the petitions of the religious. If God exists and has the power to work miracles, why are not the prayers of the devout who are ill or in danger answered in a way that confers greater longevity on them than on atheists? By the same contention, Mormons (centered in Utah) and Shintoists (centered in Japan), who are among the longest living people when categorized by religion, may have a mock right to claim that they have a special rapport with God.

DeVore[42] recounted the following legend:

> The Bishop of Worcester once returned from a debate at the British Association for the Advancement of Science to explain "the terrible theories of Mr. Darwin" to his scandalized wife. On hearing the claim that we might be descended from apes, the good woman is reported to have exclaimed, "Oh dear, let us pray that is not so. But if it is so, let us hope that it does not become generally known." (p. 87)

The principles of evolutionary theory have been thoroughly confirmed. More than a century of unsuccessful refutations have demonstrated the truth of Darwinism. As discussed by Mayr[134], Darwin's *On the Origin of Species* was in the main a refutation of the idea of special creation. Evolution is the only process by which the rich variation of life on Earth could have arisen. Weak arguments about special creation have no influence on the modern scientist, thanks to the work of Darwin.

Occasionally I do encounter laypersons whose thoughts on the origin of the diversity of life are pre-Darwinian. I rarely make the effort to disillusion them unless they have a sincere inquiry.

As it has been defined in astronomy: "Hydrogen is a light, colorless, odorless gas that given enough time turns into people". We know that carbon and the other heavy elements in our bodies were fabricated in the dense centers of ancient collapsing stars. In turn, the carbon-based organic chemicals of which we are composed were synthesized in the atmospheric conditions that prevailed on primitive Earth, a process which has been duplicated in the laboratory. And the final form of our behavior and morphology has been shaped by organic evolution. As Julian Huxley pointed out, after billions of years of evolution, the universe is becoming conscious of itself, and it is able to understand something of its past history and its possible future. This observation by Huxley was astute, but he carried the point too far when he asserted that the supreme task for humans was to increase conscious comprehension and to use it to guide future events.

If we are going to condone religion, would not a religion that incorporates evolutionary principles and the evolutionary ethic be even more desirable than existing religions? If not based on evolution, then a religion based on the worship of a fertility god or fertility goddess might contribute to the increased fitness of its devotees. The ancient Egyptians had Hathor, their goddess of sky and fertility, and Min, their god of virility and generation. Min was normally portrayed as a male figure with his penis erect and wearing a headdress with two tall plumes. How different would our practice of reproduction be if his image replaced the icons presently used in the Christian church? That thought of replacing one god with another, more progenitive god, inspires a question regarding the ultimate value of truth in terms of reproductive success, which will be discussed in a following section. But such a religion would be adaptive for its adherents for some time. Would this religion be called the Church of the Evolutionary Ethic? What would be its tenets? Perhaps they would include not only a fertility god and goddess, but also coitus as a sacrament, prohibition of contraception and elective abortion, the encouragement of the practice of proception, and descendant worship. Ancestor worship is an attribute of many cultures, and it may help to define and bind kinship groups, perhaps to the benefit of the members. Descendant worship would seem to be a more direct pathway to increasing reproductive success, but it does not play a part of any culture with which I am familiar. How might we promote such a progenitive religion and what would be the signs of its growing popularity? In a crude measure, we shall know the frequency of converts by the number of bumper stickers reading "HONK IF YOU LOVE DARWIN".

A final point about religion is its genetic basis. Some people might be inclined toward religious belief for genetic reasons just as some people are inclined to do mathematics well for genetic reasons. If religious behavior has been or is adaptive as discussed herein, it is possible to imagine selection for genes predisposing individuals toward religion in a way that increased the frequency of this trait in the population. Thus, in addition to the spread of religion as a self-perpetuating culturgen, the maintenance or spread of the trait in the population may be in part due to natural selection.

Life-lesson: Religion is wrong, but it may be good for you.

Namely, it is likely to increase one's reproductive success. However, beware of high variance in reproductive success as a function of religion. When religious beliefs are good (as in the case of the Hutterites) there is hardly anything better for helping an individual to maximize reproductive success, but when religious beliefs are bad (as in the case of the Shakers), there is hardly anything worse for reproductive success.

Interspecific questions

Humans are as concerned about interspecific interactions as an omnivorous species should be. We eat plants and animals, dote on our pets, and sometimes become concerned over animal rights when inspired by activists. What does an evolutionary analysis tell us about these interactions? Darwin[38] pointed out that natural selection can never generate anything for the sole benefit of another species. Animal rights activists would need to elucidate the benefit of animal rights for humans to put the concept on a sound evolutionary basis. Humans have domesticated animals and used some of the species as sources of food and clothing for about eight thousand years. Long before that, indeed for millions of years, humans hunted wild animals to meet their needs, and long before that, human ancestors went through an insectivorous stage. Use of animal products has been a primary component of human survival in the past. Therefore, we cannot possibly look for historical precedence in arguing for the sanctity (in the sense of right of freedom from exploitation) of animal life. The big five domestic animals (horse, cow, sheep, goat, and pig) are used widely around the world by diverse cultures. Achieving protected status for them, as some of the more ardent animal rights activists desire, seems impossible. But another question should be addressed here: Are there grounds for abstaining from the use of a product (such as meat, leather, or animal-tested pharmaceuticals) that required the killing of an animal? Darwin[38] expressed the view that in nature species compete against other species, and that this competition led to considerable suffering and death. With this idea in mind I submit that there are no clear evolutionary grounds for the objection to the killing of other common species. There might be grounds to argue against killing of some other species to the point of extinction, particularly if they were or could be useful to humans. Patterns of reliance on animal protein in the human diet are likely to change in the future (when the human population is larger than now) as we shorten the human food chain in order to utilize plant energy more efficiently. This trend will limit the breeding and, in effect, limit the killing of domestic animals. If people in other cultures of the world ate like Americans do, e.g., living at the end of a long food chain and consuming large quantities of meat, less than half of the current world population could have been fed on the record harvests of 1985 and 1986[54]. When food shortages do occur, Americans, like the majority of other humans, will adopt a diet that shortens the food chain and contains greater quantities of calories derived directly from plants.

There is an important, fitness depleting trend in America toward accepting reproduction substitutes. Americans spend one billion dollars a year on baby food, but spend a considerably larger eight billion dollars a year on dog and cat food[199]. About one and a half billion of the total expenditure on pet food is spent on luxury "superpremium" brands. They cost approximately twice as much as ordinary pet foods -- but do pets really need them? As Sussman[199] reported:

> ... the most common nutritional problem veterinarians see is obesity, not illness due to a nutrient shortage. Half of American dogs and perhaps a quarter of cats waddle through life as furry dumplings. (p. 98)

Those same resources that make our pets obese could be used instead to adequately feed ten million hungry children around the world perpetually -- with money left over to give them clean water and primary health care as well. At first it seems strange that we should pamper our Abyssinian cats while children die in Ethiopia (modern day Abyssinia) every day from preventable causes generated by extreme poverty, poor nutrition, and inadequate primary health care. When I first saw a bumper sticker with the message: "I love Abyssinians," I thought that it was a compassionate expression of solidarity with people in an ancient and troubled land -- then I realized the vehicle owner was referring to his cats! It is consistent, perhaps, with inclusive fitness theory that Americans should care first for their immediate family, then for more distant family and friends, for neighbors, for fellow Americans, and last of all unrelated, unfamiliar people on the other side of the world. But should we really place our pets near the top of that list of people for whom we care? My hypothesis is that we are being manipulated by our pets and that they are a set of domestic animals that have turned the tables: They co-opt rather than contribute to our reproductive effort. Domestication of animals occurred because it provided a resource utilizable by humans. In a statistical distribution of the net effects of all species domesticated by humans, it is not surprising that the least valuable (in terms of providing utilizable products), i.e. pets, would actually incur a net cost on humans instead of any benefit at all. Another point is that our pets have a daily opportunity for direct manipulation of our emotions, whereas the forty thousand children who die around the world each day of mostly preventable causes are remote and do not have a direct opportunity to influence us. I would argue that we should redirect the effort expended in supporting and breeding pets to the care of our own children. Can we stop our clinging to reproduction substitutes and set ourselves free?

The question of whether the keeping of pets is mutualism or parasitism can be asked. In other words, is the relationship of benefit to both the pets and their human keepers, or of benefit to only one? Humans are always of use to the domestic pets they keep. The question is whether the pet serves a useful function for the humans. Examples of functional pets are: working sheep dogs, dogs bred for sled transportation by the Eskimo, or kept for human food as among the Aztecs (the Mexican hairless dog was bred as a source of protein and fat) and by the Chinese, and guide dogs for the blind. There are many examples of harmful pets. Caged birds in the home are associated with increased risk of lung disease and psittacosis, a disease contracted from the dust of feathers or excreta of infected birds. Dogs in the home are a common source of serious, disfiguring bites to children. More than 2 million dog bites are reported each year in the U.S.A. Dogs can transmit a number of diseases to humans, including rabies, which is fatal, and dog roundworm, which is a rare cause of blindness in humans. Among the Turkana people, who live around Lake Rudolf in eastern Africa, dogs are a definitive host for a tapeworm (*Echinococcus* sp.) which, in the larval stage parasitizes its human keepers as intermediary hosts and causes the disease echinococcosis. The adult tapeworms give the dogs little trouble. It is the humans who suffer when they become infected by accidentally ingesting canine tapeworm eggs. After a long period of unnoticed growth, large parasitic hydatid cysts are formed in the liver, lungs, bones, brain, and other organs. Treatment by drugs and surgery is moderately successful. When untreated, as it often is in eastern Africa, the result is that the hydatid cysts, some the size of basketballs, disfigure and kill the human victims.

Horses kept for the genteel pleasure of riding are more dangerous than sharks, based on the relative rates at which they maim and kill Americans. Here is an alternative to bear in mind: In Europe, horsemeat is a delicacy, and American slaughterhouses will pay in the range of five hundred dollars for a horse which will eventually appear on tables in France. Take the five hundred dollars and spend it on proception. In truth, the vast majority of American pets fall into the harmful category. Even though many Americans allow their dogs to sleep with them in their beds, it is hard to imagine that many use their dogs as blankets as do Australian Aborigines on cold nights. Americans are also imaginative in their rationalizations for keeping pets. One popular excuse for keeping dogs is for protection. But a surprising number of people who keep dogs for protection have their dogs stolen from the homes or cars that they are supposed to be guarding.

Humans first domesticated animals because of the benefit to themselves.

Through a process of coevolution, both humans and animals were changed. The process of coevolution has turned many of our pets into parasites that manipulate us for their own benefit. Much can be said of how we are manipulated by other organisms that we encounter. Parasites often manipulate their human hosts. Cholera bacteria produce a toxin that causes severe diarrhea in the infected human. By this means the cholera infection is spread to other people via the fecal-oral route. With a little imagination the distinction between pet and parasite is blurred in the expression: "The tapeworm is the perfect pet; it goes where you go, it eats what you eat". Of course, an important point to keep in mind is that a tapeworm is a much less costly pet to keep than the average dog. While few people would have reservations about taking an anthelmintic to rid themselves of a tapeworm, and while many people endorse the campaign to neuter dogs, few are prepared to take the step necessary to completely rid themselves of this costly parasite and have euthanasia performed on their dog, even though most chapters of the SPCA will provide that service *gratis*. People are so manipulated by their dogs that I doubt that many will follow my advice. "Man's best friend" is really "man's best parasite" when placed in the modern setting of the American family home. I doubt that these paragraphs will rid Americans of the pets that parasitize them so unremittingly, and that is because the strategies of the parasitic pets are so artful. For example, take the "cute response" that young pets like puppies and kittens have evolved to evoke and misdirect human parental care. They mimic the visual and auditory stimuli of a human baby thereby eliciting a human care response. By tapping into parental investment tendencies, these parasitic pets have succeeded in finding a veritable eternal fountain of care, because such parental investment tendencies serve an essential and perpetual function of human reproduction. Among the more bizarre interactions between Americans and their pets is the provision some people make for their pets in their will. People confer their parrots on relatives (with the concomitant risk of lung disease); they provide trust funds for their dogs; they leave the family home to the cat. Among the more extreme examples of a lack of rational thinking in terms of reproductive success is people who run into burning buildings in order to rescue their cats. Such behavior does not make a great deal of sense from the human viewpoint.

Life-lesson: Keep no pets. Have another child or help a relative raise another child instead.

Chapter 7: Competition

Aggression

I would like to examine aggression in a phylogenetic perspective. Aggression and even the killing of conspecifics is common in the animal kingdom. It is not only humans who kill their own kind. Indeed, things that distinguish humans from their nearest nonhuman primate relatives are the low rates of aggression, the infrequency of killing of conspecifics, and traditions to deal with homicide. For example, homicide is only the ninth leading cause of death in America. In comparison, the adult male anubis baboons in the Masai Mara population that I studied had on the average three life-threatening encounters of escalated male-male aggression every day! These bouts of escalated aggression are probably the most common cause of death for adult males. My point is not that aggression leading to homicide is desirable, rather that aggression leading to homicide is comparatively infrequent in humans. The final point, regarding traditions to deal with homicide and its aftermath, is that they seem to be lacking among the nonhuman primates I have observed. An adult male killed in escalated aggression is allowed to lie where he fell, for the scavengers. A dependent infant who is killed will often be dragged along for a few days by its mother, then finally left behind during a troop progression.

It appears clear that improved nutrition increases rates of male-male aggression among primates. As habitat quality improves, male-male competition increases for access to mates. Rates of escalated male-male conflict are positively correlated with annual rainfall[162]. For example, by rough comparison male anubis baboons in the wet habitat of Masai Mara, Kenya, are ten times as aggressive as male hamadryas baboons in the dry habitat at Harar, Ethiopia. The relationship between rainfall and aggression is straightforward. As rainfall increases and improves habitat quality, searching and handling costs for food items decreases, increasing portions of the time budget and energy budget that are available for nonfeeding activities. The rate of male-male conflict increases with increasing habitat quality, because males are better able to meet the high energetic costs of aggressive behavior. In particular, rates of escalated aggression are expected to increase in the context of competition for access to females. Males are better able to meet the costs of competition as described above, and females are an object of competition that increases in value with increasing habitat quality, because the females have a greater amount of reproductive effort to expend per unit time.

Associated with the advantage provided to the individual during male-male competition, the degree of sexual dimorphism in body mass increases with increasing rainfall in baboons. The difference in size between male baboons and female baboons varies widely among habitats. Males may be between 72 percent larger and 216 percent larger than females. Male baboon body mass increases geometrically as a function of adult female body mass. In dry, energy poor habitats, baboons incur high searching and handling costs in foraging. A large portion of the energy budget is expended on the acquisition of new food sources. In wetter and energy richer habitats, smaller percentages of the total energy budget are required for feeding, and more energy may be diverted to reproductive effort.

Starvation reduces rates of aggression, contrary to the common assumption. Rhesus monkeys on Cayo Santiago, Puerto Rico, showed a dramatic reduction in aggressive behavior when their main source of artificial provisioning was cut off by shipment failures. Of course, when food is in short supply, competition for food sources may be reduced or enhanced, depending upon the nature and distribution of the food resources. But among primates, aggressive competition over food resources is usually a small part of the total aggression profile.

While humans are somewhat removed from the kind of ecological determinism that shapes baboon social behavior, we are not entirely free of it. One would not expect a correlation between male-male aggression in human societies and local annual rainfall, as appears in baboon societies. The lesson for human behavior that we learn from ecological determinism is that recent increases in the quality of diet available to Americans is, overall, desirable in terms of maximizing reproductive success. But an unavoidable consequence is the increase of male-male aggression in direct attempts to gain access to females or in indirect attempts to do so, such as aggressive displays relating to status, gang ''territory'' and so forth. This behavior is conspicuously evident among some young Americans where school-age violence is a newly emergent ''luxury'' behavior that could not have been afforded by earlier generations with less plentiful and less dependable food sources.

It has not always been recognized that the primate model of nutrition and aggression applies to human behavior, and that we should expect higher rates of aggression among us as we improve nutrition. Early theories in anthropology suggested that protein deprivation was a cause of aggression in human societies (e.g., Harris[89]). However, counterexamples like the Yanomamö Indians of South America reversed the hypothesis; if anything, rates of aggression are *positively* correlated with protein consumption[24].

In humans and other animals there are kinship effects in competition. The cost of competition to a competitor is considered in the competitive cost-benefit inequality[164], if a competitor is a relative. The result is reduced competition among relatives. Relatives are selected to exaggerate costs of competition to themselves. But if the object of competition is of sufficient value and alternative reproductive strategies are limited, then even high regression coefficients of relatedness can be overridden. In sororicide among honeybees, sisters with a regression coefficient of relatedness of $^3/_4$ compete to the death over which will inherit the hive.

The primary object of competition that leads to escalated aggression in most nonhuman primate societies and most non-Western human societies is females (see examples: Popp[163] and Chagnon[24]). The evolution of social dominance occurs because each individual in the social system strives for a social status that provides it with access to limiting resources. Competition for dominance does not improve the species in any broader sense[164]. There is merely selection for those traits that confer intrinsic competitive ability on the individuals who possess them.

Wealth and social status

At present there is an inverse relationship between wealth and reproductive success in most modern societies. In America the decline in the fertility gradient with increasing income is steep. Women in families earning over $35,000 have a thirty three percent lower total fertility rate than women in families earning less than $10,000. The present provides a unique opportunity to maximize reproductive success. As an individual, choose adaptive behaviors and let the life-lessons herein be your guide. As a member of a family, explore areas of overlapping fitness that allow each member to maximize his or her reproductive success. As a member of a business, you should be trying to maximize reproductive success, not profit, in your daily operations. That pattern may well be on the horizon for American businesses. We see the precursors of such a future adaptive strategy in today's common workplace behaviors, e.g., appointing a son to the family business, promoting a daughter preferentially, or hiring a girlfriend. Indeed, we accept such nepotism as entirely normal, even though we rarely give thought to its implication for reproductive success. If wealth depresses fertility, is an alternative medium of exchange needed in order to promote progenitiveness? Perhaps not if we learn to convert the monetary value of goods and services into reproductive success value, the ultimate currency. Modern Americans have trouble understanding the tradeoff of wealth for life and vice versa. I prefer in thinking about this tradeoff to emphasize not the economic value of a life (which is the way it is commonly put) but, instead, the reproductive success value of economics. At the moment the conversion would be irregular and imperfect, with some goods and services being of high monetary value but low reproductive success value and others being of low monetary value but high reproductive success value. It is certain that reproductive success value of goods and services has predominance over monetary value in any rational system based on evolution. Ultimately, the monetary value of goods and services would fall in line with reproductive success value. I recognize that this assertion, that wealth is a liability in America in an evolutionary sense, goes against conventional wisdom and that even fellow anthropologists may be incredulous. The two concomitants of wealth, prestige and fame, are also largely reproductive liabilities. But the commonplace, erroneous expectation that modern economic success should be positively correlated with reproductive success may be just another sad legacy of Social Darwinism. This true inverse relationship between wealth and reproductive success has far-reaching implications for American life, as we shall see in a following section on charity.

Life-lesson: Instead of obsessively pursuing more wealth, use what you have to maximize your reproductive success.

Along with the inverse relationship between wealth and reproductive success, there is also an inverse relationship between social status and reproductive success in most modern societies. Fisher[60] wrote:

> ... the socially lower occupations are the more fertile, we must face the paradox that the biologically successful members of our society are to be found principally among its social failures, and equally that classes of persons who are prosperous and socially successful are, on the whole, the biological failures, the unfit of the struggle for existence, doomed more or less speedily, according to their social distinction, to be eradicated from the human stock. (p. 241)

Based on a study of the average number of children per person in *Who's Who*, Fisher[60] pointed out that the key indicator of how much one's fertility is depressed by social status is the amount of social promotion. Among those individuals whose social promotion is most striking, the fertility is lower than it is for individuals of the same status but for whom their social promotion was less.

Law, liberty and justice

The first order of business in this section is the issue of reproductive rights. Every individual has a right to as few or as many children as she or he wishes. Reproductive rights may have to supersede other rights sometimes taken for granted, e.g., the right to more than adequate nutrition for all. I do not deny that unrestrained quest for reproductive success may raise ethical questions. For example, it may threaten some existing cultural values. The American preference for large quantities of animal fat and animal protein will not be sustainable at high population densities. The commonly sought goal of prosperity, if it remains a commonly sought goal, will be difficult to achieve, though each additional child represents only a small decrement in the country's prosperity and only at high population densities. Progenitivism could, conceivably, also instigate the formation of a pernicious government with an anti-reproduction agenda, because the government's self-perpetuation and stringent control over people are undermined by unregulated reproduction. Thus, by exercising progenitivism we may thereby endanger this very same, most essential, primary value. Any kind of forced or coercive control of fertility creates difficult ethical dilemmas. Yet, such policies may nevertheless arise in the future in America as they have already in China.

Cultural values opposing progenitivism are simply a type of culturgen. There is much latitude for their replacement, exchange and extinction. And the attempts of unrelated individuals to encourage you to not reproduce are exactly what you should expect. Is the missionary-like zeal of the people advocating reproductive restraint altruistic? Only if the restraint on their own reproduction and the reproduction of their relatives is more than the restraint they urge upon unrelated people. In the main, the promulgation of contraception and abortion is either a spiteful behavior or a selfish behavior. Carrying this form of cynicism to an extreme, one may not be entirely surprised when individual environmentalists, the parents of many in private lives, publicly encourage other people in the spirit of ecological concerns to refrain from reproducing. This tendency may be appropriately named the "breeding hypocrisy hypothesis": Encourage unrelated people to control their numbers while attempting to maximize the number of children that you and your relatives produce. It just might be a successful reproductive strategy in these strange times.

At present there is something of a social backlash against parents who do not support their children. There is the possibility of coming change in welfare laws affecting women with dependent children. For example, there is a trend on a state by state basis to deny welfare recipients additional welfare benefits for additional children born to the mother while on welfare. Some maintain that poor women get pregnant just to become eligible for welfare support. Political conservatives maintain that the promise of welfare support, to the extent that it promotes pregnancies among unmarried mothers, is facilitating a self-destructive choice by these women. Of course, according to the evolutionary ethic, the exact opposite is true: Welfare facilitates a good choice. But in technical terms we do not know for certain if current welfare payments are too low or too high to maximize the reproductive success of the recipients. It is possible that they are too high, and that a reduction in welfare support will result in an increase in fertility among the recipients and former recipients who are disenfranchised. Welfare, including food stamps, now accounts for approximately three percent of the federal budget. It is a step in the right direction of eliminating the social pathology of extreme variance in income in America, which hurts the rich and poor alike. Both the rich and the poor gain reproductive benefits from the welfare system. The logic of this argument is explained in the section on philanthropy and charity.

One high technology proposal to deal with absentee fathers who do not support their children is the use of genetic profiling to determine paternity and then to extract child support by means of legal intervention from fathers who do not provide it voluntarily. That might improve the finances of these children, but will it increase their reproductive success? Over thirty years after President Johnson's war on poverty, the tables have turned, and it is now commonplace for individual Americans and their leaders to begrudge welfare support to needy families. One point to keep in mind is that the unemployed mother receives less welfare support for the addition of another dependent child to her family than the tax deduction allowed to a working parent with a dependent child.

Crime and punishment

The three most common punishments for violations of the law in America are fines, imprisonment, and the death penalty. I shall examine each in turn. It is common knowledge that these forms of punishment administered by our legal system have failed conspicuously to eliminate or even reasonably control crime. I propose that is the case because we have ignored the evolutionary implications. Let us first consider the punishment of a fine. Fines provide a proximate disincentive to crime because most people are inclined to want to preserve their wealth -- parting with wealth is a form of negative reinforcement. That psychological model is the usual explanation for fines as a useful form of punishment. But in direct opposition to this line of thinking, fines are actually an ultimate incentive at another, more fundamental level of causation. Unless the person fined is greatly impoverished, fining him is actually doing him an evolutionary favor, because there is an inverse relationship between wealth and reproductive success. A financial bonus as punishment for a crime would provide a proximate incentive but an ultimate disincentive. I conclude that neither fine nor bonus can be a truly effective deterrent to crime. The ideal disincentive would make a crime distasteful to the senses through negative reinforcement *and* would be maladaptive. In contrast, the ideal incentive for a behavior would be tasteful to the senses through positive reinforcement and would be adaptive. However, since individuals differ in the state of their life history parameters, no practical, single treatment of disincentive or incentive seems applicable to all. For example, food deprivation might be a true punishment for some (both distasteful and tending to reduce fitness), but to others, e.g., the morbidly obese, it would be a benefit! The consequences of imprisonment and the death penalty are also variable. At risk perhaps of overstating the case, some prisoners benefit, in the ultimate sense relating to their fitness, from imprisonment by virtue of the fact that they "dry out" from alcohol abuse or from abuse of illicit drugs, or by receiving more or fewer calories, or by receiving needed state-sponsored medical care. The death penalty is obviously more broadly negative in both the proximate and ultimate effects, but it can hardly be considered an applicable sentence for all crimes. And, surprisingly, it also shows some variation in its effects. For example, it is not totally preposterous to imagine a psychopathic murderer on death row, who is plotting to have his own family killed, being better off in most respects, including the evolutionary consideration of his own inclusive fitness, by permanently removing the threat that he poses to them. I conclude that this analysis, which shows both the ineffectiveness and inequity of punishment, seems to undermine the simplistic notion in Western culture stating equal punishment for equal crime. It also calls into question the very definition of punishment. In turn, these flaws illuminate a paradox regarding the real consequences of the entire practice of justice and law in America today. An alternative system of law and justice, based on evolutionary principles as well as the current model of positive and negative reinforcements, merits further study. But somehow, to an anthropologist, at least, that alternative system of justice seems itself to be unjust, because that which lowers one's reproductive success is bad according to the evolutionary ethic. Of course, in a strict interpretation, it might be argued that it is bad for the criminal but good for those imposing the punishment and good for other members of society as a whole whose reproductive interests are thereby protected.

In the 1990 U.S. Census there were 2,356 people on death row in America. Between 1930 and 1988, 3,963 people were executed in America. This number is insignificant in comparison to the total American population of 248,709,873. The issue of the death penalty is an emotionally and politically charged one. In this analysis we can suggest that certain conditions could exist that made it adaptive for an individual to trade his life for a fitness gain, e.g., the defense of the lives of a group of relatives with lethal aggression, with the actual loss of the actor's life being imposed by legal sanction. Furthermore, other individuals could find it adaptive to impose that legal sanction. In a sense we all trade years of our life for the ability to reproduce, whether potential or realized, as we learned earlier. Killing of conspecifics is a regular event in human and nonhuman primate societies. It is a source of amazement to many that even among human cultures that express the utmost reverence for living things, like the Hindus who sweep away insects from the ground in front of them as they walk, their members would systematically murder their own newborn daughters in the process of biasing the sex ratio toward sons.

Politicians and police take credit, often with considerable fanfare, for the reduction in the rate of major crimes in America in recent years. But the observed crime reduction is really a consequence of demographics, and it is an aging population that is moving out of the ages most prone to committing crime that is actually directly responsible. Therefore, politicians and police are responsible only in the sense that their repressive policies are antigenitive and have depressed fertility and thus contributed to this demographic shift. This truth is one that politicians and police do not want their constituencies to know. Instead, they prefer to mislead the public into believing that they are effectively combating crime. Higher status, higher budgets, and larger salaries are three of the motivations for perpetuators of this misinformation.

In an ideal system of government, of, for and by the people, citizens would make laws to increase their reproductive success. But of course any reproductive strategy must take into account the social environment in which it is employed. Based on the principle of the evolutionary ethic, members of a society can form agreements in the shape of laws to reconcile reproductive conflict of interests. In this way, our simplified system of one ethic would become the foundation of an entire legal system. Laws pertaining to reciprocity, marriage, property rights, corporations, partnerships, and crime would arise readily from all people seeking to make agreements to assure the maximization of their reproductive success. Take the example of laws against homicide. It is easy to imagine circumstances under which two or more people could increase their reproductive success if they entered into a binding contractual agreement prohibiting murder. Such a binding contractual agreement could, with the same theoretical justification, be extended to hold for all of society in the form of a legal code. As a result, we would have a society that was more civilized than other nonhuman primate species. We might even have a society with greater pacific stability than our present one. So fear of regression under the rule of the evolutionary ethic to a primitive state of rampant, self-serving, murderous aggression is not founded. To the contrary, fine points of law regarding contracts and compromises, in the form of binding agreements on all desirable issues, would be assessed for their implications for reproductive success, and would be ratified if found to be in the reproductive success interests of the proposed participants, perhaps many of them state and nationwide. Americans often confuse law and morality. A law establishes a sanction. The sanction places a fitness contingency on our behavior. The law and the behavior are moral if they are in accordance with the evolutionary ethic. In this way progenitivists do not object to culture establishing social order beyond what genes alone can do; the objection arises only when it is against the interests of genes.

Let us define as perverted that which is unnatural and lowers reproductive success. When defined in this way, most perversions have a large cultural component. When we look at the truly perverted atrocities in human history, e.g., human sacrificial killing and mass annihilations, we can see for the most part that they were primarily the product of culture, not genes, and that they benefited no one's reproductive success. Thus, it is ironic that many people should commonly associate rule by genetic interests with tyranny and injustice. In contrast, I expect the application of the evolutionary ethic to bring an increase in civility, freedom, and dignity to our lives. I see a potential inconsistency in the thoughts of those who would maintain that the "bad" that humans do is not in our genes and who at the same time would object to the evolutionary ethic. One cannot easily maintain both objections. If crimes like genocide are not genetically determined, then would not rule by genetic interests offer a way of sure improvement of our moral code? I call this question the "evolutionary ethical dilemma". It exists only for those who doubt the evolutionary ethic and who also believe that humans are not intrinsically "bad".

Parricide

We have covered infanticide in a previous section. It is not the only form of lethal aggression within the family. For example, matricide occurs among the social bees and wasps[14]. In human societies, parricide is the stuff of royal legends. For example, King Edward III of England was implicated in the grizzly murder of his father, King Edward II[30]. In some species of spiders and insects the young feed on the body of the dead or dying mother.

Homicide rates

Lorenz[123] seems to have gotten it entirely wrong when he imagined the existence of an inhibition of killing conspecifics among animals. His speculation gave rise to the false conclusion that only humans kill their kind. In fact, the opposite is true; by nonhuman primate standards, humans are exceptionally peaceful.

Familial aggression

Corporal punishment within the family, either of a child or of a spouse, is a perplexing subject. We need to know more about the fitness implications of these behaviors before we can decide if the outcome is good or bad. Familial conflict is a timely subject, in that it has received increased attention in the last decade. It may be that American values are changing. It does seem that what once would have historically been considered normal familial discipline might now be considered criminal abuse in some cases. One important variable in measuring the adaptive significance of these behaviors is legal sanctions, both old and new, that aim to regulate familial behavior.

Xenophobia, racism, and war

Competition between groups of organisms, whether they be humans, baboons, lions or hyenas, seems to be a common consequence of natural selection. Individuals from other populations (or subpopulations) are more likely to be viewed by the members of one's own group as competitors because they are only distantly related. This genetic distance between tribes or races in humans and between troops of baboons, prides of lions and clans of hyenas may be a large part of the explanation for intergroup aggression, tribalism, racism, and xenophobia. Hamilton[86] wrote:

> ... I hope to produce evidence that some things which are often treated as purely cultural in man -- say racial discrimination -- have deep roots in our animal past and thus are quite likely to rest on direct genetic foundations. To be more specific, it is suggested that the ease and accuracy with which an idea like xenophobia strikes the next replica of itself on the template of human memory may depend on the preparation made for it there by selection -- selection acting, ultimately, at the level of replicating molecules. (p. 134)

Hamilton[86] suggested that there are genetical (as well as cultural) reasons why intergroup migration and marriage should decrease intergroup hostility among humans. Simply stated, intergroup marriage increases the relatedness among groups and that increase in relatedness decreases the net benefits that can be obtained through aggressive competition. But Hamilton[86] did not make an important point: Increases in intergroup migration and marriage should also increase *intra*group hostility. This prediction follows from the fact that with outbreeding the regression coefficients of relatedness decrease among members of a group. Along this line of thinking, I have wondered if children of mixed marriages are more selfish and more self-centered in familial relations than the children of parents of similar genetic background. For example, would children of mixed marriages show greater weaning conflict than other children?

History shows that America is a country of substantial prowess in and of considerable propensity toward war. When is war just? When it furthers reproductive success, not when it only promotes a culturgen like a political or economic system. Perhaps more so in the discussion of this form of behavior than in any other, a distinction should be drawn: To offer a biological explanation of it is not necessarily to suggest that it is a desirable characteristic for modern society -- it might very well have biological roots but still be bad for people touched by it according to the definition of the evolutionary ethic. One view of wars is that men do fight them to further their reproductive interests. But another view is that conflicting culturgens in the form of ideas motivate opposing armies to fight each other, without necessary benefits accruing to either side. Consider the Vietnam war in this regard. Americans fighting in Vietnam engendered many Amerasian children, but it is not clear that the number of children engendered was greater than the number that would have been engendered by the Americans if they had stayed in America. The alternative view is that two grand ideas, capitalism and communism, each superculturgens, were in opposition in the Vietnam war. Could the war have been a battle of culturgens using soldiers as their hosts and agents rather than a strategic exercise in achieving a clearly definable human goal? Perhaps the ferocity of war is so great because it is a combination of different gene/culturgen complexes battling for supremacy.

Slavery

In true slavery, the reproductive success of the slave is reduced. This condition is met in slavery (dulosis) in a number of species of ants. Wilson[221] provided a detailed description of slavery in ants, and I shall not consider it further here. Interracial slavery among humans is presently limited to the Sudan, where young Nilotic people of the south are kidnapped and enslaved by Semitic people of the north. The going price for a slave is the equivalent of twenty dollars. The definition of a true slave is also met by the wetnurse. In a sense she is the ultimate slave -- her reproductive effort is tapped directly. Once associated primarily with the infants of white slave-owners being suckled by black slaves in the South, wetnursing has made an alarming resurgence as a product of the pro-breastfeeding movement in America today. Humans of other cultures have been known to similarly squander their reproductive effort. Women of ancient Siam would breastfeed young sacred white elephants for religious reasons. Women of New Guinea breastfeed young swine for economic reasons.

Now a broader kind of slavery occurs in America. We are enslaved by fitness reducing culturgens. Our goals should be to emancipate humans from these fitness reducing culturgens.

Strategic aggressive competition

During aggressive competition, as well as during some other aspects of the life history, there is selection for the exaggeration of variables in the cost-benefit competitive inequality. The remaining paragraphs in this chapter review an analysis of aggressive competition by Popp and DeVore[164].

Individuals may exaggerate their competitive ability -- thus making it appear that they have an increased probability of winning the competitive encounter and causing the competitor to quit the competition early. Piloerection (body hair standing out on end) in chimpanzees and thick mantles of hair in anubis and hamadryas baboons and manes in male lions are examples of how individuals can exaggerate their competitive ability by appearing to be larger than they really are.

An individual may also exaggerate the value of a disputed resource. Such exaggeration suggests a disparity between how the actor and the competitor value the object of competition, giving the actor a competitive advantage. For example, among some birds and some fish sham nest-building and sham nest-tending behavior occur during agonistic encounters. The real or imagined presence of a nest for the actor would ordinarily confer a competitive advantage on the actor, because he or she has more to gain and to lose in the encounter than the competitor, as explained by Popp and DeVore[164].

An actor may also exaggerate the probability of winning the competitive encounter. Such an exaggeration suggests to the competitor that expenditure of his time, energy, and the risks assumed are not rational because of his decreased chance of winning. Such an exaggeration could easily occur through projecting a confident, self-assured manner before and during the conflict.

Concealing the costs of competition can also be adaptive during a competitive encounter. Hiding injuries from the competitor and not feeling pain during the conflict as an adaptation to effectively hiding injuries that would ordinarily be painful are two examples of how the costs of competition may be concealed. Lost feeding time is another type of cost. In response, the evolution of displays of sham feeding behavior by a wide range of animals during aggressive encounters makes adaptive sense.

Another strategy useful in aggressive competition is for the actor to exaggerate the regression coefficient of relatedness between himself and the competitor. While individuals are likely under most circumstances to have a relatively fixed conception of relatedness to opponents, it does appear to be a variable in the cost-benefit competitive inequality that is sometimes exaggerated. Territorial intruders sometimes attempt to adopt the scent of the territorial holders by rubbing on scent deposits. Among humans the inappropriate evocation of the kinship idiom in terms of address occurs [164], e.g., "Brother, can you spare a dime?"

Certain sets of exaggerations are expected to occur when the actor and the competitor are relatives. One is to exaggerate the value of the resource to the actor. The actor portrays a desperate, exaggerated need for the object of competition. The gaping mouths and waving heads of nestlings competing for a food item brought back to the nest by a parent is a possible example. Among humans, desperate begging and pleading for the object of competition is likely to occur.

Another principle of aggressive competition is the exaggeration of the costs of competition to the actor when the competitor is a relative. Actors are expected to feign serious injury, or higher rates of costs of conflicts to themselves, during a fight with a relative. For example, one would expect, based on this model, that siblings have a lower threshold for vocal complaints and cry more often and more intensely when roughhousing among themselves than when doing so with unrelated children. This strategy is particularly effective if a related potential mediator, like a mother, is made to witness the display. Crying and tattling to mother about the behavior of a sibling makes a lot of sense in terms of an evolutionary theory of aggressive competition.

The form of exaggeration among mates depends upon the degree of linkage of their fitness. They may be outright competitors in some respects if the fitness linkage is low, or they may be linked by close cooperation and altruism as shown by actual relatives, if the fitness linkage is high. In other words, to the degree that there is fitness overlap between mates, they will be less inclined to exaggerate.

Chapter 8: Demography and Ecology

Human population growth

Demographers know and they often tell us that humans cannot continue a positive rate of population increase indefinitely. The human population will have a rate of growth very close to zero in the long-term. Cohen[27] stated that this drop to near or below zero population growth rate must occur at most within a century or so. The cause for this zero growth rate will eventually be due to limiting resources, unlike the pattern currently observed in Western countries which have a near zero growth rate for cultural reasons. Since the time of the advent of agriculture, the human population of Earth has increased by approximately 50,000 percent. But now, in developed countries including the United States and all of Western Europe except Ireland, fertility is at an all-time low[174]. The human population is growing at 94 million people a year. About 93 percent of births are in Africa, Latin America, and Asia. In absolute numbers this rate of growth is the greatest in history. The Earth could not support the 694 billion people that would exist in the year 2150 if present fertility rates continue[27]. At present the human population of Earth is six billion and by rough estimates might eventually reach 70 billion to 700 billion. One estimate suggested that the total human impact on global net primary productivity including direct human consumption, indirect co-option, and suppression of photosynthetic production is 25 percent[54]. This estimate, if correct, would suggest that the human population growth curve is rapidly approaching the asymptote. Some maintain that there are too many people on Earth already. But we progenitivists must question: "Too many, by what definition?" No doubt that there could be too many people in terms of preservation of endangered birds like the California condor and the whooping crane, but are there too many in terms elucidated in the evolutionary ethic? The evolutionary ethic holds true regardless of the size of the population. Furthermore, the fact that the human population continues to grow is an empirical observation that fails to support the hypothesis that the world is overpopulated.

It is important to state unequivocally that overpopulation is *not* the goal of the philosophy herein supported. Achieving a larger population than there is at present is merely a by-product; in the broad sense it does not do anything for us. But at the same time striving to achieve reproductive success, even in a population that is stationary or declining due to population pressure, is good. In one prediction in many imaginable future demographic scenarios for the human population on Earth, people envision a population boom followed by a population crash. This imaginary scenario leads to the question: Is the maximization of reproductive success good, even if it leads to lowered reproductive success in the future? Even if maximizing reproductive success in the present leads to reduced reproductive success in the future, e.g., through the imagined coming population crash, it is not grounds for altruistic, voluntary reproductive restraint. Rather, one should try to maximize reproductive success anyway. Here is the reason: The operation that is undergoing natural selection is for the increase of the frequency of one's genes in the population. Selection for this operation occurs whether the population is increasing, stationary, or decreasing. Furthermore, solitary, altruistic, voluntary restraint in reproduction, even if it did prevent a population crash (and in fact it will not), never accomplishes an increase in the frequency of one's genes -- by definition it is the opposite of that operation. So if the commonly proposed response (altruistic, voluntary reproductive restraint) in fear of the boom and bust scenario is based on a fallacious argument, what is the root of this line of incorrect thinking? It is in the often implicit assumption that humans are trying or should try to maximize their sustainable population size. While reproducing to the point of boom and bust may sound counterintuitive and perhaps even unappealing, it is true that it is adaptive for the individual to always strive to maximize reproductive success. And is it not better to act on the basis of what is true and adaptive, rather than maintaining that it has no right to be true? The more we learn of these things the more it will help us to apply the evolutionary ethic. One can imagine that the principle of maximizing reproductive success could be maintained for each individual, and the population number could be reduced, if, by some bizarre, mandatory mechanism, the contribution of each individual's genes to the next generation were reduced by the same proportion from the maximum they would have achieved to some lower figure. But this end would be impossible in the sense that offspring are discrete entities not infinitely divisible. Rounding errors alone would lead to considerable discrepancy. Unlike in some other systems of ethics, where human values are threatened by overpopulation, the evolutionary ethic holds firm regardless of the size of the human population or the direction and rate of its growth. The progenitivist views expressed in this book notwithstanding, the world population will eventually reach a zero rate of growth. But regardless of whether the population rises or falls, progenitivism and the evolutionary ethic remain.

So even as the human population reaches the carrying capacity, the principle of maximizing reproductive success still holds. The difference is that at the carrying capacity it becomes more difficult to produce large numbers of offspring that survive to reproduce themselves. Some people who write about demography and ecology maintain that the human population has already exceeded the carrying capacity and that we are presently living on fossil fuel reserves in numbers greater than will be permanently sustainable. Does this possibility invalidate the argument to maximize reproductive success? No, it does not. It simply suggests that at some time in the future it will be even more difficult to produce large numbers of offspring that survive to reproduce themselves. When we turn to the best of human population studies for guidance on the carrying capacity of Earth, that guidance is lacking. In a review of Cohen[28], Nordhaus[154] wrote:

> Hence, after hundreds of pages of analysis and mathematics, we conclude that the number of humans the earth can durably support lies somewhere between one billion and one trillion; that the number changes over time and with technology; and that the factors determining the number are a complex and poorly understood interaction of land, water, social institutions and ingenuity. (p. 13)

This finding is supportive of the progenitive cause. With such a wide range in the estimate of Earth's carrying capacity, it is difficult to embrace the alarmist view that humans must take Draconian measures to control their population growth now. Instead, I would argue that each individual should strive to maximize reproductive success in engendering the billions of offspring that are sure to be produced in subsequent generations.

Human population growth rates will decline to near or below zero in approximately a century. Just when a scientific idea becomes widely accepted by the public, it is often proven to be false. The idea of ''the threat of overpopulation'' will follow that course. Nevertheless, it is ironic that we should discover the progenitivist philosophy herein described only at the end of a two million year period of population growth. The real meaning of life is only just dawning upon us as we are about to enter the period of great constraint on population growth, thus reducing our ability to reproduce freely. However, even in the presence of reproductive constraints we will still fulfill our purpose in life by maximizing reproductive success. On an optimistic point, the opportunities to reproduce over the next few decades are unique, largely because so few of us are doing so.

The future decline in population growth rates can occur because of fewer births or more deaths before the age of reproduction. Because natural selection does not have foresight, traits promoting population control will not be selected merely because they will provide some ''benefit'' in the future. Furthermore, as previously discussed, group selection is an exceedingly weak mechanism in natural populations. Abstaining from individual reproduction for the benefit of the species is a trait that is unlikely to evolve. Malthus[130] explained that the human population grows geometrically while the food supply grows at a slower arithmetic rate. He predicted that the human population would ultimately be limited by food deprivation and misery. He may yet be correct -- no population can maintain a level above that which is supported by its food supply. But it is more likely that he will be proven correct about the human population eventually reaching a zero rate of growth, but will be incorrect about the means. Primate populations under natural conditions are usually limited by contagious diseases like tuberculosis before they reach the carrying capacity of their environments in terms of food resources. Will the human population follow this pattern?

Many objections to progenitivism will no doubt be raised. For it is clear that if one is maximizing one's reproductive success, one cannot be putting other traditional goals first. Environmentalism seems so right when considered in isolation. But in the light of the evolutionary ethic, it is no longer a credible philosophy, at least in the extreme form of environmentalism for the environment's sake. Environmentalism is just one goal that is displaced as the primary one. Others including financial security, health, women's liberation in the narrow sense, educational achievements, the preservation of our civilization, hedonism and quality of life are all challenged as main objectives in life, too. Furthermore, progenitivism rejects the belief that we do not need to maximize reproductive success because there is less danger in modern times that children will not survive to reproduce. Take the issue of quality of life. Some might maintain that by controlling our population numbers the people who do live will have a higher quality of life. That view is challenged by progenitivism which maintains that the quality of life is significant in an evolutionary context only to the degree that it enhances reproductive success.

As with many cultural trends of our time, I take issue with environmentalism. I am not proposing retrograde anti-environmentalism, but rather the formation of environmental policy that is conducive to producing conditions that are friendly to individuals attempting to maximize their reproductive success. I am especially not condoning the endangerment of rare species or their habitat for crass economic interests, as seems to be the current argument in politics for the repeal of the Endangered Species Act. Perhaps in years to come the ultimate task of environmentalism will be to optimize the carrying capacity of Earth for the human population. Squandering natural resources for its own sake makes as little sense as preserving natural resources for its own sake. But using resources to reproduce is the business of all living things. The human population may continue to grow until it reaches the carrying capacity of Earth. This final carrying capacity will be dependent in part on how we interact with the environment. If we are judicious in the use of resources like topsoil and fossil fuel, we can help to increase that final carrying capacity. During the interval until such time that we reach final carrying capacity we can increase reproductive success. Although not necessarily a goal of progenitivism, the carrying capacity of Earth can be maximized by minimizing per capita consumption. While establishing a minimum threshold of resource consumption allowing life and reproduction is desirable, squandering resources for the sake of conspicuous consumption is not. It is possible that the average American is consuming a thousand times more energy than is needed to maximize reproduction. If our consumption of manufactured goods and energy far exceeds the level required to maximize reproductive success, what possible ultimate justification can there be for such consumption?

Environmentalists are best employed to achieve this end of maximizing our reproductive success within the limitations of the ecosystem. They will be enlisted as efficiency experts to manage natural resources and thereby maximize the Earth's carrying capacity for humans and, more importantly, to enhance their reproductive success directly. To the extent that domesticated species or wild species compete with human reproduction, e.g., those species that are net consumers of primary productivity that could be harnessed by humans, they should be displaced. While this view is not an encouraging one for the prospect of preserving maximum biodiversity, it is a logical extension of the evolutionary ethic. Many of the species on Earth will be displaced, but a few of the most useful and most hardy will survive, and they will need the careful nurturing of the applied science of ecology. We must preserve those species of utility to human reproduction. For example, those species will include food species, species that provide essential ecosystem services (such as the production of atmospheric oxygen and decomposition) and those plants and animals that provide us with biophilic pleasures which have adaptive components. Preservationists often propound the view that all life is sacred. That is a view reminiscent of Spencer's life ethics of yesteryear, in which all life was considered "good". The view offered in this book is in contrast. Many of the species on Earth have negative fitness effects on humans through parasitism and competition. Should the protozoan that causes malaria, the cholera comma-bacillus, or the leprosy bacillus actually be preserved? Would not the eradication of the tobacco plant result in a net benefit for humans? Was it wrong to displace the indigenous prairie and forest species in the process of creating the American farm belt? We might ask the question that is the key to discrediting the preservationist philosophy: What net costs should we be willing to incur to preserve other species? If net costs are measured in terms of reproductive success, then the answer is none! Environmentalism for the environment's sake is simply *passé*. But, environmentalism for the sake of one's reproductive success is justified. The point is made well by contrasting conservation and preservation. A conservationist philosophy can make sense if it aims at furthering one's reproductive success at the present or in the future. A preservationist philosophy does not make sense when it advocates preservation of nature for its own sake. I feel that this point contains a basic truth, but unlike the message from some environmentalists, it does not contain the kind of apocalyptic vision that some Americans seem fond of embracing when it comes to the environment. For lack of impending doom for humanity in my message, it may not be as easily perpetuated as the alternative.

Reproducing at high rates will not be easy when population densities are 100 times higher than today, but that is the natural outcome of doing what we were evolved to do. We should attempt to perpetuate no aspect of our environment unless it increases our reproductive success. We should continue to try to maximize our reproductive success regardless of population densities.

Life-lesson: Regardless of the direction and rate of population growth, practice maximization of reproductive success.

It would obviously be nice if one could have it both ways and simultaneously vigorously support communal population stabilizing measures while maximizing reproductive success one's self. By maximizing one's own reproductive success and discouraging reproduction in unrelated members of the population, the rate of increase in the frequency of one's genes in the population might be furthered. In practice there are problems with such a strategy. People tend to believe their own arguments. Encouraging others not to reproduce might actually curtail one's own reproduction. See the discussion of other mechanisms including feedforward in a following section.

Ecological considerations

The human population is part of the global biotic community, and human influences are in some ways self-destructive. But this pattern is not justification for the misanthropic beliefs held by some environmentalists in which humans are likened to a plague on Earth. Another unrealistic model held up to people in modern Western cultures is that of the noble savage living in tune with his environment. North American Indians in pre-Columbian times are often held up as an example of peoples living in harmony with their surroundings, but in fact they wrought major ecological change on the forests and grasslands of North America and helped exterminate a number of species of big game by over-hunting. If the evidence from recently living hunter-gatherers is relevant, the North American Indians gave birth to more children per woman than do Americans now. Ecological considerations have, do, and will always play a part in human reproductive strategies. Perhaps at a time of ecological conditions that are less propitious than at present, natural mechanisms to reduce fertility will be actuated in humans to avoid offspring wastage. The evolutionary principle behind these mechanisms is that one is selected to try to produce the number of offspring, small or large, one can raise successfully to maturity in order to avoid wastage of reproductive effort. The result will be a decline in the rate of human population growth. This natural method of fertility control has evolved in humans, and it is this control that keeps the human population within the carrying capacity of our environment and at the same time achieves maximum reproductive success.

Cohen[27] explained what may be the ultimate ecological limitation to human population growth:

... human populations may be limited by land (for farming, living, and recreation), food (from marine as well as terrestrial sources), fresh water, energy, or biological diversity (to provide ecosystem services such as decomposition of organic wastes, the regeneration of oxygen, and natural enemies for pest species).

Naturally, different limiting factors may interact. For example, high-intensity fertilization of farmlands may pollute water supplies while increasing food yields. (p. 116)

I would add to the above list what may be the most important limiting factor in human population growth: disease. As mentioned previously, evidence from my studies of wild nonhuman primate populations indicate that they for the most part are limited in numbers by disease, having developed strategies (allowed by their high intelligence) to elude predators, and having avoided the limitations of food shortages for the most part by adopting eclectic diets. If humans follow this model, large die-offs of occasional frequency will keep our numbers in check before we entirely destroy the environment's capability of supporting human life. The applicability of this model is strengthened as the human population grows because of the density dependent characteristics of many diseases and epidemics. In other words, as the human population grows, humans become increasingly susceptible to the ravages of disease.

The Gaia hypothesis, that the Earth including living matter, air, oceans, and land surface form a living organism[124], leads to objections: The first set of objections is that the Earth is really nothing like a living organism. It has no life history strategy, no discrete genetical mode of inheritance, most telling -- it does not reproduce. If we refer to the Earth as a living organism, the term ''living organism'' loses all meaning in the sense of how it is traditionally defined in biology. In the second set of objections, Williams[219] argued convincingly against the Gaia hypothesis by pointing out that there is no evidence that a metaphorical invisible hand actually manipulates evolution so as to produce results favorable to organisms. Even if the invisible hand were doing so, it would not justify the claim that Gaia is a total planetary being which practices homeostasis.

There is another concept, often not recognized by the layperson, that purports to explain a logical basis for nature worship. Humans, chimpanzees, pottos, rats, birds, turtles, fish, clams, insects, worms, trees, mushrooms, bacteria, and all other currently living organisms are the most recent link in a chain of evolution going back 3.5 billion years to the beginning of life. In this sense, all species are distant cousins. For example, humans diverged from chimpanzees as recently as six million years ago. Should we not treat these other species as though they are related, with altruism, in order to assure that they survive and reproduce? While it it poetic to say that we are ''brother'' to the elm tree, the answer to the question is no. The members of these living species are too distantly related to us to warrant altruistic behavior. Once again as Darwin[38] stated the principle succinctly: Natural selection can never generate anything for the sole benefit of another species. Earth and nature worship does not make evolutionary sense, but Earth and nature utilization does.

Paradox: maximize reproduction voluntarily or involuntarily

As individuals we shall choose to strive to maximize our number of offspring or they will be maximized by natural selection. People of the type that choose not to maximize their reproductive success will be replaced by those who choose to and by those who do so because they have not the power to choose at all. Choose to do so or be compelled to do so, that is the real choice we face in terms of maximizing reproductive success. It might also appear that another view has some truth to it as well: We shall voluntarily control our numbers or our numbers will be controlled by environmental limits. The combination of these two views is that in the long run we shall maximize our reproductive success *and* we shall be controlled by environmental limits. To believe that we could rise above this natural state in which all animals exist is self-aggrandizement on a species-wide scale. The optimal and indeed only plausible strategy is to raise the maximum possible number of children to the stage of sexual maturity -- not too few or too many. Too few would not fully expend the reproductive effort that is available and would be selected against. Too many leads to mortality or depressed fertility in the offspring and the subsequent wastage of reproductive effort on nonviable or nonreproductive offspring. It wastes reproductive effort that could have been more productively allocated to a fewer number of offspring and would be selected against. The culturgen of altruistic, voluntary reproductive restraint can be perpetuated in only a part of the population and only for a limited time. Another part will include those who are unable or unwilling, for whatever reasons, to carry this culturgen. They will continue to reproduce without altruistic, voluntary restraint. Depending on a number of variables including heritability, fertility rates, etc., this group in noncompliance may increase in proportion to those that practice altruistic, voluntary restraint. This consequence was anticipated by Hardin[87] when he wrote:

> At the moment, to avoid hard decisions many of us are tempted to propagandize for conscience and responsible parenthood. The temptation must be resisted, because an appeal to independently acting consciences selects for the disappearance of all conscience in the long run, and an increase in anxiety in the short. (p. 1248)

It may not be a lack of conscience *per se* that is actually selected for, but another trait that makes carrying the culturgen of conscience unlikely. Why should this result be so? Gould[75] offered an imaginative explanation of how natural selection is constrained by the current form of an organism. Rather than seeing organisms as spheres, ready to be rolled in any direction by genetic selection, he sees them as polyhedrons with facets that represent constraints for which direction and how far selection may tumble them. Evolutionary change is neither necessarily optimal nor does it always offer the primary control on evolution. This argument does make some assumptions about the amount of genetic variability and the channeling of traits, but on the whole it is a useful one. With this model in mind we can imagine that there may not be a straightforward pathway of allelic substitution to achieve the simple "disappearance of all conscience". Rather, a more elaborate route for selection involving pleiotropic effects of the genotype are ultimately selected, many of which have nothing to do with conscience, but which in part or whole have that final result. For example, selecting against intelligence increases fertility in the sense that the choice to use contraception may not be made consistently, and this pathway might be an indirect one to the elimination of conscience.

The above points on altruistic, voluntary, reproductive restraint show the duplicity in the message of population control advocates who urge people to have fewer children. They depict that it will make a difference in world demography, when in fact it has no measurable impact at all. Compensatory mechanisms simply lead to the increase in another person's reproduction to negate your decrease in reproduction.

Advocates of population control think that they are promoting a practical solution. What they do not realize is the existence of a theoretical limitation. They recognize one truth: If we fail to control our population growth, it will be done for us by nature. But they are unaware of the existence of a perverse corollary: If we fail to maximize our reproductive success, it will be done for us by evolution. Evolutionary biology teaches us that the notion of a species voluntarily controlling its numbers is the stuff of group selection legend. That humans can do so could be nothing more than imagination. It is not only a question of *should* we try to reduce rates of reproduction but also a question of *can* we for the long-term. If we can, I do not know the evolutionary mechanism by which we may do so. I challenge population control activists to provide a model of altruistic, voluntary, population control that is consistent with the principles of modern evolutionary biology. Citing short-term cultural mechanisms for population control is not enough, because ultimately they are shaped and changed by evolution to patterns that are adaptive for the individual in accordance with epigenetic rules. People who recommend population control often do so because of the narrow ecological constraints, but they ignore the evolutionary implications. This oversight is a considerable one, since nothing makes sense in biology (including population biology and ecology) without evolution, to paraphrase Dobzhansky. Put in its simplest form, here is the ignored evolutionary implication: We know that in humans, fertility is heritable, and also that we are selected to maximize reproductive success. Fisher[60] calculated for data on reproduction in England among the upper social classes in the 19th century, that fertility was 39.1 percent heritable, with the remainder of the strong correlation among grandmother, mother and daughter fertility being due possibly to cultural components of causes like religious doctrine, moral environment or social ideas. Even in countries with an overall negative rate of population growth, there are minority subpopulations that are growing rapidly. In time these subpopulations may increase and be transformed into the majority through the very attribute that they exhibit, high fertility. Thus, the target of voluntarily controlling rates of reproduction is an elusive one. In the entire history of life on Earth, we have not a single example of a species voluntarily controlling its numbers. So what is the evidence that humans can do so? There is no evidence that any organism, including humans, can be designed by natural selection for any purpose other than maximizing the representation of its own genes in future generations.

Fisher[60] wrote:

> ... among our contemporaries, at least, differences in heritable disposition play so large a part in the determination of fertility, that somewhat large modifications of temperament must be brought about by reproductive selection within a span of ten generations, that is within a relatively short historical period. We have seen that by no means extreme genotypes have rates of reproduction in a ratio higher than 2 to 1, and if for simplicity we imagine a population consisting of two strains, which, having equal mortality, differ only to this extent in fertility, it is easy to see that the numbers of one type relative to that of the other will, in ten generations, be increased over a thousandfold. To put the matter in another light, if at the beginning of the period the population consisted of 97 per cent. of the less fertile and 3 per cent. of the more fertile strain, in 5 generations the two strains are brought to an equality, and in 5 more their situations are reversed, so that the less fertile strain is represented by 3 and the more fertile by 97 per cent. of the population. Civilized man, in fact, judging by the fertility statistics of our own time, is apparently subjected to a selective process of an intensity approaching a hundredfold the intensities we can expect to find among wild animals, with the possible exception of groups which have suffered a recent and profound change in their environment. We may therefore anticipate that a correspondingly rapid evolution has taken place within historical times in the appropriate mental attributes. (p. 218)

You have probably heard it; you may even believe it; the overpopulation myth is a powerful culturgen, and it could cost you reproductive success. The point you need to remember is that maximizing one's reproductive success does not necessarily lead to overpopulation. The converse is also true. Failing to maximize one's reproductive success does not necessarily prevent overpopulation. Evolutionary biologists know that when all individuals in a population strive to maximize their reproductive success, it does not necessarily mean that the population is growing. Nor does it mean that they live in misery with overpopulation. Natural populations of animals and plants, including our hominid ancestors, for millions of years have shown adaptations designed to maximize reproductive success yet lived in populations close to stationary in terms of growth. Even when the human population stops growing, it will continue to be adaptive to maximize one's reproductive success. So when population control advocates seek to achieve zero population growth, they almost always enlist the wrong mechanism: altruistic, voluntary reproductive restraint. Zero population growth will eventually be achieved without altruistic, voluntary reproductive restraint and striving to maximize reproductive success by individuals will continue. I do not propose that people should have children they cannot feed and who would starve to death in childhood. That would be maladaptive and is a perfect example of the kind of reproductive restraint that is favored by natural selection, i.e. practicing restraint so as to maximize reproductive success. People who breed too profusely when food resources are limiting will leave fewer descendants, not more. Thus, under very narrow conditions it is better to have fewer children and to nourish them well enough for them to survive and reproduce, thereby increasing your reproductive success, than to have many who perish prior to maturity and reproduction. However, true to my thesis, I must warn that the average American is grossly underreproducing at present. Not too few children and not too many children is the rule, but it happens to be the case that in the present environment Americans can hardly ever have too many. Indeed, were the current state of human nature different, by chance, so that we produced too many offspring, which in turn prevented us from maximizing our reproductive success, I would be urging reproductive restraint in this book. Environmentalists are dangerously mistaken when they deny that humans will and should attempt to maximize their reproductive success. I do not protest this antigenitive message only because it is intellectually dishonest, but also because of its consequences if applied. Might we take a moment to ponder: What good can come from such a falsehood? Can a concept so fundamentally wrong serve any environmental objectives, whatever they might be?

The greater the reproductive restraint and the longer the time before it shows a benefit for future generations of relatives, the more difficult it is to promote through natural selection. This fact argues against the possibility that reproductive restraint will evolve in humans for the benefit of generations in the distant future. But humans already have many mechanisms that regulate their reproduction for the sake of maximizing their own reproductive success. However, these existing mechanisms are based on the sound principles of maximizing individual fitness and inclusive fitness, and do not rely on the weak group selection arguments usually invoked in appeals for altruistic, voluntary reproductive restraint. It is hard to imagine that humans will or should show altruistic, voluntary reproductive restraint until such time that their immediate relatives, say children and grandchildren, stand to benefit from it rather than unrelated members of the population. But such behavior would be in accordance with inclusive fitness theory, and individuals would each be attempting to maximize their reproductive success, not curtail it, through a strategy of regulating their reproduction.

Some aspects of environmentalism are self-perpetuating culturgens. Beware of the feel nice approach to conservation typified by plant-a-tree campaigns and adopt-a-whale drives. They have popular appeal, so they spread, but in fact they are useless, or perhaps worse than useless because they divert time and energy from solutions to the real ecological problems. Instead, demand effective action by the government to conserve essential resources. New standards to reduce wastage and increase efficiency for industry and transportation would be a helpful start. While environmental impact statements may serve a useful function when considering development projects or changes in public policy, reproductive success impact statements are even more important and should be required on the same occasions.

Chapter 9: Evolution of Philoprogenitiveness

Charles Darwin was a devoted father to his ten children. While we cannot be entirely certain of Darwin's personal motivation in engendering his large number of offspring, in the past most people had children because they were a by-product of sexual intercourse, not out of a desire to be a parent. Then came the new technology of modern birth control. Parenthood no longer depended on an intense sexual impulse, but rather on the intellectual decision to choose to have children. This second drive is a weak one in many people, especially in technologically advanced cultures. Love of offspring or a desire for posterity has to be weighed against the perceived costs of having children. The evolution of philoprogenitiveness, i.e. love of perpetuating one's genes or love of producing offspring, would seem to be a possible consequence of these new selection pressures. C. G. Darwin[36] suggested that any race of people who could forgo automobiles and instead invest the savings in producing additional children would soon populate the world. The motive would be inconsequential -- it could be principle, some creed, or simply stupidity -- but their numbers would increase nonetheless. Indeed, how many Americans do make the choice either to buy a new car or to have a baby? An upper-middle class American child born today will cost approximately three hundred thousand dollars to raise to adulthood. That figure includes the essentials of life such as housing, food, and medical care, but it does not include the cost of college. Since most of the children in the world receive only a fraction of that amount of financial support, we might ask ourselves if we Americans are overemphasizing the financial investment in our offspring. While Americans could likely raise their children for less, that alone would not necessarily increase the number of children produced. The fundamental error that Americans make is to trade the opportunity to maximize reproductive success for the opportunity to acquire material goods like cars.

Reproduction in modern times depends on having an urge to be a parent, the love of having offspring and a desire for posterity. Romantic love and sexuality, once an efficient bonding mechanism and method of fertilization for the facilitation of reproduction, have been circumvented by some new culturgens. Now for reproduction to occur, it generally requires a desire to have a baby *per se*. Some of the proximate mechanisms are a desire to make a baby to love, to make a baby to be loved by, to bring the parents closer together, or to raise the status of the parents (primarily in other cultures).

Since the procreative drive found presently in many humans is failing to maximize reproductive success, individuals who overcome this failing will proportionally increase their type in the population. If the spontaneous wish of some people to have children has a genetic basis, then natural selection can increase the frequency of that trait. The consequence will be the spontaneous wish in more people to have children. This wish to have children might occur as a sense of lack of purpose when childless, as a feeling that something significant is missing from life, as a need to express nurturing behavior, as a strong desire to leave heirs, as a desire for genetic continuity with the next generation or as a recognition that extinction of a bloodline is irreversible. Regardless of the mechanism, genes that code for general progenitive desires would seem to have an advantage over those genes that code for specific behaviors, and the frequencies of the genes coding for general progenitive desires would seem likely to increase.

It is instructive to consider what degrees of reproductive success can be accomplished by humans. The fatherhood record generally cited[57] contained figures that are impossibly wrong: 525 sons and 342 daughters are claimed for an 18th century emperor of Morocco. Even with a secondary sex ratio in the population that was strongly biased in favor of males (say 110:100), the odds against this reported disparity in sons and daughters being real are astronomical. Daughters were likely systematically underreported. The motherhood record appears more credible: The greatest known number of children born to a woman is 69, many were multiple births. This mother was a Russian peasant in the 18th century[57]. These figures are small in comparison to what could be achieved by one modern male billionaire who had a strong sense of philoprogenitiveness and the help of many mothers. Economically, and with the use of artificial insemination, he would be able to engender and support ten thousand children. But consistent with the fitness depressing effects of wealth, the world's richest men and women actually have few or no children at all.

Some environmentalists tell us as a group to control our numbers. What is the alternative to doing something about the growing human population? The answer is simply to default and do nothing. Nature will take its course and population growth will eventually be suppressed through density-dependent selection. Evolutionary biology tells us, as individuals and as kinship groups, that if we maximize the number of offspring we produce, we will be represented in future generations. The viewpoint from evolutionary biology and the viewpoint from ecology may be in total disagreement on this point of the importance of maximizing reproductive success. But as explained previously, the viewpoint from evolutionary biology takes precedence because evolutionary biology provides many of the underlying principles for ecology. Ultimately, a stationary population with intense intraspecific competition, sexual selection, and mortality selection will prevail. The maximum number of offspring that can be raised successfully will decrease. Family size will decline. Parents will reduce their target family size to achieve the most effective distribution of the available reproductive effort if mortality during the development of offspring is too high. However, parents will increase their target number of births if mortality during the development of offspring decreases.

Environmentalists see us in a world where K-selection is operating and object with dismay when r-selection strategies are employed by other people. I use the terms K-selection and r-selection in the way described by Pianka[159]. K-selection occurs when a population is at its carrying capacity, and r-selection occurs when a population is in its positive growth phase. I argue that the human population is still experiencing more r-selection than K-selection. The progenitive message in this book is applicable to both. However, the more that steps to control population growth through altruistic, voluntary restraint succeed, the more important is the message in this book. This conclusion follows from the fact that if steps to control population growth do not succeed, then people must be reproducing well for one reason or another. Some people who fail to maximize their reproductive success rationalize it by saying that they are pursuing a K-selection strategy of investing well in each of the few offspring they produce. Perhaps so, but that K-selection strategy is a mistake in the current r-selection world of human reproduction. We know that from the fact that the children at the high end of the distribution of parental investment in America in turn produce fewer, not more, children themselves.

I inquired earlier: "Why advocate maximizing reproductive success?" And I responded with: "It is the meaning of life. It is that which we are designed by evolution to do." Let us examine the question from another viewpoint. Below is a description of the world in which many of us will admit we live. It provides a listing and brief negation of many of the reasons we may think of as our purpose in life.

- We live for life's sake -- but life is short and such a meaning implies that life does not have lasting value.
- We live to worship and glorify gods -- but gods do not exist.
- We live to attain a fitting place in an afterlife -- but life after death is an illusion in the form of a particularly potent culturgen.
- We live to serve our country -- but our leaders have lost their way and we openly question much of our governmental policy.
- We live for justice -- but it is ill-served by the judicial branch of government.
- We live for money -- but there is rarely enough.
- We live for love -- but it is too rare.
- We live for peace -- but ethnic strife, religious conflict and war abound.
- We live for sex -- but sex for the sake of sex is incomplete.
- We live for our vocation -- but work does not seem important enough to dedicate one's entire lifetime to it.
- We live for happiness -- but we do not know how to find it and when we do find it, it does not last.

Huxley[106] wrote:

> ... the prospect of attaining untroubled happiness, or of a state which can, even remotely, deserve the title of perfection, appears to me to be as misleading an illusion as ever was dangled before the eyes of poor humanity. (p. 44)

So why advocate maximizing reproductive success? The answer can be reduced to a set of fitness equations. Perpetuation of our kind and contributing to future generations is the only real long-term reward. *We live to maximize reproductive success.* And what is life if you are not reproducing? Two acceptable alternatives come to mind: 1. You may be growing so as to achieve overall higher reproductive success in the future, or 2. you may be helping relatives to reproduce. This listing does not provide many options, and any other conceivable option would have to lead to higher overall reproductive success in the way that the two mentioned options can.

Americans are often concerned with doing things -- anything -- well. Quality and excellence are the battle cry in nearly every aspect of our lives. So let us consider what doing things well means in terms of the evolutionary ethic.

· To live well is to maximize one's reproductive success.
· To die well is to confer maximum inclusive fitness on relatives in the act.
· To marry well is to choose a mate who will help you to maximize your reproductive success.
· To parent well is to maximize your number of grandchildren. That means that supportive nurturing of your child as an individual makes sense only up to a point that your children as a group produce the maximum number of grandchildren.
· From the life history equation we may consider four more variables: to feed well, to grow well, to maintain well, to reproduce well. All are evaluated in terms of their consequence for maximizing reproductive success.

Why not advocate a policy that achieves a sustainable population? Because natural selection favors those individuals who maximize their reproductive success. Maximization of reproductive success now may or may not lead to extinction of one's genes at a time in the future. If *future* extinction of our genes is dependent on current rates of reproduction, the absurd position in which we find ourselves is that the alternative is to refrain from reproducing and have our genes become extinct that way at the *present*. If future extinction of our genes *is not* dependent on reproduction now, then the underlying assumption in the argument to refrain from reproducing is not valid. It is likely that the extinction of the human race is not dependent on the reproductive behavior of individual humans.

If producing as many relatives as possible is the goal, the skeptic might ask why should the evolutionarily-minded not work at a sperm bank and contribute the maximum number of samples possible? Why not advocate spite, perhaps even lethal aggression, toward unrelated members of the population? There are rational answers to these questions. Spite works as an evolutionary strategy only where populations are small, the cost of spite to the actor is small, the recipient is unrelated and the cost of spite to the recipient is high. A form of spite, in which the cost to the actor is small but the cost to the recipient is potentially high, is the proselytizing of messages designed to curtail the reproduction of unrelated people. This form of spite graduates into selfishness under some form of density dependent population regulation -- the actor benefits through an increased share of some limiting resource. The frequency of such behavior is likely to increase as the population grows and resources become scarce. But the general model of spiteful behavior as viewed by evolutionary biologists suggests that it requires rare and unusual conditions for it to be adaptive. On the subject of donating sperm to a sperm bank, I know of no major theoretical objections to it. Obviously, it is a frequency dependent strategy; it returns high reproductive success only when the number of men employing it is small.

We have addressed the question of why not kill unrelated people to promote one's inclusive fitness, in a response to a challenge of this philosophy associated with environmentalism. Accordingly, it is only fair that we ask a similar question about the philosophy of environmentalism: Why not kill one's children, as well as one's fetuses *in utero*, in order to control overpopulation? I doubt that the environmentalist movement has a response to that question which could be called an integral part of their philosophy. Rather they are likely to take refuge in some other philosophy or system of morality, e.g., Judeo-Christian values. Taking such refuge is testimony to the lack of scope of environmentalism. In contrast, the evolutionary ethic provides an explanation of why we should not murder, as described in the above paragraph on spite. Western society has laws that provide a strict sanction against murder. An act of murder followed by these sanctions usually lowers the actor's reproductive success (in the terminology of the model of spiteful behavior, the costs to the actor are elevated). In this way, the laws against murder, or any law, can be seen to be just another part of the social environment that needs to be considered when devising a strategy of optimal behavior.

Extinction

Darwin[38] recognized that extinction and natural selection go hand in hand. A great majority (about 99.9 percent) of the billions of species of life that have ever lived on Earth are now extinct[168]. There remain today perhaps ten million species of animals and two million species of plants on Earth -- and even had humans never evolved, all would eventually perish. Humankind is, no doubt, greatly accelerating this process of extinction[223]. We may eradicate a quarter of all living species within

Chapter 10: Other Current Topics in Evolutionary Context

Happiness is a desirable goal for the individual only in the sense that it is achieved by acts increasing one's inclusive fitness. People are often surprised at how feelings of even great happiness are ephemeral. Why do not even exhilarating feelings last? ''I will be happy for the rest of my life'' is a feeling that many have had at least once. Why was that expectation in error? Evolutionary biology has the answer. This short-term satisfaction occurs because life is a process of reproductive success maximization, not satisfaction maximization. No matter what one achieves in terms of reproductive success it is not adaptive to stop trying, because perhaps with more time and effort even more reproductive success can be achieved. The latency period depends on the biological function of the behavior and the adaptive significance of the timing of its repetition:

· A breath -- a few seconds
· A swallow reflex -- a few minutes
· A meal -- a few hours
· Sexual intercourse -- a few days for the average American
· Ovulation -- a few weeks
· A new head of hair -- a few months
· A new, long-term romantic love relationship -- a few years

The philosophy that states: "Don't worry; be happy" makes some sense, because the behaviors inspired by unhappiness in America are often strategic errors that lead to lower reproductive success. For example, unhappy marriages often lead to divorces, and unhappiness with one's personal finances often leads to an attempt to increase one's wealth. Both responses are likely to decrease the individual's reproductive success. Often in America the happiness associated with romantic love seems all too brief and shallow. We become bored and find fault with our partner after time, even though that person may be an otherwise entirely suitable mate. And we often treat the symptom of unhappiness in love with divorce. But in treating the symptom we usually fail to treat the disease: failure to reproduce.

Love

Love is a proximate mechanism to confer benefits on mates and relatives and in turn gain reproductive success oneself. In this sense it is not something to be maximized in itself. In the Christian interpretation, love is an expression with special significance in bringing one close to God. The progenitive view is that love is a tactic to increase one's inclusive fitness. At the risk of oversimplifying, love can be divided into a number of different types: 1. as a mating drive with implications for individual fitness; 2. as a bond with relatives with implications for inclusive fitness; 3. as a bond with friends with implications for reciprocal altruism. Love (whether romantic, or for relatives, or for friends) is a bonding mechanism to further reproductive success. If one could reproduce successfully without love, then love need not be invoked. The loveless marriage or a male-female relationship that is based on sexual gratification rather than love is as valid as a marriage or relationship based on deep love if the reproductive success achieved is identical. Indeed, in the complex and changed environment in which Americans find themselves today, entirely too much time and energy is devoted to looking for love *per se*. In the modern environment, the bonding that occurs in love has become a goal in itself rather than a means to achieve a goal (reproductive success), as it was earlier in human evolution. In this sense the quest for true love by many Americans takes pathological proportions. Rather than increase reproductive success, the pathological search for true love reduces it.

Cross-cultural comparisons

In some cultures marriage is an economic relationship, without the Western concept of romantic love. The arranged marriage involving a man and woman who do not know each other seems to be a successful means of procreating in some societies, based on the stability of such marriages and the number of children they produce. In other cultures, brideprice, rather than romantic love, is commonly the bond between a husband and wife. Sometimes it is useful to consider brideprice not as a purchase of the bride herself, but rather as a purchase of the claim to her reproductive role. This second view is supported by the fact that the bride comes with a warranty of fertility. In many African societies if a wife proves to be infertile, the family of the woman must provide a younger sister without brideprice, or the original brideprice must be returned. The economic relationship in marriage is also clear from other formalized modes of acquiring a mate in other cultures. These include dowry (the transfer of something of financial value to the husband's family from the wife's family), suitor service (services provided by the husband to the wife's family), gift exchange, inheritance, and adoption.

Divorce in non-Western society

Only a small fraction of marriages among non-Western peoples are for life. Hobhouse et al.[96] found that only 4 percent of a sample of 271 societies forbid divorce; more than 71 percent permit it at the will of the husband, wife or both; and 24 percent allow it for specific causes, e.g., infidelity, infertility, etc. In this cross-cultural perspective, marriages in America have been inordinately stable, and increases in divorce among American couples in recent decades have simply been a regression to the cross-cultural mean.

Divorce and reduced fertility

A lower rate of divorce would likely contribute to higher fertility in America. The average marriage in America lasts slightly less than five years. The figure of 4.9 years is close. Previous divorces substantially increase the risk of future divorce if the individual remarries. Considering the great time and effort allocated to the breakup of a marriage under the current laws and social customs, and considering also that about fifty percent of all marriages end in divorce at present, a new form of marriage -- one that would increase reproductive success -- might be indicated. Perhaps a form of contract marriage, lasting for five years, which would dissolve spontaneously if not renewed, might be a preferable alternative. I realize that one component of pair bonding and traditional marriage is the illusion of permanence of the bond. Thus, it might be necessary to have some figure of speech associated with these contract marriages to put oneself and one's mate in the mood. The phrase "I will love you forever" is the customary lie told in America prior to traditional marriages. A variation on that theme might suffice, for example, "I will love you for 4.9 years". This line of thinking, if carried further, would take us to the subject of lies that need to be told for evolutionary reasons. And remember, from the perspective of many divorced people marriage is not so great, but the *children* it provides certainly are wonderful. See the section on misinformation among mouthbreeding fish for an example of a lie that not only benefits but is essential to the reproduction of both the male who deceives and his mate who is deceived by him.

Entertainment and leisure

Unrealistic models of behavior and inappropriate goals are commonly portrayed in the mass media. In addition, the mass media in America are a source of abundant misinformation and provide a rich set of examples of self-perpetuating culturgens. The evolution of social interest in sex and violence is exploited by the media with the routine portrayal of gratuitous sex and violence on television and in cinema. Under the natural conditions humans evolved, watching real events of this kind had important survival and reproductive consequences. Television and cinema simulate them with sufficient reality that our largely innate drive to watch them is triggered. Things that we have been selected to watch during the vast time of human prehistory include: hunting, gathering, food, water, eating, tool making, sexual behavior, predators, fire, and aggression. These topics accordingly contribute disproportionately to the mass media coverage. People speculate about the correlation between violence portrayed in the media and violence in our communities. The relationship is causal. The media play a role in promoting aggression by teaching techniques and contexts. Counter to the main point of this argument, one clearly good thing about television and cinema is that the large dose of sexually explicit portrayals makes American children aware of their own sexuality earlier than the sexually repressive ideal culture of their parents would have them be. This early awareness of sexuality is an important step in maximizing reproductive success.

Spectator sports are immensely popular in America today. The closest that spectator sports come to any of the items in the above list is aggression, since sports are ritualized forms of aggressive competition. It is quite unlikely that the intense interest shown by the average American man in spectator sports is adaptive today; rather, it is vestigial in the sense that observing aggressive behavior facilitated learning about aggressive techniques in historical and prehistorical times. Mass media program selections are of course driven by viewer ratings and advertising revenues. Even for the most despicable rubbish now broadcast, one might ask this question: "If the viewers want it, why not give it to them?" The truth is that not many people have the ability to answer that question. But it is ultimately a question of what is good for the broadcasters and for the viewers. Though no data exist relating television program selection to viewer reproductive success, it is difficult to imagine that most of what is broadcast in America today could be considered fitness enhancing (with the obvious exception of the fact that the vast amount of time spent in television viewing is time not spent in increasing income or furthering education). By emphasizing the deviant and the dysfunctional, television brings depictions of behavior to the public that serve as near perfect negative role models. Regrettably, the aberrant behaviors portrayed are sometimes indirectly offered as viable alternatives to maximizing reproductive success. A brief thought about television viewing is all that is required to show that Americans allocate too great a portion of their time budget to it. Next to time spent working and sleeping the most common activity is television viewing.

Philosophy

One of the key functions of any philosophy is to provide an explanation for the ultimate causes of events, states, conditions, and behaviors in our daily life. Many philosophies are quite old and predate the scientific revolution. Symons[200] made an interesting observation on this subject:

> Scientifically acceptable views of ultimate causation have existed for a relatively brief period of time, and have not superseded older theories of ultimate causation to the extent that science has superseded mythology in ... [issues] of proximate causation. (It is not unknown today for a scientist not directly involved with evolutionary biology to hold essentially the same views on ultimate causation that were held by desert nomads 3000 years ago.) (pp. 59-60)

Diverse philosophical systems are ubiquitous, even after more than a century of Darwinism. This observation is contrary to what one might expect, considering that Darwinism could be a powerful unifying principle, were the world of humans more rational than it is at present. In a following section we discuss why philosophies are so multitudinous. In this section I shall discuss some specific aspects of modern philosophies in terms of the evolutionary ethic and their evolutionary consequences. I argue that these other philosophies, and the behaviors they promote, can lead to mistakes in life.

Capitalism *versus* Marxism

Capitalism is simply an economic system in which trade and industry are controlled by private owners. It is one of the philosophies that compete for our adherence. Along with the commonly concomitant philosophies of the political right, it has recently experienced a considerable worldwide increase. Certainly it is firmly entrenched in America. To the extent that it generates abundant resources required for reproduction, capitalism is to be recommended. However, to the extent that it distracts the individuals in its society from the primary task at hand, i.e. maximizing reproductive success, it is to be criticized. Materialism and capitalism seem to go hand in hand in practice. And accumulation of material goods and wealth for their own sake is a detriment to fitness, as we have previously mentioned.

Marxism, once thought to be the economic system of the future by leftist intellectuals, is on a worldwide decline. Marx and Engels[131] were fixated on some narrow issues, mainly on a proletarian owned industrial economy and economic equality. And they were idealists in their objections to worker servitude to a capitalist economy, though they did not object on grounds of endangerment to reproductive success, which I would believe to be the correct source of objection if one is to be made. Unfortunately, countries inspired by their philosophy have installed worker servitude to bloated bureaucracy, instead, often with their own negative effects on reproductive success. Apologists for Marx say that there has never been a true Marxist state and that his writings have been misinterpreted and misapplied. However, I have objections to his *bona fide* writings, not just to how others have applied them. For example, rather than guarantee reproductive rights, he appears to curtail them, as in his proposal to abolish marriage and prohibit inheritance. In practice, Marxism often goes hand in hand with high rates of elective abortion and suppressed reproductive success as observed in the former U.S.S.R., in China, and in former Soviet Block countries like Hungary, for reasons that do not appear to be an actual part of the official dogma but that are nonetheless a consequence of this social system. Ultimately, a major cause of the demise of Marxism as practiced in formerly communist Russia is the culturgens of bureaucracy. Any economy burdened as heavily as that one was by officialdom is bound to fail and to inspire a consumer revolt.

Democracy

The U.S.A. is a democratic republic. That means we have majority rule but with guarantee of minority rights. For example, people with brown eyes, the majority, cannot deport people with blue eyes, a minority, by a popular vote. I would like to consider an aspect of the electoral process, the process on which all democracies are based, in a cost-benefit analysis. If I am not mistaken, it undermines the process from an evolutionary perspective. Let us begin with the fact that the chance of making the deciding vote in any major election is less than the chance of being killed in an automobile accident on the way to the polling booth. Imagining other possible costs for voting, the fitness disincentive for voting might be quite considerable. What is the potential fitness gain in voting? Even if your vote does make a difference by some extraordinary fluke, there is not any reason to believe that the typical candidate or typical ballot issue will increase your fitness. Skeptics usually reply to this argument with the question: "What if everyone felt that way?" The answer is that if everyone agreed with this argument, then there would be fewer votes, the value of a single vote would increase to a point where it might then be worth the effort to cast your ballot. For whatever reasons, the majority of Americans do not vote and the percentage of voters is decreasing -- if this trend continues, one day voting may be worthwhile. I do not deny that it might make sense to actively campaign for a cause or to run for political office if you can influence the behavior of others *en masse*, but it must meet the criterion of enhancing your fitness.

In America, past and present, we often subordinate the values that we associate with democracy, like freedom, liberty, dignity, truth, and justice. Since we are likely to continue to do so, we should do so for the right cause, i.e. in a tradeoff for reproductive success.

Determinism *versus* "free willism"

In the battle for human minds, one of the most difficult obstacles that this book will face is the battle for supremacy between the philosophies of determinism and "free willism". Though rarely thought of by laypersons, these opposing ideologies actually underlie many of the conflicts of opinion in modern Western thought. For example, determinists tend to be atheists, and "free willists" tend to be religious. This dichotomy is less well-known, but it is as important to American life as other dichotomies such as the political left *versus* the political right, Democrat *versus* Republican, and idealism *versus* cynicism. Indeed, the unclear thinking about determinism and "free willism" contributes to the further splits within these other dichotomies. But from a scientific perspective the facts are clear. Genetics and environment are responsible for all human traits. What we do, what we think, and what we are all have deterministic causes. There is no true randomness or role for gods -- all effects have causes at the human level of interaction. Though many people intuitively believe in free will, the explanation for their misunderstanding is straightforward. The evolution of intentionality as a function of the human brain to allow us to make choices designed to enhance reproductive success is what many people confuse for a God-given ability to exercise free will.

Determinism is scientifically true and "free willism" is false, but that does not mean that the former is or will be more widespread than the latter. Among other things, a deterministic view of life can lead to a problem: Intellectuals holding this philosophy can be paralyzed by inaction from knowing that all their behaviors are effects of previous causes and are, in this sense, predetermined. Accepting procreation as the defined meaning in life helps to avoid the paralysis and might in turn increase the spread of determinism. In this way, determinism might lead to higher reproductive success than "free willism". For reasons that I cannot fully justify according to the evolutionary ethic, it is pleasing that something which is logically correct should also be good, i.e. maximizing reproductive success. Perhaps at the highest levels of fertility, truth is more conducive to increasing reproductive success than falsehood. But clearly that is not necessarily so at low to moderate levels of reproductive success. Culturgens based on blatant falsehoods that promote fertility are ubiquitous in the reproductive climate in America today. It may surprise the reader that the evolutionary ethic does not redefine the words "truth" and "falsehood" the way it redefines "good" and "bad". But according to the evolutionary ethic, truths are not always good and falsehoods are not always bad.

Stoic ethics

Stoic ethics, the philosophy of Rousseau, Taoism, and many other belief structures advocate "doing what comes naturally" or "living according to nature". The naturalistic fallacy applies to these philosophies in that they equate "natural" with "good". Doing what comes naturally has some obvious merits (e.g., it may lead to satisfaction), but it has some limits, too. When environments change then behaviors that are adaptive change. What feels natural may no longer be adaptive. A personal example may state the objection more vividly: During my 15 years of life in Africa I observed a great deal that was natural but *not* good, according to the system of ethics I had at the time and have now. For example, the killing of conspecifics is natural and quite common, especially among our closest relatives, the nonhuman primates. Even with our greatly simplified system of the evolutionary ethic in which those things improving one's reproductive success are good, it is possible to find things in nature which are not good, i.e. natural phenomena which reduce one's fitness such as most types of parasites, disease, and accidents. So I disagree with the hypothetical suggestion of Symons[200] that:

> One can define "good" as that which is produced by natural selection. (p. 61)

I am much more in agreement with Symons'[200] hypothetical suggestion that:

> An individual thus would be acting ethically as long as it was maximizing its inclusive fitness. (p. 61)

As a matter of fairness, the similarity between the above quotation and the content of the evolutionary ethic does not imply that Symons[200] endorsed the evolutionary ethic as presented herein. In fact, from the original context of the above quotation, it appears that Symons[200] rejected the inference.

Hedonism

Hedonism may lead to pleasant sensations but pleasure is not what we are in the business of maximizing. Nor should we be maximizing the opposite: personal abstention from pleasures and the willful self-infliction of pain. If modern humans did not find themselves in a recently and considerably changed environment, then the pursuit of pure hedonism would presumably be nearer to the optimal strategy. This assumption follows from the fact that sensations of pleasure and pain evolved as motivators in the pursuit of limiting resources and the avoidance of injury. But since paleolithic times there have been many environmental changes, in part brought about by human cultural change (e.g., advances in technology); consequently, we are not perfectly (or perhaps even well) adapted to the present environment. Thus, the pursuit of purely hedonistic goals may at times act against an individual's reproductive interests. For example, partaking in caviar and champagne, as incredibly satisfying to the senses as it is, is likely to be correlated with reduced reproductive success, because of its class and economic associations. And while such an indulgence may not be the cause of reduced reproductive success, neither is it the cause of increased reproductive success as would be indicated by the great pleasure it provides, if there were the primitive correlation between pleasure and reproductive success. The point is that even foods do not produce pleasure in proportion to their healthfulness and eventual impact on our reproductive success anymore. Primitive tastes for fat and sugar have gone awry in a dietary world where they are no longer rare nutrients to be sought but rather abundant to the extent of being problematic. Excessive self-denial is not the correct road either. In this sense, the pursuit of pleasures is out of step with the pursuit of reproductive success. Will the two operations converge again in the future? Perhaps they will if rates of cultural change slow and the gene frequencies which provide the genetic basis for feelings of adaptive pleasure evolve to provide optimal strategies in the changing environment. Lumsden and Wilson[126] suggested that it may take genes about a thousand years to track a new culturgen.

Utilitarianism

Utilitarianism maintains that we should try to promote pleasure or, in some versions, happiness, and to reduce misery. According to that philosophy, an act is right if it does at least as much to increase pleasure or happiness, and to decrease misery, as any possible act or inaction. The same argument with which we dismiss hedonism applies to utilitarianism. People often mistake the drives that bring us pleasure, such as hunger, thirst and libido, as well as other tendencies such as self-preservation and parental care, for the ultimate cause directing us to the ultimate goal of our behavior. But, in fact, evolution is the ultimate cause of our behavior and maximization of reproductive success is the ultimate goal. These drives and tendencies serve only as proximate mechanisms through which reproductive success was once maximized in previous generations.

Natural law

Natural law is a concept common to many religions. It maintains that we should do that which is in accordance with the will of God. Among the problems encountered with this philosophy is the assumption of the existence of God, which is no longer taken for granted at our modern level of scientific knowledge and intellectual development. Some maintain that the question of the existence of God is not within the realm of scientific inquiry. I disagree. Scientists, if they wish, may study the universe using the scientific method and ask two questions: Is there a need to invoke the presence of God to explain its existence and its properties, and is there evidence of the physical presence of God? The secondary problem is in establishing a valid and reliable means of ascertaining what *would be* the will of God, if he exists. There have been perhaps a hundred thousand religions over the span of human history and prehistory. This large number of religions is in no way indicative of truth in religion in general. Instead, this number represents just a small fraction of the trillions of culturgens that have existed based on falsehoods. The remarkable diversity of moral codes embraced by these many religions, from the necessity of cannibalizing one's dead relatives (endocannibalism) after giving the corpses sufficient time to putrefy in order to appease their spirits, to the total immersion of living human bodies in water in order to purify their souls by washing away original sin, indicates clearly if God did exist and did communicate his will to humans, that his will is bizarre and at times highly self-contradictory. In the span of religions known to anthropology, there is no universally shared system of values or morals or identity of deities or creation myths. To accept any of them preferentially is highly idiosyncratic behavior from a scientific viewpoint.

Let us consider a point of some emphasis in this book in terms of natural law, i.e. contraception. Advocates of natural law usually maintain that contraception is unnatural because it thwarts God's intention that sexual intercourse lead to reproduction; therefore, they argue that it should be condemned. In disagreement, Wilson[222] argued that reproduction is not the primary role of sexuality in humans, unlike in the majority of other species, and that contraception should not be condemned. He felt that the belief that it is unnatural is based on a failure of theologians to understand ethology. I am in agreement with Wilson on this issue in that I feel that contraception should not be condemned because it is unnatural. However, because sexual intercourse is the means of reproduction (among other things in humans), I feel that contraception should be condemned because it almost always lowers reproductive success. Wilson[222] was correct in terms of the interpretation of the complex role of sexuality in humans. At the same time, natural law theologians condemn contraception, which I must interpret as good according to the evolutionary ethic.

The Protestant ethic

The Protestant ethic is a set of values held to be the ideological basis of the capitalistic system that extols the necessity and desirability of work and thrift. It holds that work has intrinsic value. It maintains that diligent work is not only a key to productivity and wealth, but that it is a method of avoiding vice. The question once again is what are the fitness implications for practitioners of this philosophy? Work may often lead to productivity in the sense of generating goods and services useful in reproduction, but it does so by a surprisingly circuitous route. Namely, and in violation of the second point in the Protestant ethic, work does not well explain the accumulation of wealth. Rather, there is an inverse correlation between weekly hours of employment and income. The people working the longest hours generally have the lowest incomes, and the people working the shortest hours generally have the highest incomes. Therefore, since long working hours are correlated with low income, and since low income is correlated with high fertility, then long working hours correlates with high fertility. On the other point concerning vice, at present we are unable to validate the claim that work prevents it, because vice in the conventional sanctimonious sense no longer exists under the evolutionary ethic. Bad is that which leads to reduced reproductive success. And even in this sense it is not clear that work always prevents bad consequences. For example, one might be overly dedicated to work in a way that caused one to fail to allocate time and resources to reproduction at an optimal level.

There is another argument that is germane to the Protestant ethic -- it is undermined from within. Some view work as having intrinsic value above all else, and they view support of the lazy and unproductive members of society as wrong. But a paradox arises from this attitude, because if work does have intrinsic value, then it makes sense for an individual to volunteer to work in order to support another lazy, unproductive individual.

Constitutional law

Constitutional law is conspicuous in its failing to address issues of an individual's reproductive success in favorable terms, or to address them at all. The Second Amendment of the Constitution of the United States guarantees the right to bear arms. Regrettably, there is no article or amendment of the Constitution that guarantees the right to bear children. Such an amendment would prevent a reactionary move to deny poor people, especially those on public assistance, the right to choose their family size. The fifty-five delegates who met in 1787 to draw up the Constitution and the Bill of Rights did not see fit to specifically guarantee the right to breathe or eat, either. Perhaps they assumed that reproduction was so fundamental a right that it needed no guarantee. Of course, there is no problem with that assumption until the right is denied. The time has come for a new Amendment of the Constitution -- one that guarantees the right to maximize reproductive success -- it would read:

The maximization of reproductive success is an undeniable right afforded to all.

Until such an Amendment of the Constitution is ratified we cannot depend on the executive, legislative, or judicial branches of government to govern in accordance with the evolutionary ethic and progenitivism. But, in the meantime, we may be able to call on the average citizen in the course of jury duty to refuse to enforce any law which does not increase his reproductive success, and to enforce with certainty those laws that do.

Humanism

Humanism in its many forms generally denies that there is a meaning of life that is to be sought for and found. Rather, humanists generally maintain that the meaning of life is something that we create, not discover. Or they state more directly that life has no meaning *per se*[119]. In this sense, humanism contrasts with the evolutionary ethic and progenitivism. Humanists also maintain that in a world of humanism, religion will be obsolete, and they reject the divine origin of morality. Thus, humanism serves as a counterbalance to religiosity and natural law in America today. Unfortunately, humanism rejects religion outright without allowing for the beneficial effects some religions may have on reproductive success. At the same time, humanists often embrace contraception and elective abortion, both of which are strongly antigenitive. I cannot conclude that there is much in humanism that would appeal to the evolutionary ethicist, since the modes of analysis of the two disciplines are entirely different. This fact is made the more strange by the claim that both fields might make: Their aim is to serve humanity. One problem with humanism is that it appears to lack a clear unifying principle. The evolutionary ethic and progenitivism has ''maximize your reproductive success,'' an axiom from which all other rules follow in that philosophy. On the other hand, humanism appears to be a patchwork of human rights and inclinations without hierarchical structure. Sometimes, those inclinations, such as rejecting the traditional dualism of mind and body as part of their manifestos[118], are germane to any modern scientific philosophy. But that is no substitute for a source of tenable philosophical authority such as evolution provides for the evolutionary ethic.

Nationalism

Nationalism as it has been practiced in the recent past is not in accordance with the evolutionary ethic. That humans might always exist in cultures, and that those societies in which the cultures exist might organize themselves into nations, has been part of human history for a few thousand years. Nations might conceivably serve the reproductive interests of the people of which they are comprised. But they can never be correctly viewed as integrated and harmonious, nor can they be viewed as political entities for which reproductive sacrifice ought to be made. It has been recognized in the U.S.A. for a few decades that inequity in the social system cannot be justified on the grounds that it is for the benefit of the nation. It is now time to recognize that a nation's only legitimate purpose is to foster an environment in which individual citizens can maximize their reproductive success.

Freudian theory

Freudian theory has some obvious problems: The death wish and the notional sexual conflict within the family are two examples -- they are ridiculously out of touch with evolutionary thinking. While Freud claimed that he was inspired by Darwin, it takes great imagination to find manifestations of that inspiration in Freud's published works. We have had the scientific tools required to debunk the Freudian notions of death wish, Oedipus complex, boys being afraid that their fathers might castrate them, and penis envy by girls, before they were ever written. The tools were provided by Darwin[38]. On Freud's interpretations of dreams[63], the best explanation of apparent symbolism in them may be the recognition of weak cognitive associations of objects according to their shape and function and the neural pathways by which their mental images are connected. The assertion that dreams are Freudian is a self-fulfilling prophecy -- if you think of a symbolic relationship, it is so in your subconscious mind. Some people notice they have never had a recognizable Freudian dream until they read Freud[63] on dreams. Then, being consciously aware of the imagery, it begins to affect their dreams.

Social Darwinism

Social Darwinism, a now discredited notion from the last century, should never be confused with true Darwinism or with my theories of the evolutionary ethic and progenitivism. Social Darwinists believed that social injustices visited upon the lower class were justified in a broader sense by the maxim ''survival of the fittest''. It also maintained that social privileges enjoyed by the upper class were their natural right. Further, Social Darwinists believed that social stratification was promoting a beneficial selection process and that exploitation of the less economically fortunate among us was befitting. These beliefs were held in absence of any data that would indicate that the lower social class was innately deficient in some broader sense. All we know is that they are economically deprived and that this condition is correlated with other conditions such as lower educational status and poorer health. The stark contrast between my views and Social Darwinism is that I do not argue that the reproductive imperative exists for the benefit of any particular social class or for the benefit of society as a whole, for that matter. I do not argue that one social class is inherently better than another or that it should be entitled to differential reproductive rights or perhaps any differential human right. Consistent with Darwin's argument,

I believe that evolution has no purpose. It is not my theory that bears similarity to Social Darwinism, but rather some currently popular, antiquated views about social welfare held by Americans who are right of the political center, that do bear this similarity.

Eugenics

The eugenics movement, popular around the turn of the century and an element in many modern social views, was concerned with the control of human reproduction to produce a superior breed of human. "Superior breed" usually meant a person of great intellectual power, physical vigor and European ancestry -- in short, the most efficient type of human by Victorian standards. What eugenicists failed to appreciate was that natural selection itself would choose the most efficient type of human according to the criterion of reproductive success. The philosophy espoused herein is the opposite of eugenics. It does not propose commitment to any particular type or race of humans. Rather, it is by survival and reproduction that all will prove if they are the fittest. Darwin[38] made it clear that differential survival and reproduction are the only criteria of fitness thus to survive. This statement sounds strange to many people when they first encounter these criteria, and that is because of the subtle thread of eugenics that runs through our culture even today. One of the fears of eugenicists is that the human race is somehow undergoing devolution through genetic degradation in the modern world with the relaxation of old selection pressures by civilization. But the point is that when an old selection pressure is eliminated, new traits become adaptive in its absence. Fear of "survival of the unfittest" is the underlying concept in eugenics. But survival to reproduce is the criterion, not the outcome, of fitness. In other words, the fittest *must* survive and reproduce -- and I mean this statement in the sense that it is the definition of the word "fittest," not in the sense that it is a call to undertake needed action to ensure that they do. Stripped of the conceptual rigor of its main propositions, the eugenics movement is clearly exposed as motivated by a subjective desire to mold all humans in the shape of an unscientifically, preconceived, ethnocentric ideal. On a related subject, I would like to make an attempt to remove a popular misconception. It seems that current usage of the phrase "the survival of the fittest" is the opposite of what Darwin intended when he borrowed the phrase from Spencer. For modern Americans the phrase invokes images of the strong vanquishing the weak in a battle to merely exist. The chief error here is the incorrect assumption that "fittest" refers to physical fitness or prowess in battle, when, in fact, it refers to those individuals with the greatest reproductive success, the combined outcome of their survival and reproduction. We are left with the conclusion that for humans, as well as all other life, proficiency in surviving and reproducing, by whatever means, is the only trait which natural selection favors necessarily.

Biological reductionism

Biological reductionism can mean many things. For example, it can mean that human behavior is reduced to fundamental biological components. Reductionism is a philosophy that portrays complex data or phenomena in simple terms. In some cases it occurs with oversimplification. One form of biological reductionism suggests that the ultimate nature of humans can be found in their reflexes and drives. How does the philosophy supported herein differ from that view? That form of biological reductionism maintains that humans have a fundamental nature, and at the same time it may assert that a system of ethics must accept humans for what they are. The foundations of human behavior being rooted in serving a biological need seems to some to be adequate justification for that behavior. Therefore, eating, drinking, sleeping, coitus, and perhaps many other behaviors are sanctioned and hold special significance in defining what humanity ought to do according to some reductionists. Here is the contrast between the progenitivist philosophy of this book and reductionism. Progenitivist philosophy does not turn to reflexes and drives for an ultimate justification of human behavior, as reductionism does. Rather, progenitivist philosophy maintains that any behavior is good if it maximizes reproductive success. Evolution *per se*, not the existence of a drive to perform a natural function like eating or drinking, is believed by the evolutionary ethicist to offer the ultimate purpose and justification for our actions. This claim is not a denial that optimal strategies for feeding, drinking, sleeping and mating can be and should be pursued, but rather that they make sense only in the context of a broader evolutionary strategy of attempting to maximize one's reproductive success. Of course, it can be argued that believing evolutionary biology to be the source of explanation for some anthropological phenomena, as I do believe, is just another form of reductionism. That is true in the sense that physics is the source of explanation for some of the observations in chemistry. Used in that way, biological reductionism is nothing more or less than germane science with synthesis.

Genetic engineering

Genetic engineering has come under attack by a coalition of religions, with the charge that it represents an attempt to play God. Genetic engineers respond that, instead, it is an attempt to be first-rate physicians. If genetic engineering increases one's reproductive success, then by the definition of the evolutionary ethic it is good. I discussed in a previous section how humans are not obliged to reproduce a gene in their genotypes if it is deleterious. For the most part genetic engineering at present is the practice of dealing with rare, deleterious alleles. Naturally, there is a potential for conflict of interests between these rare, deleterious alleles that are engineered out of existence, and the humans who do or would bear them. One way to resolve the fate of genetic engineering itself is to imagine the existence of a gene which predisposed its carrier to practice genetic engineering. Mathematical modeling of the frequency of such a gene in an environment which it, in part, helped to create would resolve the question of whether genetic engineering is adaptive from the viewpoint of a gene. Such mathematical modeling is beyond the intended scope of this book. But intuitively, the great lengths to which genes have gone to replicate themselves without change or error suggest that the genes themselves would be opposed to human intervention of a random nature. However, if rare, deleterious alleles were always targeted for genetic engineering, then the average gene might benefit. All the above applies only to the futuristic alteration of the human genome. It does not apply to the use of genetic engineering on other organisms, which, in fact, makes up the bulk of the genetic engineering work today. There is some opposition to this work on other species, even on bacteria. The matter is honestly not worth serious debate. Those who oppose the genetic engineering of other organisms are simply Luddites who wish to deny all humanity access to the benefits of this powerful, constructive tool that will provide new pharmaceuticals to cure human disease and increase crop yields.

Revisionist history

Revisionist history is a recurring theme in the documentation of events over time. Mass support for unjust regimes in Russia, German Democratic Republic, Sudan and Ethiopia existed only to evaporate as soon as the regimes fell. The same theme is repeated in America, though to a lesser extent. Few people spoke ill of former FBI director J. Edgar Hoover until he was dead, and then came an avalanche of news reports, books, and jokes about his eccentric and unlawful tendencies. This pattern of revisionist history is rooted in natural selection. There is selection to act adaptively, not necessarily truthfully. In fact, we may not be particularly well designed to either perceive or to perpetuate the truth about certain subjects. Survive and reproduce in the current environment is the mandate. Attempt to assess the current environment and change it only to the extent that it maximizes one's reproductive success. Hypocritical support of the powers that be may be precisely in the actor's best interest, only to change when politics change.

Morality

Through misclassification, morality has long been defined as a spiritual rather than physical matter. Increasingly, it appears that any practical morality cannot be free of an anthropological basis. Human thoughts are determined by our environment and genetics, and because concepts in morality are the product of human thinking, they, too, are rooted in environment and genetics. Human values are deeply anthropocentric. Some species of ants produce trophic eggs[221], which are designed to be consumed as food by relatives. If humans had evolved from these hymenoptera instead of from primates, human cultures might have institutionalized the habit of cannibalizing the ova of relatives as a behavior that was completely natural, right and proper. Instead, we consume milk in infancy and in some cultures also at other stages of life, a behavior which is viewed as acceptable clearly because it is peculiar to our mammalian heritage. Ruse and Wilson[178] raised a number of important points:

> It is easy to conceive of an alien intelligent species evolving rules its members consider highly moral but which are repugnant to human beings, such as cannibalism, incest, the love of darkness and decay, parricide, and the mutual eating of faeces. Many animal species perform some or all of these things, with gusto and in order to survive. If human beings had evolved from a stock other than savanna-dwelling, bipedal, carnivorous man-apes we might do the same, feeling inwardly certain that such behaviours are natural and correct. In short, ethical premises are the peculiar products of genetic history, and they can be understood solely as mechanisms that are adaptive for the species that possess them. It follows that the ethical code of one species cannot be translated into that of another. No abstract moral principles exist outside the particular nature of individual species. (p. 186)

In earlier times, a belief in ethics as the will of God was the foundation of morality. But times have changed. As Singer[193] stated:

> One reason why religion no longer provides a satisfactory answer to the puzzle about the nature of morality is that religious belief itself is no longer as universally accepted as it once was. But there is also another problem in locating the origins of morality in the will of God. If all values result from God's will, what reason could God have for willing as he does? If killing is wrong *only* because God said: "Thou shalt not kill," God might just as easily have said: "Thou shalt kill." Would killing then have been right? To agree that it would have been right makes morality too arbitrary; but to deny that it would have been right is to assume that there are standards of right and wrong independent of God's will. Nor can the dilemma be avoided by claiming that God is "good," and so could not have willed us to kill unjustly -- for to say that God is "good" already implies a standard of "goodness" that is independent of God's decision. For this reason many religious thinkers now agree with the non-religious that the basis of ethics must be sought outside religion and independently of belief in God. (p. x)

In thinking about morality and ethics in an evolutionary perspective, it is useful to consider the meaning of warfare, murder, infanticide, and cannibalism in nonhuman primate societies and human societies. We may come to the conclusion that our notions of morality cannot be easily removed from narrow anthropological contexts.

Among the most remarkable observations that I made in my studies in Africa was the occurrence of war among hamadryas baboons. In Ethiopia, 24 km. south of

Harar, I observed prolonged battles between the adult males of three bands of baboons (totaling a troop of 920 individuals) that shared the same large sleeping cliff. During these wars, female baboons from the harems of males in the opposing bands were stolen. These conflicts included escalated aggression and high levels of sound from the combined vocalizations of the males threatening one another in combat.

Male-male aggressive competition appears to be a major cause of mortality among anubis baboons in the Masai Mara population. That fact is not surprising considering that the adult males each enter into 3 escalated aggressive encounters on the average day. In human terms, we would have to describe the deaths as murder in many cases, because they result not from fair one-on-one combat, but from coalitional behavior in which two or more males overpower and kill a competitor in a coordinated attack after "deliberation," using signals and vocalizations to communicate. Infanticide among langur monkeys and gorillas and cannibalism among chimpanzees also appear from considerable field evidence to be elaborate, premeditated strategies.

Cannibalism among humans is a practice of historic significance. Aztecs practiced exocannibalism (eating victims from an out-group), while among the Trobriand Islanders and the Yanomamö, endocannibalism is practiced (eating people from an in-group, often relatives). Regarding communion, Christian mythology maintains that at the time of consecration bread and wine are converted through transubstantiation into the body and blood of Christ. The subsequent consumption of these sacramental foods is known to anthropologists as theophagy (literally, God-eating). The belief is that, in the process, God-like qualities (e.g., power) or God-pleasing attributes (e.g., devotion to the service of God) will be conferred on the recipient. In this sense, theophagy does not differ in purpose from the most common forms of anthropophagy, i.e. the eating of humans by humans, because in cannibalism there is usually the associated belief that the spiritual qualities or desirable characteristics of the victim will be assimilated by the cannibal. In contrast, wholesale butchery of humans by the Aztecs may have had important nutritional consequences as well as spiritual ones. The Aztecs' pattern of anthropophagy certainly appears to be different from the occasional ritualistic consumption of humans in many other societies.

The point of discussing warfare, murder, infanticide, and cannibalism in nature is that we come to the conclusion that our notions of morality cannot be easily removed from narrow anthropological contexts. Given our primate and hominid heritage, many behaviors have been exhibited by humans that would otherwise make no sense at all.

The evolutionary ethic has been some time in the making -- the logic required was not difficult but was counterintuitive. The idea of "doing what comes naturally" has diverted many thinkers in naturalistic philosophy from the crux of the evolutionary ethic. While doing what comes naturally has some appeal, it is not an end in itself. For if doing what comes *unnaturally* were, under some circumstances, to maximize reproductive success, as modern medicine does under some circumstances, then it would be adaptive to do so. Similarly, many phenomena such as parasites and predators are natural, but because they reduce an individual's reproductive success they are not good. Another point, though not a logical refutation, is that in a cross-species and cross-phyletic survey, it is clear that this mandate of doing what comes naturally can lead to actions which some people might consider atrocious.

The history of morality in America in the last few decades can be seen as a political dichotomy. Liberals view the change as an escape from repression. Conservatives view the change as a surrender to moral anarchy. Any ethical system requires one attribute if it is to exist at all: It must be capable of being perpetuated. That requirement in turn defines some other characteristics. The system requires some degree of internal consistency so that it can be applied (and in turn observed and spread). It should not detract too severely from the inclusive fitness of its adherents. Analysis based on the evolutionary ethic says that morality in America during the last few decades has been on the decline. Falling total fertility rates at a time of inordinate plenty is the justification for that viewpoint.

Government

Weak government is associated with personal freedoms. Strong government is associated with curtailment of personal freedoms. The peoples enjoying the greatest freedom are those entirely removed from government -- these people include the most remote tribes of eastern, southern, and central Africa. They have no paperwork, no taxes and no intrusions whatsoever of government regulators (or large corporations) into their lives. They live in anarchy in the sense that they lack a dominating government, but through rich traditions in their cultures and a biological basis for their behaviors, they have ordered societies.

Almost everyone who lives under the rule of a strong government, regardless of whether it is a dictatorship, former communist block country, or traditional democracy, has been wronged at one time or another by his government. The wrongs come both large and small. An erroneously imposed death penalty or a forced sterilization rates as a large but uncommon wrong. An unfair driving citation or parking ticket rates as a small but common wrong. Democracy is more a title than a practice in countries that describe themselves as democratic. Would the citizens of a true democracy really vote in favor of something as exorbitant as income tax and in favor of something as petty and annoying as parking meters? After establishing parking meters, would they then pass a law against "feeding" the meters? If safety is a human right, how do we justify our government maintaining a large nuclear arsenal in a post-Cold War age? With increasing frequency American cities are imposing curfews on our young people in a way that is frighteningly similar to the curfews once imposed by now demised communist dictatorships. Certainly in these examples the cure of strong government is worse than the disease.

What are the costs and benefits of strong government? Strong government, in order to survive, must make self-perpetuation its top priority. To this end government makes laws protecting itself. For example, it is difficult for an average citizen to bring suit against the government even when the government has committed a conspicuous crime. Similarly, governments pass laws forbidding treason. Government obtains the benefits from this protection and people bear the costs. Another general trend of strong government is that the ruling elite take more privileges for themselves and the average citizens become the victims of repression, in part to pay for those privileges. The effects of authoritarianism and civil repression should be measured, of course, in terms of the effects on reproductive success. Other cherished rights, like freedom of speech, freedom of the press, and the right to bear arms, should be viewed as only proximate social rights that might help assure freedom to maximize one's reproductive success.

The ultimate question we should ask about government is: Does government hinder or help our reproduction? Taxes on food and medicine for babies conspicuously increase the cost of raising a child. Taxes on food, health care, energy, housing, clothing, and other resources needed for survival and reproduction are another way of making supporting a family much more expensive. It is possible that these taxes reduce the financial incentive to reproduce and thus reduce the reproductive success of those taxed, even though the overall trend is greater fertility for less wealth. In fact, any policy that reduces prosperity, as taxation does, leads to a predictable increase in the death rate. For illustrative purposes in relating mortality risks induced by economic expenditures, Keeney[111] estimated that there is one induced fatality for every 7.25 million dollars spent by government. Some governments go still further. India uses coercion to reduce rates of reproduction. China uses restrictions to curtail personal choice in reproduction. The U.S. government is considering measures to restrict the reproductive rights of Americans receiving public assistance, to make some forms of public assistance contingent on not producing any more children, and to exclude wholesale some sex-age-classes (usually teenage girls with children are the target) from receiving public assistance *because* they reproduced.

While there is much to be said in favor of anarchy, some persuasive arguments also exist in favor of the establishment of a bare-bones government (perhaps similar to the government envisaged by the authors of the Constitution of the United States). Which taxes should we approve in order to finance its operation? Examples of acceptable taxes might be a luxury sales tax, a pet tax, a tobacco tax, a tax on advertisements in the mass media, a tax on contraceptives, a tax on divorce, a tax on education past eighth grade, a tax on cereal grains, a tax on urban living, a tax on political organizations and political campaigns, a tax on spectator sports, and a tax on elective abortions. A tax on elective abortions might appropriately be set in the range of what it would cost to raise the child if it were allowed to survive, about three hundred thousand dollars among the upper-middle class. It is important not to generate too much revenue through these taxes, because governments through the ages have proven their inclination and ability to grow to expend any amount of revenue, no matter how large. Big governments are also well known for their ability to confiscate resources that could be better used by the populace that they proclaim to serve. In America, new heights in government spending have been achieved, to the extent of spending trillions of dollars creatively borrowed from future generations.

Populations in countries with the most ineffectual governments (mostly in Africa) have the highest growth rates. Populations in countries with the most organized and powerful governments (mostly in western Europe and North America) have the lowest growth rates. The observed difference in population growth rates is explained in part as the cost of supporting government. A government benefits as a superculturgen if it can divert the reproductive effort of its citizens. The diverted energy and resources are then used to support the government itself, to provide the lavish lifestyles of the ruling elite and to defend the ruling elite through a defense system build-up and by acts of war. I encourage future researchers to examine the effects of government on reproduction.

It is true that a government can also be endangered by a prolonged negative population growth rate -- because it ultimately leads to a situation where there is nobody left to be governed. Just such a trend has occurred in some countries with very big government. To avoid demise, such endangered governments institute remedial measures to increase rates of population growth. For example, reproductive rates can be increased through social and economic incentives for having a baby. Immigration rates can be increased through liberalization of regulations controlling the influx of foreigners. Pronatalist policies in Sweden (where the total fertility rate at 1.6 in 1983 was well below the replacement rate) entitle parents to 18 months of paid leave after the birth of a child. Swedish national health insurance covers hospitalization costs plus 90 percent of the income a worker loses when he or she is ill, including for work days lost when caring for a sick child. Education, from day care to university, is low-cost in Sweden.

A government's existence can be threatened by overpopulation, and it can be expected to take drastic and repressive measures to limit fertility, as observed in China today with the rule of one child per family, forced birth control and forced abortion. In America we generally believe at the present that the right to procreate is so fundamental that the government should not offer forceful interference. But some kind of repressive governmental intrusion into our reproductive lives may become more common in the future. Official repression of reproductive rights could in turn inspire the unfolding of a powerful drive toward philoprogenitiveness in the people subject to the restrictions. In the future, the conflict between despotic governments attempting to deny the right to reproduce and the desires of individuals who wish to have children can be expected to increase.

The ideal government from the viewpoint of the evolutionary ethic would be one in the minimal tradition, there to serve individual reproductive interests. In fact, it can be argued that government's first responsibility is to the reproductive success of its citizens. An ideal government must be small because it would otherwise consume too many resources that could be used in maximizing reproductive success. Politicians and laws would similarly conform to principles that maximize the reproductive success of individual citizens. Instituting such reforms to this end might well be a cause worth pursuing. To allow shortsighted politicians and special interests to maintain our heading on the present course is to abrogate what increase in freedom we might have to maximize our reproductive success. For example, take the selection of nominees for the post of Surgeon General. Why are they so often outspoken on reproductive matters? Unfortunately, not because of a desire by the government to promote reproductive success. These nominees are not fertility experts, as they should be to satisfy the cause of progenitivism. Rather, they are chosen to fit the hidden agenda of promoting contraception and abortion that goes with the position. Consistent with this antigenitive policy, one recent nominee for Surgeon General during the Clinton administration built his career largely on suppressing the reproductive success of teenagers. The linkage between the post of Surgeon General and antigenitivism would be fine material for an *exposé*.

Arts and sciences

Intelligent application of the scientific method is a powerful means of obtaining knowledge. Why has there been a running assault on it over the centuries right up to the present? The main reason is that it challenges the validity of other culturgens. Perhaps the worst assault on the scientific method in recent memory was the subordination of science to political ideology in the former U.S.S.R. under the influence of Trofim D. Lysenko. Religious ideology, too, both in the past and present, often attempts to undermine scientific thought.

Knowledge can either aid or hinder reproduction. Having spent most of my life in pursuit of knowledge, I firmly believe that there are many things that should not be known, i.e. in fact anything that reduces one's reproductive success. For example, knowledge on how to manufacture, distribute, and use intrauterine birth control devices (IUDs) is disastrous to fertility. A corollary of this rule is that there are some falsehoods that we are better off believing. For example, the political gullibility of the masses seems to be adaptive sometimes, in that it furthers acquiescence to almost unstoppable power, opposition to which might result in reduced reproductive success.

Should we support or oppose new technologies? The answer depends on the implications of these technologies for individual reproductive success. For example, it is my opinion that there should be a moratorium on research for new contraceptives and new abortifacients. Technology can only solve our problems to the extent that it can favorably influence the variables in our life history equations.

Lenin said: "Art belongs to the people". The evolutionary ethic imparts: "Art belongs enhancing the reproductive success of the people". Should the sole criterion for art be that it is aesthetically pleasing? Historically, art sometimes fulfilled religious and political purposes. Could it not fulfill the purpose of enhancing the artist's and the patron's reproductive success?

The people in our most learned professions are among the least fertile[60]. The principle of allocation suggests that they under-reproduce because of intellectual pursuits which compete with reproduction. There can be competition between cultural inheritance and genetic inheritance. Above a minimum amount required to survive and reproduce, culture can begin to inhibit genetic transmission. Part of culture consists of self-perpetuating culturgens. They do not require heritability. They can pass from individual to unrelated individual. Self-perpetuating culturgens are most effective when they cause the carrier individual to do nothing else in life but to transmit them. These may be ideas or part of the material culture, e.g., wealth or knowledge. They are the most extreme form of cultural baggage. Fisher[60] wrote:

> We may remember that the Latin word *Proletarii* for the class of citizens without capital property meant in effect "The beggars who have children", and that numerous, though perhaps ineffective laws, of the early Empire, were designed to encourage parentage among the higher classes. (p. 241)

It is likely as true today as it was in ancient Rome that because the proletariat do not have capital property they are therefore free of a certain form of cultural load that such property brings to the bourgeoisie. The cultural elite may also simply over-intellectualize the process of reproduction, thereby reducing their fertility. The fact that a "brainchild" can be a reproductive substitute is suggested in the very choice of the word. In fact, for the ordinary American individual, not much planning goes into the production of offspring. This fact is a fortunate one, because planning tends to shut down production. That is why 60 percent of pregnancies in America are unplanned.

Humans are not the only organisms with knowledge. And based on a definition of science in which it is the ability to make accurate predictions about the future based on past events, we are not the only ones with science. Anubis baboons in Masai Mara appear to have a rudimentary science of astronomy that allows them to predict and modify their behavior according to nighttime levels of lunar illumination. Baboons recognize and modify their behavior in accordance with the phases of the moon. They prefer to sleep high in the tallest trees of the forest near the ends of lateral branches to avoid predation by leopards, which are excellent climbers and often hunt at night. They can protect themselves from leopards (and even intimidate them) when there is adequate light, but they cannot see as well as leopards when it is dark. Seasonally the baboons feed in small, wild African olive trees. And they return to the sleeping trees before nightfall most of the lunar month. But when the moon is full, the nighttime illumination is bright enough for a human to read a newspaper by it. Baboons anticipate that the moon will be bright before nightfall and before the moon has risen, and do not return to their usual sleeping trees. Instead, they stay at the olive groves to feed during the night and to save a long, costly progression to and from the sleeping trees, knowing they are able to protect themselves from leopards in the bright moonlight. Although there is obviously a genetic component to this behavior, it is sufficiently complex to have a large environmental component, including observational learning from other troop members in perpetuating it and a basic understanding of lunar cycles. It is a case of nonhuman science benefiting its practitioners, and an example of how early human intellectual development might have benefited rather than hindered human reproductive success.

Energy

Current patterns of energy consumption are based on economic cost-effective use. This pattern should be replaced with one based on reproductive success effective use. We are currently in the process of a massive drawdown of cheap fossil fuels. While some of this energy is used in the production and transport of food and for other purposes that might assist our reproduction, most of it is wasted in a superfluous, even dangerous, fashion. While commercial energy is not limiting to reproduction at the present, it is possible to imagine future shortages that may impact the Malthusian parameter of population increase, m, if alternative sources of energy such as nuclear fusion are not found. It is diachronic competition[21] in a sense: We are now using resources that cannot be renewed which might be saved instead for the reproduction of our relatives in future generations.

In the future we shall rely on some alternative sources of energy. Solar energy is nearly competitive with conventional energy sources, and wind energy already is. Nuclear power, including current fission techniques, and, if hopes are realized, fusion techniques, seem to be uniquely suited to delivering safe, cheap electricity.

Though it is counterintuitive, you are much safer sitting in a nuclear power plant than sitting in your automobile. Nuclear power plants emit less pollution than oil-fueled power plants and emit less radioactivity than coal fueled power plants. The chief risk associated with the use of nuclear power around the world is the increase in the number of countries that have the materials and means to construct nuclear weapons. Proliferation of thermonuclear devices is undesirable in almost every aspect because of its potentially disastrous effects on reproductive success.

Our machines do a tremendous amount of work compared to what humans can do unaided, but a lot of that work is superfluous to maximizing reproductive success. The enormous gulf between humans and their machines is illustrated by this example: If all Americans together did intense physical work to generate power, they could only power one small city with the energy generated by their labors. The evidence for much superfluous work by machines in America comes from the past and the present. Prior to the industrial revolution, only the waterwheel and the windmill provided mechanical sources of energy. Yet, in the complete absence of electricity, motor vehicles, fossil fuel powered machines, nuclear power and other products of a postindustrial economy, they were able to produce three or four times the number of children that Americans do now. Similarly, the average American consumes about a thousand times the energy that the average Ethiopian does. Yet, the average Ethiopian has four times the number of children that the average American does. This observation leads to an important point for conservation of resources. If this tremendous historical increase in mechanical work has not increased our reproductive success, what justification is there for it? Affluence for its own sake is a preposterous proposition because it robs the present generation and future generations of resources that could be used for reproduction.

Every few years there is a major, day long, power failure in an American city, followed by a spike in the number of births in that city nine months later. Obviously, the people with nowhere to go and nothing to do during the power failure turn to sexual intercourse for recreation. This phenomenon, amusing as it might seem at first, actually reveals something sinister: Our ordinary routines in American life are so maladaptive that even a minor disaster can improve them.

Personal finance

The basic assumption in life history strategies is that time and energy are limiting currencies in the attainment of reproductive success. The basic question in life history strategies is: "What is the individual's optimal distribution of the expenditure of time and energy for reproductive effort, considering that reproduction is a competing variable with growth and maintenance in the life history, and that ultimately there is a tradeoff of survivorship for reproduction?" Among humans, in addition to time, energy, and reproductive success we also have new, imperfectly assimilated forms of currency. For example, in America we have Federal Reserve notes, commonly referred to as ''money''. But it is not commonly recognized that this new form of currency has no real intrinsic value. Its worth from an evolutionary viewpoint is entirely determined by its ability to be exchanged for time, energy, and reproductive effort in the old system of currency. In managing one's personal finances it is of paramount importance to have a clear goal in mind -- namely maximizing one's reproductive success. Without such a goal there is an increased likelihood of performing some other operation on the life history in the course of pursuing another, inappropriate goal such as maximizing wealth, body weight or longevity. At the present, it appears that Americans are indeed dying rich, fat, and old. So engrossed in this new system of currency, Americans are leaving far fewer descendants than they could actually have produced. A detailed analysis of how one might best manage one's personal finances is beyond the intended scope of this book. But the one trend that is clear and requires comment is that individuals in all economic classes appear to be failing to exchange their financial assets for reproductive effort, and in this way buy reproductive success. A little conscious deliberation by anyone on how to take the financial resources available and use them to produce and raise the largest number of children possible would be a major step toward solving the problem.

Gambling

The probability of a ticket being the winning one for the grand prize in the Texas State Lotto is 1 in 15,890,700. Like many state lotteries, the Texas State Lotto requires that all six numbers drawn out of the range of numbers from one to fifty match to win the grand prize. With the prevalent attitude being one of disfavor toward taxation, it is strange that state-sponsored lotteries are so popular. On a national level they took in 34 billion dollars in 1993. The mean return for players in the lottery is less than the mean wager (in fact in most games only about half the amount wagered is returned to winners), but the variance in the amount returned is higher than the variance in the amount wagered. In this sense, state lotteries do not offer what would be described as ''fair bets,'' because the price of the wager is disproportionately high compared to the size of the prize times the probability of winning it. A better use for the money spent on gambling would be to redirect it to the costs of raising additional offspring. But this statement is not to say that playing the lottery is maladaptive. In the strange environment in which we currently live there is an inverse correlation between wealth and reproductive success. In this sense, if you are dedicated to gambling look at it as a dependable way to reduce your wealth and thereby increase the number of children that you have, rather than hold the unrealistic notion that it is a way to get rich. Four hundred billion dollars is spent on gambling in America each year. That may not by itself be enough to turn around the low rates of reproduction in America, but it is a large step in the right direction. It is amusing to imagine how an anthropologist from another planet might interpret casino gambling. Casinos, with their cathedral-like edifices, small altars where money and tokens are offered by the patrons during regular visitations, the elaborate, highly repetitive rituals performed, the trance-like state of the patrons, and the certainty with which the patrons leave their money behind, might look to him for all purposes like a hallowed ceremony for ridding oneself of fitness-depressing wealth. One interesting phenomenon is the reverse lottery -- a circumstance in which a person is paid to accept a higher chance of death. Indianapolis race car driving is an example. Why are reverse lotteries not more common?

Vocation

Of course the ideal vocation is the one that maximizes reproductive success. Sufficient data on that subject do not appear to be available, but farming is positively correlated with reproductive success in many places in the world, including the U.S.A. I have also casually observed that the employees of fast food restaurants, while engaged in a relatively low social status occupation, appear to reproduce well and early. I cannot help but wonder about the average reproductive success of evolutionary biologists. Darwin certainly got this field off to a strong start in the struggle for survival with his ten children. I would guess that average modern evolutionary biologists, who have not yet had the opportunity to embrace the new evolutionary ethic herein, have fewer offspring than the average American, but not so few as the greatly depressed number of their fellow academicians.

The National Institute of Occupational Safety and Health reported that the accidental death rate of all U.S. occupations is seven per 100,000 workers annually. Saporito[182] reported that, in comparison, crab fishermen in Alaska have what is probably the most dangerous occupation in the U.S. They experience accidental death rates of 660 per 100,000 workers annually -- almost 100 times the national average. Contrary to what it might seem, a risky vocation should not necessarily be avoided. Instead, it should be undertaken at times of low extended reproductive value and only with a compensating fitness differential, i.e. a payment of reproductive success in exchange for life lost.

Occupations that threaten fertility, the fetus *in utero*, or that require sterilization must generally be avoided. For example, U.S. industry has a history of banning fertile women from certain jobs such as those with high exposure to lead, in turn leading some women to seek sterilization in order to obtain or keep those jobs. Women doing so are never making a good choice.

Suicide rates vary by occupation. Once physicians were at the greatest risk. Now law enforcement personnel are at greatest risk. Law enforcement personnel are so prone to suicide that it exceeds the other risks associated with the job; they are more likely to die by their own hand than in the line of duty.

Philanthropy and charity

There is a question regarding gifts of money from one person to another: Is there positive spin-off from some forms of philanthropy and charity? We generally assume, perhaps too hastily, that the recipient of the monetary gift benefits, but that is not necessarily so when benefit is measured in reproductive success. And we wonder if the donor might be benefiting in some way, too. The remarkable philanthropy of the Rockefeller family is an interesting case. It would be cynical to overlook the possibility that they took personal satisfaction in giving to charity with the belief that something right was being done. But their gifts also helped to secure a source of political power and social influence that may well endure for a number of generations of their descendants.

Does charity pay off in a broader way? Having and maintaining excessive wealth is a cause of cultural load, because wealth is a culturgen that reduces reproductive success by the principle of allocation as well as by other mechanisms. The adaptive strategy, if you have too much wealth, is to get rid of it. Perhaps Americans should consider adopting the obscure custom of the potlatch of the Northwest Coast American Indians, in which the wealthiest members of the tribe take great pleasure in a ceremony in which they give away most of their wealth to other members of the community. Anthropologists have been puzzled by this custom for decades, some suggesting that it is a means by which the giver elevates his status, but I would interpret it as an ideal strategy of reducing the potlatch giver's cultural load. In the Rockefeller example above, it is obviously only a small step in the right direction of reducing net worth and increasing fertility. But few Americans are faced with a cultural load in terms of wealth of that magnitude.

In this serendipitous discovery there is a **life-lesson: The wealthiest people can benefit their reproductive success by giving, and the poorest people can benefit their reproductive success by receiving.**

This asymmetry provides a somewhat remarkable rational basis, which is consistent with the evolutionary ethic, for the practice of charity among related and unrelated people alike. In this system, charity would be directed by people with more wealth than the optimum for reproductive success to people with less wealth than the optimum for reproductive success. At the present, the optimum family income for maximizing reproductive success is near the middle of the range of what is currently defined as poverty in America. The current official poverty line in America is an income of $15,000 a year for a family of four. So there is some opportunity for adaptive charity in terms of donations from middle class people and upper class people to the very poorest people in our society. Charitable transactions based on this principle might reach ten percent of America's gross domestic product and do a tremendous amount of good in the process. The limiting factor is an insufficient number of poor people below the optimal income for reproductive success. There just are not enough of them to absorb all the wealth that the comparatively rich people need to shed for their own good. We might consider enhancing our foreign aid to the people in the poorest countries in the world once suboptimal poverty in America is eliminated. With the 1.3 billion impoverished people in the world, many of them below the optimal income for maximizing reproductive success, there is a great opportunity for Americans to practice fitness enhancing charity abroad. For individual Americans who want to practice charity on a global scale, I have observed the International Red Cross and the Catholic Relief Services doing fitness enhancing work among the very poor in Africa, and you might consider making a donation to them. Of course, there are other international aid organizations, but many of them foist contraception and abortion on the recipients of the aid. Although they are well intentioned, well intentioned behaviors are rarely enough. We cannot anticipate much assistance from the U.S. government in facilitating this international aid effort, because the U.S. government commonly makes the mistake of giving that aid to the foreign governments, many of which are antigenitive, instead of giving it directly to the people in foreign countries.

Current proposals for welfare reform need to be evaluated with the same mode of analysis. In asking if society's safety net is working, we must define its goals. Welfare should serve the reproductive interests of the recipients *and* of the providers, i.e. taxpayers. The current system of welfare is clearly serving the reproductive interests of the providers, because it lowers their net income through taxation to an amount closer to the optimum income for maximizing reproductive success. However, it is not clear that the current system of welfare is serving the reproductive interests of the recipients, because the average amount received by recipients may not be the optimal income for reproductive success. The financial assistance actually provided could be at the optimal level, too large or too small. Accepting the goals of maximizing reproductive success of recipients and providers, and further research into the optimal support for maximizing reproductive success, would bring unaccustomed rigor to the debate on welfare reform.

When the wealthy fail to give generously to the poor, they are showing the ultimate manifestation of false economy, because it is their own fitness that suffers as a part of the consequences.

Our present Social Security System in America is sometimes thought of as a charity to ourselves. We contribute when young and receive financial benefits when old. Unfortunately, it is not sustainable. It is moving inevitably toward bankruptcy as the American population ages and as retired recipients increase in proportion to working contributors. One of the primary reasons that the Social Security System will go bankrupt is that the people who will collect the insurance have failed to produce enough children to pay into the fund. In old age we are often dependent on our children and, if there are too few of them, the burden on each is great. Averaging the burden by contributing to and drawing from a communal Social Security Fund neither alters the fact of the dependency on our children nor does it make the burden any less. Similar to the situation in non-Western cultures at the present, many of the elderly in our country will require the direct economic support of their working children in the future. As in the Third World, having children will be a means of buying security for old age in America. Social Security will be defunct, the elderly will be too old to earn an income, but may be capable of providing some services important to reproductive success, e.g., child care in the home for the children of their children who in turn support them. More than any single factor, I expect that the failure of the Social Security System will lead the generation of baby boomers in the early part of the next millennium to conclude that they made a grave error in having so few children. Of course, individuals will not have sufficient numbers of their own children to care for them in old age. But because everyone on average failed to reproduce sufficiently, there will be a chronic overall labor shortage that aggravates the situation.

Much is made of the value of an egalitarian society in America. But a society with excess wealth and an inverse relationship between wealth and reproductive success is a better society if wealth is concentrated in a few unfortunate individuals, thereby leaving the majority free to reproduce without hindrance. Political parties advocating the relative growth of the middle class and upper class are accordingly misguided. It is even imaginable that the few individuals who serve as a repository of great wealth in such a society might serve society's purposes as a whole, even though those few individuals fail their own reproductive interests. This system is the inverse of that found in eusocial insects, in which control of resources is concentrated in the large castes of workers and reproductive rights are centered in very small groups of reproducing individuals.

Communication and misinformation

Nonverbal

In the animal world, a large part of the communication is misinformation. In species where competitors modify their aggressive competition as a function of their opponent's body size, exaggeration of body size is expected to evolve. This type of misinformation about body size in animal communication has been generally appreciated since Darwin's time. But Popp and DeVore[164] pointed out that their cost-benefit analysis of aggressive competition makes new predictions about misinformation and exaggerations, which need not be limited to morphological structures. They may, instead, include any of the variables that they delineate in their cost-benefit functions for aggressive competition. In this model, competitors are expected to exaggerate the value of the disputed resource, perhaps by mimicking higher levels of motivation during the competition than they, in fact, felt. Or a competitor may exaggerate the value of winning an encounter by misrepresenting the circumstances under which the encounter occurs. Sham incubation behavior, sham nest-building behavior, and sham nest-tending behavior are common in birds and fish. Once thought by ethologists to be nonadaptive "displacement" activities (assumed to be the result of high levels of motivation or conflicts between drives), they take on new strategic significance with this mode of analysis. Popp and DeVore[164] explained:

> ... the presence of a nest or eggs would usually imply higher benefits from winning the encounter for their owner than for the intruder, and individuals who advertise such asymmetry when it exists, or delude an opponent into believing that such asymmetry exists through sham behavior, will have a competitive advantage. (p. 326)

Misinformation may have more than a small effect on fitness. Among ovophile mouthbreeding fish of eastern Africa, at the time of spawning the female follows the male to the spawning pit, lies on her side, and releases one or more eggs. She immediately takes them into her mouth. The male then lies on his side and displays his anal fin. The male has decoy egg spots on his anal fin, and the female tries to gather them. In this way she sucks sperm into her mouth and the eggs are fertilized. Thus, fertilization of the eggs is made possible by a strategic piece of misinformation from the male. Without this misinformation the fertilization rate might be considerably lower. This example is a nice one of misinformation benefiting both the actor and the recipient.

Creeper males in sticklebacks are males that mimic female stickleback appearance and behavior. Instead of defending a territory, building a nest, and courting females, they approach the nest of a territorial male as though they were a female ready to lay eggs. When courted by the territorial male they enter the nest, but instead of laying eggs they deposit sperm on the eggs laid there by a previous female. In this example, misinformation occurs to the benefit of the actor and to the cost of the recipient.

The evolution of misinformation, exaggeration and mimicry demonstrates that there is no intrinsic value to truth. What value truth has is a consequence of its fitness effects on an individual in its interactions with its social, biotic and physical environment. While truth is praised as part of the ideal culture in America, it is less prevalent in the real culture than the ideal would have. In non-Western cultures there often appears to be an indifference to truth from the Western perspective. Among animals misinformation is often so common that it becomes a pronounced feature of their societies itself.

Language

Language has a large cultural component, and words are culturgens. Sublinguistic thought like emotions or intuition may not be culturgens. We shall learn in a following section how culturgens cannot be trusted to assist us in maximizing our reproductive success. Can sublinguistic thought be trusted more than thought based on language? Unfortunately, probably not, since the environment has changed so much since the neural pathways producing those thoughts evolved. In this section I shall assume that human language is more than culturgens using us for their own purposes. I shall assume that language can under some circumstances serve the purpose of the speaker or listener, e.g., misinformation. Have you ever been slighted or insulted and found yourself strangely ignoring it or pretending that it did not occur? Saving face, as it is called, is a fine art in some cultures. It makes sense, especially when you are accidentally slighted. Social psychology teaches us that people who treat you poorly consequently think less of you. The strategy then to make people think well of you is simple: If you are slighted, cover up the fact.

When we wish to consider misinformation in human communication and how it is perpetuated, there is no better example of it than the culturgens associated with lying politicians. Why do they dominate the current political scene? We need to imagine two alternatives: first, honest politicians who will always tell the truth, no matter how unpopular or damaging to their careers; second, lying politicians, who have no respect for the truth, but instead will say anything that will promote their careers. Further, imagine that the political issues involved are sufficiently complex that there is no recognized authority on truth and falsehood, thereby making penalties for dishonesty unlikely and even recognizing dishonesty difficult. Which politicians get elected? The liars do. So it is not surprising that all politicians holding elected office are liars. The election process without checks ensuring veracity is a sieve that guarantees this outcome. Fortunately, the situation is far from lost; there is utility in this pattern. The exact opposite of what politicians say is often the truth, so they are valuable in this way as inverse barometers. I do not intend to argue that the morality of the evolutionary ethic maintains that politicians should not lie, rather if they do lie, the lies should be ones that increase the reproductive success of their constituents. Nevertheless, I conclude that one of the most important rights afforded to Americans is the right not to participate in the political process. Today, Americans are exercising that right in record numbers. If the trend toward a declining number of voters is reversed, it should be to provide an enormous disincentive to lying politicians who suppress the reproductive success of their constituents.

Social behavior

One useful way of analyzing social behavior is through a fitness cost-benefit model. Trivers[206] has been a long-time advocate of this approach and stated:

> [Social traits] affect at least one individual other than the possessor of the trait, so the simplest social theory begins with two individuals. We imagine that one individual, the actor, initiates some action that affects a second individual, the recipient. We measure the effects in units of reproductive success; that is, we measure whether the behavior increases the reproductive success of the actor (benefit) or decreases it (cost) and we measure the same thing for the recipient. Neglecting zero effects, we have at once four kinds of social acts: the actor confers a benefit but suffers a cost (altruistic), the actor gains while inflicting a cost (selfish), both parties gain (cooperative), and both parties suffer (spiteful). (p. 41)

Altruism

Among humans, altruism appears to occur on a sliding scale based on costs to the actor, benefits to the recipient, and the regression coefficient of relatedness. While altruism is something that is cherished at all times, practical necessity when times are difficult is well recognized as a cause of abandoning altruism and morals to which one would otherwise adhere. The future of human rights (and of the growing animal rights movement) are largely dependent upon the well-being and security of the potential practitioners of altruism in the society. For example, a sound nutritional and economic footing allows some people in our society to advocate and practice a strict form of animal rights, but in non-Western societies such attempts to put animal rights on the agenda are not only ignored but scorned -- some societies cannot afford the luxury of feeding their cats gourmet cat food, or feeding them at all for that matter. Instead, in some places cats are viewed as proper food for humans. In many non-Western societies animals are for work and to eat;

the pleasure, pain and quality of life of these animals is of no consequence to the people who own them. Rather than concern themselves with superfluous altruism toward animals, the people of some societies struggle to maintain interactions among themselves that are usually considered the bare minimum for human dignity. Desperate circumstances lead to desperate human behavioral strategies. Sometimes the cost of altruism to the actor is too great to bear, even when it would seem trivial under normal circumstances. Turnbull[207] described his conclusion after studying the Ik tribe in eastern Africa, whose society and families had collapsed during a famine:

> ... kindness, generosity, consideration, affection, honesty, hospitality, compassion, charity ... it seems that, far from being basic human qualities, they are superficial luxuries we can afford in times of plenty, or mere mechanisms for survival and security. (pp. 31-32)

Turnbull[207] published his study of the Ik tribe of Uganda. They had lost their traditional hunting grounds and primary means of subsistence, and their social behavior degenerated into entirely self-serving actions -- even parental care of dependent offspring was lacking. Turnbull[207] stated:

> The Ik ... were as unfriendly, uncharitable, inhospitable and generally mean as any people can be. (p. 32)

Some of those aspects of humanity that we cherish most, like altruism, are displayed according to the sliding scale of cost-benefit on which the Ik fall at the extreme end.

The bias that we show in directing altruism toward members of our families rather than among the community at random, is well recognized and occurs for genetic reasons. Parent-offspring altruism is just a special case of altruism where the actor and recipient are very closely related and the asymmetry of benefits and costs are high. Contrary to the claims of individuals who oppose a sociobiological model of behavior, there is evidence for a genetic basis of some altruism. Nest cleaning behavior by worker honeybees involving two components, uncapping of a cell containing dead brood and removing of the dead brood, is dependent on homozygosity for two separate recessive genes[176]. Rothenbuhler[176] also reported racial differences in stinging behavior of honeybees, and while not apparently controlled by the same loci as nest cleaning behavior, the genetic basis of this ultimate form of altruism, death by self-sacrifice in defense of one's relatives, cannot be seriously doubted. It is not surprising that for the most rigid, genetically determined forms of altruism we must look at interactions among close relatives. It is only under such social conditions that the predictability of costs, benefits, and regression coefficients of relatedness are high enough to create a selection pressure that drives a gene to high enough frequencies in a population to be observed. Among humans the pattern is the same. The fact that mothers hold their crying infants and breastfeed them has a large genetic component, perhaps the largest of all forms of altruism observed in humans, and obviously it is a form of parent-offspring altruism.

There is a minor paradox regarding the shared genes among all humans and their implication for altruism. We are all indeed at least distant relatives. Dobzhansky[44] made an argument similar to the following one. An individual has 2 parents, 4 grandparents, 8 great-grandparents, and 16 great-great-grandparents. Calculating the number of ancestors each person has 38 generations back produces an astounding number of progenitors for each of us at that stage: 274,877,906,944. This number is far greater than the current world population or the world population at that distant time, and in fact greater than the total number of humans who have ever lived. Keyfitz[113] estimated the total number of people who have lived was 69 billion at the time of his publication. It follows from this argument that we are all close or distant relatives by virtue of sharing some of the same ancestors. A complete genealogy would show everyone related in a complex web of shared descent. Because we share most of our genes in common with other members of the human race, why is it that regression coefficient of relatedness mediates altruism? At first it would appear that inclusive fitness theory is undermined by the fact that we are all relatives. Why are we not altruistic to everybody? Why is there no genetic basis for species directed altruism? Why do we not treat distant relatives like relatives? The solution to the problem lies in how many living relatives we have and how closely they are related. As a consequence of sexual reproduction in a stationary population not undergoing selection, we each have a number of relatives in our generation equal to about $1/2$ the reciprocal of any regression coefficient of relatedness. For example, siblings in the absence of inbreeding share a coefficient of relatedness of $1/2$, so $1/2$ the reciprocal of the coefficient of relatedness gives us 1 sibling on average. First cousins are related by $1/8$, so we have 4 of them on average, second cousins are related by $1/32$, so we have 16 of them on average, third cousins are related by $1/128$, so we have 64 of them on average, fourth cousins are related by $1/512$, so we have 256 of them on average, fifth cousins are related by $1/2048$, so we have 1024 of them on average, and so forth to large numbers, such as fifteenth cousins with whom our relatedness is so remote that we are unlikely to share any genes at all in common on an individual by individual basis, and who number more than a billion. This calculation, as specified, assumes an absence of inbreeding and an absence of selection, which is unrealistic in real populations. But the point of the exercise is to give some indication of how very distantly related most of our relatives actually are. It is difficult to imagine the evolution of a social behavior that could differentiate between a fifth cousin and an unrelated individual. Fifth cousins and more distantly related individuals share so few genes in common with an actor that the regression coefficient of relatedness approaches 0. In addition, the mechanism for, and the cost of ascertaining, such genetic relationships further suggest that we are likely to treat distant relatives as though they were unrelated.

Any set of genes that mediates species-directed altruism is vulnerable to replacement by mutations that mediate altruism according to the regression coefficient of relatedness, even though the first set of genes provides greater overall benefit for the species. The concept of evolutionarily stable strategies[133] seems to apply. Social behavior mediated by the regression coefficient of relatedness is the stable strategy. Interestingly, it includes a calculation for inbreeding which is not present in simpler models of degree of relationship.

The exact kind of altruism observed in practice is a function of mutation rates and the differential rates of population growth produced by the different types of altruism. But can a gene for species altruism ever replace a gene for altruism based on the regression coefficient of relatedness? Why is it that not everyone displays the kind of altruism shown by Jean Valjean toward an orphaned Cosette in the novel *Les Misérables*[102]? The answer seems to be that we are selected to act in accordance with cost-benefit inequality described by Hamilton[85] in which the cost of altruism to the actor is weighed against the benefit and the regression coefficient of relatedness to the recipient. The actor and the recipient in an altruistic social behavior will have a different viewpoint about which altruistic social behavior is good. Even from the viewpoint of the evolutionary ethic the actor and the recipient may have different concepts of what is good. If the act maximizes the inclusive fitness of the actor, it is good for him. If the act maximizes the inclusive fitness of the recipient, it is good for him. But the two operations are not identical unless the actor and recipient share a $b_{AR} = 1$, e.g., they are monozygotic twins.

From this discussion of altruism we can draw a **life-lesson: Any social behavior is good if it increases your inclusive fitness**.

In the case of altruism, $C < b_{AR}B$ must be true, where C is the cost to you, the actor, b_{AR} is the regression coefficient of relatedness between the actor and the recipient, and B is the benefit to the recipient.

J. B. S. Haldane, it is said, anticipated an essential element of inclusive fitness theory. Gould[74] wrote:

> Haldane, arguing about altruism one evening in a pub, reportedly made some quick calculations on the back of an envelope, and announced: "I will lay down my life for two brothers or eight cousins." (p. 262)

Obviously, Haldane had recognized an approximation to the regression coefficient of relatedness in the absence of inbreeding, namely, that one is related to one's brother by $1/2$ and to one's cousin by $1/8$. Further, he had extrapolated the social implications of these fractions in a vivid example.

One of the strangest forms of altruism that I have personally observed is the behavior of the honeyguide, a mostly African genus of bird. Honeyguides are so named because they tend to lead humans to wild beehives, and I was amazed to have just such an experience in Kenya. With this behavior the birds provide considerable assistance to human honey hunters. Honeyguides feed on honeycomb and its contents (brood, pollen and honey), having the ability to digest the wax itself. According to folklore, the human honey hunters should leave some honeycomb behind after harvesting the hive to reward the honeyguide for its assistance, or the honeyguide will take revenge on the humans and lead them to a lion or to a venomous snake on some future hunt. In this way, the original altruistic guiding behavior by the bird is reciprocated by the human. Such patterns of reciprocal altruism have been described and analyzed by Trivers[203].

The expression "only the good die young" may have some truth in it, when good is defined according to the evolutionary ethic, considering the increased risk of mortality that is associated with reproduction. The phrase could also, perhaps, be restated as "only the altruistic die young".

Cooperation

Cooperation in a sense is the simplest social act to execute in practice because both individuals are theoretically willing participants. With both individuals accruing a benefit, it provides immediate or long-term fitness enhancement for the participants. See the discussion by Trivers[203] on the subtlety of a form of long-term cooperation that he calls reciprocal altruism.

Selfishness

One aspect of selfishness that surprises all but the cynical among us is that it is theoretically unbounded among unrelated individuals. The regression coefficient of relatedness between the actor and the recipient of the social act is the only theoretical limitation to the asymmetry of benefits and costs incurred in true selfishness. I say "true selfishness" in order to distinguish it from cooperation with delayed returns of benefits, which is of course mediated by the rules of reciprocal altruism as discussed by Trivers[203].

Spite

Spite is a valid strategy in a small population of unrelated individuals. But this condition is a difficult one to meet, because the smaller the population, generally, the more closely related the members. For a vivid example of the constraints on using spiteful behavior strategically, consider the negative political campaigns that have become increasingly common in America. Negative political campaigns, in which the method is to attack one's opponent rather than to extol one's own positive attributes, only make sense when the number of candidates is small. That is true because campaign resources are better allocated toward extolling one's own attributes when the number of opponents is sufficiently large that they cannot be all discredited with smear tactics.

Women who have an elective abortion are spiteful in a specially unwise way from the evolutionary perspective, i.e. they incur a cost on themselves and on a *relative* (the unborn fetus). The aborted fetus is the victim of spiteful behavior. And abortion protesters are technically true altruists, as bizarre as it might seem. They probably incur a cost to themselves to enhance the reproductive success of another, often unrelated, individual.

The fitness cost-benefit analysis of social behavior has broad implications for the occurrence of altruism in humans and other animals. As Trivers[206] stated:

> If Copernicus dethroned us from the center of the universe and Darwin from the center of organic creation, then work on the evolution of altruism has dethroned us once again, making altruism more general than we had appreciated and more deeply self-serving. This has been a painful realization for some, generating minor spasms of resistance to this way of thinking. (pp. 46-47)

Cost-benefit analysis is a clarifying influence and a refreshing approach to the analysis of behavior. It has been used successfully elsewhere including in consideration of parental investment[204], altruism[85], feeding[185] and aggression[164]. This cost-benefit analysis has application to our daily routines.

Life-lesson: One should judge people by a single parameter for strategic social behavior: how well they will help you to maximize your net inclusive fitness in interactions with them.

Other attributes of interpersonal relations like love, friendship, loyalty, honesty, reciprocity, and financial dealings must serve this end of maximizing inclusive fitness in order to be validated as criteria for modifying your social behavior.

The evolutionary ethic and progenitivism as social traits

Those of us who subscribe to the evolutionary ethic and progenitivism are amused when we hear the claim from others who do not: "I certainly do not intend to maximize my reproductive success, or to reproduce at all, for that matter". This amusement comes from the fact that we recognize that the claim is filled with empty protest -- the speaker is in fact likely to have children or relatives he assists in reproduction in the future. But the amusement also comes from knowing that if the threat is kept, it harms the speaker himself the most, and increases the opportunity to maximize reproductive success for someone else, likely one of our descendants, in the distant future. For it is true that, under certain conditions in a population, the failure of one individual to reproduce aids the reproduction of another. Along these lines, there may be some who feel that the evolutionary ethic and progenitivism should be kept a guarded secret, or at least not actively disseminated for popular consumption to unrelated individuals. Certainly social theory does not mandate that you confer *altruistic* benefits upon unrelated members of the population by sharing this message. This point gives rise to a question on the establishment of progenitive laws: Why should they be established to benefit others? The answer is: They should not, but they should be established and supported by you because of the positive effect on *your* reproductive success. You may have noticed how converts and teachers in other walks of life are the most avid practitioners of the philosophy that they embrace and impart. That is just one mechanism that explains how you would benefit from openly advocating for others the philosophy advanced herein. Humans are not entirely rational, as this mechanism shows, and we do well to acknowledge that fact and to exploit it when promoting the evolutionary ethic and progenitivism. Another mechanism is that by proselytizing, you are creating a social environment in which it is acceptable for you to openly display the traits leading to high reproductive success. Social traits have a way of affecting their own frequency with positive or negative feedforward. I expect that while the evolutionary ethic and progenitivism are rare that the feedforward will be primarily positive.

Chastity and celibacy

If chastity, celibacy, environmentalism, or homosexuality cause a person to fail to reproduce, it is the equivalent of prereproductive *death* of that person in terms of its evolutionary consequences, with the exception of reproductive effects on other individuals such as relatives. With such strong sanctions, we might consider how these nonreproductive states of existence ever occur at all. Homosexuality is discussed in the next section and environmentalism was discussed in a previous chapter. Here I shall consider chastity and celibacy. The most successful example of chastity working as an evolutionary strategy is the case of the eusocial insects and their sterile workers. Among the eusocial species it appears that sterile workers gain a reproductive benefit themselves by providing aid to their mother in producing sisters and brothers rather than trying to produce their own daughters and sons. Among the hymenoptera, eusocial life with sterile castes has evolved independently a number of times. This fact is based on their unusual mode of sex determination:

They are haplodiploid. As a result, males have no fathers and females are more closely related to their sisters ($^3/_4$ of their genes in common) than to their own daughters ($^1/_2$ of their genes in common). Thus, it makes adaptive sense for a female to be sterile and assist her mother in reproducing more sisters than to strike out on her own and raise daughters.

In some species, chastity is not voluntary, but is the result of competition for social dominance with respect to breeding among close relatives. The fertility of the subordinate individuals is suppressed by a combination of behavioral, nutritional and chemical means. Among humans, chastity is defined as the avoidance of sexual intercourse. It can be a strategy to enhance future reproductive prospects within some environments and to gain greater future reproductive success at the cost of present reproductive success. For example, chastity might allow the tracking of resource availability through time or it might enhance a future or existing pair bond. Or chastity may be imposed upon an individual by a parent along the lines of intergenerational competition for breeding opportunity that occurs when both parent and offspring are of reproductive age. Most commonly in humans, chastity is imposed by self-perpetuating culturgens. Celibacy in the strict definition of the word is to be in an unmarried state, often for religious reasons, and does not technically require chastity.

Homosexuality

Homosexuality in nonhuman primates is often misinterpreted. The mounting behavior observed in baboons between males is an expression of social dominance, not of sexuality. Similarly, penis grabbing among baboons is another expression of social dominance. But in other species there is clearly a sexual and reproductive significance of homosexuality. Pygmy chimpanzees, among the sexiest of all primates, seem to use a great deal of sexuality, including homosexuality, as a bonding mechanism within their groups. Trivers[206] described lesbian pairs in five species of gulls based on the fieldwork of Kovacs and Ryder[116] and of Hunt et al.[104] and others. The females court each other, build a nest, defend a territory and take turns sitting on the eggs, which both females lay. Between one in ten and one in twenty eggs is fertile, showing that extra-pair copulations are sometimes occurring with males in the colony. Although lesbian pairs are reproducing at a suboptimal rate in comparison with heterosexual pairs, it may be better than not reproducing at all if, for example, there is a shortage of males available with which to form pairs. Among male African bedbugs homosexuality takes a peculiar twist. Copulations among bedbugs involve what are described by entomologists as traumatic insemination, in which the exoskeleton of the female is pierced by the male. In a strange scenario, male-male rape using the same technique has been observed in these bedbugs. Remarkably, the behavior appears to be adaptive for the rapist. His sperm migrate to and enter the vas deferens of the victim, and they then appear in the ejaculate during subsequent copulations between the victim and females! It is with some satisfaction that I learned of the confirmation of the observations in the last sentence[62], because I had predicted at a Harvard University seminar precisely this adaptive scenario when I first heard of the then unexplained pattern of male-male rape in this species.

There is a key question yet unresolved: At what rates do human homosexuals (and their close relatives) reproduce? Weinrich[213] argued that homosexuals in human societies can confer inclusive fitness benefits on relatives and thus perpetuate their type -- in a sense he views them as a functional equivalent of sterile workers among eusocial insects. I do not know if the evidence on this matter is conclusive at the moment. Perhaps the hypothesis is not fully supported at the present, but the concept could be a valid reproductive strategy that homosexuals should consider employing. In another approach, Wilson[222] hypothesized that homosexuality is a balanced polymorphism with heterozygote advantage.

Contrary to the commonness of homophobia in America, tolerance of male homosexuals by heterosexual males would seem to make biological sense, because, in effect, they increase female availability to heterosexual males. But it is perhaps understandable that heterosexual males would be offended by unwanted propositions from homosexual males and that they would feel indignation at the attempt of a transvestite or transsexual to falsify his true sex class. It is possible to imagine truly rare instances where heterosexual men could lose reproductive success by unwittingly becoming involved with a surgically altered female impersonator. Still, the adverse reaction of heterosexual men to homosexual men seems out of proportion to the relatively uncommon threat to fitness. In a small percentage of cases of homophobia, it is clearly a symptom of the mental illness paranoia, but of course that cause can only be considered a proximate one. Tolerance of female homosexuals by heterosexual females would seem to make biological sense, too, because in effect they increase male availability.

Miscellaneous fertility factors

A popular misconception in America is that many marry too young and get pregnant too often, when in fact these conditions are very rare from an evolutionary viewpoint -- indeed the precise opposite is commonly true.

Bongaarts[12] provided a framework for the quantitative analysis of proximate determinants of fertility in the form of intermediate fertility variables like contraception, elective abortion and sterility. His examples of Korea and the U.S.A. show clear trends over time that can help to explain the observed rate of decline in reproductive success experienced by those populations. His framework could be considered a basic resource for progenitivists who wish to understand and influence rates of human reproduction.

Sexism and racism

The definitive refutation of sexism, and one that I have never heard cited in that context, is Fisher's sex ratio principle[60]. This principle assures evolutionary equality in terms of parental expenditure of the sex classes. Higher male mortality means that the average male at conception and at birth has a lower extended reproductive value than the average female has at conception and at birth (primary and secondary sex ratio is greater than 1:1). Subsequently, at the time of sexual maturity males are fewer than females (sex ratio is less than 1:1), so the average male in this age class has a higher extended reproductive value than the average female. In addition to these differences in extended reproductive value, there is the phenomenon of higher male variance in reproductive success and in many other parameters (body weight, income, height, etc.). I conclude that, because the relative extended reproductive value of human males and females varies with age, that it is incorrect to claim that either is superior in any evolutionary sense, unless one is willing to be specific about the precise age and extended reproductive value of the age/sex classes being discussed. Because the extended reproductive value of males and females varies over the life history, it is incorrect to say that one sex is innately superior to the other. Naturally, in keeping with the progenitive philosophy of this book, it is assumed that the sole method of validating one's evolutionary worth is through reproductive success. That view is at odds with old style feminism. But some modern feminists argue that the emphasis placed on fertility control by environmentalists and antigenitivists in achieving women's rights is misplaced. They feel that the real problems are gender inequality and poverty. Indeed, in an evolutionary sense a true women's liberation would be the right and opportunity for women to reproduce as they choose without control or coercion from men. And to the extent that the women's movement is more concerned, inappropriately, with political and economic empowerment than with reproductive empowerment, we must ask: To what end?

Evolution is the ultimate ''court'' judging the success of subspecific, i.e. racial, variation within humans. The recent expansion of Bantu and Hamitic people inside Africa and to other continents indicates that they are demographically the greatest of recent population success stories. The only criterion that approaches objectivity in judging the success of a race is the Malthusian parameter of population increase. Those populations that are expanding have, or do, something that makes them superior at reproducing. In turn, that affects the proportion of the human gene pool that their genes represent and the duration of the representation, which are two other parameters for measuring the impact of an individual or population on a species.

Age/sex class roles

In addition to different age/sex class specific behaviors that comprise primary sexual function, there are other conspicuous differences among the primates according to the age and sex of the actor. Among baboons, it is primarily adult males that are involved in predation on other mammals and in consumption of the meat. Active troop defense against predators is also a behavior exclusively shown by adult and subadult male baboons. Age/sex class specific behaviors like these examples are a consequence of natural selection acting on life history strategies.

Metal working is the most male-dominated activity in a cross-cultural comparison of human societies. All cultures have a division of some roles into age specific/sex specific categories. Sex roles in behavior are also common in species that lack culture. Among birds, males and females often take different food items according to their size and bill shape. For example, female raptors are generally bigger than their mates. Males and females hunt and bring back to the nest prey of different sizes. Among the social insects, sex is a primary determinant of caste. Among the hymenoptera, the worker castes are comprised only of females.

Recreation

Perhaps the most important suggestion for recreation is the rediscovery of sexual intercourse as a pastime. Another strategic use of leisure time, as commonplace as it might sound, is playing with your children or your young relatives, so that at the end of the day they are tired from physical activity and from learning, and go to sleep naturally without protest. Use the opportunity to teach them the evolutionary ethic and to impart the progenitive philosophy.

Technologies: tools and machines

The evolution of tool-use had adaptive significance. It is so important in human evolution that the primary way anthropologists measure the degree of a culture's technological advancement is by the degree of sophistication of its cutting tools. *Homo erectus* had a cutting tool technology that was stable and largely unchanged for hundreds of thousands of years. In sharp contrast, *Homo sapiens* underwent rapid change in cutting tool technology in the times of transition from paleolithic to mesolithic to neolithic, in the Bronze Age, Iron Age, and in the flourish of cutting tool advancements of the postindustrial technology of the 20th century.

Artificial intelligence, machine intellect, to date does not appear to be antigenitive *per se*. But future developments could pose a problem. This problem arises in the area of self-reproducing machines -- ones that can reproduce themselves as artificial life forms. It would probably be best if the development and deployment of these machines were prohibited in order to avoid the theoretical possibility of competition between humans and these new "life forms". In our technologically oriented society, our standard for measuring accomplishments seems to be how well something or someone works. Sometimes efficiency, economy or profitability are additional standards by which we judge ourselves or our inventions. These standards are usually substitutes for a more meaningful standard, i.e. the consequence on reproductive success. Self-reproducing machines, while perhaps efficient and perpetual, would serve no purpose at all if they eliminated humans in pursuit of efficiency in a fashion that is now the stuff of many science fiction scenarios.

Life-lesson: Support measures that help in the conservation of resources like energy resources and that discourage the manufacture of superfluous consumer goods.

Clothing and decoration

Clothing is a recent cultural adaptation. When it is combined with our indoor lifestyle it can lead to vitamin D deficiency. Vitamin D is ordinarily synthesized by the skin when exposed to sunlight. Indeed, light skinned populations of humans probably evolved their skin color in part to ensure adequate vitamin D synthesis in northern latitudes. It is recommended that vitamin D supplements be started for infants in America. This supplement is particularly important for individuals who tend to stay indoors and who have dark skin. Unpigmented skin is well adapted to northern latitudes for another reason. It is more resistant to damage from frostbite.

Women are now the more decorated sex in Western cultures. In preindustrial times the situation was reversed -- men were the more decorated sex. Men were selected to attract women in a way similar to the pattern of sexual selection employed by birds in which males appear in elaborate plumage of bold colors. Indeed, over human history the plumage of birds has often been used by humans as a type of adornment. The new trend of female adornment is an indicator and consequence of hypergamy and extreme male variance in the ability to provide for a family that came with the industrial age. Extreme male variance leads to a rather unusual state for a primate in Western humans in which females compete for access to optimal males. Hypergamy is not the necessary rule in human societies. In some societies men can have concubines of low class but in marriage proper the wife is always expected to be of higher status than her husband, and a man may have to postpone marriage for many years to achieve this end[121]. This system of women marrying down is called hypogamy. The amount of a woman's brideprice varies according to the rank status of the patrilineage to which she belongs[121]. Jinghpaw aristocrats sell their daughters to men of lower social class outright; Gauri and Lakher disdain to do so, they merely permit their social inferiors to have sexual access in return for the payment of tribute fees (brideprice).

Jewelry is found in almost all cultures, it is for the most part decorative along the lines of increasing sexual attractiveness. Some jewelry makes a statement about the reproductive status of its wearer. Among the Masai of eastern Africa there are beautiful necklaces of blue Venetian glass that are given to a grandmother each time a grandchild is born. In America, jewelry often makes an economic or class statement. But for the most part Americans are bilked when buying jewelry. For example, diamonds have a purchase price that is artificially inflated by a worldwide diamond cartel. If one wants to enhance one's appearance with jewelry, either for decorative purposes or for making an economic statement, gold is the right medium. Unlike diamonds, it truly is scarce and in part for that reason it has real, durable monetary value, as well as an attractive appearance that is recognized by many cultures. In an informal worldwide comparison, it appears that people who adorn themselves with gold have higher fertility than do those who use diamonds. The cause appears to be a correlation with other cultural variables, like the presence of brideprice.

Hair dyeing and use of cosmetics to cover wrinkles in the skin are blatant tactics to disguise aging and to appear younger, with a higher extended reproductive value. Removal of facial hair in men may serve the same purpose, or it may be to signal adolescence and the consequent noncompetitiveness with other adult males over mates.

Tattoos seem to be increasing in frequency in America. They make a lot of sense if you are a Polynesian. It would be interesting to study the question of a possible correlation between tattoos and reproductive success.

Residence

Murdock[146] in a study of 250 societies learned that the frequency distributions of different types of residence were: 58 percent patrilocal, 15 percent matrilocal, 9 percent matri-patrilocal, 8 percent bilocal, 7 percent neolocal, and 3 percent avunculocal. Americans are neolocal, i.e. the husband and wife take up a new place of residence, away from both of their families. As for the frequency of this type of residence in other societies, it is not common as shown above at 7 percent. It is just another way that Americans are out of the ordinary in their social behavior. Neolocal residence denies a husband and wife some of the kinship support that would be available from one or both sides of the family with any of the other forms of residence. As much as we protest the intrusion of our mothers-in-law into our lives, the lack of this extended family contact may be part of the reason that so many American marriages struggle and fail to both endure and to produce children. And of great relevance to the central theme of this book, it must be noted that neolocal residence is the least supportive type of residence in matters of child care, for the simple reason that in other systems of residence, a relative is almost always on hand to help with baby-sitting or other needed assistance. The alternative, day care for children, presents serious problems to many American families; they feel forced to leave their children in the hands of unrelated people providing less than perfect care.

Rural living appears to lead to improved prospects for survival and reproduction in America. The haze of small particle air pollution that hangs over some American cities reduces longevity. That is one reason why rural living leads to greater longevity than city living. Regardless of where you live, it is important for your survival to have a home. In a study in Philadelphia, homeless adults were found to have an age-adjusted mortality rate nearly four times that of the general population[95].

According to the 1990 U.S. Census, Utah has the greatest number of persons per family with 3.67. That figure is an indicator of the strongly progenitivist tendencies of the people of Utah, many of whom are Mormons. The same census shows that Mississippi has the highest percentage of births to teenagers, 20.7 percent. Finally, the same census indicates that the District of Columbia has the highest percentage of births to unmarried women, 61.7 percent. Note that these states are not the highest in longevity. Quite the contrary, the District of Columbia has the shortest life expectancy, with Hawaii being the most longevous state[195]. Hawaii ranks low in percentage of births to teenagers, 9.4 percent, and in births to unmarried women, 22.2 percent. Crude birth rates are available for all states, but it is well known that they are not an accurate measure of fertility; they are not corrected for variations in the age and sex distribution of different populations. They are only a rough estimate of fertility. With that in mind, we can examine the figures for states with high crude birth rates and those with low crude birth rates. Overall the United States has a crude birth rate of 14.9 per 1000 members of the population according to the U.S. Census. The three states with the highest crude birth rates are Utah, 21.2, Alaska, 20.7, and California, 20.4. The two states with the lowest crude birth rates are West Virginia, 12.7 and Iowa, 13.9. In comparison, the Hutterites as studied by Eaton and Mayer[51] had a crude birth rate of 45.9.

The choice of a country in which to live is more complex than simply choosing the one with the highest rate of population increase. It is a question of both the current rate of reproductive success that can be achieved in different countries at the present *and* in the future. Thus, ignoring immigration for a moment, the U.S.A., while providing a relatively poor cultural environment for reproduction, has a high long-term potential for continued population growth. In contrast, China offers poor long-term potential for future growth. Allowing for emigration, Ethiopia has both the highest sustainable rate of population growth and a strong tendency for its inhabitants to emigrate to other countries, thereby allowing future reproduction in novel environments. Despite Cold War propaganda to the contrary, Ethiopia is a pleasant place to live, especially from the viewpoint of the evolutionary ethic. The right strategies for Ethiopians, rather than live in Ethiopia full-time, is to spend part of each generation there and part in a Western country. In this way they can benefit from resource availability, citizenship, and mobility by association with a First World country, but maintain their cultural ties and progenitive values by contact with their place of origin.

Chapter 11: Cultural Evolution

Life forms have a built-in capacity to survive relative to environments that they have experienced in previous generations. Cultures consist, in part, of a set of ways of meeting the survival needs of individuals. For example, humans have specific biological needs and limits of tolerance. While these vary from population to population due to genetic variations in behavior and morphology, all cultures tend to provide for these demands of human nature. When they fail to do so, the culture and the people in it tend to go extinct. We do not know how many cultures in human prehistory and history have failed this test, but if the loss of indigenous languages is a measure, then this process of joint extinction of cultures and peoples has occurred tens of thousands of times. This thought is a sobering one since within our own American culture we often feel secure, and we can hardly imagine that our culture could or would show a critical failure, endangering itself and us along with it. The point here is that a culture can be a maladaptation as well as an adaptation. The old belief in anthropology that culture is here to serve us dutifully and benevolently is not the picture of culture that is now emerging.

Durham[49] made an interesting point about cultural evolution and sociobiology:

> [A problem with early models of sociobiology] ... is the assumption that the process of genetic selection is responsible for any phenotypic diversity for which it can be made to seem responsible. Although it is true that genetic selection does favor the evolution of adaptive phenotypes, ... cultural evolution can do the same. If so, then the adaptiveness of a phenotype tells us nothing about whether it evolved genetically or not. (p. 157)

The fact that cultures evolved has been appreciated by anthropologists for generations. Cavalli-Sforza and Feldman[23] gave a complete description of how differences between cultures evolve. New cultural characteristics arise through "mutation," which may be due to deliberate innovation or error in copying an old characteristic. Existing cultural characteristics may be transmitted, actively or passively. Existing cultural characteristics may fluctuate in cultural drift. Members of the culture may make decisions which influence the frequency of cultural characteristics. The frequency of cultural characteristics may also be affected by natural selection, based on the fitness consequences of the characteristic for its bearers.

The great majority of Americans are certainly not consciously trying to maximize their inclusive fitness. Whether the people of any culture have done so is not known -- the classic ethnographic studies of now greatly changed or vanished non-Western cultures predate the concept of inclusive fitness, so it was not studied by early anthropologists at the only time it could have been well-researched. Even individual fitness, a concept available since Darwin's publication of *On the Origin of Species* in 1859, was rarely a subject of inquiry during the study of now lost cultures. It seems plausible that some cultures did include people who consciously attempted to maximize their inclusive fitness and certainly many included people who unconsciously did so. Furthermore, I predict that Americans are moving at present toward such a fitness maximizing culture. There are two reasons; the first is regression to the mean. In other words, we shall do so because we have gone so far in the opposite direction, with antigenitivism reaching the point where at times we have failed to reproduce enough even to maintain the replacement level of our population, that we now have the prospect of moving toward progenitivism. A mechanism by which this infertility trend may be reversed is by a reduction in the contraceptive prevalence, at present near ceiling levels; if contraceptive prevalence changes, it can only decrease. The second reason is that the evolutionary ethic is a truth whose time has come. But maximizing inclusive fitness requires extinguishing other competing culturgens, and they do not go without a fight. How easily will Marxists or Christians put aside their culturgens, including philosophies and goals, to make way for an unfettered application of the evolutionary ethic?

One challenge that anthropologists and informed laypersons should accept is to find out what culture has been up to -- learn how it has shaped our environments, molded our bodies, directed our minds and altered our gene frequencies. With this knowledge we can better get about the business of maximizing our own evolutionary success. The more that we learn about the mechanisms of cultural determination, the better we shall be able to work for ourselves instead of blindly promoting the perpetuation of our culture itself. Of course, any human trait is the product of genetics and environment, and culture is a very important part of the human environment. With this thought in mind I do not propose the unattainable eradication of culture, rather the control of culturgens that are deleterious to our reproductive success. We should reject outright the simplistic view that cultures are merely a set of ways of meeting the survival needs of individuals. Let us consider a broader traditional view of culture: All cultures establish ways of providing food, shelter, technology, economies, sex relations, trade, enculturation, defense, war, world view, and often government. The extent to which these listed cultural attributes benefit human members of the culture and the extent to which these attributes benefit the perpetuation of the culture itself are not entirely clear at a cursory inspection. Among other things, we shall explore components of culture that better fit the definition of self-serving culturgen than benevolent server of humankind.

Culture as a maladaptation

Cultures, too, have their ''needs'' which must be met by the members of each society if the cultures are to survive. Sometimes these needs may be in conflict with the best survival and reproductive interests of the individuals in them. One need is for the enculturation of individuals, specific aspects of which may or may not be to the fitness benefits of the individual. Another need is to provide devices that help to ensure cultural survival through perpetuation of the culturgens of which it is composed. Another need is to control the biological functioning of the human members of the culture in a way that perpetuates the culture itself. For example, cultures control and regulate reproductive behavior as a means of reproducing new members for the cultural group. This control and regulation by culture is most obvious when we view the traditions of another culture. But we can feel them, nevertheless, in our own culture if we are perceptive. Take the subject of sexual inhibitions. A cross-cultural examination of the anthropological record indicates that traditional American culture imposes greater sexual inhibitions on its members than is usual, but in recent decades the real culture has been moving away from this position. Perhaps a time will come when our culture will no longer attempt to imbue the peculiarly repressive sexual norms of now living Americans upon each new generation. Rather than modify the natural expression of sexual behavior among our youth, older generations might be encouraged to promote progenitivism at a young age.

Americans immerse themselves in superfluous consumer goods and services, but in spite of the abundance of available resources, total fertility rates in America indicate that Americans are surely violating the evolutionary principle that individuals should attempt to raise as many children as will maximize reproductive success. What is the cause for this disparity between abundant resource availability and low fertility? In part the cause may be a simple tradeoff: investing in consumer goods and financial instruments instead of investing in children. Another explanation follows from the principle of allocation: Time spent seeking material assets (or intellectual assets, for that matter) competes with time that could be allocated to parenthood. But the relationship between culturgens and reproductive success is more complex than that, as we shall see in the following section.

Culture is a manipulator of its human hosts. It does so by rules, regulations, laws, physical necessities, customs, and material realities. We take for granted that cultures, through laws and institutions, regulate human behavior. Increasingly, cultures do so without regard for the welfare of human reproductive concerns. Humans are particularly susceptible to varying degrees of manipulation by culture, from mild to extreme, because human behavioral biology is constructed by evolution to require a component of culturgens. For example, the structure of the speech centers of the brain have a genetic basis, but they require the learning of a culturally transmitted language in infancy. Human ancestors once had no language, only vocalizations and gestures like those found among nonhuman primates. The evolution of language capability was obviously an important advance with selective advantages, and language ability became fixed in the entire species. Once human language was firmly established, it had considerable latitude to transmit culturgens in the form of verbal concepts. Some of these concepts then reduced reproductive success, and were able to do so as long as the resulting reproductive success was not as low as the fitness of an individual with no language capability at all in a human world where language dominates. In the end, language provided a smaller increment of fitness than it theoretically could have, because of these fitness reducing culturgens.

Culture evolves by its own rules because culturgens, such as wealth and language, can be a form of extragenic inheritance. They may or may not lead to maximizing reproductive success. They are not transmitted entirely like genes from parent to offspring. They may be inheritable and/or infectious. Most newly created culturgens have a negative or neutral effect on the reproductive success of their hosts. Most fail to establish themselves for more than a brief time and are nearly insignificant aspects of a culture. In addition to innovation of culturgens there is diffusion of culturgens. They can spread more readily through diffusion than through repeated innovation if the culturgen is self-perpetuating. They have a better chance of succeeding than newly emergent culturgens in new cultures because they have already been tested and proven successful in another culture. The way that cultures share culturgens is analogous to the way organisms share genes in order to reproduce.

Coevolution of genes and culture

Anthropologists have understood that culture is a new force in human evolution, but Lumsden and Wilson[127] argued convincingly that culture's capacity to transform heredity is far greater than has been generally appreciated. In contrast to the conventional scenario in which culture replaced genetic evolution, they argue that genes and culture coevolve. Lumsden and Wilson[126] defined coevolution as a change in the epigenetic rules (defined below) due to changes in gene frequencies, or changes in culturgen frequencies due to the epigenetic rules, or both. Murdock[146] wrote:

> The imperious drive of sex is capable of impelling individuals, reckless of consequences while under its spell, toward behavior which may imperil or disrupt the cooperative relationships upon which social life depends. The countless interpersonal bonds out of which human association is forged, complex and often delicately

balanced, can ill suffer the strain of the frustrations and aggressions inevitably generated by indiscriminate competition over sexual favors. Society, therefore, cannot remain indifferent to sex but must seek to bring it under control. Possibly in man's long history there have been peoples who have failed to subject the sexual impulse to regulation. If so, none has survived, for the social control of sex is today a cultural universal. Our sample societies reveal not a single exception. (p. 290)

Murdock[146] above spoke of social organization in an old fashioned sense as if it were a kind of superorganism unique to humans, benevolently putting our otherwise chaotic lives in order. We now know that his assumptions are not true. Culture does not regulate sex for the benefit of the group or the individual. If Murdock[146] was making the point that cultures might be shaping the behavior of humans for the benefit of the culture itself, I will not deny that possibility. In fact, there are many examples of how culturgens are using humans for the culturgens' purposes. Another point is that other animal societies such as those of the social insects and the nonhuman primates, to mention a few, do not show random or erratic sexual behavior or erratic social behavior in a broader context, even though they lack human culture. In fact, animal societies show precisely the same organized solutions as an inherent property of mating strategies, regardless of whether they are comprised of baboons or humans. Animal societies tend to show mating patterns comparable in nature to those of humans: monogamy, polygyny, polyandry, and promiscuity. Darwin[37] alluded to the comparability of humans and other animals in an even broader philosophical sense when he wrote:

> Origin of man now proved. -- Metaphysic must flourish. -- He who understands baboon ~~will~~ would do more towards metaphysics than Locke (p. 539).

Lumsden and Wilson[127] discussed gene-culture coevolution in a refreshing, analytical light. They described it as an interaction between genes and culture in which culture is shaped by biological imperatives and biological traits are simultaneously altered by genetic evolution in response to cultural change. Here is how the process works: Some properties of the human mind result in a linkage between genetic evolution and cultural history. Human genes affect the way the mind is formed, e.g., the way stimuli are sensed, the way information is processed, the way memories are stored and recalled, and the context under which emotions are displayed. Lumsden and Wilson[127] described these processes and called them "epigenetic rules". Epigenetic rules follow directly from human biology, and they help to shape culture. The other part of gene-culture coevolution is the effect that culture has on gene frequencies. We learned in a previous discussion of social selection that culture could indeed create an environment in which selection for specific genes occurred, for example genes for twinning or for albinism. But at this point gene-culture evolution comes full circle, because certain epigenetic rules are the cause of individuals adopting cultural choices and, in turn, those cultural choices cause them to survive and reproduce more successfully than individuals with other epigenetic rules. In this way the genetic bases for epigenetic rules are perpetuated differentially.

Is the Lumsden and Wilson model of gene-culture coevolution applicable now to human populations? Yes, but coevolution is occurring slowly. The problem is that the process is swamped with recent, rapid cultural changes. Lumsden and Wilson pointed out that coevolution of this kind requires about a thousand years. But that is slow in comparison to the rate of cultural change in the last thousand years, leading me to conclude that their model applies better to any other thousand year period in human prehistory or history than to the last thousand years. Because of the model's limited applicability to the present, we need to search for a new model. Like the Lumsden and Wilson model, this new model recognizes that genes and culture reciprocally dovetail in a coevolutionary process. But this new model allows a weakening of the link between epigenetic rules and the actual expression of a cultural trait. For as we have observed over the last thousand years, rapid, great cultural change without much underlying genetic change is a reality. Once aspects of culture are freed from tight linkage with genes, something interesting happens. We must begin to view some individual aspects of culture as entities with self-interests in perpetuating themselves; their existence is no longer the necessary product of epigenetic rules and their consequences on the fitness of genes have less relevance to their own frequency. This new model is disturbingly close to one that Lumsden and Wilson[126] seemed to criticize: one in which culturgens that encode for specific behaviors leap between individuals and colonize the brain as pathogens invade hosts. Yet it differs and gains validity from the fact that it incorporates a role for the acceptance of the culturgen by the host according to epigenetic rules, even though the role of epigenetic rules is somewhat diminished.

I have suggested that culturgens have traits *vis-à-vis* their interactions with humans that may enable their perpetuation and replication. Two models of human-culturgen interactions are the predator-prey relationship and the host-pathogen relationship. The predator-prey relationship is the most appropriate description in circumstances where the culturgen kills humans outright. Examples include the electric chair, the gas chamber, and thermonuclear devices. The host-pathogen relationship is more common, and includes any fitness reducing association between humans and culturgens. Tobacco and contraception are two examples.

Cloak[26] has suggested that cultural instructions may be considered parasites on humans. They evolved with the autonomy of a separate organism. Dawkins[40] expressed a similar view when he discussed survival of cultural traits that are advantageous to themselves. Symons[200], Ball[6] and Durham[49] considered another aspect of cultural traits as parasites. They hypothesized that we should expect resistance to them just as resistant individuals are selected by the existence of disease. Symons[200] wrote:

> Dawkins argues that bits of culture are, like viruses, self-replicating parasites on human beings, but his analogy shows precisely why this view must be incomplete: in environments containing pathogenic viruses, selection favors the most resistant individuals. (p. 308)

I am inclined to side with Dawkins in this difference of opinion, partly because the analogy of self-replicating parasite so aptly describes some culturgens, but also because Symons was wrong when he stated that "selection favors the most resistant individuals". Natural selection actually favors the fittest individuals, not the most resistant ones, and this difference becomes important when there are negative pleiotropic effects of resistance. For example, an innate inhibition to learn a deleterious culturgen might likewise inhibit the learning of something beneficial, with the net fitness effect being lower than in individuals lacking the resistance. This claim is not inconsistent with the possibility that culturgens which parasitize us may, under some circumstances, advance the development of defenses in us, their hosts.

I would like to formally introduce the term "cultural load". It is in a sense the cultural equivalent of the concept of "genetic load". Cultural load is the combined loss of fitness imposed upon an individual by deleterious culturgens. Natural selection will favor those individuals who reduce their cultural load when the net result is an increase in fitness. I wish to make it clear that I am not establishing a new kind of reverse false dichotomy, in which cultural influences are viewed as sinister, and genetic influences are viewed as righteous. Instead, I am describing culture as having components that may enhance fitness, may leave fitness unaffected, or may detract from fitness. Cultural load is those components of culture that detract from fitness. Eaton and Mayer[51] asked some questions relevant to understanding my concept of cultural load:

> How many children can a group of human beings have if they reproduce up to the limit of their biological capacity and live through their entire period of potential fertility? This concept also facilitates the answer of the corollary question: How many children are *not* produced by a group of human beings because some of their cultural values, customs or habits interfere with biologically possible reproduction? (p. 219)

By my definition, those children not produced because of the interference of a culturgen on biologically possible reproduction is a measure of the cultural load. In other words, cultural load is the reduction in fitness imposed upon an individual by deleterious aspects of culture. I propose that it is something that humans should be in the business of trying to reduce. Reproducing early and often, in spite of cultural restraints, is the solution. What fertility can be achieved in America without cultural load? At present the total fertility rate in America is about 2. I also previously discussed the example of the Hutterites, a well nourished, healthy population who use no artificial contraception, and they have a total fertility rate of about 10. When we add proception to the reproductive strategy, a well-nourished population might achieve a total fertility rate of about 20. Thus, even with avid philoprogenitiveness, total fertility rates are not infinite; instead they would reach a peak of approximately 10 times the current total fertility rate. In this way we can see that cultural load reduces American fertility by about one order of magnitude at the present time.

Some ideas and many aspects of our material culture are self-perpetuating even though they do not lead to higher reproductive success. For example, contraception, abortion, smoking, delayed marriage, licit and illicit habit-forming and addictive drugs (nicotine, alcohol, cocaine, opiates) are prevalent in spite of their tendency to reduce reproductive success in many cases. Perversely, a kind of "selection" can occur for increasingly potent, increasingly addictive, and increasingly fitness depressing culturgens such as illicit drugs. Though they are outright dangerous to reproductive success, they perpetuate themselves by the behavior modification that they induce in users. While harmful overall, the effects of alcohol abuse or illicit drug use cannot be considered entirely bad in every individual case, because the state of intoxication induced by them is sometimes directly responsible for acts of adaptive sexual intercourse that would not have otherwise occurred and which resulted in pregnancies.

Among the American culturgens with the highest rate of spread to non-Western technologically unadvanced societies are tobacco and fundamentalist Christian religion. Among the most common American culturgens based on their prevalence in our society are probably artificial fibers. The most virulent American culturgens are contraception and elective abortion, because they have a direct and devastating effect on fertility.

Some falsehoods, by the very nature of the message they carry, are perpetuated and are thus widely accepted. Dawkins[40] pointed out that blind faith is self-perpetuating by the fact that it discourages rational inquiry into its own validity. This aspect of blind faith in a culturgen seems to be a powerful one if its commonness in human life is a measure. Religions, cargo cults, financial bubbles, occultism, magic, and matters of healing assisted by spiritualism all involve a measure of blind faith. The adherence of the believers to these philosophies is strengthened by it.

Some truths, by the very nature of the message they carry, are not perpetuated and are therefore largely unknown. Too much wealth is a common cause for failure to maximize reproductive success among Americans. This truth is hard to perpetuate because everyone wants more wealth, and few desire, in the current environment, to actively maximize their reproductive success. A genuine secret is a culturgen that cannot be perpetuated, even if it contains an important truth. A genuine secret can be contrasted with a rumor, which, depending upon its credibility and sensationalism, is a culturgen that is well perpetuated. Rumormongers are the agents that perpetuate this culturgen. Dreams are culturgens whose adaptive significance is not entirely clear. One hypothesis is that they provide useful exercise to the eye muscles during REM sleep. I propose an explanation why they are so quickly forgotten and fail to be transmitted most of the time. They are forgotten so that they do not serve as false memories that would confuse the dreamer's waking view of reality. Our ability to forget our dreams is one reason why we can function while awake. But there is another, external problem for the human brain: Bogus ideas in the form of flotsam travel around the world in our material culture of mass media, and from mind to mind. Why are our minds not filled with nonsense? To an increasing extent our minds *are* filled with nonsense. Crossen[32] pointed out how America has become a culture of misinformation. Citation of facts in the mass media are not merely often wrong, they are sometimes deliberately wrong. This manipulation of facts creates a special category of culturgen: the perpetuated misinformation culturgen. Whether such a culturgen is fitness enhancing or fitness reducing depends upon the nature of its interactions with humans. How great a burden of misinformation flotsam can we carry? The answer to that is complex for a variety of reasons. Some knowledge of the real world is required to survive and reproduce. Our mental capacities and our time budgets cannot support an infinite amount of nonsense culturgens and still be able to function in accordance with the necessities of life history strategies. If these culturgens of misinformation are a burden, then why have human brains not evolved the ability to purge culturgens that have negative effects on reproductive success? There is no doubt that since culture first appeared, a great portion of our intellect has been dedicated to coping with them. Perhaps filtering through culturgens has been a source of selection for reflective and contemplative aspects of human rationality. From my studies of nonhuman primates, I conclude that they have remarkable intellects, but none of them have true culture. This observation leads one to speculate that the conspicuous increase in encephalization in humans over other primates indicates the tremendous cognitive effort required to contend with culturgens. This discussion suggests that a possible adaptive advantage for less than perfect memories exists: They are a way to purge the brain of nonsense culturgens. May it not be only our dreams that are selectively forgotten, but also other culturgens that have a negative effect on our fitness? For example, sexual morals ingrained during many years of development are often forgotten with surprising ease in the passion of a teenager's first sexual behavior.

Life-lesson: Reduce your cultural load.

One can be burdened with a cultural load so great that it is impossible to reproduce at all. Sadly, that is the situation in which many Americans find themselves. Our bodies and our intellects have evolved in part as a response to and to cope with culture. However, we can be strained by too great a burden of fitness reducing culturgens, and reduced reproductive success necessarily follows.

The relationship between humans and culture as a host-parasite association explains many aspects of modern life such as birth control, popular music and fashion in clothing. Some religious orders have celibate priests. Let us think of celibate vows as a culturgen. This celibacy culturgen may effectively contribute to its own perpetuation by preventing the priests who carry it from being distracted by family matters and by impelling them toward more effective transmission of the culturgen. See Dawkins[40] for an eloquent discussion of celibacy among priests. A final note on this matter is that there is a striking analogy for the mode of perpetuation of the celibacy culturgens among priests in the animal world, pointed out by Ball[6]. It is a class of parasites that makes it a first order of business to castrate its host, thereby making the host unable to reproduce, but in so doing extending the life of the host beyond the time normal for a reproducing member of its species, and also making available to the parasite the energy that would have been normally used by the host in reproductive effort. This consequence is to the detriment of the host and to the benefit of the castrating parasite, which obtains the use of its host for an extended time in which it can live and reproduce. Similarly, the castrati of the middle ages, who were boys castrated before puberty in order to preserve their prepubescent soprano or contralto singing voices, are an example of how perpetuating a culturgen, i.e. boy's choral music, can occur at a great cost to individual reproductive success.

Most culturgens lack a mode of inheritance and a means of reproduction (cultigens, not to be confused with the word culturgen, are an example of an exception -- they are the species which humans have domesticated). Thus, the historical leverage that evolution has in shaping generation after generation of living organism does not exist for culturgens. Gold jewelry is a culturgen appreciated and sought after by the members of many cultures. But it has no genetic code and no means of self-reproduction. Thus, in accordance with gold's relative scarcity in the Earth's crust, it is a scarce commodity in normal human life. This book is a culturgen, and even though it cannot reproduce, it can be replicated by the publisher if the demand for it is sufficient. Like any publication, if it is enjoyable, or important, or interesting, or controversial, it will help to promote its own dissemination. From another viewpoint, this book may be an example of a culturgen that selects against itself, even though its purpose is to increase the fitness of its readership. The process of selection against itself is straightforward. The tendency to read books of nonfiction is positively correlated with years of education. Years of education are inversely correlated with fertility. Thus, much of the readership for this book will be high in education and low in fertility. To the degree that their low fertility is associated with a feeling that it is right or proper, they may have a world view that is contrary to the progenitivist philosophy herein communicated. Thus, the readership for this book may, for the very reasons they *are* the readership, be hostile to it. If you find yourself rejecting outright the views herein, why not reflect on the possibility that the variables in your life that lead you to pick up this book also preselected you to be an objector to some of its contents? Consider that the more you object to this philosophy, the more you are likely to need it. It is reasonable to assume that a member of the Amish community will never read this book, but with their progenitive culture they have no need for it. In contrast, the people who do read this book probably have an endangered genetic legacy that cries out for it. These thoughts about the intrinsic nature of culturgens lead us to some rules established by Dawkins[40] for designing a meme (his terminology for a concept close to a culturgen) with high evolutionary success. It should have longevity, fecundity, and copying-fidelity. Not surprisingly, these are the same parameters for the evolutionary success of organic systems like genes.

Durham[48] suggested that cultural evolution generally retains those attributes which increase, or at least do not decrease, the abilities of humans to survive and reproduce. I believe that he is in error in the sense that he does not mention the abundance of culturgens that do decrease the abilities of humans to survive and reproduce. While the mathematical modeling required to properly illustrate this point is beyond the intended scope of this book, an explanation in prose is offered. A culturgen may have a positive, neutral or negative fitness effect on its human carrier. For example, a positive culturgen would be one that contributed to sexual intercourse in teenage years. An example of a neutral culturgen is Roman Catholicism. It has both progenitive and antigenitive components, and its practitioners around the world have a reproductive success that is close to the mean for their societies when corrected for income levels. Examples of negative culturgens are a vasectomy and a tubal ligation. Our goal as individuals should be to acquire and maintain culturgens in our phenotypes that have positive fitness effects, and to rid ourselves of culturgens that have negative fitness effects. Reducing cultural load is desirable from the evolutionary perspective. There are many ways that cultural load reduces reproductive success. It may divert resources from reproduction, e.g., the acquisition of luxury cars and diamonds instead of children. It may undermine the will to reproduce, e.g., through environmentalist philosophy. It may impair fecundity, e.g., the behavioral pathology of artificial contraception. It may kill us, e.g., use of tobacco. It may kill our children, e.g., elective abortion of unborn offspring and infanticide. It may reduce our rates of sexual intercourse, e.g., Americans find the time for watching dreadful television situation comedies daily, but not for fifteen minutes of sexual intercourse a few times a week for the majority. In fact, the average American in the age range of 18-59 years has sex (not defined solely as sexual intercourse) only 6 or 7 times a month[139]. Also, devoutly religious Americans have lower rates of sexual activity, including marital intercourse, than religiously inactive people[115]. It may reduce the energy available for reproduction (though in the modern Western environment energy *per se* is not often limiting), e.g., the culturgens that contribute to the condition anorexia nervosa, depleting a woman's stored energy and making reproduction difficult or impossible. It may serve as a child substitute, e.g., "Video Baby," a videotape of a newborn commercially available and aimed at couples who do not have a child of their own. According to the demographic transition theory to which many population growth planners subscribe, as per capita income increases, people substitute consumer durables, like televisions and automobiles, for children. It may reduce the time available for reproduction, e.g., pursuing an advanced university degree during the peak reproductive years of twenty to thirty, instead of reproducing. It may shorten the reproductive life, e.g., since suicide in America is by culturally determined means and because it also occurs in clusters of time and space, the existence of suicide culturgens, transmitted from person to person, sometimes with the assistance of mass media, is a hypothesis worth examining. Stories about artists who killed themselves to increase the value of their paintings or about writers who killed themselves in order to promote their books are common. But dying for culturgens like paintings or books does not make evolutionary sense. Considering the many forms of cultural load, it is little wonder then that so many healthy Americans of reproductive age are either unprepared for reproduction, averse to reproduction or outright hostile to reproduction.

In a further classification of culturgens, they may be virulent or nonvirulent. Contraception was mentioned above as virulent. A nonvirulent example would be the Susan B. Anthony dollar coin. Hundreds of millions of them sit in Treasury Department warehouses, unwanted by Americans as a medium of exchange and therefore, unlike other media of exchange, they are unable to impact our reproductive success.

Culturgens may also be placed into one of four classes based on the culturgen's effect on the human carrier's reproductive success and on the culturgen's own perpetuation. The first class is cooperator. A culturgen that is a cooperator has a positive effect on its human host's reproductive success and has a positive effect on the culturgen's own perpetuation. An example of this type of culturgen is fertility drugs. A second class is altruist. A culturgen that is an altruist has a positive effect on its human host's reproductive success and has a negative effect on the culturgen's own perpetuation. An example of this type of culturgen is defective condoms. Culturgens in this class are rare because no culturgen can exist long while conferring benefits on its bearers and costs on itself. A third class is selfish. A culturgen that is a selfish one has a negative effect on its human host's reproductive success and has a positive effect on the culturgen's own perpetuation. An example of this type of culturgen is tobacco use. A fourth class is spiteful. A culturgen that is spiteful has a negative effect on its human host's reproductive success and has a negative effect on the culturgen's own perpetuation. Examples of this type of culturgen are paleolithic tools (stone tools of a kind used in the distant past by our hominid ancestors) in the modern environment, and the Dalkon Shield IUD, an IUD with dangerous complications that reduced the reproductive success of human users which, in turn, reduced its own perpetuation to effectively nil when it was recalled by the manufacturer. Another example is the cookware made of lead in ancient Rome. A simple rule is to view all culturgens with suspicion, and acquire them only if their class is cooperator or altruist with a positive effect on human fitness. How did humans get into the trap in which they are so thoroughly parasitized by culturgens with negative fitness effects? The answer is fairly straightforward: To be open to culturgens that may increase one's fitness may expose one to infection from culturgens that decrease fitness.

Some genes perpetuate genes, as in the case where genes for the formation of teeth also promote genes that put components into saliva that are ideal for buffering and protecting teeth. Some culturgens perpetuate culturgens: Beer promotes the bottles and cans which contain it. Some genes perpetuate culturgens, such as those that code for the morphological structures which in turn provide language ability. In Czar Peter the Great's attempt to modernize Russia, he made a directive that all men should shorten their beards. However, they were allowed to keep a long beard if they wore a medal showing that they had paid a heavy tax for the privilege. By a rather circuitous route, the genes for beards perpetuated a medal. Some culturgens perpetuate genes: The presence of dairy products in the diet selects for genes that cause adult lactase production.

The great struggle now in human evolution is the battle between gene and culturgen. That is different from the first few million years of human evolution in which culturgens in the form of simple tools and language where overwhelmingly positive assets, and when the battle was gene against gene and culturgen against culturgen. In this battle I suggest that we should attenuate the culturgens responsible for cultural load, rather than vainly attempt to eliminate culture. I am not recommending a cultural purge in the style of the Chinese cultural revolution, in which notional impediments to political or social progress were rooted out as part of official policy. Rather, I am making an appeal, mostly to individuals, to take self-interested action.

Bennett[7] provided an anomalous anthology in his popular work about virtues. It is anomalous because it is highly literate, and because it advocates total subservience of the individual to moral culturgens. It is an entire book dedicated to the dissemination of moral culturgens, some of them parasitic, mostly to the minds of young people. I recognize that Bennett[7] published in a *genre* different from the one in which this book is published, but that cannot excuse the mindless repetition of self-serving, fitness depleting culturgens. However, there is a point about virtues worth noting: They may have once had translation tables to adaptive strategies, e.g., it is not hard to imagine that old style virtues once led to the efficient use of time, energy or reproductive effort in the process of maximizing reproductive success. A fair question might be: Does the evolutionary ethic condone any virtues at all? Yes, those that lead to the maximization of the individual's reproductive success. An entire branch of ethics might well be devoted to the discovery of these new, fitness-friendly virtues.

The above example of the dissemination of moral culturgens by a book is one showing that enculturation, i.e. the process of learning culture as a child, is not entirely the benevolent process that many anthropologists think it is. Traditionally, it is viewed as a process that turns a brutish infant into a civilized adult, and of course that sounds desirable when considered superficially. But actually the process does something else as well. It burdens the child with culturgens, some malignant, in the process. Some of these culturgens may be with the child for the remainder of his life, and he is likely to pass on to the next generation those that are of the self-perpetuating parasitic class of culturgens. The lack of total benevolence of a culture becomes more apparent to the American adult with the experience of international travel. There, acculturation, i.e. the process of learning the ways of a different culture, can have its painful moments that are filled with consternation. Anyone spending an extended time in another culture experiences it. The source of the conflict may be in part an incompatibility between the culturgens of the new culture and those of the old, but it also may be the incompatibility of primordial drives with the culturgens of the new culture.

The cost of transmitting a culturgen between people may be divided between the carrier and the recipient. If acceptance of the culturgen is against the recipient's inclination, the cost of transmission may be born by the carrier, and accomplished by intrusive means such as inculcation. This pattern is demonstrated in coercive ideologies like religions that employ active recruitment techniques in which the costs are initially born by the carrier, e.g., the Jehovah's Witnesses' devotees in their long trek from door to door with their religious literature, looking for potential converts. If the recipient is a willing one, the cost of transmission may be born by the recipient. Seeking membership in an exclusive club involves expenses born by the inductee. Yet another set of costs associated with the culturgen may be encountered after transmission, depending on whether the culturgen has positive, neutral or negative fitness effects. While it is true that the transmission of culturgens with negative fitness effects occurs at a considerable cost to humans, the culturgens have attributes that extract these costs, not only those of transmission *per se*, but also the long-term costs to the host. There is a related phenomenon concerning the transmission of culturgens which are against the natural inclination of humans. They extract time and energy from the carrier in order to inculcate and maintain themselves as an aspect of culture that is unnatural. However, they may have any of the three possible fitness outcomes for the recipient: positive, neutral, or negative. With reference to a previous section on the fallacy of equating natural with good, it is clear that some ''unnatural'' culturgens, but with positive effects on reproductive success, might well be resisted by potential hosts out of natural inclination.

In a strange twist, Ehrlich and Ehrlich[54] suggested that if society is to come to grips with population growth, it will have to do so through cultural evolution, i.e. through an increase in frequency of culturgens with a negative effect on reproductive success in the culture. While it is clear that Ehrlich and Ehrlich[54] supported the concept that aspects of culture *can* reduce reproductive success, they are in error when they imply that they *should* be used to reduce reproductive success. Prescribing culturgens that are fertility parasites for the fertile is more confused than prescribing tapeworms for the obese (a once common treatment intended to cure obesity). Here is another comparison. Before the acceptance of the germ theory of disease there was no concept of sterile operating conditions, and surgeons took great pride in the accumulated pus and blood on their operating garb from successive operations. Before the acceptance of the evolutionary ethic, some people will continue to go to great lengths to thwart the function of their reproductive organs. One day we will universally recognize that practice to be as misguided as the surgical procedures of old. A sense of moral superiority often goes with the culturgens leading to the expression of concern about overpopulation or about too many single mothers. For example, Ehrlich and Ehrlich[54] reported that they instituted social sanctions against their own relatives by denying birthday gifts to any child past number two in a family. Such a sense of moral superiority is an illusion according to the evolutionary ethic. It is also unclear that actions like denying a child birthday gifts will actually reduce the child's reproductive success, or any individual's reproductive success for that matter.

Here are three examples of people supporting self-perpetuating culturgens that are parasitic and which reduce the bearer's reproductive success: the priest who is celibate; the teenager who fatally overdoses on an illicit, addictive drug; the fashion model who nearly starves herself, becomes anorexic and cannot conceive.

Much of the ambiguity and uncertainty in our lives is caused by culturgens conflicting with primordial drives. For example, there can be a source of conflict in the choice of staying up late and watching television programs designed to beguile you (a culturgen) or getting enough sleep (a primordial drive). For another example we need only consider a choice that is at the heart of the evolutionary ethic: making cumbersome preparations for artificially inhibited sexual intercourse with a contraceptive (a culturgen) or having natural, spontaneous sexual intercourse (a primordial drive). It is noteworthy that contraceptive promoters try to make the American public feel that not using a contraceptive, e.g., a condom, is a sign of laziness or of recklessness. They ride roughshod over the truth, i.e. that a real and momentous conflict between the culturgen and the primordial drive exists. Furthermore, almost any proximate mechanism that prevents one from using a contraceptive, e.g., embarrassment, fear of side effects, lack of knowledge, inconvenience, or expense, is a valid way of achieving the evolutionary ethic. Note carefully, this call is not one for an increase in sexually transmitted diseases, rather it is a mandate to be informed about the state of health of your sexual partner.

During the peak of the Black Power Movement in the sixties and seventies there was the often heard call by black activists to members of their race to outbreed the class of white oppressors. Whether or not they hearkened to this call, the minority black population has increased substantially from those times to the present. The 1990 U.S. Census indicated that the black population has been growing at more than twice the rate of growth for whites (white = 6 percent; black = 13.2 percent). Some other minority groups, such as Asians and Hispanics, are also increasing their representation in the population. By the guiding principle of reproductive success, these populations clearly have what it takes to succeed. This trend raises the questions of not only does race influence fitness, but does race identification, e.g., slogans, pride, and camaraderie, influence fitness?

"The Lord will provide" is an interesting culturgen and perhaps a useful motto in overcoming a psychological, culturally imposed obstacle to fertility. This obstacle is the pursuit of excessive resource availability and predictability before having a child. Another interesting culturgen is the name "Chastity". It seems strange that parents should name a child "Chastity". Interestingly, it is a more common first name than last name. Could this fact be a result of the name Chastity inspiring chastity in its bearer (as was the intent in the historical origins of the name), with the result being the inherited last name leaving fewer or no descendants to bear it and perpetuate it? First names, of course, are given and have a lower heritability than last names in Western society.

Self-deception can be defined as an individual deceiving himself, or being in one state of mind that precludes consciousness of another more truthful, contradictory state of mind. Trivers[206] presented an evolutionary model for the explanation of self-deception. He suggested that deceit is more convincing if there are no detectable indications of deceit in the deceiver. The best way for a deceiver to be convincing in his deceit and not show indications of deceit is to believe the lie himself. While his model has merit, I propose what is a more common cause of self-deception in humans but not in other organisms. I suggest that culturgens may be the source of misinformation that in turn leads us to false conclusions about our state of mind or body, and that in the absence of these culturgens we would have a truer picture of reality. For example, many Americans believe that they have a guardian angel watching over them. Some Eskimos believe that they have become possessed by a snow devil in a culturally specific psychosis. Psychosis in general might be viewed as the self-deception of an abnormally functioning brain and the insane culturgens it carries. Psychotropic drugs like cannabis induce a feeling of well being and euphoria that is not in accordance with the true state of the individual. In modern and historic times faith healers, quacks, fortunetellers, victims of extraterrestrial abduction, rainmakers, self-proclaimed witches, prophets, and exorcists all are likely examples of persons experiencing extensive self-deception. It seems reasonable to posit a strong cultural component to the examples of self-deception given in that last sentence. In these cases it would appear that superculturgen belief structures take possession of the mind, greatly altering the world view and limiting the capability of rational thought.

Advertisements are culturgens, and they really are capable of modifying human behavior. The majority of beer commercials on television have such characteristics that they would seem to be best suited to appeal to cretins. But they must be selling beer, or the breweries would make a change, since they are driven by the profit motive. Could it be that beer commercials are designed to appeal to people who are mentally impaired by virtue of the fact that they are already intoxicated or because they have brain damage from long-term alcohol abuse? Such viewers would be customers of high consuming potential, and appealing to them rather than to astute nondrinkers would be much more important for sales.

Gould[74] wrote:

> If the world displays any harmony and order, it arises only as an incidental result of individuals seeking their own advantage .... (p. 12)

This statement is true if natural selection acting on gene frequencies is the only determinant of behavior. But we have discussed in detail in this section the extragenic factors of culturgens which are often behaviors or which modify behaviors. For example, I can imagine a culturgen that promoted world peace for its own purpose of having larger numbers of individuals (than in a world at war) with whom to cooperate.

Superculturgens and subcultures

Superculturgens, which are a group of culturgens that are transmitted and held in a tight cluster, and subcultures, which are the cultural attributes of a subpopulation of people, tend to merge into each other. Philosophies like that of fundamentalist Christianity are examples, but of course that is just one subset of religious philosophies within Christianity, which in turn is just one subset of philosophies of religion, which in turn is a subset of philosophy. It is perhaps reasonable to speculate that there have been millions of philosophies that could be categorized out of human knowledge and belief over the period of our prehistory and history. Why have there been so many? There are two main reasons: They tend to perpetuate themselves and they tend to bifurcate into new philosophies with geographical or social isolation.

Superculturgens do not always coexist in harmony. One interesting phenomenon is when a superculturgen employs a human zealot to actively harm another superculturgen or another superculturgen's human representatives. Attacks on the heads of religions or political movements by conspirators of other religions or political movements are examples. Terrorism is often of this form. Not surprisingly, the superculturgen and the individuals on the receiving end are usually motivated to extreme levels of condemnation and retaliation by the attacks.

Let us consider systems of ethics as superculturgens. The disparate views among ethicists themselves about how an act can be justified and what makes it "good" or "bad" can be disconcerting at first. It will be some time before the evolutionary ethic could, under the best of circumstances, prevail and supplant older, more traditional systems of ethics. In the interval, we need to understand that the disagreement among ethicists is not surprising; different schools of philosophy and ethics are superculturgens battling for supremacy in our minds. Sometimes, they have considerable roots in epigenetic rules, and sometimes they have fitness implications for their human hosts, but almost always they are self-perpetuating subcultures.

Cultural determination of a genetic trait

I have already discussed the social selection of the genetic traits of twinning and albinism. Another example of social selection is the ability of the adults in some human populations to tolerate the ingestion of milk, to produce lactase and to be capable of lactose absorption. This subject has been a long considered topic by anthropologists. Durham[49] did a thorough analysis of how adult lactose absorption has coevolved in a complex interaction between culture, noncultural environment and genes. The keeping of animals suitable for milk product, latitude, and adult lactase production are correlated. Durham[49] concluded, and I concur, that this example is an unusually clear one of culture causing genetic change.

Genetic determinism of a cultural trait

One of the best examples of the genetic determination of a cultural trait is the incest taboo discussed by Lumsden and Wilson[126] and by others. The avoidance of close inbreeding accomplished by the incest taboo is a mechanism to increase reproductive success by the avoidance of inbreeding depression and the expression of rare, recessive, deleterious alleles. An innate aversion to mating with close relatives, especially those with close social contact during the years of development, has evolved as a proximate mechanism. In turn, cultures around the world have taken this innate aversion to incest and incorporated it into the ethos, sometimes with subtle reshaping and manipulation. Ethos is a rich combination of traits that have evolved by cultural evolution and biological evolution as well as being both environmentally and genetically determined.

The tendency to exalt the in-group, e.g., culture or subculture, and to depreciate the out-group, is known as ethnocentrism. Perhaps originally associated with feelings of superiority in one's tribe, it has become more broadly characteristic of all social groups, e.g., "team spirit," "local pride," "college spirit," "religious intolerance," "racial prejudice," and "nationalism"[146]. All cultures cultivate ethnocentrism -- they must or they perish by being absorbed into another culture after contact.

Patriotism and martyrdom

Patriotism is a motivational factor in defending the culture and its political leaders as well as the citizens themselves, on occasion, and has similarities to ethnocentrism. But perhaps more than with ethnocentrism there is a deliberate attempt made by leaders to cultivate patriotism at times when it is considered useful, as in times of warfare. Although a model has been advanced for modern warfare as an inclusive fitness maximizing strategy, I do not find it credible from the existing evidence. That leaves us with an alternative explanation for patriotism: That it is a culturgen which is deliberately perpetuated and spread by the culture itself. I do not doubt, however, that such attempts to promote patriotism do not miss the opportunity to further its acceptance by eliciting feelings of loyalty and solidarity. Such feelings in older, more natural social environments would have been reserved for members of the human kinship group, which may have been used in primitive warfare, not unlike that displayed by hamadryas baboons today. And what about people who die for their religious beliefs? The average American's attitude toward such people is highly ethnocentric. If the martyr is one in the distant history of Christianity, he is treated with hushed reverence. But if the martyr is one in the current events of the Muslim struggle for religious predominance, he is treated with scorn. However, if we put aside these emotions evoked by culture playing with our limbic systems, it is clear that all martyrs are the tragic pawns of sinister, fitness depressing culturgens.

It is right to love your country if so doing maximizes your reproductive success, but at the same time hate your fitness suppressing government. Martyrdom is always bad because it is the sacrifice of reproductive success for the purpose of perpetuating a culturgen, i.e. religion. But patriotism may be good. When does patriotism make adaptive sense? When there is a large out-group against which a competitive advantage can be gained, and when the reproductive benefits of patriotism are fairly distributed among the patriots. A small population of closely related individuals would naturally promote patriotic behavior.

Traditional, non-Western cultures have not changed so much or so fast that the people living in them have genes that are out of touch with their culturgens. As a result these people have a low cultural load and, consequently, high fertility. It is common in the West to denigrate non-Western cultures as primitive and to list high fertility as just another of their undesirable attributes. But let us recall an important principle in anthropology: Non-Western cultures are not primitive; they differ only in that they are relatively technologically unadvanced. For example, their languages, kinship relations, and religions are just as modern and complex as ours. Americans sometimes refer to non-Western cultures as primitive, not so much out of an intention to insult, but out of ignorance. From the viewpoint considering the importance of reproductive success of the members of a culture, our ethnocentrism is without foundation -- non-Western cultures are more successful in terms of this critical parameter than America.

Perhaps since the rapid cultural change of the neolithic age our minds have been in the grips of primitive dogma. For these ten thousand years, and especially so in the last hundred years, our lives have been ruled by culturgens, not by evolutionary strategy. In terms of the potential to enhance reproductive success, one culture may not be the same as another. Among other things, cultures provide technologies and behavioral strategies for resource extraction. And in the fine points of resource extraction they may differ considerably, one culture being better suited to doing so in a specific environment. That is the ultimate measure of a culture -- how successful it is in helping individuals to turn resources into reproductive success. Sometimes we judge cultures by their arts, military power, tools, longevity or the extent of their geographical distribution. But these criteria are only meaningful in the context of the evolutionary ethic in terms of their impact on reproductive success.

Chapter 12: Conclusions

The future holds a more populated, less resource-rich planet Earth. For the present and foreseeable future, it is the only planet we have. Colonizing space and other planets does not now appear to be a possibility. But the space program offers the only possibility of ever being able to colonize other planets and other solar systems in the distant future. Although the prospects are not promising, they are the only prospects for survival of humans after the demise of Earth. The space program is useful in another way: It provides a way to rid ourselves of current, fitness reducing, surplus wealth and, at the same time, it provides potential long-term benefits. By necessity, humans will eventually leave Earth via the space program or perish.

The world is a long way from a comprehensive policy for the control of population growth. The International Conference on Population and Development in Cairo in 1994 is testimony to that fact. There, delegates were preoccupied with arguing over the moral status of contraception and abortion, and they consequently failed to reach consensus on a 20-year-plan for development, or for management of population growth. In the absence of action by this world body or any other one, it is clear that reproductive choices will remain in the domain of the individual around most of the world for some time. Reproduction may or may not be recognized as the fundamental human right that it is, but it is a reality in practice in view of the ineptitude of those who seek to regulate it and deny it. If a new world reproductive order does eventually come, let us hope that it is a progenitive one instead of the fitness depressing schemes now in the minds of international leaders.

Evolutionary trends in humans extrapolated: At least twice before, human destiny has been changed by the evolution of a new race in Africa which then expanded to populate the entire Earth. This process may be in the early stages of repetition with the recent Bantu expansion around the world and the current Hamitic expansion at a rate higher than that of all other races.

What can everyone do to promote fertility? In a study by Jones et al.[110] of fertility in developing countries, they arrived at some conclusions about what factors depress teenage fertility. The inverse of those factors might do quite well to promote teenage fertility. Listed below are those policies that would help to *elevate* the teenage birth rate:

· Low levels of socioeconomic modernization
· A lack of openness about sexuality
· A relatively small proportion of household income distributed to the low-income population by wage structure
· A low minimum legal age for marriage

· Generous maternity leaves and benefits
· Overall progenitivist policies designed to raise fertility
· Religiosity

The following factors promote adult fertility:

· Rural living
· Less education
· Less income
· Fewer working women
· Less abortion due to legal prohibition
· Less use of modern contraceptive techniques
· Early marriage
· Birth of first child to young parents
· Less divorce
· Less bachelorhood and less spinsterhood
· Less openness about homosexuality and lesbianism
· Less cohabitation among unmarried couples
· Lowering the financial costs of raising children
· Ignorance of the doctrine of environmentalism

What is ultimately needed in order to understand how to promote reproductive success is a multiple regression analysis of the independent variables that explain the variance in the dependent variable, fertility. Which independent variable explains the greatest amount of variance in reproductive success? Might it be the extent to which no contraceptives are used? Might it be the extent to which proception is employed? Other independent variables of importance include income and education. Even though extensive data for the variables that contribute to reproductive success have been analyzed for baboons using stepwise multiple regression[162], this form of analysis does not appear to have been employed often in the study of human reproductive success. This fact is an unfortunate one, because among baboons such an analysis proved to be revealing. I analyzed 25 independent variables in behavior, morphology and physiology in male baboons in terms of their ability to explain variations among males in the dependent variable, consort and copulation success, a high correlate of reproductive success. The stepwise multiple regression equation explained 99.48 percent of the variance in the dependent variable. Eight independent variables were significant in the stepwise multiple regression, and twelve independent variables had correlation coefficients with consort and copulation success that were significant at the p less than 0.05 level. Such a quantitative study of American reproductive patterns would be of considerably more value than the qualitative studies that now prevail. Bongaarts[13] came close to the desirable type of analysis to which I refer. He reported that a small number of intermediate fertility variables are responsible for the variation in fertility levels in a wide range of populations. Four factors: Proportion married, contraception, elective abortion, and postpartum infecundability explain 96 percent of the variance in the total fertility rate in his study of 41 diverse populations. It is interesting to note that the intermediate fertility variables that he analyzed are a comprehensive listing of proximate fertility determinants, and as such it is only through them that social, economic, and cultural conditions can affect fertility.

Below I present a hypothetical progenitivist agenda in order of decreasing likelihood of acceptability by the average American:

· The U.S. is twenty-third in infant mortality in the world; should this ranking be improved through better maternal and child health care? Or should we allow American children to die from easily preventable causes?
· Should community support programs to ease the burden on teenage parents be initiated?
· Should larger tax breaks for dependent children be given?
· Should incentives be offered for having a baby, like paid leave and free medical care for expectant mothers and children?
· Should more careful controls be placed on medications and technologies that endanger reproductive health?
· Should sales tax be abolished on food, medicine and apparel for children?
· Should there be a redistribution of national wealth and resources to actively reproducing people?
· Should contraception and elective abortions be banned? There *was* a time in recent U.S. history when elective abortions and distributing contraceptives were illegal in many states.
· Should people who are reluctant to have a child be coerced? We are coerced to pay our income tax and obey traffic laws -- why not coercion to reproduce?

Laws requiring use of seat belts, use of motorcycle helmets and prohibiting suicide are common in America. Many states have the death penalty. Society obviously can mandate life and death -- could it not also mandate reproduction in the future? I ask all the above questions not because I advocate an affirmative answer to them, but because they provide provocative concepts of counterbalance to the existing antigenitivist policies in America today. An affirmative answer to the above questions may be appropriate to the degree that the following questions are answered in the affirmative: Is antigenitivism a cultural plot to enslave us all? Does it aim to redirect our reproductive effort in order to perpetuate culturgens such as our government, consumerism and postindustrialism? Given the remarkable manipulative powers of superculturgens, it is not surprising that corporations and government bureaucracies take on lives of their own. Perhaps a hypothetical progenitivist agenda like the one above containing strong measures is indicated to combat them.

I propose that we replace the gold standard in medicine, which measures the efficacy of a treatment by the extent to which it increases survivorship, with what I call the *platinum standard*, which measures the efficacy of a treatment by the extent to which it increases reproductive success. This platinum standard can be applied to medical treatment, behaviors, products and so forth. Although the two standards may overlap under some circumstances, i.e. when increased longevity leads to increased reproductive success, the two standards are not identical and the platinum standard should take precedence. The standard of maximizing reproductive success for a patient is not one only for physicians. Other professions should treat their clients similarly. Investment counselors, lawyers, nutritionists, dentists, and university professors are other examples of professions that require their own platinum standard. How far does the platinum standard go? It should be applied in all professions where the benefit in reproductive success to the client is greater than the cost of the application in reproductive success. Until such time that the platinum standard is widely accepted, you have no choice but to be the guardian of your own reproductive success without assistance. Even prostitution, the oldest profession after hunting and gathering, will be transformed by the platinum standard. In the place of high risk, low-fitness-return sex now associated with prostitution, women of this vocation will instead sell their surrogate motherhood services. In the process, a prostitute would have to be changed into a healthy egg donor or surrogate who took good care of the fetus *in utero*.

In the immediate future as in the recent past, environmental (including cultural) change may continue to outpace biological evolution. Dawkins[41] stated:

> Adoption and contraception, like reading, mathematics, and stress-induced illness, are the products of an animal that is living in an environment radically different from the one in which its genes were naturally selected. (p. 36)

What new challenges from a largely self-made environment await our species? Could the challenge now be to broadly face the cultural load that we bear and accept the unfolding of a new, reproductive success-friendly ethos? Perhaps the reproductive success revolution will not come out of a scientific approach as exemplified by this book, but rather out of an intuitive or emotional revolt to the tight grasp which culturgens with negative fitness effects have on us.

So much has been written that is contrary to the spirit of the evolutionary ethic, against progenitivism and opposing evolutionary interpretations of human life, that an entire book might be composed simply of negations of those objectionable statements. There is no doubt that with the publication of this book those objections, driven by the complex interactions of culturgens with humans, will increase, not decrease in number. This prediction is based on the fact that never before has an evolutionary interpretation of human life been combined with a progenitivist philosophy and with the evolutionary ethic as introduced herein.

There has been much speculation in this century about the negative effects of modern society on the human gene pool. Some argue that the genetic load is increasing and that desirable traits like high intelligence are actively selected against. But our concern should instead be about the rapid and great increase in cultural load. If you are interested enough to be reading this book and to see the logic in its arguments, then by all means your contribution to the gene pool would be appreciated! If, on the other hand, you contest the contents of this book, then by all means restrict your reproduction. For example, to anyone who obnoxiously and militantly asserts (for whatever reason) that people should curtail their reproduction, I say: "By all means, do refrain from having children yourself". There are other points that need to be made about the readership of this book -- they are the people who most need the evolutionary ethic, and they are also the people who are least able to comprehend it, because their relatively high level of intellectual development has burdened them with fitness depressing culturgens in the form of tenacious ideas about what is right and proper concerning restraining reproduction.

It is an old theme that humans are destined to participate in their own evolution. Gene frequencies among human populations will change as a function of both unconscious and conscious reproductive choices. We know that evolution is occurring now in the American population because gene frequencies are changing from generation to generation. Gene frequencies have changed in America over the centuries, but this change is in a large part due to immigration rather than to natural selection. The time will come when humans will actively participate in directing these changes.

In the future, more people will adopt with enthusiasm a lifestyle that leads to reproductive success, just as many today have a lifestyle that is centered around physical fitness or religion. It is already common for people to say that they have their priorities right, in that they put their families first. Progenitivism is an extension of that concept, and it changes the *cliché* into a practical, adaptive strategy.

A listing of the life-lessons in review

That which increases one's reproductive success is good; that which decreases one's reproductive success is bad; that which has no effect on reproductive success is neutral.

Eat plenty of fruit, vegetables, and lean animal protein. Eat few cereal grains.

If you are cosmetically obese (less than 100 percent over your ideal body weight), do not worry about it. Instead, use the stored calories to raise additional children. If you are morbidly obese, consider a diet and an exercise program. Your weight goal is that which maximizes your reproductive success, not necessarily that which makes you look nice or be healthy.

See that your children get a good eighth grade education.

Age is not the life history variable that you should be maximizing. Life is a tradeoff between longevity and reproductive effort. And because, other things given being equal, higher reproductive effort leads to higher reproductive success, one should accrue and expend reproductive effort at the expense of longevity.

Use an inclusive fitness maximizing approach to estate planning.

Avoid smoking tobacco, unless you are a teenager who would otherwise not be having sexual intercourse.

If you are a man, find a fertile woman; if you are a woman, find a virile man.

The truth of the fact that we should not maximize the amount of food we eat has slowly become apparent to the average American. By the same slow process Americans will realize that we should not maximize our wealth, education, longevity, physical fitness or any variable other than reproductive success. Too much of anything can lower reproductive success.

Individuals should not use any form of contraception.

Practice proception.

Never have an elective abortion. You would be killing an individual with whom you share $1/2$ of your genes in common.

Bottle feed your baby.

Start reproduction early, preferably at puberty, have a long reproductive life, and maximize your reproductive success.

Religion is wrong, but it may be good for you.

Keep no pets. Have another child or help a relative have another child instead.

Instead of obsessively pursuing more wealth, use what you have to maximize your reproductive success.

Regardless of the direction and rate of population growth, practice maximization of reproductive success.

The wealthiest people can benefit their reproductive success by giving, and the poorest people can benefit their reproductive success by receiving.

Any social behavior is good if it increases your inclusive fitness.

One should judge people by a single parameter for strategic social behavior: how well they will help you to maximize your net inclusive fitness in interactions with them.

Support measures that help in the conservation of resources like energy resources and that discourage the manufacture of superfluous consumer goods.

Reduce your cultural load.

Catchwords for progenitivism

Because any practical philosophy or social movement requires catchwords to promote it, in closing I submit the material below to further the cause of the evolutionary ethic and progenitivism. The direct applicability of these catchwords is not as high as that of the previously listed life-lessons, nor is it intended to be. Rather, the catchwords are designed to provoke thought and to inspire progenitive action. Both the life-lessons and the catchwords are paramount for the establishment of a new, reproductive success-friendly ethos, the former primarily at the level of the individual and the latter primarily at the level of the population.

A prediction: Those people who apply the herein life-lessons, either deliberately in accordance with this book, or by happenstance, will populate the Earth with their descendants. Those people who reject the life-lessons will become extinct.

A moral rule: In our newly found and greatly simplified moral climate, we have a functional rule. In the final analysis, one's actions can be regarded as good or bad according to whether or not they enhance one's reproductive success.

A precept: Life is merely an artifact of evolution -- maximizing reproductive success is why we are here. Humans were designed for a purpose by evolution, to maximize reproductive success. I would think myself guilty of belaboring the obvious were I not fully aware that this essential fact will have considerable difficulty in gaining broad acceptance.

A battle to be fought: The ultimate evolutionary battle now facing humans is the battle between an individual's genes and fitness reducing culturgens. The present American culture is like a fire. And it is human bodies and minds that keep it alive. Instead of being consumed by culture, those bodies and minds could be serving their own genetic self-interests by maximizing reproductive success.

A call for change: We will neither allow our world to be the laboratory for culture any longer, nor our own lives and reproductive success to be the experiment. In a sense, holders of the evolutionary ethic are freedom fighters against fitness reducing culturgens.

A principle: Maximize reproductive success in all you do.

A habit: When faced with decisions, we should make a habit of asking: Which option will increase our reproductive success? The broad guidelines of the life-lessons presented herein cover many of the important aspects of compliance with the evolutionary ethic. It is advisable that readers focus their compliance with the evolutionary ethic by application of these life-lessons. Considering the flagrant disregard in America today for maximizing reproductive success, it is difficult to imagine that too much devotion to the evolutionary ethic could soon be a problem. But it is theoretically possible that one might become over zealous in analyzing the reproductive consequences of every detail of one's life. Such over-analysis could incur costs in time, energy, and intellectual processing that might actually reduce, not increase, reproductive success. The question of how much effort to spend on gathering and processing information that is useful in tracking reproductive strategies comes under the broader heading: What price knowledge? which is discussed in a previous section. I do not mean to imply that Americans have invested too much in the study of optimal reproductive strategies. On the contrary, it is unfortunately true that the fitness consequences of many specific behaviors, certain consumer choices, individual lifestyle preferences and so forth are neither conspicuously obvious nor the subject of study. What is needed is a kind of reproductive success analysis, which rates human behaviors and culturgens according to their role in the increment or decrement of reproductive success, in the way that *Consumer Reports* rates products that Americans are likely to encounter, in terms of economic value and utility. And in the same way that consumer advocacy has appeared in the last few decades to monitor abuses of consumer rights, we need reproducer advocacy to monitor abuses of reproducer rights, and to help the individual achieve the goal of maximizing reproductive success. A new cadre of reproductive success advisers is also needed. They will be drawn from the fields of anthropology and evolutionary biology, with those disciplines providing the theoretical foundations. Demography, medicine, and economics would provide some of the data relevant to designing optimal reproductive strategies.

A demand: Holders of the evolutionary ethic make a single demand on society -- the liberty required to allow them to maximize their reproductive success. I have a vision of the proper function of society: to serve its members in maximizing their reproductive success. A consequence of progenitivism is the establishment of a new societal order. For example, we must have a national campaign to encourage pregnancies among teenagers, and births outside marriage. Such a campaign neither need necessarily render the institution of marriage obsolete, nor alter marriage's long held traditions. After widespread acceptance of the evolutionary ethic, American society will change. But we should not fear that change, because we have no valid reason to wish to perpetuate any past, present or future form of society except to the degree that it maximizes our reproductive success. And so, my fellow Americans: Ask not what you can do for your country -- ask what your country can do for your reproductive success. One aspect of my argument that staunch believers in natural selection at the level of the gene or the individual may have objection to is the progenitivist theme which I advocate should permeate every aspect of society. The members of no other species concern themselves on a large scale with the reproductive success of unrelated members of their populations. Rather, their behaviors function to maximize their own individual reproductive success. Why do I suggest that a different pattern is appropriate for humans? There are two reasons. First, I have a professional obligation to *all* my readership to advocate strategies that will benefit them. I can hardly maintain that all of America should function in a way that maximizes my own personal reproductive success, even though such a scenario, if realized, would produce a truly remarkable outcome for my fitness. Secondly, there are mechanisms in human behavior that seem to cause people to emulate the ideas that they promulgate, with the result that participating in a campaign for a fitness-oriented society may be one of the best ways to motivate an individual to maximize his own reproductive success. I discussed this second point in a previous section in terms of feedforward.

A slogan: A reproductive organ is a terrible thing to waste.

A celebration: We have Earth Day yearly, but do not have a similar celebration or commemoration of reproductive success. I propose that a Fitness Month be added to the calendar. It could be scheduled for the month in which the fewest conceptions occur in each country, since humans tend to show a slight trend toward seasonal breeding in the current environment, which may not be adaptive.

A charity: Just as there are environmental charities and charities sponsoring aspects of our culture such as the arts, there will be progenitive charities.

A societal goal: Turn the pursuit of fitness into a revolution, and defend it with any and all means consistent with maximizing one's reproductive success.

A criterion: Reproductive success is the sole, incomparable criterion for measuring the desirability of a trait.

A guiding principle: We have entered a new world, where the maximization of reproductive success, the fundamental guiding principle for all human endeavors, is known and certain.

A motto: People of the world, maximize your reproductive success! You have nothing to lose but your cultural load.

Glossary

Adaptation: an aspect of behavior or morphology that equips an individual to survive and reproduce.

Affine: a relative by marriage.

Allele: an alternative form of a gene.

Altruistic behavior: a social act that occurs at a cost to the actor and confers a benefit on the recipient, where cost and benefit are measured in reproductive success.

Amenorrhea: delay of onset or abnormal cessation of menstruation.

Animistic belief: the belief that humans share the world with other beings which are extraordinary, extracorporeal, and mostly invisible.

Anthelmintic: medicine to kill worms.

Anthropology: the study of humans including their behavior, morphology, culture, history, evolution, prehistory, and material artifacts.

Antigenitive: a trait or characteristic leading to antigenitivism.

Antigenitivism: a philosophy against perpetuating one's genes and against maximizing one's reproductive success.

Antigenitivist: a practitioner or policy of antigenitivism.

Archaeology: the study of the material culture of past human life through the recovery and examination of physical remains.

Artifact: a product of artificial character due to extraneous agency. For example, pins are artifacts of pinmakers, and life is an artifact of evolution.

Assortative: selection on the basis of likeness.

Australopithecus afarensis: an early australopithecine.

Australopithecus **spp.**: a genus of fossil hominids that lived 4-1.3 million years ago. They had a cranial capacity less than half that of modern humans.

Avunculate: the special social and economic relationship between a man and his sister's children found in some cultures.

Avunculocal: a custom of residence in which a married couple live with or near a maternal uncle of the husband.

Bilocal: a custom of residence which permits a married couple to live with or near the parents of either spouse.

Brideprice: gifts or payments provided in some cultures by the groom or his family to the bride's family at marriage.

Calorie: a unit of energy in food, in technical terms a kcal. (a kilocalorie is a unit of 1000 calories), or the amount of heat required to raise the temperature of one kilogram of water one degree centigrade.

Chromosome: a rod-like structure found in cells bearing genes.

Cirrhosis: the third stage of liver deterioration seen in heavy drinkers in which liver cells have died and hardened and have permanently lost their function.

Clitoridectomy: the excision of the clitoris, usually for ritualistic purposes.

Coevolution: a change in gene frequency in one population in response to the effects of a second population, followed in turn by a change in gene frequency in the second population in response to effects of the first population. Alternatively, it is a change in gene frequency in a population along with feedback in a change in culture.

Consanguine: a relative by blood.

Cooperative behavior: a social act that occurs at a benefit to the actor and confers a benefit on the recipient, where benefit is measured in reproductive success.

Cross-cultural comparison: a comparison of the attributes of different cultures.

Cross-phyletic comparison: a comparison of different kinds of animals based on the major divisions in the animal kingdom known as phyla.

Culturgen: a relatively homogeneous group of transmissible mental constructions or their products, as used by Lumsden and Wilson[126, 127].

Cultural evolution: a change in culture over time, represented by a change in the frequencies of culturgens in a culture.

Cultural load: an individual's reduction of fitness imposed by deleterious culturgens.

Culture: the integrated sum total of learned behavioral traits characteristic of the members of a society.

Deterministic: of the philosophy of determinism, a cause and effect relationship between variables, so that aspects of life can be explained by previous causes.

Diploid: a characteristic of organisms, including humans, whose cells (apart from the gametes) have two sets of chromosomes, and thus have two copies of the basic genetic complement.

Dowry: gifts or payments provided by the family of the bride to the groom at marriage in some cultures.

DNA: deoxyribonucleic acid; the molecular foundation for heredity.

Endogamy: selecting a mate from within the group.

Ephemeroptera: the order of insects that includes the mayflies.

Epigenesis: the process of interaction between genes and the environment that ultimately results in the anatomical, physiological, cognitive, or behavioral traits of an organism, as used by Lumsden and Wilson[126, 127].

Epigenetic rule: any regularity during epigenesis that channels the development of a trait in a particular direction, as used by Lumsden and Wilson[126, 127].

Environment: all of the external influences acting on an organism.

Estrus: a time of sexual receptivity in the female.

Et al.: and others, from the Latin *et alii*.

Ethnographic present: a style of writing in which the present tense is used in reference to descriptions of cultures, even if the action is clearly in the past.

Ethnography: a description and comparison of cultures.

Ethnology: the study of cultures.

Ethos: the character of a people in a specific culture.

Eusocial: the condition of a group of social insects displaying cooperative care of young, reproductive division of labor with sterile workers, and overlap of generations, as used by Wilson[221].

Evolution: descent with modification due to the change of gene frequency in a population over time.

Evolutionary ethic: the fundamental moral principle which asserts that which increases one's reproductive success is good; that which decreases one's reproductive success is bad; that which has no effect on reproductive success is neutral.

Exogamy: selecting a mate from outside the group.

Expressivity: the degree to which a genotype produces a phenotypic effect.

Extended reproductive value: expected future number of offspring (reproductive value) plus the expected future contribution made to the production of offspring by relatives devalued by the regression coefficient of relatedness.

Fecundability: the probability of conception per month.

Fatty liver: the first stage of liver deterioration seen in heavy drinkers involving fat accumulation that interferes with the distribution of nutrients and oxygen to the liver cells.

Fecundity: the physiological capacity to reproduce.

Fertility: the realization of the capacity to reproduce.

Fibrosis: the second stage of liver deterioration seen in heavy drinkers in which scar tissue replaces functioning liver cells.

Fidelity: faithfulness in reproduction.

Fitness: reproductive success or the number of offspring raised to maturity.

Founder principle: a phenomenon which occurs when the smallness of the number of founders of a population give rise to a genetic drift effect.

Gamete: a reproductive cell -- an ovum or sperm.

Gene: a basic unit of inheritance; a section of DNA capable of coding for a polypeptide chain (a polypeptide chain is a molecule of amino acids linked together by peptide bonds).

Genetic drift: the random fluctuation of gene frequencies in a finite population between generations.

Genetic load: the average number of deleterious alleles per individual in a population.

Genetic profiling: a laboratory technique of determining the genetic relationship between individuals, usually using blood samples and often referred to as ''genetic fingerprinting''.

Genotype: the genetic constitution of an organism.

Hemizygous: a genetic locus present in only one copy, as in sex-linked genes in the heterogametic sex, e.g., X-linked genes in human males.

Heritability: the variation in a trait in a population due to heredity as opposed to environmental factors.

Heterogametic sex: the sex possessing a pair of non-homologous sex chromosomes, e.g., X and Y chromosomes in human males.

Heterozygotic: having different alleles on a pair of chromosomes.

Hominid: a human-like primate who belongs to the family of Hominidae, or to either of two genera: *Homo* spp. or *Australopithecus* spp.

Hominoidea: the gibbons, great apes, and humans.

Homologous chromosome: a member of a pair of similar chromosomes.

Homozygotic: having the same alleles on a pair of chromosomes.

Homo erectus: The direct ancestor of modern humans. Fossils of this species differ from modern humans in having a prominent brow ridge and lacking a forehead.

Homo sapiens: all modern humans of all races belong to this single species.

Hypergamy: marriage of a woman upward from a lower social class or caste into a higher one.

Hypogamy: marriage of a woman downward from a higher social class or caste into a lower one.

Ideal culture: a people's verbally expressed standards for behavior, which may or may not be translated into normal behavior.

Incest: sexual intercourse between relatives.

Inclusive fitness: the number of offspring raised (fitness) plus the contribution made to the number of offspring raised by relatives devalued by their regression coefficient of relatedness.

Infanticide: the killing of infants.

In utero: within the uterus.

In vitro: Latin for "in glass"; fertilization inside a "test tube" instead of inside the body.

Invalidicide: the killing of invalids.

Levirate: the marriage of a woman to her deceased husband's brother.

Life history: the pattern of distribution over time of the evolutionarily significant events of growth, maintenance and reproduction for an individual.

Life-lessons: practical guides for living.

Matriline: lineage based on tracing descent through the maternal line.

Matrilocal: a custom of residence whereby a husband lives with his wife, either in the house of her parents or in a nearby dwelling.

Matri-patrilocal: a custom of residence whereby a married couple first lives with or near the parents of the wife and later lives with or near the parents of the husband.

Mesolithic: the "middle stone age," a cultural period of human prehistory between the paleolithic and and neolithic.

Moiety: a societal division in which there are only two sibs, so that every person is necessarily a member of one or the other.

Monozygotic twins: twins produced from a single zygote which are therefore genetically identical.

Morphology: the form and structure of an organism.

Mutualism: mutually beneficial association between different kinds of organisms.

Natural Selection: the differential survival and reproduction of variants of a species and its evolutionary effects over generations.

Neolithic: the "new stone age," a cultural period of human prehistory known for improved techniques in fashioning stone tools and coinciding with the appearance of settled cultivation and animal husbandry, beginning about 10,000 years ago.

Neolocal: a custom of residence in which a married couple lives independent of the location of the parental home of either partner, as is typical of American culture.

Paleontology: a branch of anthropology that involves the study of human life from the geological past.

Patriline: lineage based on tracing descent through the paternal line.

Patrilocal: a custom of residence in which a married couple lives with or near the parents of the husband.

Patronymy: a custom in which children take the name of their father.

Paleolithic: the "old stone age," an immensely long cultural period of human prehistory lasting for two million years beginning with the earliest pebble tools.

Penetrance: the percentage of individuals possessing a particular genotype who show the associated phenotype.

Pentadactyl: having five digits on the hand or foot.

Phenotype: an observable characteristic of an organism as determined by the interaction between the genotype and the environment.

Philoprogenitiveness: love of perpetuating one's genes or love of producing offspring.

Phylogeny: the line of descent through evolutionary history of a species or higher taxonomic group.

Pleiotropic effect: one gene controlling seemingly unrelated features.

Polyandry: a form of marriage where one woman has two or more husbands, usually brothers.

Polygyny: a form of marriage where one man has two or more wives.

Polymorphism: the existence within a population or species of different forms of individuals.

Popular: for the general public.

Prehensile: capable of grasping.

Primate: a member of the order of mammals that includes humans, apes, monkeys, and prosimians.

Proception: behavior in which the goal is to achieve conception, as used by Miller[141].

Progenitive: a trait or characteristic leading to progenitivism.

Progenitiveness: a trait or characteristic of progenitivism.

Progenitivism: a philosophy in favor of perpetuating one's genes to maximize one's reproductive success.

Progenitivist: a practitioner or policy of progenitivism.

Real culture: a people's actual behavior in their total round of living.

Regression coefficient of relatedness: a mathematical expression of the number of genes shared by common descent between two individuals. .

Reliability: the ability of a research method to produce the same results when used repeatedly under the same conditions.

Religion: a set of doctrines, rites, and rituals to appease and entreat the objects of animistic beliefs (see Animistic beliefs above).

Reproductive effort: energy expended in the process of attempting to reproduce.

Reproductive success: inclusive fitness or the contribution of genes to the next generation.

Reproductive value: expected future number of offspring.

Senilicide: the killing of the aged.

Sex ratio: the ratio of males to females in the population, usually with reference to an age class: primary sex ratio (at conception), secondary sex ratio (at birth), tertiary sex ratio (at sexual maturity).

Sexual dimorphism: a difference in behavior or morphology between the sexes, e.g., a different mean body mass.

Sib: a kin group which acknowledges common descent but for which it is not always possible to trace the actual genealogical connection between individuals.

Selfish behavior: a social act that occurs at a benefit to the actor and confers a cost on the recipient, where cost and benefit are measured in reproductive success.

Singleton: a single offspring born alone.

Social Darwinism: a discredited theory in sociology that maintains sociocultural advance is the product of intergroup conflict and competition and that the social elite (people possessing wealth and power) are biologically superior.

Sociobiology: the scientific study of the biological basis of social behavior in all kinds of organisms, including humans.

Sororal polygyny: the simultaneous marriage of two or more sisters to one husband.

Sororate: the practice whereby a sister marries the widowed husband of her deceased sister.

Species: a group of organisms capable of interbreeding and producing fertile offspring.

Spiteful behavior: a social act that occurs at a cost to the actor and confers a cost on the recipient, where cost is measured in reproductive success.

Spontaneous abortion: a miscarriage or loss of fetus during a pregnancy.

Stereoscopic: giving a three-dimensional effect.

Superculturgen: a group of culturgens that are transmitted and held in a tight cluster.

Validity: the ability of a research method to measure what it is thought to be measuring.

Vestigial: describing a trait that is a vestige (no longer used or needed) of what once existed as an adaptation.

Wife lending: the custom whereby a husband extends to a household guest the sexual favors of his wife as a symbolic gesture of brotherhood or hospitality.

Zygote: the cell resulting from fertilization of an egg by a sperm.

References

1. Alexander, R. D., 1979. *Darwinism and human affairs*. University of Washington Press: Seattle. 317 pp.

2. Alexander, R. D., 1987. *The biology of moral systems*. Aldine de Gruyter: New York. 301 pp.

3. Amann, R. P., 1970. Sperm production rates. In A. D. Johnson, W. R. Gomes and N. L. Vandemark, eds. pp. 433-482. *The testis* Volume I. Academic Press: London.

4. Ayer, A. J., 1990. *The meaning of life*. Charles Scribner's Sons: New York. 212 pp.

5. Baker, R. R and M. A. Bellis, 1993. Human sperm competition: ejaculate adjustment by males and the function of masturbation. *Animal Behaviour* 46:861-885.

6. Ball, J. A., 1984. Memes as replicators. *Ethology and Sociobiology* 5:145-61.

7. Bennett, W. J., 1993. *The book of virtues: a treasury of great moral stories*. Simon & Schuster: New York. 831 pp.

8. Bermant, G., 1976. Sexual behavior: hard times with the Coolidge effect. In M. H. Siegel and H. P. Zeigler, eds. pp. 76-103. *Psychological research: the inside story*. Harper & Row, Publishers: New York.

9. Biocca, E., 1970. *Yanoáma: the narrative of a white girl kidnapped by Amazonian Indians*. E. P. Dutton & Co.: New York. 382 pp.

10. Blank, R. H., 1993. *Fetal protection in the workplace: women's rights, business interests, and the unborn*. Columbia University Press: New York. 225 pp.

11. Blumenschine, R. J. and J. A. Cavallo, 1992. Scavenging and human evolution. *Scientific American* 267(4):90-96.

12. Bongaarts, J., 1978. A framework for analyzing the proximate determinants of fertility. *Population and Development Review* 4:105-132.

13. Bongaarts, J., 1982. The fertility-inhibiting effects of the intermediate fertility variables. *Studies in Family Planning* 13:179-189.

14. Bourke, A. F. G., 1994. Worker matricide in social bees and wasps. *Journal of Theoretical Biology* 167:283-292.

15. Brewer, M., M. Bates and L. Vannoy, 1989. Postpartum changes in maternal weight and body fat depots in lactating vs nonlactating women. *American Journal of Clinical Nutrition* 49:259-265.

16. Brown, P. J. and M. Konner, 1987. An anthropological perspective on obesity. *Annals of the New York Academy of Sciences* 499:29-46.

17. Bruce, H. M., 1959. An exteroceptive block to pregnancy in the mouse. *Nature* 184:105.

18. Bruce, H. M., 1960. A block to pregnancy in the house mouse caused by the proximity of strange males. *Journal of Reproduction and Fertility* 1:96-103.

19. Butler, S., 1877. *Life and Habit.* 1923 edition. E. P. Dutton & Company: New York. 263 pp.

20. Camus, A., 1957. *The fall.* Alfred A. Knopf: New York. 147 pp.

21. Catton, W. R., Jr. 1980. *Overshoot: the ecological basis of revolutionary change.* University of Illinois Press: Baltimore. 320 pp.

22. Cavalli-Sforza, L. L. and W. F. Bodmer, 1971. *The genetics of human populations.* W. H. Freeman and Company: San Francisco. 965 pp.

23. Cavalli-Sforza, L. L. and M. W. Feldman, 1981. *Cultural transmission and evolution.* Princeton University Press: Princeton. 368 pp.

24. Chagnon, N. A., 1983. *Yanomamö: the fierce people.* Third edition. Holt, Rinehart and Winston: New York. 224 pp.

25. Chopra, D. 1993. *Ageless body, timeless mind: the quantum alternative to growing old.* Harmony Books: New York. 342 pp.

26. Cloak, F. T., Jr., 1975. Is a cultural ethology possible? *Human Ecology* 3(3):161-82.

27. Cohen, J. E., 1992. How many people can Earth hold? *Discover* 13(11):114-119.

28. Cohen, J. E., 1995. *How many people can the Earth support?* W. W. Norton & Company: New York. 532 pp.

29. Cohen, J. S., S. D. Fihn, E. J. Boyko, A. R. Jonsen and R. W. Wood, 1994. Attitudes toward assisted suicide and euthanasia among physicians in Washington state. *The New England Journal of Medicine* 331:89-94.

30. Costain, T. B., 1962. *The three Edwards: a history of the Plantagenets.* Doubleday & Company, Inc.: Garden City, New York. 419 pp.

31. Crook, P., 1994. *Darwinism, war and history.* Cambridge University Press: Cambridge. 306 pp.

32. Crossen, C., 1994. *Tainted truth: the manipulation of fact in America.* Simon & Schuster: New York. 272 pp.

33. Daly, M. and M. I. Wilson, 1981. Abuse and neglect of children in evolutionary perspective. In R. D. Alexander and D. W. Tinkle, eds. pp. 405-416. *Natural selection and social behavior: recent research and new theory.* Chiron Press: New York.

34. Daly, M. and M. Wilson, 1983. *Sex, evolution, and behavior.* Second edition. Wadsworth Publishing Company: Belmont, California. 402 pp.

35. Daly, M. and M. Wilson, 1984. A sociobiological analysis of human infanticide. In G. Hausfater and S. B. Hrdy, eds. pp. 487-502. *Infanticide: comparative and evolutionary perspectives.* Aldine: New York.

36. Darwin, C. G., 1953. *The next million years.* Doubleday & Company, Inc.: Garden City, New York. 210 pp.

37. Darwin, C. R., 1838. Notebook M. In P. H. Barrett, P. J. Gautrey, S. Herbert, D. Kohn and S. Smith, eds. pp. 520-560. *Charles Darwin's Notebooks, 1836-1844*. 1987 edition. Cornell University Press: Ithaca.

38. Darwin, C. R., 1859. *On the origin of species by means of natural selection, or the preservation of favoured races in the struggle for life.* John Murray: London. 502 pp.

39. Darwin, C. R., 1871. *The descent of man and selection in relation to sex.* John Murray: London. 423 and 475 pp.

40. Dawkins, R., 1976. *The selfish gene.* Oxford University Press: Oxford. 224 pp.

41. Dawkins, R., 1982. *The extended phenotype.* Oxford University Press: Oxford. 307 pp.

42. DeVore, I., 1977. The new science of genetic self-interest. Interviewed by S. Morris. *Psychology Today* February:42-88.

43. Diamond, J., 1992. *The third chimpanzee: the evolution and future of the human animal.* HarperCollins Publishers: New York. 407 pp.

44. Dobzhansky, T., 1973. *Genetic diversity and human equality.* Basic Books, Inc.: New York. 128 pp.

45. Dominey, W. J. and L. S. Blumer, 1984. Cannibalism of early life stages in fishes. In G. Hausfater and S. B. Hrdy, eds. pp. 43-64. *Infanticide: comparative and evolutionary perspectives.* Aldine: New York.

46. Dorjahn, V. R., 1958. Fertility, polygyny and their interrelations in Temne society. *American Anthropologist* 60:838-860.

47. Downhower, J. F. and K. B. Armitage, 1971. The yellow-bellied marmot and the evolution of polygamy. *American Naturalist* 105:355-370.

48. Durham, W. H., 1978. Toward a coevolutionary theory of human biology and culture. In A. L. Caplan ed. pp. 428-448. *Sociobiology debate: readings on ethical and scientific issues.* Harper & Row, Publishers: New York.

49. Durham, W. H., 1991. *Coevolution: genes, culture, and human diversity.* Stanford University Press: Stanford. 629 pp.

50. Eastman, N. J. and E. Jackson, 1968. Weight relationships in pregnancy. 1. The bearing of maternal weight gain and pre-pregnancy weight on birth weight in full term pregnancies. *Obstetrical & Gynecological Survey* 23:1003-1025.

51. Eaton, J. W. and A. J. Mayer, 1953. The social biology of very high fertility among the Hutterites: the demography of a unique population. *Human Biology* 25:206-264.

52. Eaton, S. B. and M. Konner, 1985. Paleolithic nutrition: a consideration of its nature and current implications. *The New England Journal of Medicine* 312:283-289.

53. Eaton, S. B., M. Shostak and M. Konner, 1988. *The paleolithic prescription:*

a program of diet, exercise and a design for living. Harper & Row, Publishers: New York. 306 pp.

54. Ehrlich, P. R. and A. H. Ehrlich, 1990. *The population explosion*. Simon & Schuster: New York. 320 pp.

55. Emanuel, E. J. and L. L. Emanuel, 1994. The economics of dying - the illusion of cost saving at the end of life. *The New England Journal of Medicine* 330:540-544.

56. Etchason, J., L. Petz, E. Keeler, L. Calhoun, S. Kleinman, C. Snider, A. Fink, and R. Brook, 1995. The cost effectiveness of preoperative autologous blood donations. *The New England Journal of Medicine* 332:719-724.

57. Facts on File, 1991. *The Guinness book of records 1992*. Guinness Publishing Ltd.: New York. 320 pp.

58. Fallon, A. and P. Rozin, 1985. Sex differences in perceptions of desirable body shape. *Journal of Abnormal Psychology* 94:102-5.

59. Findlay, S., 1989. Buying the perfect body. *U.S. News & World Report* 106(17):68-75.

60. Fisher, R. A., 1930. *The genetical theory of natural selection*. 1958 revised and enlarged edition. Dover Publications, Inc.: New York. 291 pp.

61. Flamm, B. L., 1990. *Birth after cesarean*. Prentice Hall Press: New York. 197 pp.

62. Forsyth, A., 1986. *A natural history of sex: the ecology and evolution of sexual behavior*. Charles Scribner's Sons: New York. 190 pp.

63. Freud, S., 1900. *The interpretation of dreams*. 1950 translated edition by The Modern Library: New York. 477 pp.

64. Friedman, G. D. and A. L. Klatsky, 1993. Is alcohol good for your health? *The New England Journal of Medicine* 329:1882-3.

65. Frisch, R. E., 1975. Demographic implications of the biological determinants of female fecundity. *Social Biology* 22(1):17-22.

66. Frisch, R. E., 1988. Fatness and fertility. *Scientific American* 258:88-95.

67. Fuchs, C. S., M. J. Stampfer, G. A. Colditz, E. L. Giovannucci, J. E. Manson, I. Kawachi, D. J. Hunter, S. E. Hankinson, C. H. Hennekens, B. Rosner, F. E. Speizer, and W. C. Willett, 1995. Alcohol consumption and mortality among women. *The New England Journal of Medicine* 332:1245-50.

68. Gadgil, M. and W. H. Bossert, 1970. Life historical consequences of natural selection. *American Naturalist* 104:1-24.

69. Gallup Poll, 1985. Religion in America -- 50 Years: 1935-1985. *The Gallup Report* No. 236 (May). Princeton.

70. Galton, F., 1872. Statistical inquiries into the efficacy of prayer. *Fortnightly Review* 18(65):125-133.

71. Gaulin, S. J. C., 1985. The use and abuse of sociobiology. *The Behavioral and Brain Sciences* 9:193-194.

72. Gaziano, J. M., J. E. Buring, J. L. Breslow, S. Z. Goldhaber, B. Rosner, M. VanDenburgh, W. Willett, C. H. Hennekens, 1993. Moderate alcohol intake, increased levels of high-density lipoprotein and its subfractions, and decreased risk of myocardial infarction. *The New England Journal of Medicine* 329:1829-34.

73. Gille, H., 1987. Social and economic implications. In J. Cleland and C. Scott, eds. pp. 986-1010. *The world fertility survey: an assessment.* Oxford University Press: Oxford.

74. Gould, S. J., 1977. *Ever since Darwin: reflections in natural history.* W. W. Norton & Company: New York. 285 pp.

75. Gould, S. J., 1980. Is a new and general theory of evolution emerging? *Paleobiology* 6:119-30.

76. Gould, S. J., 1993. A special fondness for beetles. *Natural History* 102(1):4-12.

77. Gould, S. J., 1994. The power of this view of life. *Natural History* 103(6):6-8.

78. Graham, J. D., B.-H. Chang and J. S. Evans, 1992. Poorer is riskier. *Risk Analysis* 12:333-7.

79. Greenberg, E. R., J. A. Baron, T. D. Tosteson, D. H. Freeman, G. J. Beck, J. H. Bond, T. A. Colacchio, J. A. Coller, H. D. Frankl, R. W. Haile, J. S. Mandel, D. W. Nierenberg, R. Rothstein, D. C. Snover, M. M. Stevens, R. W. Summers and R. U. van Stolk, 1994. A clinical trial of antioxidant vitamins to prevent colorectal adenoma. *The New England Journal of Medicine* 331:141-7.

80. Guralnik, J. M. and G. A. Kaplan, 1989. Predictors of healthy aging: prospective evidence from the Alameda County study. *American Journal of Public Health* 79:703-709.

81. Haaga, J. G., 1989. Mechanisms for the association of maternal age, parity, and birth spacing with infant health. In A. M. Parnell, ed. pp. 96-139. *Contraceptive use and controlled fertility: health issues for women and children.* Committee on Population, National Academy Press: Washington, D.C.

82. Hamilton, E. M. N., E. N. Whitney and F. S. Sizer, 1991. *Nutrition: concepts and controversies.* West Publishing Company: St. Paul. 554 pp.

83. Hamilton, J. B., 1948. The role of testicular secretions as indicated by the effects of castration in man and by studies of pathological conditions and the short lifespan associated with maleness. In G. Pincus, ed. pp. 257-322. *Recent progress in hormone research* Vol. III. Academic Press Inc.: New York.

84. Hamilton, W. D., 1966. The moulding of senescence by natural selection. *Journal of Theoretical Biology* 12:12-45.

85. Hamilton, W. D., 1972. Altruism and related phenomena, mainly in social

insects. *Annual Review of Ecology and Systematics* 3:193-232.

86. Hamilton, W. D., 1975. Innate social aptitudes of man: an approach from evolutionary genetics. In R. Fox, ed. pp. 133-155. *Biosocial anthropology.* John Wiley & Sons: New York.

87. Hardin, G., 1968. The tragedy of the commons. *Science* 162:1243-48.

88. Hardin, G., 1972. *Exploring new ethics for survival: the voyage of the spaceship* Beagle. The Viking Press: New York. 273 pp.

89. Harris, M., 1974. *Cows, pigs, wars and witches.* Vintage Books: New York. 276 pp.

90. Harris, M., 1989. *Our kind: who we are, where we came from, where we are going.* Harper & Row: New York. 547 pp.

91. Harrison, D. E. and J. R. Archer, 1987. Genetic differences in effects of food restriction on aging in mice. *Journal of Nutrition* 117:376-382.

92. Hatcher, R. A. and J. Trussell, 1994. Contraceptive implants and teenage pregnancy. *The New England Journal of Medicine* 331:1229-30.

93. Heath, D. B., 1987. A decade of development in the anthropological study of alcohol use: 1970-1980. In M. Douglas ed. pp. 16-69. *Constructive drinking: perspectives on drink from anthropology.* Cambridge University Press: Cambridge.

94. Henry, L., 1961. Some data on natural fertility. *Eugenics Quarterly* 8:81-91.

95. Hibbs, J. R., L. Benner, L. Klugman, R. Spencer, I. Macchia, A. K. Mellinger and D. Fife, 1994. Mortality in a cohort of homeless adults in Philadelphia. *The New England Journal of Medicine* 331:304-9.

96. Hobhouse, L. T., G. C. Wheeler, and M. Ginsberg, 1975. *The material culture and social institutions of the simpler peoples.* Arno Press: New York. First published by Chapman & Hall Ltd., 1915; reprinted by Routledge & Kegan Paul Ltd., 1965. 299 pp.

97. Hoebel, E. A., 1966. *Anthropology: the study of man.* McGraw-Hill Book Company: New York. 591 pp.

98. Hölldobler, B. and E. O. Wilson, 1990. *The ants.* Belknap Press: Cambridge. 732 pp.

99. Howell, N., 1979. *The demography of the Dobe !Kung.* Academic Press: New York. 389 pp.

100. Hrdy, S. B. and G. Hausfater, 1984. Comparative and evolutionary perspectives on infanticide: introduction and overview. In G. Hausfater and S. B. Hrdy, eds. pp. xiii-xxxv. *Infanticide: comparative and evolutionary perspectives.* Aldine: New York.

101. Huck, U. W., 1984. Infanticide and the evolution of pregnancy block in rodents. In G. Hausfater and S. B. Hrdy, eds. pp. 349-365. *Infanticide: comparative and evolutionary perspectives.* Aldine: New York.

102. Hugo, V., 1862. *Les Misérables.* 1976 edition translated by N. Denny.

Penguin Books: New York. 1232 pp.

103. Hume, D., 1739. *A treatise of human nature*. L. A. Selby-Bigge, ed. 1888 edition. Clarendon Press: Oxford. 709 pp.

104. Hunt, G. L., Jr., A. L. Newman, M. H. Warner, J. C. Wingfield and J. Kaiwi, 1984. Comparative behavior of male-male and female-female pairs among western gulls prior to egg-laying. *The Condor* 86:157-162.

105. Hutchinson, G. E., 1959. Homage to Santa Rosalia or why are there so many kinds of animals? *American Naturalist* 93(870):145-159.

106. Huxley, T. H., 1894. Evolution and ethics. In J. Paradis and G. C. Williams, eds. pp. 57-174. *Evolution and ethics*. 1989 edition. Princeton University Press: Princeton.

107. Irons, W., 1979. Cultural and biological success. In N. A. Chagnon and W. Irons, eds. pp. 257-272. *Evolutionary biology and human social behavior*. Duxbury Press: North Scituate, Massachusetts.

108. Jackson, D. D., 1994. The art of wishful shrinking has made a lot of people rich. *Smithsonian* 25(8):147-156.

109. Jain, A. K., 1977. Mortality risk associated with the use of oral contraceptives. *Studies in Family Planning* 8(3):50-54.

110. Jones, E. F., J. D. Forrest, N. Goldman, S. Henshaw, R. Lincoln, J. I. Rosoff, C. F. Westoff and D. Wulf, 1986. *Teenage pregnancy in industrialized countries*. Yale University Press: New Haven. 310 pp.

111. Keeney, R. L., 1990. Mortality risks induced by economic expenditures. *Risk Analysis* 10(1):147-159.

112. Keeney, R. L., 1994. Decisions about life-threatening risks. *The New England Journal of Medicine* 331:193-196.

113. Keyfitz, N., 1966. How many people have ever lived on the Earth? *Demography* 3(7):581-82.

114. Keyfitz, N., 1994. Influence of human reproduction on environment. In K. L. Campbell and J. W. Wood, eds. pp. 331-346. *Human reproductive ecology: interactions of environment, fertility, and behavior*. The New York Academy of Sciences: New York. Vol. 709.

115. Kinsey, A. C., W. B. Pomeroy, and C. E. Martin, 1948. *Sexual behavior in the human male*. W. B. Saunders Company: Philadelphia. 804 pp.

116. Kovacs, K. M. and J. P. Ryder, 1983. Reproductive performance of female-female pairs and polygynous trios of ring-billed gulls. *The Auk*: 100:658-669.

117. Kurland, J. A., 1979. Paternity, mother's brother, and human sociality. In N. A. Chagnon and W. Irons, eds. pp. 145-180. *Evolutionary biology and human social behavior*. Duxbury Press: North Scituate, Massachusetts.

118. Kurtz, P., 1973. *Humanist manifestos I and II*. Prometheus Books: Buffalo. 31 pp.

119. Kurtz, P., 1980. Does humanism have an ethic of responsibility? In M. B.

Storer, ed. pp. 11-35. *Humanist ethics: dialogue on basics.* Prometheus Books: Buffalo.

120. Lauersen, N. H. and C. Bouchez, 1991. *Getting pregnant: what every couple needs to know.* Rawson Associates: New York. 347 pp.

121. Leach, E. R., 1961. *Rethinking anthropology.* The Athlone Press, University of London: London. 144 pp.

122. Lee, N. C., H. B. Peterson and S. Y. Chu, 1989. Health effects of contraception. In A. M. Parnell, ed. pp. 48-95. *Contraceptive use and controlled fertility: health issues for women and children.* Committee on Population, National Academy Press: Washington, D.C.

123. Lorenz, K., 1966. *On aggression.* Harcourt, Brace & World, Inc.: New York. 306 pp.

124. Lovelock, J. E., 1979. *Gaia.* Oxford University Press: Oxford. 157 pp.

125. Luke, B., 1994. The changing pattern of multiple births in the United States: maternal and infant characteristics, 1973 and 1990. *Obstetrics and Gynecology* 84(1):101-106.

126. Lumsden, C. J. and E. O. Wilson, 1981. *Genes, mind and culture: the coevolutionary process.* Harvard University Press: Cambridge. 428 pp.

127. Lumsden, C. J. and E. O. Wilson, 1983. *Promethean fire.* Harvard University Press: Cambridge. 216 pp.

128. Lunn, P. G., 1994. Lactation and other metabolic loads affecting human reproduction. In K. L. Campbell and J. W. Wood, eds. pp. 77-85. *Human reproductive ecology: interactions of environment, fertility, and behavior.* The New York Academy of Sciences: New York. Vol. 709.

129. Malinowski, B., 1932. *The sexual life of savages.* Routledge & Kegan Paul Ltd.: London. 506 pp.

130. Malthus, T. R., 1798. *An essay of the principle of population.* In P. Appleman, ed. 1976 edition. W. W. Norton & Company, Inc.: New York. 260 pp.

131. Marx, K. and F. Engels, 1848. *The communist manifesto.* 1948 translated edition by New York Labor News Co.: New York. 75 pp.

132. Mayer, P. J., 1982. Evolutionary advantage of the menopause. *Human Ecology* 10(4):477-494.

133. Maynard Smith, J., 1982. *Evolution and the theory of games.* Cambridge University Press: Cambridge. 224 pp.

134. Mayr, E., 1991. *One long argument: Charles Darwin and the genesis of modern evolutionary thought.* Harvard University Press: Cambridge. 195 pp.

135. McGervey, J. D., 1986. *Probabilities in everyday life.* Nelson-Hall: Chicago. 269 pp.

136. McNeilly, A. S., C. C. K. Tay and A. Glasier, 1994. Physiological mechanisms underlying lactational amenorrhea. In K. L. Campbell and J. W. Wood,

eds. pp. 145-155. *Human reproductive ecology: interactions of environment, fertility, and behavior.* The New York Academy of Sciences: New York. Vol. 709.

137.   Mead, M., 1977. *Male and female: a study of the sexes in a changing world.* Morrow Quill Paperbacks: New York. 477 pp.

138.   Mendel, G., 1865. Experiments in plant-hybridisation. 1965 translated edition. Harvard University Press: Cambridge. 41 pp.

139.   Michael, R. T., J. H. Gagnon, E. O. Laumann and G. Kolata, 1994. *Sex in America: a definitive survey.* Little, Brown and Company: Boston. 300 pp.

140.   Miller, F. G., T. E. Quill, H. Brody, J. C. Fletcher, L. O. Gostin, D. E. Meier, 1994. Regulating physician-assisted death. *The New England Journal of Medicine* 331:119-123.

141.   Miller, W. B., 1986. Proception: an important fertility behavior. *Demography* 23(4):579-594.

142.   Mock, D. W., 1984. Infanticide, siblicide, and avian nestling mortality. In G. Hausfater and S. B. Hrdy, eds. pp. 3-30. *Infanticide: comparative and evolutionary perspectives.* Aldine: New York.

143.   Moore, G. E., 1903. *Principia ethica.* Cambridge University Press: Cambridge. 232 pp.

144.   Morris, D., 1967. *The naked ape: a zoologist's study of the human animal.* McGraw-Hill: New York. 252 pp.

145.   Mosher, W. D., 1985. Reproductive impairments in the United States, 1965-1982. *Demography* 22:415-430.

146.   Murdock, G. P., 1949. *Social structure.* The Macmillan Company: New York. 387 pp.

147.   National Center for Health Statistics, 1970. Mortality from selected causes by marital status. *Vital and Health Statistics* Series 20, No. 8, Parts A and B. 55 and 47 pp.

148.   National Center for Health Statistics, 1993. Advance report of final mortality statistics, 1991. Monthly vital statistics report 42:(2)1-64 Public Health Service: Hyattsville, Maryland.

149.   National Institute of Alcohol Abuse and Alcoholism, 1986. *Toward a national plan to combat alcohol abuse and alcoholism: a report to the United States Congress.* National Institutes of Health, Public Health Service, U.S. Department of Health and Human Services: Rockville, Md. 81 pp.

150.   National Research Council, 1980. Recommended dietary allowances, 9th ed. Report of the Food and Nutrition Board, Assembly of Life Sciences. National Academy Press: Washington, D.C. 185 pp.

151.   National Research Council, 1989. *Diet and health: implications for reducing chronic disease risk.* Committee of Diet and Health. National Academy Press: Washington, D.C. 749 pp.

152. Neumann, P. J., S. D. Gharib, M. C. Weinstein, 1994. The cost of a successful delivery with in vitro fertilization. *The New England Journal of Medicine* 331:239-43.

153. Newcomb, P. A., B. E. Storer, M. P. Longnecker, R. Mittendorf, E. R. Greenberg, R. W. Clapp, K. P. Burke, W. C. Willett and B. MacMahon, 1994. Lactation and a reduced risk of premenopausal breast cancer. *The New England Journal of Medicine* 330:81-7.

154. Nordhaus, W. D., 1996. Elbow room: a biologist ponders future population growth. *The New York Times Book Review*. January 14, 1996:12-13.

155. Orians, G. H., 1969. On the evolution of mating systems in birds and mammals. *American Naturalist* 103:589-603.

156. Ornish, D., 1990. *Dr. Dean Ornish's program for reversing heart disease*. Random House: New York. 631 pp.

157. Packer, C. and A. E. Pusey, 1984. Infanticide in carnivores. In G. Hausfater and S. B. Hrdy, eds. pp. 31-42. *Infanticide: comparative and evolutionary perspectives*. Aldine: New York.

158. Pershagen, G., G. Åkerblom, O. Axelson, B. Clavensjö, L. Damber, G. Desai, A. Enflo, F. Lagarde, H. Mellander, M. Svartengren and G. Astri Swedjemark, 1994. Residential radon exposure and lung cancer in Sweden. *The New England Journal of Medicine* 330:159-64.

159. Pianka, E. R., 1970. On r- and K-selection. *American Naturalist* 104:592-597.

160. Pirsig, R. M., 1991. *Lila: an inquiry into morals*. Bantam Books: New York. 409 pp.

161. Polaneczky, M., G. Slap, C. Forke, A. Rappaport and S. Sondheimer, 1994. The use of levonorgestrel implants (Norplant) for contraception in adolescent mothers. *The New England Journal of Medicine* 331:1201-6.

162. Popp, J. L., 1978. Male baboons and evolutionary principles. Ph.D. thesis. Department of Anthropology, Harvard University: Cambridge. 237 pp.

163. Popp, J. L., 1983. Ecological determinism in the life histories of baboons. *Primates* 24:198-210.

164. Popp, J. L. and I. DeVore, 1979. Aggressive competition and social dominance theory: synopsis. In D. A. Hamburg and E. R. McCown, eds. pp. 317-338. *The great apes*. Benjamin/Cummings Publishing Company: Menlo Park.

165. Potter, R. G. and S. Millman, 1985. Fecundability and the frequency of marital intercourse: a critique on nine models. *Population Studies* 39(3): 461-470.

166. Potter, R. G. and S. Millman, 1986. Fecundability and the frequency of marital intercourse: new models incorporating the ageing of gametes. *Population Studies* 40(1): 159-170.

167. Pugh, G. E., 1977. *The biological origin of human values*. Basic Books, Inc.: New York. 461 pp.

168. Raup, D. M., 1991. *Extinction: bad genes or bad luck?* W. W. Norton & Company: New York. 210 pp.

169. Reijnders, L., 1978. On the applicability of game theory to evolution. *Journal of Theoretical Biology* 75:245-247.

170. Reimer, G. M., 1994. Radon and lung cancer. *The New England Journal of Medicine* 331:1098.

171. Rennie, J., 1994. Trends in genetics: grading the gene tests. *Scientific American* 270(6):88-97.

172. Richards, R. J., 1987. *Darwin and the emergence of evolutionary theories of mind and behavior*. University of Chicago Press: Chicago. 700 pp.

173. Roscoe, J., 1907. The Bahima: a cow tribe of Enkole in the Uganda protectorate. *Journal of the Royal Anthropological Institute of Great Britain and Ireland* 37:93-118.

174. Ross, J. A. and E. Frankenberg, 1993. *Findings from two decades of family planning research*. The Population Council: New York. 101 pp.

175. Rossing, M. A., J. R. Daling, N. S. Weiss, D. E. Moore and S. G. Self, 1994. Ovarian tumors in a cohort of infertile women. *The New England Journal of Medicine* 331:771-776.

176. Rothenbuhler, W., 1964. Behavior genetics of nest cleaning in honey bees. IV. Responses of F_1 and backcross generations to diseased-killed brood. *American Zoologist* 4:111-123.

177. Ruse, M., 1986. *Taking Darwin seriously*. Basil Blackwell: Oxford. 303 pp.

178. Ruse, M. and E. O. Wilson, 1986. Moral philosophy as applied science. *Philosophy* 61:173-192.

179. Ryder, N. B. and C. F. Westoff, 1971. *Reproduction in the United States 1965*. Princeton University Press: Princeton. 419 pp.

180. Sachs, B. P, P. M. Layde, G. L. Rubin and R. W. Rochat, 1982. Reproductive mortality in the United States. *Journal of the American Medical Association* 247(20):2789-2792.

181. Sakagami, S. F. and Y. Akahira, 1960. Studies on the Japanese honeybee, *Apis cerana cerana* Fabricius. VIII. Two opposing adaptations in the post-stinging behavior of honeybees. *Evolution* 14:29-40.

182. Saporito, B., 1993. The most dangerous job in America. *Fortune* 127(11):131-140.

183. Scheig, R., 1970. Effects of ethanol on the liver. *American Journal of Clinical Nutrition* 23(4):467-473.

184. Schoenborn, C. A. and B. H. Cohen, 1986. Trends in smoking, alcohol consumption, and other health practices among U.S. adults, 1977 and 1983. *Advance Data from Vital and Health Statistics of the National Center for*

Health Statistics, No. 118. Department of Health and Human Service Publication PHS 86-1250. 16 pp.

185. Schoener, T. W., 1971. Theory of feeding strategies. *Annual Review of Ecology and Systematics* 2:369-404.

186. Schultz, A. H., 1938. The relative weight of testes in primates. *The Anatomical Record* 72:387-394.

187. Seligman, M. E. P., 1994. *What you can change and what you can't: the complete guide to successful self-improvement.* Alfred A. Knopf: New York. 317 pp.

188. Shakespeare, W., 1606. *The Tragedy of Macbeth.* In *The Harvard Classics: Elizabethan Drama.* C. W. Eliot ed., Volume 46, 1938 edition. P. F. Collier & Son Corporation: New York. 463 pp.

189. Shapiro, J. P., 1993. Bonds that blood and birth cannot assure. *U.S. News & World Report* 115(6):12-13.

190. Short, R. V., 1994. Human reproduction in an evolutionary context. In K. L. Campbell and J. W. Wood, eds. pp. 416-425. *Human reproductive ecology: interactions of environment, fertility, and behavior.* The New York Academy of Sciences: New York. Vol. 709.

191. Silber, S. J., 1991. *How to get pregnant with the new technology.* Warner Books: New York. 390 pp.

192. Simpson, G. G., 1949. *The meaning of evolution.* Yale University Press: New Haven. 364 pp.

193. Singer, P., 1981. *The expanding circle: ethics and sociobiology.* Farrar, Straus & Giroux: New York. 190 pp.

194. Slovic, P., B. Fischhoff and S. Lichtenstein, 1980. Facts and fears: understanding perceived risk. In R. C. Schwing and W. A. Albers, eds. pp. 181-214. *Societal risk assessment: how safe is safe enough?* Plenum Press: New York.

195. Smith, D. W. E., 1993. *Human longevity.* Oxford University Press: New York, 175 pp.

196. Smith, R. M., 1988. Natural fertility in pre-industrial Europe. In P. Diggory, M. Potts and S. Teper, eds. pp. 70-88. *Natural human fertility: social and biological determinants.* Macmillan Press: London.

197. Spencer, H., 1879. *Data of ethics.* David McKay, Publisher: Philadelphia. 334 pp.

198. Stossel, J., 1994. Are we scaring ourselves to death? ABC News.

199. Sussman, V., 1991. No sign of recession at Fluffy's mealtime. *U.S. News & World Report* 111(16):98.

200. Symons, D., 1979. *The evolution of human sexuality.* Oxford University Press: New York. 358 pp.

201. Tannahill, R., 1980. *Sex in history.* Stein and Day: New York. 480 pp.

202. Thoreau, H. D., 1854. *Walden; or life in the woods*. Ticknor and Fields: Boston. 357 pp.

203. Trivers, R. L., 1971. The evolution of reciprocal altruism. *Quarterly Review of Biology* 46:35-57.

204. Trivers, R. L., 1972. Parental investment and sexual selection. In B. Campbell, ed. pp. 136-179. *Sexual selection and the descent of man 1871-1971*. Aldine: Chicago.

205. Trivers, R. L., 1974. Parent-offspring conflict. *American Zoologist* 14:249-264.

206. Trivers, R. L., 1985. *Social evolution*. Benjamin/Cummings Publishing Company: Menlo Park. 462 pp.

207. Turnbull, C. M., 1972. *The mountain people*. Simon & Schuster: New York, 309 pp.

208. Verner, J. and M. F. Willson, 1966. The influence of habitats on mating systems of North American passerine birds. *Ecology* 47:143-147.

209. Vining, D. R., 1985. Social versus reproductive success: the central theoretical problem of human sociobiology. *The Behavioral and Brain Sciences* 9:167-216.

210. Wagner, R. H., 1993. The pursuit of extra-pair copulations by female birds: a new hypothesis of colony formation. *Journal of Theoretical Biology* 163:333-346.

211. Watson, J. D. and F. H. C. Crick, 1953. A structure for deoxyribose nucleic acid. *Nature* 171:737-738.

212. Weinberg, S. K., 1955. *Incest behaviour*. Citadel Press: New York. 291 pp.

213. Weinrich, J. D., 1976. Human reproductive strategy: the importance of income unpredictability, and the evolution of non-reproduction. Ph.D. dissertation, Harvard University, Cambridge. 231 pp.

214. Wilcox, A. J., C. R. Weinberg and D. D. Baird, 1995. Timing of sexual intercourse in relation to ovulation: Effects on the probability of conception, survival of the pregnancy, and sex of the baby. *The New England Journal of Medicine* 333:1517-1521.

215. Willett, W. C., 1994. Diet and health: what should we eat? *Science* 264:532-537.

216. Williams, G. C., 1957. Pleiotropy, natural selection, and the evolution of senescence. *Evolution* 11:398-411.

217. Williams, G. C., 1966. *Adaptation and natural selection: a critique of some current evolutionary thought*. Princeton University Press: Princeton. 307 pp.

218. Williams, G. C., 1989. A sociobiological expansion of *Evolution and Ethics*. In J. Paradis and G. C. Williams, eds. pp. 179-214. *Evolution and ethics*. Princeton University Press: Princeton.

219. Williams, G. C., 1992. *Gaia*, nature worship and biocentric fallacies.

American Naturalist 67(4):479-486.

220. Williams, G. C. and R. M. Nesse, 1991. The dawn of Darwinian medicine. *The Quarterly Review of Biology.* 66(1):1-22.

221. Wilson, E. O., 1971. *Insect societies.* Belknap Press: Cambridge. 548 pp.

222. Wilson, E. O., 1975. *Sociobiology: the new synthesis.* Belknap Press: Cambridge. 697 pp.

223. Wilson, E. O., 1992. *The diversity of life.* Belknap Press: Cambridge. 424 pp.

224. Wislocki, G. B., 1942. Size, weight and histology of the testes in the gorilla. *Journal of Mammalogy* 23:281-87.

225. Wolraich, M. L., S. D. Lindgren, P. J. Stumbo, L. D. Stegink, M. I. Appelbaum and M. C. Kiritsy, 1994. Effects of diets high in sucrose or aspartame on the behavior and cognitive performance of children. *The New England Journal of Medicine* 330:301-7.

226. World Bank, 1994. World Bank works to stem deaths during childbirth. Associated Press, May 8, 1994.

227. World Fertility Survey, 1984. *World fertility survey: major findings and implications.* Alden Press: Oxford. 61 pp.

228. World Health Organization, 1989. *Preventing maternal deaths.* E. Royston and S. Armstrong, eds. World Health Organization: Geneva. 233 pp.

229. Wu, F. C. W., 1988. The biology of puberty. In P. Diggory, M. Potts and S. Teper, eds. pp. 89-101. *Natural human fertility: social and biological determinants.* Macmillan Press: London.

230. Zimicki, S., 1989. The relationship between fertility and maternal mortality. In A. M. Parnell, ed. pp. 1-47. *Contraceptive use and controlled fertility: health issues for women and children.* Committee on Population, National Academy Press: Washington, D.C.

Index